W9-CHR-042

Contents

For Ines for everything

SOCIALISM AND EUROPEAN UNITY

The Dilemma of the Left in Britain and France

MICHAEL NEWMAN

JUNCTION BOOKS   LONDON

© 1983 Michael Newman

First published in Great Britain by
Junction Books Ltd
15 St John's Hill
London SW11

ISBN 0 86245 103 5 (hard)
    0 86245 104 3 (paper)

Printed in Great Britain by
Biddles Ltd, Guildford, Surrey

Preface

This book originated from a feeling of dissatisfaction with much of the discussion of the EEC by the left in Britain. My hope was that some of the issues might be elucidated by a study which both set the current debate in a context of historical development, and compared British attitudes with the substantially different ones held in the French labour movement. My purpose has therefore been both to explain and to evaluate the policies which have been followed in the two countries.

Given the scope of the work it has inevitably been necessary to be selective. Little attention has been paid to developments in other European countries and parties despite their importance in shaping the process of West European integration; and emphasis has been placed on those events which have had particular political significance for the left. This means, for example, that I have discussed the controversy over the proposal for a European Defence Community at some length in the French context, while saying very little about EURATOM. However, some further factual information on West European integration which could not be included in the text is given in the two appendices, and those who wish to study particular questions in more depth are referred to the extensive footnotes.

One stylistic device requires explanation. As its opponents point out, the European Community is not synonymous with Europe. However, it appeared awkward always to use a longer term and I have therefore written Europe as 'Europe' when discussing the Community.

Finally, I would like to acknowledge all the help that I have received while working on this project. First I must thank two authors whose books were published after I had begun my own research on the subject: R. Pinto Lyra for *La gauche en France et la construction européenne* (Librairie générale de droit et de jurisprudence, 1978) and L.J. Robins for *The Reluctant Party – Labour and the EEC 1961–75* (G.W. & A. Hesketh, 1979). Both works contain invaluable information, insights and references which greatly eased my own task. A further vital source was *Britain and Europe since 1945* (Harvester Primary Social Sources, The Harvester Press, 1973–continuing) – a vast microfiche collection of statements and publications by British parties and pressure groups. I was able to use this at the European Documentation Centre in the Polytechnic of North London and I should like to thank the library staff there for their advice with this and other sources. I am also very grateful to the following for help with source material: Angela Raspin of the British Library of Political and Economic Science, Stephen Bird and David Lowe of the Labour Party, Professor Loïc Philip of the University of Aix–Marseilles, and Brian Thomas of the Polytechnic of North London.

I owe a great deal to the Polytechnic, which granted me sabbatical leave in 1978–79 and I should like to express my gratitude to those who made this possible and, in particular to my colleagues in the European Studies Division. I was also helped by the staff of the Institut d'Etudes Politiques at the University of Bordeaux, where I spent my sabbatical year, and especially by Professeur Jacques Lagroye who allowed me full access to the Institute's facilities. I would also like to thank The British Academy (Thank Offering to British Fund) which granted me a European Research Fellowship for my time abroad.

Geoff Pugh acted as my Research Assistant from 1980–82 and I am very grateful to him both for helping with the research on the British side and for taking over some of my teaching responsibilities so that I could finish the book. I would also like to thank Joanne Foakes of the Law Department of the Polytechnic for her helpful suggestions on Appendix II, and Amanda Harris for her quick and accurate typing.

Above all I want to thank my family: my mother for typing most of the book, my father for reading it so carefully and commenting constructively on content and style, my children, Kate and Hannah for lending me their rubbers (a lot of rubbing out was necessary!) and Zack for being so cheerful. Ines, my wife, not only made the whole book possible, but also vastly improved it by constant discussion of the subject matter and incisive criticisms of each draft chapter. It is to her that I dedicate it.

Introduction

In terms of population size, relative power and recent international experience, there are striking similarities between France and Britain, yet their national political development and outlooks diverge sharply, and their relationship has seldom been harmonious. It is therefore natural to ask: how is it that two neighbouring states can be so similar and yet so different? This question acquires particular significance in relation to the process of West European integration, for there have been sharp contrasts in the reactions of the two nation-states to their common predicament in the post-war era.

In 1945 both France and Britain were former great powers with world empires, but were not overshadowed by the United States and the Soviet Union. Since they were the only two major states in Western Europe which were, in theory, fully sovereign, their unity would have enabled them to influence the pattern of post-war political and economic development in the region. Instead they embarked on radically different courses, and their relationship was often very strained. This was most evident during the 1960s when de Gaulle twice vetoed British entry into the EEC, but even since the passing of that era, there have been frequent Anglo-French disputes within the Community. Indeed the public in each nation-state has been led to regard the other as the principal obstacle to co-operation in Western Europe.

Such differences are perhaps less important now in European and world terms than they were in the early post-war period. The revival of West Germany as a major force has meant that France and Britain are no longer preeminent within Western Europe, and the growth of other power blocs, particularly in China and Japan, has reduced the relative weight of the whole European continent in the world. However, both France and Britain remain significant medium-range powers in economic, military and political terms, and developments in either country inevitably affect Western Europe as a whole. Moreover, the area of the European Community is the greatest geographical concentration of economic strength in the world. It therefore follows that Anglo-French unity – were it possible – could still influence the course of European history.

Such observations become particularly poignant with regard to the subject of this book: the evolution of the 'European' attitudes and policies of the parties of the left in the two countries. Had the Anglo-French left been united on the issue in the early post-war period, the pattern of integration and of subsequent European development could have been very different. And even now cross-national agreement could lead to the transformation of the European Community and greater socialist influence throughout Europe. However, even to suggest such a possibility appears naive, for the divergencies between the two nation-states in the post-war era have been reproduced in their respective labour movements, and cross-national unity has been conspicuous by its absence.

Parties of the left have found it notoriously difficult to define their attitudes to West European integration, and the situation has been particularly complex in France and Britain. For the majority of the post-war period French Socialists and Communists have been bitterly divided on the issue, with the former strongly favouring integration and latter in total opposition to it. Even in more recent times, when a degree of compromise has been attained, substantial differences have remained. In Britain, the vacillation of the Labour Party on the EEC, particularly at leadership level, has become a renowned feature of political life and, in general, the party has remained hostile to both the concept and practice of integration. In each country the formulation of policy by the left has been problematic, and there has been a complex relationship between the 'European' attitudes of the left and those of non-socialist forces within the nation-state.

This study analyses the development of such attitudes in each country throughout the post-war era. It raises three major questions: (1) Why has West European integration posed such problems for the left in both France and Britain? (2) Why do the dominant forces on the French left now accept Community membership whilst their counterparts in Britain reject it? (3) Is there any possibility of cross-national unity by the left on the issue? The most common answer to the first question is that, despite their theoretical commitment to socialist internationalism, parties of the left are actually highly nationalistic and have found it more difficult to adjust to the demands of European internationalism than those of the centre and right. Such accusations have often been propagandist in nature, emanating from the European Movement itself or from right-wing parties seeking an electoral advantage by discrediting their political opponents. However, the charge has also been made from the left, most notably in a brilliant polemic by Tom Nairn, who argued that the bedrock of the Labour Party was nationalism and that its attitude to the EEC could be understood only if this basic characteristic were appreciated.[1]

Certainly both the French communist party (*Parti communiste français*) and the Labour Party have manifested a strong tendency to condemn West European integration in chauvinistic terms. However, the assertion that hostility to 'Europe' necessarily stems from 'nationalism' is oversimplified and this study will seek to show that the negative attitudes exhibited by some of the left are too complex to be labelled with this single term. On the other hand, it is clear that socialist internationalism has proved far more difficult to practise than many, including Marx and Engels, had anticipated. Part of the explanation for the dilemmas of the left over the question of integration lies in this wider problem.

In the century between the publication of the Communist Manifesto – with its claim that the workers had no country – and the first steps towards the establishment of an integrated Western Europe there were isolated cases of genuine working-class internationalism. However, the general trend was surely in the opposite direction. The collapse in 1914 of the Second International – established largely to prevent war between German and French workers – epitomised the weakness of international solidarity in a cathartic moment, but underlying processes were already cementing the workers to the West European nation-state in a less dramatic but more enduring way. For while capitalism remained in control, the increased provision of social services and the development of mass parties and mass culture were leading workers to perceive their own interests as bound up with those of the nation and its political institutions. ·

Left-wing political parties naturally played a role in moulding this form of consciousness as well as responding to it. Indeed, the more fully they became integrated into the existing political and social system, the more national their outlook tended to become. Nor was this counteracted by the formation of communist parties since, after the early 1920s, the main function of their proletarian internationalism was to serve the interests of the Soviet State, as defined by Stalin. Parties of the left had thus encountered enormous difficulties in the pursuit of socialist internationalism even when the dominant forces in West European societies appeared to take a relatively straightforward view of the national interest as the pursuit of national power in its economic, political and military dimensions. The attempt by those forces to uphold their interests in new ways after the Second World War therefore caused the parties of the left still greater confusion.

That the ownership of capital became increasingly international and military forces were ceded in apparent perpetuity to the Western alliance under supreme American control presented the left with acute problems in any case. But the yielding of political and economic powers to semi-supranational bodies in Western Europe perhaps provided the greatest challenge of all: if the reconciliation of socialism and the nation was already problematic, what path should be adopted when the dominant forces partially abandoned the nation-state? There was no obvious answer and there was (and is) no united response. Denunciations of West European integration, with the implication that there was some special virtue in the existing national institutions, not only presented centre and right-wing forces with a propaganda target (the 'nationalism of the left'), but also involved the risk of ignoring the objective reality of the increasing internationalisation of power. On the other hand, acceptance of the process could facilitate the economic and political strengthening of capitalism, thereby making the attainment of socialism still more difficult.

For some Marxists the means of breaking out of this impasse would appear to lie in the revolutionary overthrow of all forms of capitalism – national and international. But this study deals with the major parties of the left, which seek power primarily through electoral means within the existing political systems and for them the revolutionary spectre is neither desirable or practicable. They are thus forced to operate within a national and international environment which is non-socialist. Defence of threatened national interests can be one response to the difficulty. Internationalism or 'Europeanism' on a non-socialist basis can be another. Perhaps more often the first strategy is an attempt to combine a defence of perceived national interests with a form of socialism, while the second aspires to socialistic goals in a wider framework. This study will show that each of these forms of behaviour has been exhibited at various times by sections of the left in each country. However, there are long-term trends towards national defensiveness in Britain and 'Europeanism' in France and this contrast was epitomised in 1981 when the Labour Party voted overwhelmingly for British withdrawal just after the French Socialists and Communists in the first left-wing government for at least 25 years announced their intention: 'actively to support the participation of France in the European Community, in its institutions and its common policies, while respecting French freedom of action and legitimate interests'.[2]

This leads to the second major question: why has there been this divergence between the leading parties of the left in the two countries?

The most immediately obvious way of explaining the contrast would be to argue that, in each country, the left is simply defending the national interests and it is these that differ between the two nation-states. This interpretation certainly helps to clarify both the past and present behaviour of the left in the two countries. Thus between the late 1940s and the formation of the EEC, British policy-makers in general believed that the national interests lay outside an integrated Western Europe and the Labour Party adhered to this viewpoint. Meanwhile the French Socialists shared a widespread national opinion that French interests could best be advanced within such a bloc. Since then, French Socialists (and later Communists too) have accepted the consensus viewpoint that French interests benefit from EEC membership, while the British labour movement, like much of the population, has continued to believe that the Community is ill-suited to the needs of Britain and that her interests could be pursued more adequately outside it. However, if left-wing parties simply reflected the divergent national interests of the two states it would mean that socialist considerations played no part in their policies. This is not the case. In both countries party attitudes to 'Europe' have included specifically socialist elements and, as has already been argued, even when a policy has been justified in terms of the national interests such considerations have often been present. When, for example, the Labour Party claimed that withdrawal was necessary for the defence of British interests, its concept of national interests was clearly not shared by the Establishment, which favoured the continuation of Market membership.

If the divergence cannot be fully explained by perceiving the policies of the left as reflections of national interests can it be understood in terms of proximity to a socialist viewpoint on the one side and distance from it on the other? In other words, is there a socialist viewpoint on West European integration in terms of which the policies of the left in each country and the divergencies between them can be gauged? Without necessarily adhering to the view that there could be a pure socialist perspective, fully autonomous from all national considerations and influences, this study holds that there are distinct socialist priorities involved in the question, and that these have played a part in policy formulation.

It therefore traces the extent of such influences on the parties and shows, perhaps predictably, that specifically socialist considerations have been of the greatest importance on the left of the Labour and French socialist parties and in the *Parti communiste française* and of the least importance for the leaders of the Labour Party and French *Parti socialiste*, particularly when in power. However, despite the assertion of many in the British Labour Party, it does not follow that the British labour movement is more socialist than that in France because it is more hostile to the EEC. In fact, those with similar positions on the ideological spectrum will still tend to differ, in accordance with nationality, on 'Europe'. For example, to a typical member of the Labour left it is manifest that the EEC is wholly devoted to the furtherance of capitalism and is undemocratic while, to his counterpart in the French Socialist Party, whose general conception of socialism may be very similar, it is equally obvious that, although the Community may have grave faults, it is only on the European level that social justice, internationalism and independence from the USA can be established.

The 'European' attitudes and policies of the parties of the left can thus be fully explained neither in terms of their adherence to national interests nor to socialism. Rather they must be seen as the product of a complex and variable interaction between the two. Moreover, their perspectives must also be analysed in terms of their own historical development within the nation-state, and the contrasting impact of West European integration upon France and Britain. For history has been of crucial importance in shaping the response of the left.

This leads to the third question: is there now any possibility of attaining cross-national left-wing unity on the issue?

Clearly, understanding between these two movements, especially if simultaneously in government, could do much to transform the Community. And if the EEC could move in a socialist direction – if it were possible to build a European Community without the Treaty of Rome – impetus would be given to the European left as a whole, perhaps even meaning that the East–West division might eventually be transcended and real European unity established. At present any such prospect appears utopian. Even the first stage – the recognition that the working classes in the two countries might have common interests – depends on the resolution of vast differences in material circumstances and mental attitudes. Nevertheless, in the Conclusion it will be asked: can the left in France and Britain learn lessons from one another, thus bringing about the possibility of socialism and European unity? Or must they continue to play out the historic destiny of the two nation-states and act as troubled neighbours?

Notes

1 Tom Nairn. 'The Left Against Europe?'. *New Left Review*, September/October 1972, later published by Penguin, 1973.
2 *The Times*, 25 June 1981.

Part One

1

The Fourth Republic and West European Integration

Modernisation without Consensus

The Fourth Republic now has a poor reputation in France. The country is held to have been characterised by economic backwardness and a profound political instability leading to a bewildering succession of short-lived governments and the final collapse of the regime in 1958. Foreign policy is seen to have been at least as disastrous, not only because of the Algerian revolution or even the humiliation of military defeat in Vietnam, but because France appeared to be a wholly subordinate entity in international affairs. Yet if this image of failure is understandable, it is nevertheless misleading. In fact, despite the shortcomings of the regime, from a French capitalist perspective at least, the Republic was also a success. West European integration was both a contributory cause, and a measure, of the progress which was made.

France and 'Europe' in the Fourth Republic[1]

In 1945 a principal characteristic of France was its relative weakness. Collaboration had not only undermined its national legitimacy, but had also devastated the economy, which had increasingly served as a supplier of raw materials for the German war effort. The emphasis of the post-war government was therefore upon economic revival through renewed production. It was not, however, simply production for its own sake that was encouraged, but productivity through technical advance. The slogan of the planning commissariat, established in 1946 under Jean Monnet, was 'modernisation or decadence' and this conviction was shared by the government as a whole. By 1958 the task was well on the way to achievement. France was becoming an advanced capitalist state able to enter and benefit from the international economy. Its entry into the EEC in

3

that year symbolised the extent to which the economy had been transformed.

The relative weakness immediately after the war had also had foreign policy repercussions to which West European integration eventually offered a solution. For the French felt overshadowed not only by the superpowers but also by two neighbours: Germany and, to a lesser extent, Britain. De Gaulle's aspiration, at the end of the war, had been to solve the problem in a traditionalist manner. France was to be recognised as a great power and to acquire territories in the Rhineland, while Germany was to be held in check by the continuation of the wartime alliance. France herself was to balance identification with the West with the treaty with the USSR, negotiated by de Gaulle in December 1944. This vision rested on considerable public and political support, but it was ultimately to prove untenable.

In the first place economic considerations were to dictate an increasingly close alignment with the West at the expense of the balancing of the two superpowers, for the French economy was dependent on external support if excessive hardship were to be averted. Even with American aid the bread ration in August 1947 was to fall below the level which had been maintained during the occupation, and it was clear that, without it, the privation would have been far worse. But aid brought with it an involvement in the international capitalist economy, and economic alignment was thus a partial cause of the French entry into the Western alliance system. However, this also resulted from more specifically political factors, for France reproduced within herself the general tensions of the Cold War.

In 1944 the *Parti communiste français* (PCF), the largest force within the metropolitan resistance, had accepted the implications of the great power division of Europe when it rejected an insurrectionary policy and co-operated with Socialists, the Christian democratic MRP (*Movement républicain populaire*) and Gaullists in the elaboration of a domestic programme of social and economic reform. And after entering the post-war government the PCF constantly urged workers to participate in the battle for French production and modernisation, despite the severe fall in real living standards which accompanied the reconstruction programme. Nevertheless, many on the centre and right had never been reconciled to communist participation in the government and, as international polarisation increased, so too did domestic anti-communism. In the midst of this the only remaining advantage that non-communist forces saw in the Soviet alliance was removed when Stalin, in a bid to thwart Western influence in Germany, turned against the French claim for the economic annexation of the Saar. The USA and Britain exploited their advantage by offering France their support, thereby enabling non-communist opinion in France to follow its natural inclinations and move openly into the Western camp.

The expulsion of the Communist ministers by a Socialist-led government in May 1947 prefaced French acceptance of the Marshall Aid proposal and the start of military conversations with Britain. In 1948 Britain, France and the Benelux countries signed the Brussels Pact which formed the nucleus for the creation of NATO the next year. The accord with the Soviet Union was now effectively dead and the French state had placed its hopes in the Atlantic Alliance to provide it with security against Germany as well as the Soviet Union.

In fact, however, the German problem had not been solved. In 1947 the Americans had supported the claim for the economic annexation of the Saar in order to facilitate French entry into the Western camp, but it was soon evident that this was an isolated episode. Indeed subsequent events revealed the major American priority to be the establishment of a reliable capitalist state in West Germany and this involved the granting of concessions to the dominant forces in West Germany rather than to France. Nor could Britain be relied upon to act as a counterweight to the USA for, by 1948, the Labour Government shared American strategic views on West Germany.

If the German danger remained the priority, French governments inevitably defined the causes in terms of a further traditional problem: the lack of understanding by the 'Anglo-Saxon' powers whose 'special relationship' meant that the USA need pay no great regard to French wishes and anxieties, but could rely instead on its British lieutenant to act as its intermediary in Europe. Such considerations underlay French support for the goal of West European integration. That is, France saw it as a means of escape from a situation in which she remained preoccupied with the German problem, subordinate to Britain, and powerless *vis-à-vis* the USA.

Despite her relative weakness, France remained the strongest continental power in the west of Europe – at least until West Germany was fully established as a sovereign state. Part of the attraction of West European integration was therefore the straightforward one that French influence would predominate. However, this was not simply a matter of quasi-imperialist ambition, for French governments also believed that the creation of a West European unit would strengthen the bloc as a whole not only against communism, but also in its dealings with the USA. This latter aim was, of course, seen as crucially important while the Americans remained apparently oblivious to French fears about the revival of Germany.

As a major objective in sponsoring the moves towards West European integration in 1948–49 was to secure greater French influence, the fact that she also sought British participation might appear paradoxical. Britain was, after all, economically and militarily more powerful and politically more influential than France. Yet at this stage British involvement appeared essential if the unit were to secure political coherence and economic strength, if it were to attract the pro-British smaller powers, and if Germany were to remain in a subordinate position. Moreover, British participation appeared to offer the further advantage that co-operation on a basis of equality with France might break Britain's privileged relationship with the USA and make possible the harmonisation of Franco-British views in Washington. In all the discussions concerning the establishment of an integrated 'Europe' at this time, a major French goal was, therefore, to secure British participation on equal terms. And in 1949, when Jean Monnet was considering ways in which the French economy could be strengthened through planned internationalisation, he first suggested economic co-operation with the British Labour Government. It was the latter's adamant refusal to participate – and indeed its attempt to emasculate the moves that had been made – that led eventually to the so-called Schuman Plan in May 1950.

For three years Franco-German relations over West Germany had followed a constant pattern in which French governments began with an obdurate defence of their claims against their eastern neighbour and then gave way in the face of American *force majeure*. After the holding of the first general election in West Germany in August 1949 it appeared increasingly likely that full economic and political sovereignty would soon be restored to the new state without any controls over the use which could be made of her power. Once again it therefore seemed that France might live in the shadow of superior capitalist competition and greater military potential. The creativity of the Schuman Plan lay in perceiving a way in which German power could be controlled and harnessed to French needs.

In Bonn Chancellor Adenauer presided over a new state with enormous economic potential but a wholly uncertain political future. Its fervent anti-communism and latent strength were now sufficient to endear it to the American Government, but in Europe West Germany was still widely regarded as a pariah. Moreover, internally there were strong nationalist pressures, looking to the Adenauer Government to bring about a restoration of full sovereignty and reunification. The insight of the Schuman–Monnet team lay in the recognition of the opportunity which this apparently bleak situation offered. German coal and steel production – still the essence of industrial and military power – were destined to surpass those of France in any case. What the French team realised was that they could use powerful political bargaining counters to secure some control over, and a share in, the might of the German capitalist economy. The Schuman Plan, and the subsequent complex and detailed negotiations leading to the signing of the European Coal and Steel Community (ECSC) Treaty in 1951, defined the exact nature of the economic deal. Its political counterpart was more straightforward: by entering into a political organisation on equal terms with West Germany, France simultaneously ended the latter's position as an international outcast and weakened the potential for a revival of German nationalism.

The French state had thus made renewed Franco-German war almost unthinkable and had struck an advantageous economic bargain. In addition, French status in Washington was temporarily raised as the architect of an initiative which could greatly strengthen the Western alliance by overcoming Franco-German tension. And, from a capitalist perspective, the ECSC was a striking success and one of the factors on which the political and economic strength of the Fifth Republic was eventually to rest. However, the Coal and Steel Community was not to remain in the public eye for long.

A month after the announcement of the Schuman Plan, East–West tension reached a new peak with the start of the Korean War. The immediate response of the American Government was to strengthen its pressure for rearmament by Western Europe in general and West Germany in particular. The spectre of the resurrection of the Wehrmacht so soon after the war naturally evoked dismay and horror across a wide spectrum of political opinion in France. Squeezed between contradictory pressures emanating from Washington and the domestic environment, the French Government hastily seized upon an expedient to resolve its dilemmas: the participation of West German units in a new European Defence Community (EDC).

In the short term, public enthusiasm for the 'European idea' partially superseded hostility to the notion of a rearmed Germany; in the longer term, as the implications of the EDC became evident, and as Cold War tensions abated, opposition mounted. Finally, in a major domestic crisis amidst bitter American protests, the proposal was rejected by the French Parliament without the government of Pierre Mendès-France giving a strong lead. In view of the humiliation and reproaches which it caused, both domestically and internationally, the EDC episode could hardly be counted as a success for the French state. Yet in a longer-term perspective the experience was not totally negative.

The opponents of the EDC amongst the French elite had had two principal concerns: that France would be incorporated into a military bloc which would be dominated by West Germany, and that Britain would remain outside the unit, continuing to enjoy a privileged relationship with the USA. In other words, while the ECSC had been conceived as a means of offsetting the relative disadvantages in the French situation, it seemed that the EDC would perpetuate them. The constant calls by successive governments for British and American guarantees were thus attempts to transform the proposal and diminish the extent of French inferiority. The failure to secure sufficient concessions to overcome domestic opposition further undermined the political resilience of the Republic. Moreover, the fact that West Germany was subsequently permitted to enter NATO and rearm appeared to be a reversion to the situation which the French had originally sought to prevent with the EDC proposal. However, there were some advantages in the delay. First, by now the French state was reconciled to West German rearmament and convinced that a Franco-German accord was possible; and secondly, France had thwarted the institutionalisation of the situation of subordination to Britain. In a sense, therefore, the rejection of the EDC constituted a further stage in the overcoming of French relative weakness even if the contemporary impression was one of failure.

This disjunction between the underlying trend of increasing potential strength and the surface appearance of weakness and collapse was to continue for the remainder of the life of the Republic. At the visible level governmental instability continued while the French parliament continued to exhibit the features of an archaic petit bourgeois localism rather than that of a fast modernising industrial state. And a mood of increasingly bitter nationalism was spreading, epitomised by the growth of the extreme right-wing *Poujadiste* movement. Such emotions were to be nurtured by the further humiliation of the abortive Suez invasion in 1956 and the apparent impotence of successive French governments in the face of the constantly escalating Algerian crisis. Yet in the aftermath of the EDC, the French state had continued the strategy of the Schuman Plan and with a similar degree of success.

By the time the Messina conference was held in 1955 to reintroduce dynamism into integration (the so-called *relance européenne*), the planners in the French state institutions had come to believe that the next stage of development required greater internationalisation of the economy involving a further dismantling of the legendary French protectionism. However, no French government would surrender any of its controls over the domestic economy without securing commensurate advantages. The Socialist-led government, under Guy Mollet, was to obtain these in the negotiations for EURATOM and the EEC in 1956–57.

If both France and West Germany had reached a stage of economic development in which greater internationalisation was desirable, it was by no means inevitable that they would seek a similar organisational framework to achieve this result. Since West Germany was a highly competitive industrial nation with a great diversity of trading partners, the development of a free trading area with wide geographical boundaries would most clearly have served its interests. French trade was far more restricted, its manufacturers were competitive only in certain spheres, and it had a large agricultural surplus marketed above world prices; it would therefore favour a more limited and protected market with a guaranteed purchasing policy for its high-priced agricultural products. The EEC did not fulfil all the French demands in their entirety, but German negotiators certainly made concessions which cannot be explained on economic grounds alone.

It was evident that no common market could be established without the participation of France and, throughout the discussions, French negotiators exploited this fact to secure concessions from the other five and, above all, from West Germany. In September 1956 four prerequisites for French adherence were listed: (1) that the other states improved their social legislation so that France would not be penalised for incurring higher social expenditure; (2) that France should be allowed to continue to tax imports and subsidise exports because of the relative overvaluation of her currency and her special military expenses; (3) that special safeguard clauses should be included to help meet the French balance of payments difficulties; and (4) that the passage to the second stage of the Common Market should take place only when each state agreed that harmonisation had reached a sufficient level.

Despite the extent to which these safeguards limited the original notion of a common market, Mollet obtained substantial agreement on all of them from Adenauer in a special meeting on 6 November. Early the next year the Germans were induced to accept the continuation of the French agricultural support system and the first moves towards the Common Agricultural Policy and, in the last phase of the negotiations, they finally agreed to French (and Belgian) demands for a form of association for French overseas territories, although they really regarded this as a subsidy to French colonialism.

Why then did West Germany make these concessions? Once again the reasons were primarily political.

The EDC dispute had revived bitterness and mutual recrimination in both France and West Germany and, in 1955, had been followed by a plebiscite in the Saar in which the electorate had overwhelmingly shown its preference for reintegration into West

Germany. The campaign had often been demagogic and a reassertion of strident German nationalism appeared possible. This would naturally have been unwelcome in France; it also threatened the whole strategy of the Adenauer Government which was predicated upon close association between the Federal Republic and the West. Once again a French government had recognised the advantages which it possessed. Mollet had buried the Saar issue with astonishing alacrity and Adenauer was so keen to respond and thus demonstrate the validity of his political strategy that he was prepared to make economic concessions to the French, even at the risk of alienating German farmers and industrialists.

With the formation of the EEC, the French state had, in reality, provided a basis for solving its historic problems. Its economy had entered the stage of advanced capitalism and it had controlled the way in which foreign competition would bring about further modernisation. More specifically, it had diminished the potential threat from West Germany by establishing an interlocking economy with her, in which its own advantages would be exploited and for which it was likely to provide political leadership. Finally, with her own economic growth underway, and in unity with the Six, France was no longer disadvantaged in comparison with Britain. She had already withstood the latter's attempts to dilute the Common Market in a wider free trade area and could now exercise decisive influence over the Community in its subsequent dealings with Britain. The salient feature of French political life in 1958 was the Algerian crisis and the death throes of the Republic, so that the EEC was scarcely even noticed at the time by the public. But at a deeper level much had been achieved by 1958 and West European integration was both a measure and a cause of the success.

It was, however, a success for French capitalism rather than socialism.

The Divided Left[2]

The most fundamental reason for the ineffectiveness of socialism in the Fourth Republic was the division and, for most of the period, the mutual hostility, between the two parties of the French left.

At the end of the Second World War, the left as a whole appeared powerful: communists and socialists had been the dominating forces in the mainland resistance and, in the first post-war elections they had shown their ascendancy (in alliance with the progressive Catholic party, MRP). However, it was a theoretical power only because there was no real unity despite the appearance of accord, which had been established in the Resistance and lasted until the expulsion of the PCF ministers in May 1947. In reality the Socialists *Section française de l'internationale ouvrière* (SFIO) and PCF were wholly different parties which had exhibited bitter antagonism at various stages since the original schism in 1920. They were co-operating uneasily at the end of the war but were soon to resume their fratricidal dispute. In such circumstances socialism could not dominate French politics in either the national or international domains.

The SFIO, though in the minority in 1920, had reassumed its position as the leading party of the left during the interwar period. In theory it was Marxist in inspiration, but it was in fact very factionalised and diverse and was committed to the 'parliamentary road to socialism'. After the euphoria of the 1936 Popular Front Government under Léon Blum had given way to disillusionment, the SFIO had become increasingly ineffective, incapacitated by disputes, particularly over the question of pacifism on the one hand and resistance to fascism on the other. The political and moral decline of the party had culminated in a majority of its deputies voting for Pétain in 1940 and the participation of its former Secretary-General in the Vichy Government. The result had been its virtual disintegration. However, the Resistance had led to a revitalisation of socialist ideas and a regrouping of the party itself by supporters of the imprisoned Blum and his humanistic brand of socialism. By the end of the war the SFIO was, once again, a mass party but was now surpassed by the PCF.

In 1945, partly under the influence of Blum, the SFIO resisted a PCF call for 'organic unity' and set about the reconstruction of the country as *the* party of tripartism (i.e., alliance between the PCF, SFIO and MRP). However, the result of the first post-war election was disappointing for the party for it was placed behind both its alliance partners, and in August 1946 the SFIO congress ousted Blum's supporters from the leadership and elected the supposedly Marxist Mollet to power. In reality this change made little discernible difference to its strategic decisions and, after a Socialist Prime Minister had expelled the PCF ministers from his government, Mollet supported Blum's call in November 1947 for a 'third force' between Gaullism and communism. The party thereafter entered a series of coalition governments theoretically committed to this policy, but the almost immediate result was participation in the ruthless suppression of communist-led strikes – viewed as Soviet-backed insurrectionary threats – in 1947 and 1948.

In the longer term this policy appeared to have catastrophic effects for the SFIO. The 'third force' governments moved steadily to the right and this process was coupled with a loss of SFIO membership, particularly amongst the working classes, a decline in electoral support and general demoralisation amongst party activists. Ultimately, Mollet's attempt to secure party support for policies without socialist content – the EDC, repression in Algeria and the Suez invasion – was to lead to a major exodus from the party and internal sterility. In this sense it can be claimed that, although the SFIO was in office during the negotiations for the establishment of the EEC, socialism exercised little influence over the 'European' policy of the French Government. By now, socialist rhetoric was hardly more than a rationalisation, of an increasingly tortuous kind, for policies determined by other forces.

The PCF was a party of a wholly different kind. At the time of its formation in 1920 the Comintern had allowed the establishment of a centrist leadership in order to ensure that it became the majority organisation of the French left; but it was fully Stalinised in the late 1920s and dominated by the reliable pro-Soviet Thorez from 1930 (until his death in 1964). Meanwhile, and particularly during the Comintern's ultra-left period between 1928 and 1934, the PCF underwent a decline in support.

Its revival began with the adoption of the united front/popular front strategy in 1934, which rank-and-file communists played some part in initiating. The ideological underpinning of this policy was to exercise a real attraction both for the working classes and other groups in society, combining as it did, anti-fascism, defence of the workers and the workers' state (the Soviet Union), and a powerful appeal to national sentiment. Communism, it was claimed, represented both the interests of the workers and the nation. This formula, which was even followed in a distorted form in the period between the Nazi–Soviet pact and the German invasion of the Soviet Union, transformed party fortunes, converting it once more into the leading political organisation of the French left, with a high level of support amongst the traditional working classes and control of the trade union confederation (CGT). The Soviet grip on the party had not loosened, but Stalin's acceptance of the division of Europe gave the PCF some freedom to collaborate with other political forces. In a celebrated interview with the *Times* in November 1946 Thorez thus even went so far as to argue that there were many roads to socialism and that the Soviet model was not necessarily the most appropriate one for the French to follow. However, at the founding conference of the Cominform in October 1947 the PCF was denounced for its moderation in the preceding period and instructed to put the battle against American imperialism at the forefront of all its actions. Thereafter any potential for independence was eroded.

Adulation of Stalin and the Soviet Union, as peaceful by definition, was accompanied by denigration of Tito as a fascist; and Thorez's self-proclamation as a Stalinist was given extra credence when former leading members were expelled from the party and publicly denounced in the manner of the Eastern bloc show trials. Nor did Kruschev's revelations of Stalin's crimes in February 1956, which were in any case minimised by the PCF, make any effective difference either to its support for the Soviet Union or to its internal discipline and control. By then the Cold War might have thawed, but the capacity for independent analysis had apparently ceased to exist. Thus when some party intellectuals called for a wider debate on the issues raised by Kruschev's speech, it was proclaimed: 'The Central Committee has been mindful not to confuse free criticism with the liberty to introduce the ideas of the bourgeoisie into the party of the working class'. Thorez explained the meaning of this when he stated:

> We don't grant to men whose interventions in the interior of the party converge with attacks launched from the outside by our enemies, the 'liberty' to propagate in our ranks their destructive and anti-communist conceptions. Better still, we take the liberty to throw them out of the party.[3]

In November of the same year the *bureau politique* greeted Soviet intervention in Hungary in the following terms:

> Faced with the desperate and bestial effort of fascists, feudal interests and their allies, the church hierarchy, to restore the terrorist regime of Horthy in Hungary, it would have been inconceivable for the workers' and peasants' army of the USSR not to respond to the appeal addressed to it, while the best of the Hungarian working class were massacred, hanged and tortured.
>
> The workers of France are unreservedly on the side of the Hungarian proletariat and the Soviet soldiers who are fighting to prevent the establishment of Fascism in that country, and to consolidate socialist power.[4]

Stalinisation did not, however, mean that the PCF ceased to be the first party of the French left, for it still exercised a powerful attraction for its militants and continued to control the CGT. It even managed to maintain its electoral support with considerable success – an achievement which was all the more remarkable in view of the change in the electoral system in 1951. Yet it too experienced a decline in membership and, despite its claim to be the sole party of the working class, never secured as high a proportion of workers' support as the British Labour Party in the same period. And if the SFIO was initially weakened by ineffective participation in non-socialist governments, the PCF suffered almost as much from its total opposition to French political institutions. For although its ability to maintain mass support in strike movements and peace campaigns remained impressive, its extreme sectarianism limited its potential influence, particularly before 1953. This paradoxical position of simultaneously wielding considerable strength and yet remaining quite isolated had consequences which were sometimes tragic for the left. For its power was sufficient to make an insurrectionary threat appear credible and thus precipitate anti-communist repression, while its sectarianism led potential allies in the ranks of the SFIO to accept the Establishment view that the threat of foreign-inspired revolution must be defeated.

After 1953 there was a partial re-entry of the PCF into the mainstream of French political life. It thus offered its support (which was rebuffed) to the Mendès–France Government in 1954 and, at first, to the Mollet Government in 1956. However, there was no convergence of views and no real basis for co-operation, particularly as the SFIO had moved so far to the right by then.

It was in this situation of disunity, with the Stalinist nature of the PCF and the increasing opportunism of the SFIO, that the left as a whole failed to exert any major influence on the development of the French state during the Fourth Republic. Indeed the lack of consensus over national goals, which characterised French political life as a whole, was reproduced with particular bitterness within the left. Nowhere was this divergence more striking than in the attitudes of the two parties to West European integration.

The SFIO and 'Europe'

Atlanticism
The beginnings of the Atlanticist orientation of the French state preceded its sponsorship of, and participation in, the institutions of West European integration. What attitude did the SFIO take towards this wider process which provided the context for the development of greater unity in the West of Europe?

In the early years after the reconstitution of the SFIO in the Resistance, the ideas of Blum and his closest associates exercised a major influence over party attitudes. Blum's prison writings in *A l'echelle humaine,* for example, were smuggled out of gaol and incorporated, often verbatim, into the first party programme. At first sight, these writings appear to contain a Marxist element: for instance, Blum himself and the Socialists in general, were bitterly condemnatory of the French bourgeoisie, arguing that its pre-war and wartime foreign policy had simply reflected its attempt to preserve class rule. Such sentiments might be expected to have predisposed the Socialists to favour, at the very least, a policy of neutrality between the communist East and the capitalist West. In fact, however, this was never the case. Denigration of the French bourgeoisie was combined with a total rejection of Soviet and French communism and an idealisation of 'Anglo-Saxon' democracy. Whereas Blum blamed the selfish individualism of the French bourgeoisie for the failure of the party system in the Third Republic, he held up British party discipline and loyalty as a model even for the French working class. Moreover, he contrasted the attitude of the inflexible, defensive French bourgeoisie, who could not adapt to change, with that of the 'Anglo-Saxons' who had been capable of innovation. In fact he believed that the increasing state intervention which was evident in the USA and Britain constituted so fundamental a change in the social and economic system that the 'Anglo-Saxon' democracies were already fast becoming socialist.[5] This point was made by the whole Socialist leadership when, in September 1943, they sent a message to Roosevelt and the American people, proclaiming their dream of constructing a United States of the world in the political image of the American New Deal.[6] Similarly, Daniel Mayer, the first Secretary-General of the revived Socialist Party, was later to write:

> Even in the darkest times of 1941 we never doubted that we would triumph ... We, that naturally didn't signify ourselves alone ... but our camp, our team, England, democracy, socialism, a totality of energy and particularly of an ideal which, at that time, was still badly formed, more deeply felt than defined.[7]

This attitude was equally evident at the end of the war for, although the SFIO favoured the Soviet alliance which de Gaulle had negotiated, it also sought a counterbalance in the West. When campaigning against the fusion of the party with the PCF, Blum thus wrote:

> We have always supported the Franco-Soviet alliance. But we are also supporters, in the same way, of a Franco-British alliance and of Franco-American friendship ... Those who are leading the strange campaign of the 'western bloc' against us, are, in reality, working against a Franco-British alliance, Franco-American friendship and international organisation itself. What they want is the continuation of the system of the Three Great Powers, with France tied by a definite alliance with only one of the three – the Soviet Union. We socialists reply: the Franco-Soviet alliance, yes – but not exclusively.[8]

15

The left of the party and much of the rank and file were far more critical of the policies of the United States and Britain than Blum. Nevertheless the 1945 Congress supported the view that the development of parliamentary socialism in Western Europe, and particularly the Labour victory in Britain, made a Western orientation as important as the Soviet alliance.

Nor was the SFIO a mere spectator in the process of the Western alignment. In 1946 Blum himself was the ambassador-extraordinary who negotiated the first major American loan (the Washington Agreement of May 1946) setting underway the process which was to be so important in shifting France towards the Western camp. His advocacy of the French case in a rather hostile climate was indicative of the way in which his socialist theorising could be reconciled with capitalist priorities.

France, he argued, wanted to participate in a free-exchange system, but was unable to do so at present in view of her devastated economy. The measures of *dirigisme* which the government had adopted did not imply an abandonment of free trade for, he claimed, there was no incompatibility between the internal economic regime and external free trade. In any case, the move towards a collective economy had been taken under the pressure of circumstances analogous to those faced by the USA during the war, and the extent of the nationalisations was well-defined and limited and quite compatible with political democracy. In arguing in this way Blum was, consciously or not, taking a political stance: a fully collective economy would have found it impossible to participate in a capitalist free trade system and, by stressing the fact that nationalisations had been undertaken in a limited way because of the stringencies of the situation, he was implicitly rejecting the goal of nationalisation as a step towards socialist equity. Moreover, he concluded by emphasising that France was making every effort to help herself, but that, unless vital external help were granted, she would 'enter into one of those states of evolution whose end result could not be predicted'[9] – a passage which Alfred Grosser is surely justified in interpreting as, 'In other words, "help us or communism will triumph in France"'.[10]

It could be argued that Blum was merely making the case that his American audience wished to hear, but this seems implausible in view of his subsequent advocacy of the agreement itself and American economic policy in general. For although the Washington Agreement banned the use of import quotas by France and, through Blum's verbal assurances, implicitly limited nationalisations, he claimed that there were no ties of any kind on the loan and that the driving force of American policy was the purely disinterested idea 'that no peace was possible in the world unless the various nations [became] conscious of their interdependence and of their joint responsibility'.[11]

Subsequently he endeavoured to show the compatibility between French alignment with the Western economic system on the one hand and socialism on the other, indignantly rejecting the Soviet claim that such American loans threatened national interests. He argued that, on the contrary, the threat came from the USSR which was 'working to set up national sovereignties, which actually resuscitated the interests, instincts and dangers of economic nationalism and could lead to the emergence of two antagonistic blocs'.[12]

In view of his general attitudes it is scarcely surprising that, the next year, Blum sought to mobilise progressive opinion in favour of the Marshall Aid proposal with the proclamation that 'International socialism can now place itself at the head of a great movement of opinion in favour of the American initiative rather than rebutting it.'[13] He justified this with the argument that the organisation which would result would be a step towards the socialist goal of an international community with super-sovereignty[14] (see below, p.20). This was now identified with the emerging American–West European relationship, while the Soviet Union was held responsible for dividing Europe by refusing (and making its satellites refuse) American aid.

On both the Wasington loan and the Marshall Aid proposal, many Socialists were far more sceptical than Blum about the disinterested nature of the American offer and an extreme left group was to be expelled from the party on the latter issue. Yet there was no general inclination to refuse it. A typical view was expressed by a writer in *La Revue socialiste* of November 1947, who acknowledged the danger that the USA would seek to safeguard liberal capitalism in Europe through the aid programme, but urged that the offer must still be accepted because: 'One cannot build socialism on, by, or for the misery of the working classes.' The tasks of the French Government in these circumstances were to ensure that no conditions were attached to the aid, to enlarge the realm of economic and social democracy and to stress that the real solution to the world crisis lay in international socialism.[15]

Thereafter the Socialists were to remain strong proponents of the Western alliance, welcoming the Brussels Pact and NATO and, in general, taking a Western perspective (though not a wholly uncritical one) on Soviet policy. Ultimately, this was to degenerate to the extent that Mollet, in 1956, was to criticise the USA for failing to recognise that the French war in Algeria was necessary for the defeat of international communism. However, the Socialists' acceptance of this Western orientation was always facilitated by their support for

17

the notion of European unification, which was still more deep seated.

Europeanism before 1950

In December 1943, in a proposal for a common Resistance programme, the SFIO, again inspired by Blum, had called for a United Socialist States of Europe, as a first step towards a United States of the World. Its assumptions were twofold. First, that Nazism had been fuelled by nationalism and that similar movements could revive while the nation was regarded as the supreme entity; and secondly, that it was impossible to establish socialist reform in isolation within the nation-state since it would always be subject to external pressures from capitalist forces. In the post-war world a United States of Europe was therefore seen as essential both to control the economic, social and political factors which caused wars, and to safeguard domestic reforms. Moreover, the Socialists argued that the international organisation which should be created for these purposes must be granted extensive powers over nation-states, including even the right to veto their constitutions.[16]

At the end of the war Blum took this up with a call for a European confederation, though with a markedly West European bias and, despite Mollet's rebuttal of Blum's policy ideas, his own supporters' statement at the 1946 conference was not dissimilar:

> In the international order, the Party must aim to bring about close economic co-operation, particularly with the peoples of Europe, who are not subjected to the blocs, who have been greatly impoverished by the war, and who are now attempting the same task of reconstruction. It must state its opposition to all chauvinistic policies, whose only effect is to provoke nationalist exasperation and to multiply the causes of conflict ... Only a constructive internationalism will bring about solutions which, by transcending the national framework in the direction of federalism, will permit the renaissance of a greater working class, united in a new International and ripe for its historic mission.[17]

Long before the process of integration had become concrete, the SFIO was thus committed to the goal of European unity and, given its Western commitment, this was to mean in practice, unity in the West of Europe. Indeed the SFIO could justifiably claim to be the first French party with such a commitment. Moreover, it had a further belief which was still wholly untypical in France and which was, as has been seen, vitally important in the promotion of West European integration: a wish for reconciliation with Germany.

While a prisoner in Buchenwald, Blum had written:

I don't believe in fallen and damned races. I don't believe in it any more for the Germans than for the Jews ... All that is written and said today about the German people and their collective responsibility was said and written about the French people ... in the aftermath of Waterloo...[18]

Such sentiments were reiterated in the statements of the reconstituted SFIO and were shared by the left and right-wing tendencies within it. To be sure, the party also expressed the more explicitly socialist view that German *capitalist* forces had produced Nazism and that French and European security therefore depended on radical social and economic changes in Germany and, in particular, on the 'international nationalisation' of the Ruhr industries.[19] In practice, however, the wish for Franco-German reconciliation was to prove stronger than the demand for the overthrow of German capitalism.

Once the British Labour Government fell in with the USA in rejecting nationalisation in the Western zones, the Socialists had two alternatives: either to abandon reconciliation and to join the nationalist alliance in favour of a more repressive policy, or to argue that the SFIO's goals were attainable through French alignment with the Anglo-American position. By late 1946 this latter alternative involved a refusal to accept the evidence that the objective of the Western allies was to establish a capitalist political entity in their occupation zones but, in view of its general outlook, it was always probable that the SFIO would take this course.

By 1947 the SFIO had acquiesced, with a greater or lesser degree of enthusiasm, in the pro-Western stance of the government, and had revealed a deep-rooted commitment to integration. It could be argued that, objectively speaking, it was now accepting capitalist domination at home – through adamant support for the institutions of the Fourth Republic against working-class unrest – and inclusion in a capitalist alliance bloc abroad.[20] However, if this was the case, it was not *perceived* in this way. The 'third force' was to provide a rationale for domestic policy and the goal of West European integration was to provide an ideological justification for acceptance of the Western power bloc.

In the circumstances where the SFIO was comparatively weak, the notion of European unification, as the international expression of the 'third force', appeared extremely attractive. Not only did it provide a goal in a discouraging situation, but it was also rooted in the aspirations of socialist forces in the Resistance. The immediate historical circumstances thus harmonised with the longer-term ideological background to make the notion of a United States of Europe appear to be a natural and autonomous policy commitment.

Blum expressed this general aspiration when he wrote in January 1948:

> Between the United States, 'champions of individual liberty and the rights of man', but where the capitalist economy is fully maintained ... in all its inhumane severity, and the Soviet Union, which has destroyed capitalist private property but has also eliminated all individual, civic and social liberties, there is a place for nations which want both personal liberty and a collective economy, democracy and social justice. That is, between American capitalism – 'expansionist' as are all capitalist societies in their ascendant phase – and the totalitarian and imperialist communism of the Soviets, there is a place for social democracy, a place for socialism. It is neither an exaggeration nor a presumption to affirm that democratic socialism represents at present the predominant aspiration of old Europe, specially of Western Europe ... The international third force is therefore really a force. And, in order to act as a force, it must become conscious of itself, of its nature and of its immediate mission.[21]

Although the 1948 congress revealed rank-and-file anxiety about the implications of accepting Marshall Aid and being incorporated into a Western bloc under American control, the attraction of creating a United Europe was sufficient to secure unanimous support for an international resolution which specified that American aid could be acceptable only if it respected the democratic right of Europeans to determine their own economic and social policies, and effective only if Europeans constructed new industries based on mass production through low prices, secured by a large continental market. This necessitated the economic unification of Europe which assumed

> the unification of legislation, the concerted organisation of production, the planning of exports, the internationalisation of great basic industries; that is, it involves the necessity of a political unification meaning the creation of a supranational body, granted effective powers, based on popular opinion, the first institution of the future United States of Europe.

But:

> these efforts ... must not be turned in favour of either of the blocs. United and Independent Europe is open to all the peoples of the continent.[22]

Given the division of Europe and the extent of the alignment with the West that was already evident, the aspiration for unity of the whole continent was, by now, little more than a pious hope. Nevertheless, all the major theoretical currents within the SFIO united in providing rationales for European unification within the framework of the Western alignment.

Blum's role has already been stressed and it is sufficient to note that, until his death in March 1950, he continued to provide justifications for West European integration as 'socialist', which he promoted in practical terms by becoming a President of Honour of the European Movement in October 1948.[23] As the elder statesman of the party, and the major interpreter of the Jaurèsian tradition, he continued to exert influence with his argument that internationalism was equivalent to socialism, and that, in present circumstances, the only means of attaining this goal was through the construction of West European integration. However, in view of the fact that in 1948 a critical Marxist element remained within the party, it is unlikely that unity could have been maintained on the issue unless the left had also produced advocates of European unification. In this respect two figures were of particular importance – Pierre Rimbert and Marceau Pivert – both of whom had supported Mollet in 1946 in the effort to reduce Blum's influence and to propel the party in a more left-wing direction.

Rimbert was the party's main economic theorist and claimed to base his analysis in Marxist political economy. The pivotal point of his theory, expressed in numerous articles and a widely read book first published in 1949, was that the existence of the nation-state constituted a contradiction both for capitalism and socialism.[24] As such, socialism could not triumph without its suppression. Capitalism was characterised by the law of the falling rate of profit which led capitalists to limit production whenever profitability was threatened. But:

> At the moment when capitalism reaches the point where it must cease production, it enters into a contradiction with the interests of the nation. This contradiction is due to the division of the world into separate and sovereign nations. This division obliges each nation ceaselessly to develop its economic power in order to maintain its independence and sovereignty, particularly as modern warfare is a war of equipment, thus of production.[25]

Thus the state was increasingly forced to intervene to supplement capitalism in order to maintain its power in the international sphere. As this tendency was accentuated the national economy assumed the form of a 'statist economy' and, rather than acting as the

21

instrument of the bourgeoisie, it became the expression of class equilibrium. But the period of statist economy could be transitional only for

> the division of the world into sovereign nations does not allow a single nation to remain behind. Universal competition between nations obliges each to advance ceaselessly. This necessitates the development of socialist forms of production, for only these are capable of increasing the economic power of each nation. And the development of socialist forms of production means the march towards the rupture of the equilibrium.[26]

Thus the seeds of socialism were discernible within the capitalist state, and increasing socialisation would be forced by international competition. But Rimbert was just as convinced as Blum that socialism could triumph only on the international level. Enclosed within the national framework the statist economy could not be transcended since it would continue to face the struggle for power and survival against all other world states. Socialism could therefore triumph only if the framework of the nation-state had *already* been surpassed. Rimbert was thus arguing, apparently from a Marxist viewpoint, that the process of building an international community was at least as important a step towards socialism as was anything which occurred within the nation-state. And he became increasingly explicit in his identification of this process with the development of West European integration, within the framework established by the Marshall Plan.

The role of Marceau Pivert was perhaps of still greater importance in facilitating the acceptance of the consensus viewpoint on Europe by the party's left-wing. For Pivert was the 'revolutionary' who had been expelled from the SFIO in 1938 and had subsequently formed the *Parti socialiste ouvrier et paysan* (PSOP), at times close to Trotskyism, before being readmitted into the party in 1946. He therefore possessed powerful left-wing credentials. Moreover, he was of specific importance on the issue of Eruopean unity, as he had been president of a left–socialist international movement for the United Socialist States of Europe in 1947, which had specifically opposed any integration of Europe which might have the effect of strengthening capitalism. Yet Pivert remained prominent within the organisation when it changed its name in late 1948 to the *Mouvement socialiste pour les Etats-Unis d'Europe* (MSEUE), came under 'moderate' influence and became the most progressive wing of the European movement. His continued participation in the organisation therefore helped to prevent the development of left-wing dissidence on the issue.

Pivert provided yet another variation on a theme. Dissenting from Blum for his overt reformism and Rimbert for his economic determinism, he nevertheless argued that the creation of a United States of Europe was the major priority in order to prevent the onset of a third world war, and to build world socialism. He thus urged that the synthesis could now be established between two forms of socialism which had, until then, remained dominant:

> The socialism of 1948 must be more *democratic* than social-democracy before 1914 – more *revolutionary* than were the Leninists in October 1917. But above all *internationalist* ...
>
> International democratic socialism is leaving its infancy and entering its adolescence because it has finally found the material and economic framework, where its civilisation can blossom, *that is Europe.*[27]

Despite this revolutionary enthusiasm, Pivert's loathing for Stalinism enabled him to co-operate with the reformist right of the SFIO and liberals outside the party, and put forward arguments which, though rooted in a different perspective, yielded substantially similar conclusions. He always argued in favour of a federation of the whole of Europe, and he sometimes condemned the USA in strident terms, but his acceptance of Marshall Aid and the subsequent steps towards West European integration, effectively led him to support the establishment of a purely West European unit.

Yet if there was left-wing support for the construction of a united Western Europe, André Philip was emerging as the dominating influence on the issue and his position was unequivocally on the right of the party.[28] In November 1948 Philip became the most powerful political and intellectual influence within the MSEUE which secured recognition by the SFIO as a non-party organisation whose work should nevertheless be supported. In this position, he was able to influence SFIO policy in a direction which conformed to his own theoretical and political commitment, without apparently departing from the consensus viewpoint. Thus the July 1949 party congress adopted as its policy statement a 'Manifesto for Europe' in which Philip's influence was apparent. European unity, it argued, was an economic necessity, for there was no possibility of a real modification of the structure of trade and production or of creating vital new industries unless a large, unified market was created:

> If she remained cut up into segments, shielded behind autarchic economic policies, at the end of Marshall Aid Europe could neither retake her place in international commerce, nor avoid a lowering of her living standards, of which the working-class

23

would be the major victim.

But European unification could not be secured merely by liberal measures, such as the lowering of customs barriers. Rather, it was necessary positively to co-ordinate policies and,

> In particular, if one wants to avoid the return to cartels of private interests in the basic industries, whose harmfulness was made apparent before the war, it is vital to create European public institutions, ensuring the general direction of production, price levels and the control of investments.[29]

The objective was to establish, in all European countries, including West Germany, the pursuit of a full employment policy, guaranteeing the real standard of living of the workers, with long-term agreements on prices, purchasing contracts and production policies.

This manifesto was extremely similar to a longer report which Philip had just presented to the European Movement.[30] The fundamental argument of both was that Socialists should be prepared to co-operate with other political forces in the establishment of West European institutions, with powers to promote a degree of economic integration. This would not mean the immediate creation of a socialist United States of Europe, but the erection of appropriate institutions would mean that this aim could be realised once the 'balance of political forces in Europe opens up the democratic possibility of doing so'.[31] Given the SFIO's domestic weakness, and the comparative ineffectiveness of socialist parties in Western Europe as a whole, this strategy seemed to maintain the commitment to a socialist Europe whilst offering a hope for an immediate advance towards that end.

The argument may have been persuasive but was based on the highly questionable assumption that the new West European institutions, and their policies, could be politically neutral. Moreover, in practice Philip was prepared to go further towards the non-socialist position than the party as a whole probably realised. The whole tone of his report to the European Movement was coloured by his insistence upon the possibility of, and necessity for, finding a compromise between the state interventionist and *laissez-faire* positions amongst the protagonists of West European integration, and to this end, he accepted the necessity for an orthodox deflationary policy, whose effects were inevitably severe on the working class. Indeed his general conclusion was that the danger of national autarchy was so serious and negotiations between sovereign states so ineffective that the paramount necessity was to establish European institutions to which the common exercise of certain rights of sovereignty should be transferred.

In 1949, therefore, while the party was united on the commitment to West European integration, its strategy was increasingly influenced by Philip, whose general ideological position predisposed him to compromise traditional socialist goals in order to establish some form of West European unit. Nevertheless, there was one question which impeded the progress which Philip sought and which had definite ideological implications for the SFIO: the role of Britain.

Faith in Britain in general and the Labour Party in particular had been of immense importance to Blum and the French Socialists both during the war and in the early post-war periods. Britain and France, and the SFIO and Labour Party, had been seen as the twin pivots in the new Europe that was to be created. Indeed the proclamation of the 'third force' Europe could make sense in a political/social sense only with the participation of the Labour Government (and, to a lesser extent, that of the Scandinavian countries). Any signs of interest by the Labour Party were therefore eagerly welcomed by the SFIO whilst Labour opposition was a bitter disappointment. In general too, Labour hostility to European unity was interpreted sympathetically: that is, it was seen to stem from a socialist desire not to be embroiled in a supranational Europe based on capitalist free enterprise. The 'Manifesto for Europe' therefore deplored 'the liberal offensive against the Labour Government recently launched by "international capitalism"' and an extraordinary congress in December of the same year reaffirmed socialist opposition to all attempts to integrate Europe without Britain.[32]

Perhaps this commitment to the Labour Party and the belief that British involvement would lead West European integration to be more democratic or socialistic, was idealistic. Nevertheless, the SFIO's wish for British participation stemmed as much from political and ideological considerations as from the French national ones discussed earlier. It was an attempt to maintain some form of socialist content in the concept of a 'third force' Europe. 1950 was to be a turning point in this sense.

The Schuman Plan

Robert Schuman's proposal for a European Coal and Steel Community in May 1950 was not a purely external event for the SFIO. In 1949 Philip had suggested such a project in his report to the European Movement and had taken initiatives in the Strasbourg Assembly which had influenced Schuman. On the surface the initiative conformed so closely to the spirit of the ideas that the SFIO had advocated ever since the war that it could be regarded as an autonomous socialist policy. It combined three Socialist Party ideas: Franco-German *rapprochement;* the establishment of a supranational authority as the germ of a new international order; and international control over basic industries. If it represented a defeat for the original and more specifically socialist commitment to the 'international nationalisation' of basic industries (particularly the Ruhr), it was nevertheless apparently in line with the MSEUE's strategy of accepting proposals which provided a structure which was compatible with socialist aims. On the other hand, by its stress on supranationalism and its general commitment to the principles of free competition, the proposal was presented in such a way as to ensure its rejection by the Labour Government. How would the SFIO react in these circumstances?

At its annual congress, less than a fortnight after Schuman's announcement, the resolution, which was carried unanimously, illustrated the party's basic sympathy for the project. On the other hand reservations were also expressed. It was argued that, to be fully effective, an effort should be made to incorporate as many nations as possible, and particularly Britain, so that it did not seem to be an alliance directed against other states; the High Authority should have effective powers to impose its decisions, should contain an important degree of worker representation and should be responsible before a democratic international assembly; and the Ruhr industries should not be returned to private capitalism. In particular the party executive was urged to follow the negotiations vigilantly to ensure that a private steel cartel was not covertly reintroduced under the camouflage of the Plan.[33]

The problem of Britain was approaching its negative resolution despite SFIO wishes. In June 1950 the Labour Party called an international socialist conference in an attempt to secure support for its own position and, just before the conference sat, released a pamphlet which attacked the moves towards integration from a viewpoint which combined socialist analysis with nationalist rhetoric. (This pamphlet, and Labour's motives, will be discussed in chapter 4). The SFIO deplored the precipitous way in which the French Government had handled the negotiations with Britain, and again declared that it would never associate itself with any European policy directed against Britain. On the other hand it also expressed its regret at Labour's decision to publish the manifesto and stated that some sections of it 'reveal major modifications of attitude to the very concept of Europe, modifications with which the SFIO would never associate itself.'[34] The international socialist conference of 17 June failed to resolve the underlying conflict and the SFIO was fast reaching the position in which it was to support integration without Britain.

André Philip (with Gerard Jaquet, the other dominant SFIO figure in the MSEUE) now forced the pace on the issue. Already in May 1949 Philip had written:

> I fear that if our Labour friends pursue the realisation of socialism in a strictly national framework and disinterest themselves from the plight of Europe, it will eventually lead to a dangerous technocracy and a national socialism which will have nothing to do with our common ideal.[35]

In May 1950 Philip and Jacquet took up positions in favour of integration without Britain (for which they were reprimanded by the party executive),[36] and later the same year Philip published a pamphlet, *Le Socialisme et l'unité européenne* which was a direct and bitter critique of the Transport House manifesto. The Labour Party document, he claimed, was a blow:

> The tactlessness and contradictions of some of its statements, the expression of a nationalist isolationism which had always, until lately, been the prerogative of right-wing parties, is going to allow a fraction of the liberal bourgeoisie to pose as more advanced and more progressive than some who call themselves socialists.

He argued that despite Labour's conviction that the British economy was more socialist than that of the continental countries there was actually as much nationalisation and more public investment in France than in Britain; and France had introduced as much socialism through coalition governments as Labour, blinded by its prejudice in favour of the two-party system, had done in Britain. Besides:

> How can the Labour Party reject with horror all collaboration with a non-socialist Europe and then affirm its indissoluble solidarity, its close identity of viewpoint, its unshakeable solidarity, on the one side with the Commonwealth where ... all the governments are Conservative, and on the other with an America which, progressive as its policy is, could not be considered as the representative of a genuinely socialist ideology. In reality, none of this is serious. These arguments are only used as a pretext.

The real reason, he believed, was that the Labour Party wanted to maintain Britain's position as centre of the sterling area, in close conjunction with the Atlantic Community.

If this position is confirmed, we must, to our great regret, without waiting any longer, draw the necessary conclusions. We will still seek to obtain the adherence of our British friends to specialised economic institutions, particularly those which are seeking the planning of basic industries. But on the political level, we will no longer search for impossible compromises with them. We will prepare the organisation of a genuine federal Europe with all those who will accept it...[37]

The SFIO was not prepared to go as far as this, and in November 1950 the party's national council again claimed that European unification, without British and Scandinavian participation, would be valueless. Nevertheless, they supported the negotiations for the Schuman Plan and hoped that other supranational institutions of the same type would be created. Moreover, at the May 1951 congress, André Philip was the *rapporteur* of the international resolution, which claimed that any delay in the ratification of the ECSC Treaty would 'gravely compromise the European idea and weaken the chances of peace'.[38]

Philip's own position was that of a totally enthusiastic protagonist of the ECSC. In the same year he thus produced a propaganda pamphlet for the European Movement extolling the virtues of the proposal, and condemning the 'narrow vested interests, and obsolete traditions and nationalisms' which opposed it;[39] and he also wrote the official report for the parliamentary economic council favouring ratification of the treaty on the same economic grounds as the non-socialist elite – namely that the French economy could withstand competition and would be modernised under its impact.[40] But those who were less totally committed to integration also favoured the ECSC, and the SFIO deputies were the largest group in the national assembly supporting ratification. Even Socialists who were highly critical of the Coal and Steel Community came to substantially similar conclusions. For example, in the May 1951 issue of *La Revue socialiste*, an anonymous writer argued that the Community was conceived in a bureaucratic manner, without real worker or popular influence, and was not only incapable of providing for full employment, but could actually intensify the development of private cartellisation. Nevertheless, he maintained that the socialist attitude to it should not be negative because its creation corresponded to a real necessity for the political and economic unification of Western Europe, and it differed from a cartel since it was a public organisation. The task of European socialists was to expropriate the owners of the coal and steel industries and to give the property to a genuine European community: 'And this task seems...to be more in the interests of socialism than the rejection of the community in the name of national independence.'[41]

Acceptance of the Schuman Plan constituted a major step along the road to the emasculation of any specifically socialist conception of West European integration within the SFIO. However, the notion of Franco-German reconciliation within a supranational organisation was apparently so close to the aspirations of the Socialists during the Resistance, that it was almost inevitable that the SFIO's welcome for the general characteristics of the plan would supersede any reservations they felt about its capitalistic nature. In any case they had already abandoned the commitment to the 'international nationalisation' of the Ruhr under American and British pressure, and could therefore justifiably argue that the creation of a purely private cartel was a real likelihood, and that the ECSC was more socialistic than the probable alternative.[42]

The EDC and the Crisis of the SFIO

If the Schuman Plan exposed some of the difficulties in the SFIO's position, the Pleven Plan for a European Defence Community was to accentuate them and bring about the worst crisis in the party since that of 1940. On the one hand the plan would bring about West German rearmament to which the Socialists were overwhelmingly opposed; on the other hand, it appeared to constitute a major step towards the creation of a supranational Western Europe. The attempt to resolve this contradiction was to prove very costly.

While the vast majority of the SFIO were opposed to German rearmament in any form there was nevertheless a small minority, strongly committed to 'Europe' and the Atlantic Alliance, who favoured the idea underlying the EDC. As early as 1 December 1949 Léon Blum had seen this as the solution to the dilemma of West European defence;[43] and in August 1950, when Churchill had proposed German rearmament in the Assembly of the Council of Europe, André Philip had proposed the successful amendment which envisaged the creation of German units integrated into a unified European army under the direction of a European minister of defence and subject to the democratic control of a European assembly.

This was a minority viewpoint within the SFIO, but the party was still represented in the government when Pleven announced his project and it accepted the idea as a lesser evil than the reestablishment of an autonomous West German army. However, once the party went into opposition, and East–West tension diminished, the proposal became increasingly unpopular within the SFIO and divided it more seriously than any other party.

In general, particularly in the early stages of the dispute, the pro-European *cédistes* (i.e., those in favour of the EDC) argued that

29

the notion of a European army, based upon the integration of units, supranationalism and democratic control, constituted a major step towards the goal of a united Europe and that, although it was regrettable that circumstances had forced military integration to take precedence over economic, social and political unification, these traditional socialist goals would nevertheless be advanced by acceptance of the project. The most common initial opposition case, on the other hand, was to argue that the EDC was simply a camouflaged version of German rearmament, which involved the threat of being led into war by German revanchists in pursuit of the lost eastern territories, or of a strengthened state, bargaining between East and West, or even of a new German invasion. Moreover, some of the anti-*cédistes* used the 'European' argument themselves and claimed that military integration threatened to destroy the socialist goal of European unity by reviving German militarism, thereby destabilising the precarious democracy in West Germany, and precipitating a nationalist backlash in other West European states.

The intraparty conflict was reinforced by a complex interaction between national and international politics. For the break which had taken place between the SFIO and the Catholic MRP on the education issue in 1951 had revived SFIO enmity against 'clerical reaction', with inevitable effects upon foreign as well as domestic policy. Since the MRP, with the Christian Democrats in West Germany and Italy, were now the dominating forces in favour of a federal Europe of the Six, many Socialists purported to fear that the establishment of a supranational Western Europe would consolidate the hold of Catholicism, conservatism and capitalism. The presence of Britain and, if possible, Scandinavia, in any united Europe therefore seemed as important as ever for ideological reasons, as well as for the national ones outlined above (page 8). However, the British Conservative Government was of course no more anxious to grant control over its army to a European community than the Labour Government had been to sacrifice national control over social and economic policy.

In this acutely problematic situation, Mollet had two preoccupations. First, he was genuinely afraid that the goal of integration, to which he was fully committed, would be jeopardised if the EDC were rejected. Secondly, influenced by American threats, he feared that West European defences against the Soviet Union would be compromised unless the project were accepted. While attempting to justify the EDC in socialist terms, his strategy was thus always to seek an acceptable compromise on which party unity could be maintained. At the May 1952 congress, he concluded the debate with the formula 'neither refusal nor acceptance' and three conditions for socialist acquiescence were formulated: the creation of a supranational political authority, with limited but real powers under democratic control within a European assembly; the continued presence of American troops in Europe and American guarantees against all ruptures of the treaty (i.e., to prevent West Germany from securing autonomous control over its army); and British association.[44] However, this compromise merely reflected the contradictions within the party's position for the conditions were mutually incompatible.[45] In any case, it failed to quell the mounting opposition and, as time went on, the anti-*cédistes* gradually united on an alternative policy. Influenced both by the national considerations outlined above and by the conviction that *détente* with the Soviet Union would be possible so long as West Germany was not rearmed, they argued that the major priority should be international disarmament and the reunification of Germany. By adopting this policy the anti-*cédistes* were, in reality if not in intention, challenging the policy of integration within the Atlantic Alliance, at least as it was conceived in Washington. Given Mollet's preoccupation with strengthening the Western bloc against the Soviet Union, and his commitment to 'Europe', this was a challenge he was determined to defeat.

The dénoument took place in 1954. At an extraordinary party congress in June, Mollet was able to secure a decision in favour of ratification only by disregarding the normal voting machinery and relying on the more populous northern regions whose support for him was almost unconditional. Yet despite the fact that the congress also ruled that the SFIO deputies should be bound by its decision, more of them subsequently voted against the project than favoured it.[46] The result was the expulsion of the recalcitrant members from the executive, and their replacement by those loyal to the party decision. Finally, in December 1954 all but 18 deputies voted for the agreement which brought West Germany into NATO, but which maintained greater French control over its troops on a basis of near equality with Britain.

The bitter controversy over the EDC had dominated the SFIO for two years and was to have negative long-term effects upon the party and its attitudes to 'Europe'. The most obvious impact was to propel the SFIO still further towards the right. This is not because the anti-*cédistes* were all on the left, for some of the most prominent of them were normally reliable pro-leadership stalwarts, whose opposition on this occasion had sprung more from national than socialist considerations. Nevertheless, much of the rank-and-file hostility to the EDC was from the left and alliances with the PCF had taken place for the first time since 1947. The imposition of disciplinary measures on dissidents and the quitting of the party by intransigent opponents of the project thus increased the conformist, non-socialist inclinations of the *Molletiste* leadership.

If the effects on the party's 'European' policy were less immediately apparent, they were equally significant. First, the party, like much of the non-socialist elite now tended to become more assertive about national goals and more restive about the USA, which had appeared relatively indifferent to French interests during the EDC affair; and secondly the justification for French involvement in West European integration was to become less specifically socialist than ever.

Modernisation and the relance européenne

The shift in attitude towards the United States was discernible in the case of André Philip, although he had been one of the major supporters of the EDC within the party. To be sure, even in 1950 he had argued that an essential aim of European unification was to provide political and economic independence from the USA so that the Atlantic Alliance could become a community between near equals, rather than a system in which one power was totally dominant.[47] But at that stage he had tended to glorify the United States. Later his emphasis changed substantially. In April 1952 he expressed concern at the way in which any fluctuation in the American economy could have catastrophic repercussions on Europe;[48] a few months later he was claiming that the Americans had made a major mistake in demanding, amidst great publicity, German rearmament, for this had weakened democratic tendencies in Germany and had reduced the enthusiasm of young people for the European idea;[49] and by 1954 he claimed that American loans sometimes had a humiliating and disagreeable character and that, in general, the USA was insufficiently aware of its responsibilities and contributed to world economic instability. In these circumstances, Europe should make precise propositions to the USA

> warning it that if it is not prepared to make the necessary efforts and sacrifices that its dominant position in the world economy entails, other countries must seek the means to resolve these problems amongst themselves within a narrower framework and so create another economic equilibrium.[50]

In the event of a probable negative response from the USA, West Europe should establish itself as a unit, based on internal planning and an external policy of price stabilisation and international investment for Third World countries. Moreover he also claimed that a united Europe would be able to guarantee the western frontier of the Soviet Union – on the Oder–Neisser border, in the Sudetenland, and in the maintenance of control over East Germany. This was a departure from the American-led Western position and Philip argued that this policy would lead the USSR to realise that it too had an interest in the establishment of a strong, united Europe, capable of playing a conciliating and pacifying role between the two superpowers.

With the rightward shift of the party, Philip was also able to provide a doctrine which was far more in keeping with its practice than was Mollet's pseudo-Marxist jargon. For he, and in reality the party leadership, now advocated production, industrialisation and technical progress, coupled with social reform. The emphasis was thus close to that of the state elite: the modernisation of the capitalist economy rather than its overthrow. Once again, it was André Philip who most clearly and consistently linked this commitment to modernisation with the notion of integration in Europe.

Already in the late 1940s Philip had stressed rationalisation of production methods and the consequent prospect of a higher standard of living as a major reason for advocating integration, and these considerations had played an important role in his favourable attitude to the ECSC. But his commitment to such goals became more manifest in the early 1950s when the revisionist current, influenced both by Cold War pressures and economic and social developments, became stronger in France as in Britain. Convinced that Marxist predictions had been invalidated by events, he argued that the working class was growing neither in size nor in solidarity and that there was therefore nothing inevitable about the triumph of socialism. If it were ever to come about, he believed that this could only be as a compromise between various interests in the service of a common moral value which stressed the autonomy of man and sought to emancipate him from all forms of oppression and exploitation. This, he argued, was incompatible with the preservation of the *status quo*, for the essence of socialism was expansionist. Socialism was not primarily a matter of distributing given wealth more fairly but

> above all of creating new [wealth]. This is why it must oppose everything which keeps economic life at a backward technical level and must fight against all protection of outdated forms of production. It must associate with all who now want to bring about the technological revolution which will permit the growth of productivity and an increased standard of living for all.[51]

He asserted that this goal was realisable only if mass production methods and a planned distribution and utilisation of resources were implemented and that this, in turn, depended upon transcending the national framework and creating a united European market.

Philip's explicit contention was that the true line of division between right and left depended upon the attitude taken to economic modernisation and the nation state. All who favoured modernisation and integration in Western Europe were reliable allies for the socialists, while all who clung to anachronistic economic forms and the protection of the nation-state were really reactionaries. As the commitment to modernisation became a dominating ideological force within the SFIO, this theoretical position on 'Europe' was increasingly adopted by the party. It was, as has been shown, very close to that of the non-socialist 'modernisers', and enabled the SFIO to co-operate with other pro-European political forces in Monnet's Action Committee for the United States of Europe, and to offer full support for the *relance européenne* at Messina in 1955.

When the SFIO vote increased after four years of opposition and Guy Mollet assumed the leadership of a coalition government in January 1956, the desire for greater independence from the USA and for economic modernisation through controlled internationalisation rapidly became evident and were to be combined in the negotiations which were ultimately to lead to the establishment of the EEC (see pp. 9–10 above).

In his investiture speech in February 1956, Mollet strongly supported the idea of co-operation in the development of nuclear power in Western Europe (Euratom) and argued:

> Together, the European countries can develop by themselves their nuclear industry and thus attain the level of the two great powers. Separately, they will never overcome their backwardness
> ...
>
> We want to give Europe an energy potential equivalent to that of the two great powers of the world, and exclusively for peaceful purposes.[52]

If the wish to secure greater independence from the USA was present from the start, the crises of Mollet's period of office greatly intensified this tendency. Following the abortive Suez invasion, one SFIO speaker in the assembly debate in January 1957 argued:

> Nasser and Bulganin have taught France that we are exposed in such a way as to place ourselves more and more under American protection, while in so doing we risk finding the United States against us in the defence of certain of our vital interests ... The road to safety is that of Europe resting on Africa.[53]

American opposition to French repression in Algeria further accentuated this attitude and just after his fall from power Mollet thus combined bitter criticisms of American policy with a fervent belief in the absolute necessity for maintaining the Atlantic Alliance in order to maintain West European security against the Soviet Union. He concluded:

> Within the Atlantic Alliance, only a United Europe can claim a real independence: I stress *in* the Atlantic Alliance. It is not a question of creating a neutral Europe, but an *independent and allied* Europe, not a satellite, but an equal partner.[54]

This, he claimed, was the ultimate objective of socialist policy.

If the notion of greater autonomy from the USA influenced the policy of the Mollet Government, the belief that economic modernisation depended on European integration was of still greater importance. Each of the main SFIO speakers in Parliament, and party propaganda as a whole, thus constantly stressed that only the EEC, through its competition, would enable France to modernise its economic structures and raise its productivity so as to permit an increased standard of living and higher social security benefits. In particular, Alain Savary, in his influential report to the national assembly, adopted a very similar viewpoint to that which Philip had constantly expressed, when he claimed that France 'confined in a traditional Malthusianism does not utilise its resources to their best effect. The Common Market is openly breaking the iron collar that the demographic revival and economic growth have condemned.'[55] It was admitted that greater competition contained risks, but the SFIO argument was that it also provided an opportunity for vital modernisation – the key to economic and social progress.

While the themes stressed by the Mollet Government in its EEC policy reflected the growth of criticism of the USA and the commitment to modernisation which had developed in the party, they also revealed departures from the previous SFIO policy, which also stemmed in part from the EDC experience. First, whereas the Socialists had been committed to the notion of a federal Europe, they now tended to stress the extent to which national sovereignty would be retained within the EEC. In part this arose from the desire to appease the opponents of federalism within the country as a whole; but the EDC campaign has also shown party hostility to supranational institutions which removed important powers from the national framework. Moreover the SFIO was susceptible to the mood of intense nationalism which was now so prevalent. In this situation the SFIO leadership would have been unlikely to campaign vigorously for the kind of supranationalism that it had advocated in the 1940s, even if this had been practicable. A second difference lay in the fact that, although various SFIO speakers expressed the hope that Britain would join the EEC at a later date, her absence was no longer regarded as a factor of vital importance. Indeed Britain's attempts to secure outlets for her manufactured goods whilst maintaining the Commonwealth as her main agricultural supplier were specifically criticised.[56]. Here again British awkwardness over the EDC, following continual failure to attract British interest in 'Europe', was of importance. Moreover, economic ties with West Germany were seen to be far closer than those with Britain and, once in power, Mollet allotted a much higher priority to securing close Franco-German relations than to the Franco-British connection. Finally, despite the attempt to claim that the EEC was 'socialistic' – whether because of its interventionism, its commitment to the equalisation of social conditions, or its notion of a Euro-African community – there was in reality little trace of any specifically socialist attitude to the EEC within the SFIO in 1957. Some Socialists expressed fears about the role of French agriculture and the future of Southern France in a predominantly north European bloc, and the danger of West German economic competition, but these themes were taken up more vigorously by non-socialists.[57] The official SFIO policy was, for the moment, uncritical acceptance of the negotiated treaties, which were, of course, also favoured by capitalist modernising forces. (Appendix Two outlines the aspects of the treaties which Socialists might have found objectionable.)

Continuity and Change in SFIO Policy

It could be argued that this uncritical attitude to the EEC was implicit as soon as the SFIO committed itself to the 'third force' and European unity in the 1940s: that the deep-rooted attachment to the goal of unification would, at all stages, have produced support for any form of integration except in the realm of defence. Equally, it could be claimed that the two major theoretical influences over the Socialists' European outlook – Blum and Philip – both favoured integration for reasons which were more social–democratic than socialist and would have accepted the EEC at any time. It might therefore be concluded that nothing substantial changed in the attitude of the SFIO to 'Europe' between 1947 and 1957.[58] Although this argument has much validity, it overlooks the evolution of the party and its internal crises during the second half of this period.

Before 1950 there had been vigorous internal debate within the SFIO and, if the right remained dominant, the left still existed and subjected policies to critical scrutiny from a socialist perspective. Similarly, the strategy of the 'European' policy may always have been dominated by Blum and Philip on the right, but it had been forced to define itself in terms which were acceptable to the left in order to carry the party and, while this continued to be necessary, there remained the possibility that the more specifically socialist element within the consensus would gain influence. By the time the Schuman Plan was proposed, there had certainly been a further shift to the right, induced in part by external pressures from Britain and the USA which precluded international nationalisation of German heavy industry in the Ruhr and the notion of a 'third force' Europe. The SFIO had thus been forced to choose between integration on a non-socialist basis or no 'Europe' at all. The more evident were the effects of international pressures, the greater was the disillusionment and demoralisation of the left, thus further diminishing any specifically socialist attitudes to integration. The effects of this process were already evident in the party's attitude to the Schuman Plan but, as has been seen, American pressure for the rearmament of West Germany greatly accentuated it and brought about the crisis which was eventually to lead to the near elimination of the left within the SFIO. As a result of this, Mollet secured domination over all levels of the declining party apparatus and when he became Prime Minister in 1956, the party became a mere cypher for governmental policies. Party congresses and publications were used as means of publicising the leadership's achievements and securing votes of congratulations,[59] and dissidents and critics, now including André Philip, were unceremoniously disciplined or expelled.

By 1957 the interaction of crises in the party and French society as a whole meant that the SFIO no longer existed as an independent political force. Rather it was a vehicle for use by a government, which was implementing – or, more accurately, acquiescing in – a ruthless policy in Algeria and introducing domestic censorship on all critical journals. In this atmosphere of inflamed chauvinism over Algeria, EEC entry was far less controversial, and the majority of socialists probably viewed it as a solace from the more turbulent issues of the day.

It is therefore unsatisfactory to argue either that there was total continuity or a total break in the SFIO's conception of European unity. Rather the pressures on the party led it to evolve in such a way that the right-wing ideological tendency, which had dominated even in the 1940s, came to exclude all other elements, and eventually the possibility of criticism itself. However, one further factor was of decisive importance in influencing this tendency: the hostility to domestic and international communism. The break of 1947 therefore remains of fundamental singificance in explaining the progressive dilution of the specifically socialist element in SFIO ideology and policy.

The PCF and 'Europe'

Attitudes to the West and 'Europe' before the Break in 1947
In an important sense the SFIO had shared the underlying motivations of the French state in its attitudes to West European integration. It had thus favoured a Western alignment, *rapprochement* with West Germany and the modernisation of the economy through controlled involvement in the international capitalist system. In all three respects the PCF viewpoint was the antithesis of this dominant perspective.

Given the closeness of its ties with the Soviet Union, the party's attitude to the Western alignment, which preceded the development of West European integration, is wholly predictable. From 1941–47 its objective was to use whatever influence it possessed to maintain East–West unity, and to convince non-communist opinion that national independence depended on France alone, in close friendship with the Soviet Union – the one great power which was said to have no designs on French possessions. As tensions mounted in 1946 and 1947 the party attempted, with increasing desperation, to proclaim the benefits of the Russian alliance, without yet wholly condemning the USA. In particular, it accepted the Washington Agreement and its first inclination was to acquiesce, with major reservations, in the Marshall Aid proposal as well.[60] As will be shown, the attitude of the PCF towards West European integration was subsequently to be dominated almost exclusively by its defence of the Soviet position in the Cold War. Nevertheless PCF hostility to any such notion preceded the breakdown in East–West relations. Its attitudes at that time followed from the Communists' general perspective (see p. 12).

In 1944 the party had replied to the Socialists' proposal for a common commitment to the goal of a United States of Europe in the following manner:

> For all thinking patriots, the essential problem of international relations after the liberation is the maintenance of the unity of France and the restoration of its grandeur. The Socialist Party does not deal with this problem.[61]

Instead, claimed the PCF, the Socialists considered all sorts of fantastic schemes, forgetting that it had actually taken the 'Anglo–Saxons' four to six years to come to the aid of France, and that all talk of combinations in central Europe was anti-Soviet and 'can only end by favouring a renewed German imperialism'. The real problem, it continued ironically, was that the Socialists had far higher aspirations that the Communists. The former wanted nothing less than a United States of Europe or the world but, unless trusts were liquidated throughout the universe, this would be a 'United States of Trusts' which would lead from one dictatorship to another. The real aims should be the absolute guarantee of territorial independence, rejection of all foreign interference in French political life, deterrent punishment of war criminals, and the establishment of a security system to prevent all new German aggression against France, based on a firm *entente* with the Soviet Union. (Against the SFIO's wish for reconciliation with Germany, the PCF quoted the view of the British TUC that the German people had been responsible for aggression.) Socialist talk of the establishment of a super-state was escapism from the real problems and, if such an organisation were controlled by reactionary forces, it could lead to foreign control of French resources, the annulment of progressive domestic legislation and the ruin of the peasantry. Unless the Socialists could demonstrate how French independence and national grandeur were compatible with the idea, it must be rejected in favour of 'international agreements against the aggressor and for political and economic co-operation between peoples, based on the independence, equality and mutual respect of nations.'

These observations were written when the PCF sought full national and international unity against Nazi Germany and were therefore quite moderate in comparison with many later pronounce-ments on the subject. Nevertheless, they reveal not only the extent of the divergence from the SFIO but also the long-term themes in its hostility to the whole notion of integration. The most important of these were the defence of national independence and weaker econo-mic interests, which would be threatened by external competition; and pro-Sovietism, suspicion of the West, and anti-German rhetoric. After the war the PCF continued to combat the suggestion whenever it was made by Socialists or others, always viewing it as an ideological mask for a Western anti-Soviet bloc. However, it was the near simultaneous establishment of the Cominform with the prom-ulgation of Marshall Aid which really saw the start of a campaign which was to become increasingly intense and in which the Cold War context was to predominate over all other factors.

The Struggle Against American Imperialism and the 'Neo-Nazis', 1947–50

One of the party's leading economists set the tone for the new appraisal of the Marshall Aid proposal in January 1948:

> The aims of the Marshall Plan are multiple. First, to place the countries of West Europe under the direct control of American capitalism, to direct their production, and organise their com-

merce in order to allow American capital to invest freely, and
American goods to find suficient outlets. Then, by vassalising the
old European countries, it seeks to make them yield up ... the
colonial empires whose riches American imperialism covets.
Finally, it aims to make Europe strong for its eventual attack
against the Soviet Union.[62]

The plan was one for the liquidation of national independence,
and the SFIO's advocacy of West European integration was simply
a means of masking the war preparations of the imperialist camp:

> Blum and Ramadier, Marceau Pivert and Guy Mollet thus give a
> 'theoretical' and demagogic base to the expansionist goals of
> American imperialism. The doctrine of the 'international third
> force' ... obligingly facilitates the task of American capital, incites
> it to acts of violence and leads France into a state of vassaldom to
> the USA.[63]

Military factors were thus emphasised from the beginning, but the
signing of the Brussels Pact and the Atlantic Alliance led to an
increasing stress on the war-like purposes of all forms of integration
and a progressively more vehement insistence upon the vital necessity of recovering 'national independence'.

Although maintenance of the theory of national independence
used during the Resistance period (i.e., identification between the
working class and the nation) served the PCF's purposes once again,
the development of apparently contradictory phenomena in the
international situation necessitated certain refinements. Why was
integration in Western Europe to be deplored, while that of Eastern
Europe was to be fervently supported? Why was the struggle for
French national independence the supreme priority while the
apparently similar aim of Yugoslavia was to be denigrated? The
answer given by the PCF (and the Soviet Union) was straightforward. The inspiration behind all forms of Western integration was
identical:

> it is a question of the common defence of a social system
> threatened by the growth of the forces of genuine democracy. The
> Atlantic Pact being too obviously a war machine in the eyes of the
> people, the Council of Europe masks it with a progressive and
> peaceful facade. The first organises the reactionary western bloc,
> the second dresses it in federalist tinsel, for the use of the
> insufficiently educated masses...[64]

In opposing this new 'holy alliance' the PCF was not acting in a

nationalist manner. Nationalism was a dangerous bourgeois deviation which distorted the progressive notion of national independence
into chauvinism and which facilitated colonialism and fascism. It
was just this deviation which influenced the actions of Tito in
Yugoslavia. The struggle for national independence against the
'bourgeois cosmopolitanism' 'of yankee inspiration' was, by contrast, perfectly legitimate. However, it could be successful only if it
were integrated into the democratic and anti-imperialist camp
whose cohesion against US imperialism was essential. In order to
assure such solidarity

> It must have as its pivot the recognition of the determining role of
> the Soviet Union in the anti-imperialist front. The disavowal of
> this role by the Titoist clique has led it to sacrifice the Yugoslav
> nation, to make it a pawn on the American chessboard. The
> country of socialism is the most powerful shield against the
> feverishly active tendency of Anglo-Saxon finance capital for
> world hegemony. It is for this that the latter wants to turn Europe
> against the USSR and place the cosmopolitans at the head of the
> anti-Soviet crusade.

Thus the struggle for French national independence was actually
proletarian internationalism in action, and solidarity with the Soviet
Union was the practical application of such internationalism. In
more concrete terms, the PCF was effectively arguing that France
could secure its independence only by abandoning the western
alignment and joining the Soviet bloc.

Acceptance of this theory naturally depended upon the assumption that the USSR was socialist and a defender of all peoples, and
that all those, like Tito, who sought independence from Soviet
control, were permeated with the spirit of bourgeois nationalism.
Similarly, of course, it assumed that West European integration was
entirely forced upon Western Europe by reactionary and militarist
American imperialists with the connivance of a tiny sector of the
European bourgeoisie and their agents. Moreover, it is also notable
that the practice of the PCF failed to reveal the theoretical distinction the party had made between the defence of national independence and the bourgeois deviation of nationalism. If national independence had simply meant a struggle against foreign imperialist
domination, it might have have been expected that the enemy would
be defined in social, economic and political terms, rather than in
such a way as to play on national emotions. Yet four months later
the writer who had sought to distinguish between national independence and nationalism claimed that the first general elections in
West Germany were: 'a decisive step towards the restoration of a

German sub-imperialism capable of continuing Hitler's war on the American account',[65] while in Parliament another Communist leader expressed, in epigrammatic form, the essence of the PCF's general line for years to come: 'The American imperialists order, the neo-Nazis in Bonn propose, and the French government acts.'[65]

Of course, there was good reason to deplore the limitation of the purge which took place in West Germany and the readiness of the USA and Britain to subordinate denazification to anti-communism. Similarly, the firmly conservative and capitalist regime which took power in the Federal Republic in 1949 was naturally repugnant to the left. However, none of this is sufficient to explain the identification between West Germany and the Nazi regime which began in 1949 and became progressively more emotive, reaching its peak in the campaign against the EDC. In fact the PCF was exploiting French national prejudices and bitter war memories in order to gain support for its opposition to the strengthening of the Western alliance and the formation of an integrated Western Europe. Despite the theoretical distinctions which were offered, the PCF was using French national emotions in a similar manner to that which it denounced as bourgeois nationalism.

The Schuman Plan: 'The Continuation of Hitlerism'
When the Schuman proposal was announced, the Cold War was at its height and the overwhelming priority of the PCF was stated to be the prevention of the world war allegedly prepared by the USA. The propaganda had reached a new level of emotivity as, for example, when Francois Billoux, one of the three ministers expelled from the government in 1947, claimed:

> The struggle for peace is the patriotic battle of the French people against the American imperialists and their servants who want to submit the French nation to an enslavery and a fascist dictatorship which will be still more barbaric than that of the Hitlerian dictatorship.[67]

His early analysis of the Schuman Plan was no less alarmist and set the tone for numerous other PCF writings on the subject.

The USA, he claimed, had aimed in 1945 to take over Japanese and German imperialism in order to secure world hegemony, but had been checked by the progress of socialism and the struggle for national independence. In these circumstances the imperialists saw that the only way of securing world domination was through the launching of the third world war.

> The [Schuman Plan] is situated directly in the framework of the

preparations for the third world war which involves a more definite integration of the Germany of Bonn into the Atlantic Pact of aggression.[68]

Thus the plan was of American rather than French inspiration, and was enthusiastically welcomed by German revanchists for:

> The fusion of French and German mining and iron and steel industries places French heavy industry under the direct dependency of the war industry of the Ruhr, itself guided and controlled by the financiers of Wall Street ... German industry ... possesses the most powerful economic base. Thus this will play the directing role in the system proposed by M.Schuman and prepared by the American agent Jean Monnet ...
>
> The American warmongers want to give the revanchist Germany of Bonn a preponderant place in Europe because they are reserving for it a pride of place in the preparation of war against the peoples, the popular democracies and, in the first place, the Soviet Union.

Billoux noted that the plan would lead to closures of marginal mines and steel works, and would bankrupt small and medium enterprises, thereby increasing unemployment and German economic domination. But his economic analysis was cursory and was subordinate to the view of the ECSC as one item in the general American-dominated war economy. Similarly, Billoux claimed that the industrial deconcentration which would follow the implementation of the plan would cause the movement of workers to other regions so that the bases and strategic routes sought by the American High Command could be established.

> In eliminating certain proletarian centres, the capitalists hope to be able to destroy or reduce working-class resistance to war preparations and to the state of poverty which accompanies them ...
>
> Thus Robert Schuman, former minister of Petain, is achieving the Pétain–Hitler plan for the de-industrialisation of France. It would lead our country to become the outlet for German war industry while French workers were reduced to unemployment or starvation salaries, and French peasants could sell their agricultural products only at a loss, or export at knock-down prices.

As soon as the EDC proposal was made the French Communists launched a still more vigorous campaign and insisted that the two projects for West European integration were really only one. In

August 1951 a PCF writer thus maintained that the objective of the ECSC was to create massive unemployment and break up concentrated working-class areas in order to prepare for the constitution of a European army, which, by its cosmopolitanism, would prevent the fraternisation between soldiers and workers, make other peoples accept Nazi generals, and recruit mercenaries from amongst the unemployed.[69]

With this insistence that military considerations for anti-Soviet war were of primary importance, it was rare that detailed scrutiny of the political–economic aspects of the Schuman Plan were offered by PCF sources. A partial exception to this was in the Communist-controlled CGT's case to the committee of the Economic Council, established to consider whether the treaty should be ratified by Parliament. In this Jean Duret, a CGT economist, presented a reasoned and sober critique of the plan from the perspective of left–socialist trade unionism.

His argument was, essentially, that in periods of normal competition, the open market would mean the disappearance of the enterprises least well placed in terms of price and geographical location, thereby threatening French industry in general because French coal seams were of worse quality, and steel less rationalised, than were their competitors in the Ruhr. In cases of crises of overproduction or shortage, the position would, he claimed, be still worse, for the High Authority could fix maximum and minimum prices which would favour the Ruhr in view of its greater modernisation. All this would lead to closures and unemployment in France, while the reconversion of factories and mines to provide new jobs, which was envisaged by the treaty, seemed Utopian. Similarly, decartellisation and deconcentration were difficult to control, and no real guarantees against the reconstitution of the Ruhr complex could be given. Nor would the creation of a pool prevent the establishment of a West–European international cartel. On the other hand, since salaries and social security measures were higher in France than West Germany, harmonisation could lead only to pressures for the reduction of salaries, the diminution of social charges, the lowering of working-class living standards and progressive devaluations, coupled with the export of West German and Italian unemployment to France. French economic growth, he argued, demanded modernisation measures in Nord and Pas-de-Calais and the Lorraine, but these could come about only with government subsidies which were expressly forbidden by the treaty (except on the favourable advice of the High Authority). Moreover, the plan was envisaged as a model for similar agreements in other sectors, leading to a close interpenetration of the French and West German economies, bringing about German economic dominance with inevitable political consequences. Finally, he claimed that, even with the pool, the West European market would still be far too limited and the problem of coal and steel outlets could be resolved only by a profound reorganisation of the world market with the rapid industrialisation of less developed countries and the restoration of East–West trade links. The attempt to find a solution within continental Western Europe would inevitably bring about German domination 'already started by the present arms race and likely to be completed by the realisation of the Schuman Plan'.[70]

Nothing in this contradicted the general case of the PCF: indeed in a sense it was a translation of Communist policy into politico-economic terms for an audience for whom denunciations of American war plans and West Germany revanchism would have been useless. Following the general Communist line, it also exaggerated the disadvantages for France and overstated the probable German gains. Nevertheless, the argument was at least as plausible and reasoned as some of the wildly optimistic prognostications by the promoters of the plan. Had it been at all typical, a dialogue with the SFIO may have been possible, for although Duret's arguments bore no resemblance to those of Philip, they were not dissimilar to those used by more critical elements in the French Socialist Party. True, there was one vital difference between Duret's conclusion and that of SFIO critics: he was certain that the treaty should be rejected, while they favoured its ratification coupled with a campaign in favour of nationalisation in all member states and democratisation of the institutions. Nevertheless, the framework of analysis was sufficiently close for discussion and argument to have been possible.

However, this was almost a solitary example of this kind of analysis within Communist-controlled organisations at this time. In general, the subordination of politico-economic analysis to the preoccupation with American 'war-plans' prevented any possibility of PCF/SFIO dialogue on the subject.

The EDC: 'No to the Rearmament of a Reactionary and Revanchist Germany'

It would be an understatement to describe the PCF's campaign against the EDC as vehement, for the struggle to prevent German rearmament became the principal party preoccupation, to which all other aspects of policy, in domestic and international affairs, were subordinated. During the four-year period of its battle on the issue, its line was confusing and inconsistent, undergoing frequent changes from emotive attacks on all other forces in French political life (precipitating anti-communist repression) to the pursuit of a national alliance against the proposal. From mid 1953 onwards the latter line predominated and the PCF concentrated on building as wide a unity as possible against the EDC. As was shown earlier (see page 14), this involved concentration on parliamentary action for the first time since autumn 1947. It also meant reappraisals of all non-communist anti-*cédistes*, so that de Gaulle, who had previously been denounced as a fascist, was now regarded as a 'good Frenchman' and quoted with approval![71]

Inevitably, the further to the right the PCF went in its search for anti-*cédiste* allies, the more purely nationalist its propaganda became. But from the start the tone was highly emotive. Thus the early call for a 'wide union to say no to the rearmament of a reactionery and revanchist Germany' hit a note which was to be reiterated throughout the campaign:

> In the best of circumstances ... French soldiers would be placed under the orders of Nazi officers in order again to give Prague, and German territories beyond the Oder-Neisse, to the German militarists. The sons of the executed and massacred would be under the command of the executioners of their fathers in order to fight against the victors of Stalingrad. But the possibility that the Hitlerian criminals of war will want to restart their exploits against France before turning to the East cannot be ruled out.[72]

The emotive element remained constant throughout: a Nazi jackboot was displayed on the front cover of propaganda tracts and it was claimed that the EDC would mean the complete liquidation of national independence and its delivery to 'the executioners of Oradour and their successors and followers [who] were chanting "Deutschland über alles" and proclaiming their hatred of France and the Soviet Union'.[73] An attempt was also made to root the possibility of Franco-German war in theoretical analysis. Stalin's 'work of genius', *The Economic Problems of Socialism in the USSR*, published in 1952, which resuscitated the notion that the contradictions between the imperialist powers could prove stronger than their mutual hatred of socialism, was used in support of the argument that West Germany would turn against the weaker French imperialism before engaging in war against the Soviet bloc. Similarly, Stalin's proposal for the neutralisation and reunification of Germany – advanced as a means of preventing West German rearmament and integration into the Western bloc – was advocated as a means of creating a genuinely peaceful and disarmed Europe. Moreover this proposal was also coupled with the 'contradictions of imperialism' argument for it was asserted that, athough the USA wanted to unite and dominate the European capitalist states, this policy was threatened by the fact that the French bourgeoisie would eventually resist it in order to assert their independence and implement their own plans for capitalist development. This, it was claimed, would help to prevent the integration of West Germany into the American military bloc.[74] Such a theory facilitated the alliance with the national bourgeoisie opposed to the EDC (i.e., the right-wing nationalist alliance) but was stressed less after Stalin's death in view of the uncertainty of the subsequent Soviet policy.

In any case, theoretical sophistication was no more a hallmark of the PCF's analysis of the EDC than it was of the Socialists (pro- or anti-EDC). The general lines of its campaign followed the pattern of its wider international policy which, of course, reflected its identification between French and Soviet interests. Until 1953 American intentions were portrayed in a more lurid light than ever: for example, the growth of right-wing extremism in the Federal Republic (termed Hitlerism) and anti-communist repression in France were said to be deliberately encouraged by the USA to suppress the masses so that they could not oppose American war plans.[75]

Similarly it was claimed that the result of American policy would be the establishment of a military or fascist dictatorship on the European level![76] However, with the improvement in the international climate and the quest for an alliance with the national bourgeoisie, the emphasis shifted. The anti-German tone remained as strident as ever, but the military imperialism of the USA was emphasised less. Instead the PCF claimed that *détente* would be possible if the EDC were abandoned or rejected by the French Parliament, whereas negotiations with the Soviet Union would be made more difficult and Franco-German conflicts intensified if the project went ahead. Nevertheless, the underlying ideological framework was retained: all aspects of integration were part of the same general attempt to create 'the Europe of Hitler, but under American direction'.[77]

The relance européene: *American Imperialism or European Capitalism?*

With the disappointment of West Germany's entry into NATO, after the defeat of the EDC, PCF policy again became uncertain and variable. Its attitude to the *relance européenne* was to reflect this mood and, indeed, to reveal great confusion in analysis and propaganda.

Early in 1955 the party adopted a similar tone to that used before the relative moderation of 1953–54. Stalin was quoted in support of the view that the bourgeoisie no longer contained any liberal element, and it was claimed that the working-class struggles for national independence and improved living standards were vital if a new imperialist war and the creation of a fascist regime in France were to be prevented.[78] Similarly, Mollet and the SFIO were again said to be at the service of American imperialism, based on the most aggressive and reactionary monopoly capitalism whose aim was to create a 'unified European space' which would be a 'semi-colonial territory' and its 'centre of recruitment for its "anti-Bolshevik crusade"'.[79] Moreover, after the breakdown of the alliance with the national bourgeoisie, a campaign was launched, amidst great publicity, which asserted that the French working class was suffering from 'absolute pauperisation' in comparison with the pre-war period.[80]

However, if this seemed to constitute a step to the left, by the end of the year the party had lurched back towards the right. The Geneva conferences of July and November appeared to constitute a step towards international detente, and the election of the Mollet Government seemed to offer the prospect of domestic social reform and perhaps also of greater independence in external affairs. The Communists therefore not only supported all of the government's domestic measures, but even voted it special powers in Algeria. Almost simultaneously Kruschev threw the party leadership into confusion by his denunciations of Stalin at the February congress of the CPSU and this was rapidly followed by the development of repression in Algeria (to such a point that the PCF could not support the government's foreign policy without losing credibility), and the Hungarian and Suez crises. In short, for the PCF, as for the SFIO, the formation of the EEC became a relatively low priority in 1956–67.

The party congress of July 1956 set the tone of confusion which was to be maintained. Kruschev's optimism about peace, the strength of the socialist camp and the break-up of capitalist unity, was reiterated, and the party now emphasised negative features in the French economy, rather than the war threat, as the 'principal fruit of a foreign policy of submission to American imperialists'. On the other hand the role of France in the 'aggressive Atlantic Alliance' was denounced and the EURATOM proposal was condemned in a manner which was similar to that used against the EDC but less vehement in its tone.[81] If there was this degree of ambiguity on EURATOM, the blossoming of the *relance européene* into the more wide-ranging notion of a common market created even more problems for the PCF.

For the most part the propaganda emphasised the continuity of the *relance* with all the previous projects for European unification and asserted that 'it is the Europe of Hitler and the France of Pétain that we are being offered'.[82] Yet behind the mask of total confidence, there was clearly great uncertainty as to the correct evaluation of the *relance*. While the popular party organs took refuge in the traditional propaganda line, the more theoretical journals revealed confusion and even contradiction in their interpretations of two crucial issues.[83]

First there was disagreement as to the precise relationship between the *relance européene* and American policy. Georges Cogniot, a frequent spokesman for party policy in *Cahiers du communisme*, argued that the latest initiatives were once again American in inspiration. The US imperialists and their continental accomplices had learned from the EDC that the masses would not accept open war preparations, and had therefore disguised their latest programme 'under a pacific and constructive cover'. Nevertheless Western Europe was still being used by the Americans as a launching-pad for anti-Soviet action, including possible atomic war.[84] However, *Economie et politique* argued that, although the European economies were financially and technically too much like American tributaries for the USA to accept a genuinely independent grouping, the initiative was an attempt to resist 'the encroachments of American imperialism whose policy harms the interests of the powers of Western Europe more and more'.[85]

The second disputed issue was closely connected with the first. What was the basis of the *relance?* Was it essentially a preparation for anti-Soviet war, in which economic aspects were subordinated to military purposes? Or was it determined primarily by economic pressures and goals? The general tendency was to insist that the basic motives were political, ideological and military and then to cast doubt on such a judgement, by devoting the greater proportion of the available space to the analysis of the political economy of the projects.[86] Such ambiguity suggests that the party was beginning to believe that the latest stage in West European integration stemmed from developments in European political economy, but was not yet prepared to campaign against the treaties solely on this level. What then was the basis of the politicoeconomic critique of the EEC?

The PCF argued that the general aim of eliminating obstacles to competition based on national policy differences would facilitate the concentration of capital, and make competitive pricing policy prevail at the expense of the social and economic conquests already gained by the working class. Because of its greater strength, German monopoly capitalism would benefit from the process of concentration, while the free movement of capital meant that investment would desert France, or at least southern and western France, for West Germany. The French economy would therefore become a 'tributary' of the West German one[87] and 'a great part of our country risks de-population ... a still lower standard of living, and becoming a sort of Lozère of Europe'.[88]

Similarly, peasants would suffer terrible hardship from the process of agricultural concentration, while large-scale farmers would benefit. The realisation of the EEC would therefore be generally suicidal for the French economy.[89] Moreover, the harmonisation of social security systems involved the real risk that equalisation would be at the lowest level obtaining anywhere and this would harm the French working class, who would in any case be threatened with a massive increase in unemployment as a result of greater external competition. Likewise, the free movement of labour would mean the further export of Italian unemployment to France, while French redundant workers would have to seek employment in West Germany. The EEC therefore contained the prospect of a new period of forced labour in West Germany, and no French miner or metal worker could believe that he would live better 'as one of the 100,000 employees of Krupp, the ex-criminal of war'.[90] More generally, the growth of the reserve army of unemployed, as a result of concentration and rationalisation, would create further pressure to reduce wages and social benefits. Finally, the treaty constituted the progressive abandonment of vital economic powers – with crucial political implications – to a supranational authority, and when majority voting was ultimately introduced this would give power to the strongest. A vehemently anti-communist West Germany would thus secure control over economic policy and become the *gendarme* of France once again. The Europe that Mollet claimed to be socialist was, therefore, 'fundamentally reactionary'.[91]

There were many strands of argument in this analysis but, behind the propaganda, which continued to mix war memories with prophecies of disaster, two principal theoretical elements played a crucial role in the analyses. It was these which provided the continuity with the PCF's argument against the SFIO's proposal in 1944, with its early analysis of Marshall Aid, and with Duret's critique of the ECSC.

The first assumption was that the process of concentration, bringing with it rationalisation and modernisation, was essentially anti-socialist in raising the profitability of capital and reinforcing 'the dictatorship of monopolies'.[92] Since the Marshall Plan, ECSC and EEC all sought to increase this tendency, the PCF opposed them in the name of workers, peasants and small and middle-size business. The second assumption reinforced the first. That is, the Communists consistently argued that the French economy was too weak to withstand greater foreign competition. They therefore claimed that the process of concentration would inevitably pose a drastic threat to French industry and agriculture thereby reinforcing the harmful effects of monopolisation. These two economic assumptions then merged with the essentially political belief that the Six in general, and West Germany, in particular, were less potentially susceptible to communist influence than was France, so that the establishment of integration would accentuate the international strengthening of the right.

When the PCF presented this case and sought to defend the interests of those who would suffer from integration, it was surely arguing in a way which was absolutely legitimate for the left. Moreover, it was more accurate in holding the purpose of the EEC to be the strengthening of West European capitalism than was the SFIO in maintaining that it was a triumph for socialism. However, this is not to claim that this was the only legitimate viewpoint for a socialist.

Communist policy was, in practice, unconditional defence of the small against the large, existing methods against modernisation, and all employment against any unemployment, on the assumption that any modernisation increased exploitation and strengthened monopoly capitalism against labour. The result of this defence of threatened petit bourgeois and peasant interests was a form of nationalism rather than the international revolutionary socialism to which the PCF theoretically adhered. And this took precisely the same xenophobic form as that of Gaullism and *Poujadism*. It would, for example, be difficult to justify on any socialist grounds the contention of the 1956 party congress that: 'A campaign of "de-nationalisation" of teaching and of culture (compulsory bilingualism, "elementary" French etc.) is conducted with perseverance under the guise of "western unity" and "European Community."'[93] Such signs of chauvinism were frequently present in party propaganda and belied the political and economic analysis on which policy was allegedly based. It is debatable whether such excesses stemmed from faulty expression and misconceived propaganda or, more fundamentally, from the attempts to base party policy on an alliance against modernisation.

If Communist opposition to capitalist concentration, and thus to the EEC, was both valid and yet liable to become submerged under the weight of traditional nationalist propaganda, the SFIO's tendency to equate socialism with modernisation and 'internationalism' carried dangers from the opposite viewpoint: that is, it could simply facilitate capitalist integration by providing it with a progressive rationale. The tragedy of the Fourth Republic, from the point of view of the left, was that constructive debate between the two parties on such issues had been impossible. Had there been a serious discussion as to whether, and on what terms, socialism could favour modernisation of the French economy, and whether, and on what terms, West European integration could be beneficial, perhaps some kind of synthesis might have resulted. As it was, this dialogue never took place. Cold War pressures and the subsequent evolution of the party had led to the virtual elimination of the critical socialist element within the SFIO. Similarly, the total subordination of the PCF to the Soviet Union meant that the propaganda emphasis on 'American warmongers' completely overshadowed politicoeconomic analysis.

By the time a less emotive approach was making a cautious and temporary reappearance in some circles of the PCF in 1957, the SFIO was too demoralised and too far to the right to make any response.

Notes

1 The following are useful sources for this section: P. Williams, *Crisis and Compromise: The Politics of Post-War France* (Longmans, 1964); A. Grosser, *La Quatrième République et sa politique extérieure* (Colin, 1967); A. Grosser, *The Western Alliance* (Macmillan, 1980); F.R. Willis, *France, Germany and the New Europe, 1945–67* (Stanford, 1968); J. Rideau (ed.), *La France et les Communautés Européennes* (LGDJ, 1975); J. Monnet, *Memoirs* (Collins, 1979).

2 The following are useful sources for this section: A.J. Rieber, *Stalin and the French Communist Party, 1941–47* (Columbia University Press, 1962); *Histoire du parti communiste français* (Editions sociales, 1964); J. Fauvet, *Histoire du parti communiste francais*, 2 vols. (Fayard, 1965); D. Ligou, *Histoire du socialisme en France, 1871–1961* (PUF, 1962); B.D. Graham, *The French Socialists and Tripartism, 1944–47* (Weidenfeld, 1965); R. Quilliot, *La SFIO et l'exercice du pouvoir, 1944–58* (Fayard, 1972); R.W. Johnson, *The Long March of the French Left* (Macmillan, 1981).

3 PCF's *XIVᵉ congrès*, 18 July 1956, quoted in Fauvet, *Histoire du PCF*, vol.2, p.290.

4 Declaration by the PCF's *bureau politique*, 4 Nov. 1956, *Cahiers du communisme* Nov. 1956. (Hereafter *C du C.*)

5 Letter from Léon Blum to Felix Gouin, Oct. 1942, quoted in H. Michel and B. Mirkine-Guetzevitch (eds.), *Les Idées politiques et sociales de la Résistance* (PUF,1954), pp.124–5.

6 'Message au Président Roosevelt et au Peuple Americain' from the *comité directeur* of the clandestine socialist party, *Le Populaire*, September 1943, reproduced in D. Mayer, *Les Socialistes dans la Résistance* (PUF, 1968), pp.224–5.

7 Ibid., p.35

8 Radio broadcast of 19 October 1945, reproduced in *L'Oeuvre de Léon Blum*, vol. VI, *La Naissance de la quatrième république, 1945–47* (Editions Albin Michell 1958), pp.113–15. (Hereafter *Oeuvre.*)

9 Speech of 25 March 1946 to National Advisory Council in Washington, reproduced in ibid., p.195.

10 Grosser, *La Quatrième République*, p.218.

11 Press conference, 31 May 1946, *Oeuvre*, vol.VI, p.201.

12 'Le Problème économique international', *Le Populaire*, 16 Aug. 1946, reproduced in ibid., pp. 240–42.

13 'La position du socialisme international', *Le Populaire*, 27 May 1947, reproduced in *Oeuvre*, vol. VII, *La fin des alliances, 1947–50* (Editions Albin Michel, 1963), pp.22–3.

14 'Indépendance et non pas souveraineté', *Le Populaire*, 9 July 1947, reproduced in *Oeuvre*, vol.VII, pp.37–9.

15 Jean Lorraine, 'Les Tendances actuelles de la politique americaine', *La Revue Socialiste*, November 1947. (Hereafter *RS.)*

16 'Projet d'un programme commun', 11 December 1943, reproduced in Mayer, *Les Socialistes dans la Résistance*, pp.229–38. (For Blum's ideas, see *A l'echelle humaine*, Gallimard, 1971, pp. 143–51.).

17 'Bulletin intérieur du SFIO', Aug. 1946, reproduced in Blum, *Oeuvre*, vol. VI, pp.289–93.

18 'Notes d'Allemagne, 1943–45', in *Oeuvre*, vol. V, *1940–45* (Editions Albin Michel, 1955), p.51.

19 The SFIO and Labour Party had agreed this policy at a conference in London in March 1945 *(Labour Party Annual Report 1945):* the SFIO maintained this commitment which the Labour Government progressively abandoned.

20 D. Tartakowsky, 'Guerre froide et troisième force, 1947–54', in H. Claude, D. Tartakowsky *et al.*, *La IVᵉ République: la France de 1945 à 1958* (Editions sociales), 1972.

21 'La troisième force eurppéenne', *Le Populaire*, 6 Jan. 1948, reproduced in, Blum, *Oeuvre*, vol. VII p.150.

22 Report for SFIO's 41st *congrès national*, 15–18 July 1949.

23 For a fuller discussion of Blum's views, see M. Newman, 'Léon Blum, French Socialism and European Unity, 1940–50', *The Historical Journal*, no. 1, 1981.

24 P. Rimbert et G. Bourgin, *Le Socialisme* (PUF, 1949).

25 'Révolution directoriale et socialisme', *RS*, April 1948, p.359.

26 'Révolution directoriale et socialisme' (continued), *RS*, June–July 1948, p.145.

27 'Le socialisme fera l'Europe', *RS*, June–July 1948,p.20.

28 Philip had been a Minister of Economics in 1946 and subsequently became chief of the French delegation of the *commission économique européenne* and GATT from 1947 to 1951. He was also a member of the Strasbourg Assembly from 1949 to 1951; President of the *mouvement socialiste pour les Etats-Unis d'Europe* from 1950–64, and the director of the European Movement's youth programme. He was defeated in the General Election in 1951, but remained an influential member of the party's executive (until his expulsion from the party in 1957 following his criticisms of Mollet's Algerian policy).

29 'Manifeste pour l'Europe' passed by 41st *congrès national*, 15–18 July 1949; report for 42nd *congrès national*, pp.139–42.

30 General report on behalf of the *commission économique et sociale française* in preparation for Westminster economic conference, March 1949.

31 MSEUE declaration of November 1949, quoted by Philip in 'La Crise européenne', *Preuves*, Nov. 1965, reproduced in full in *André Philip par lui-même* (Aubier Montaigne, 1971), p.202.

32 Report of extraordinary congress of 13–14 December 1949 in report for 42nd *congrès;* Mollet reaffirmed this early in 1950 in *L'Heure de l'Europe* SFIO, 1950, pp.10–13.

33 'Motion de Politique internationale', in report for 43rd *congrès*, p.150.

34 'Decision of Comité Directeur', 13 June 1950, in ibid.

35 'L'Expérience travailliste et ses leçons', *PS*, May 1949, p.382.

36 *Comité directeur*, 13 September 1950 in report for 43rd *congrès national*.

37 A. Philip, *Le Socialisme et l'unité européenne: réponse à l'exécutif du Labour Party*, (Mouvement socialiste pour le Etats-Unis d'Europe, 1951), pp.1,9,11.

38 'Motion de politique internationale', in report for 44th *congrès national*, 22–25 May 1952, p.140.

39 A. Philip, *Pour une communauté européenne réelle: le Plan Schuman* (Mouvement européenne, June 1951), p.46.

40 *Conseil economique* (CECA, 1951).

41 P.R.,'La Communauté européenne du charbon et de l'acier', *RS*, May 1951, p.531.

42 The SFIO also believed that its attitudes were more socialist than those of the Labour Party which, it feared, was about to recognise the Franco regime. See Mollet's letter of 15 December 1950 and Morgan Phillips's reply of 9 January 1951 in report for 43rd *congrès national*, p.191.

43 'L'Armement de l'Allemagne', *Le Populaire*, 1 Dec. 1949 reproduced in *Oeuvre*, vol. VII, pp. 305–7.

44 Report of Congress of 23 May 1952 in report for 45th *congrès national*, 2–5 July 1953, p.142. For extensive discussions of the SFIO dispute over the EDC, see J. Fauvet, 'Naissance et mort d'un traité, in R. Aron and D. Lerner, *La Querelle de la CED* (Armand Colin, 1956); Quilliot, *La SFIO*, ch. 30; B. Criddle, *Socialists and European Integration* (Routledge, 1969), ch.6; R. Pinto-Lyra, *La Gauche en France et la construction européenne* (LGDJ, 1978), Part One, Subsection 1.

45 In particular, because Britain would be less likely to join if there was a supranational element. (The SFIO's position had shown a similar contradiction in 1950, with reference to the Schuman Plan.)

46 Out of 105 Socialist deputies, 53 voted against the EDC, 50 in favour, and 2 abstained. This division reflected that of the supporters of the party. See A. Girard and J. Stoetzel, 'L'Opinion publique devant la CED' in Aron and Lerner, *La Querelle de la CED*, p.144.

47 *Le Socialisme et l'unité européenne*, pp.10–11.

48 'La Crise doctrinale du socialisme en Europe', *RS*, April 1952, p.356. Yet at this stage Philip still also tended to idealise the USA. Thus simultaneously he published an article, stating: 'Those who talk of domination by Wall Street, of great capitalist power, are clinging to the analysis of the past. Since Roosevelt, and more still since Truman, the USA has become a country where the working class exert great weight on political life. It is not inconceivable that at some stage we will see it achieve … true democratic socialism' (*Études et Combats*, 3 April 1952, quoted in Ligou, *Histoire du socialisme*, pp.651–2).

49 'Les Nouvelles de l'Europe', September 1952, quoted in 'La Crise européenne', *Preuves*, Nov. 1965.

50 'Les données économiques d'une politique internationale socialiste', *RS*, April 1954, p.358.

51 'La Crise doctrinale du socialisme en Europe'.

52 'Extraits du discours d'investiture de Guy Mollet', February 1956, quoted in Pinto-Lyra, *La Gauche en France*, p.74.

53 Le Bail, *assemblée nationale*, 17 January 1957, *Journel officiel des debats* (hereafter *JO*), p. 107, quoted in Quilliot, *La SFIO*, p.588.

54 Guy Mollet, *Bilan et Perspectives Socialistes* (Plon, 1958), p.25.

55 *JO*, 25 July 1957, p.3136. (The whole report is *JO*, pp.3134–41.)

56 See, for example, Y. 'Marché commun et socialisme', *RS*, March 1957. (On the other hand, at the party congress at Toulouse, 27–30 June 1957, support was given both to the EEC *and* British proposals for a free-trade area.)

57 Apart from the PCF, the most vigorously critical force was provided by Pierre Mendès-France and the 26 radicals who had followed him when he went into opposition in May 1956. For details of his attitudes, see F. O'Neill, *The French Radical Party and European Integration* (Gower, 1981), ch. 3.

58 Both the main studies reach approximately this conclusion, though from very different perspectives. See Criddle, *Socialists and European Integration*, Introduction and Conclusion, and Pinto-Lyra, *La Gauche en France*, especially pp.117–35 and pp.153–64.

59 This was particularly marked with regard to Algeria. See decisions of 49th *congrès national* of 27–30 June 1957 in report for 50th *congrès national*, p.133.

60 See, for example, the editorials ('Notre politique') by Jacques Duclos in *C du C*, July and September 1946 and August and September 1947.

61 'Observations du Parti communiste sur le projet de Programme commun presenté par le Parti socialiste', Paris 25 April 1944, reproduced in Michel and Mirkine-Guetzevitch, *Les Idées politiques*, pp.218–38.

62 J. Baby, 'L'impérialisme americain et la France' *C du C*, Jan. 1948, p.90.

63 J. Guillon, 'Blum, agent de la réaction internationale', *C du C*, Feb. 1948, p.268.

64 J. Berlioz, 'Europe, nations, internationalisme', *C du C*, July 1949, p.814.

65 J. Berlioz, 'Le Problème allemand et la paix', *C du C*, Oct. 1949, p.1218.

66 F. Billoux, *JO, pp.6235–46, 24 Nov. 1949, quoted in Willis, France, Germany*, p.68.

67 'L'URSS et la possibilité de co-operation pacifique entre tous les pays', *C du C*, May 1950, p.72.

68 F. Billoux, 'Le Plan Schuman de guerre et les conditions d'une véritable entente franco-allemande pour la paix', *C du C*, July 1950, p.31.

69 P. Fougère, 'Le Plan americain Schuman–Adenauer de préparation à la guerre en Europe', *C du C*, Aug. 1951.

70 'La Communauté européenne du Charbon et de l'Acier'. report by André Philip for the *conseil economique*, 1951.

71 For an outline of the changes of policy, partly attributable to the long absence of Thorez through illness, see Fauvet, *Histoire du PCF*, vol.2, pp.234–65.

72 F. Billoux, 'Large union pour dire non au réarmement d'une Allemagne réactionnaire et révancharde', *C du C*, Nov. 1950, p.21.

73 Editorial, *C du C*, Oct. 1953.

74 See, for example, J–C., 'Les sophismes "européens" et les conditions d'une véritable securité européenne', *C du C*, Dec. 1953.

75 P. Villon, 'Contre la ratification des traités de guerre – lutte commune des peuples d'Allemagne et de France', *C du C*, Feb. 1953. p.174.

76 A. Stil, 'L'Internationale des traitres au socialisme', *C du C*, Dec. 1952, p.1114.

77 J-C., 'Les sophismes "européens"', p.1118.

78 C. Cogniot, 'Le caractère national de la politique du Parti communiste est une donnée de principe', *C du C*, Jan. 1955.

79 Roger Garaudy, 'La social-démocratie', *C du C*, April 1955, p.422.

80 The first article on the subject was written by Thorz in *C du C* and the theme was constantly repeated throughout the year. The timing of the campaign was, to say the least, unfortunate, for it coincided with the beginnings of the period of sustained growth in the economy. It is probable that the political motivation behind the campaign was to prevent the development of a centre–left coalition. This was the contemporary conclusion of Rimbert in 'Pourquoi le Parti communiste, a-t-il lancé la campagne de paupérisation?', *RS*, March 1956.

81 'Thèses du XIVe congrès du Parti communiste, Le Havre, 18–21 July 1956', special edn of *C du C*, p.366.

82 Speech by Marie-Claude Vaillant-Couturier, 15 Jan. 1957, *JO*, pp.19–23, quoted in Willis, *France, Germany*, p.263.

83 This observation owes much to the analysis of Pinto-Lyra, *La Gauche en France*, pp.104–11, and the references he cites.

84 'Les Nouveaux Pièges "européens"' in *C du C*, Feb. 1957, pp.183–4.

85 'La Relance européenne', *Economie et politique*, Jan. 1957.

86 Ibid. See also J. Chastagnier et P. Levy, 'Quelques aspects économiques du Marché Commun', *Économie et Politique*, April 1957, and 'Marché commun et concentration industrielle', *Économie et Politique*, June 1957.

87 Cogniot, 'Les nouveaux pièges', p.181.

88 'Marché commun et concentration industrielle', p.3.

89 Cogniot, 'Les nouveaux pièges', p.182.

90 'Marché commun et concentration industrielle', p.6.

91 'La Relance européenne', p.4.

92 'Quelques aspects économiques', p.26.

93 'Thèses du XIVe Congrès', special edition of *C du C*, p.365.

2

The Impact
of Gaullism, 1958–71

The return of de Gaulle as the saviour of France in May 1958 was to
provide a major challenge for the left. On one level this was because
the new Republic, coupled with the personal ascendancy of the
General, appeared to carry with it the risk that the decline of both
the Socialists and Communists would be perpetuated. Revitalisation
of the left was thus essential, and experience was to show that unity
would be electorally beneficial to both. However, this necessitated a
major transformation, given the parlous state of Socialist–Communist relations in 1958. The second level of the challenge was still more
profound, for de Gaulle's concept and practice of international
relations provided a vital source of legitimation and popular support
for the regime, and raised questions about the nation-state and
'Europe' which inevitably exposed the divisions on the left.[1] Foreign
policy thus rendered the attainment of left-wing unity highly
problematic, even when both Socialists and Communists believed
that it would be advantageous.

Immediately after his assumption of power, de Gaulle sought to
diminish American domination of NATO with the proposal that it
should be reconstituted as a three-power directory under France,
Britain and the USA. When this was rejected his priority became
the construction of French nuclear weapons which, he claimed,
would be independent of the USA, and this decision was later
coupled with a refusal to accede to the Test Ban Treaty of 1963. The
independent defence policy was followed up in the mid 1960s by
decisions to release France from military integration in NATO,
eventually leading in 1966 to the expulsion of American forces from
France and the removal of the NATO headquarters from Paris.

Throughout these years de Gaulle also undertook a series of
initiatives designed to heighten French world-wide influence by
dissociation from aspects of Western policy. The granting of Alge-

rian independence was exploited in an attempt to present France as a champion of Third World rights against American economic imperialism and Soviet totalitarianism, and this was complemented by an independent policy towards the communist world – recognition of communist China in 1965 and comparative warmth to Moscow. In addition, the French Government openly condemned American policy in Vietnam, took a pro-Arab position in the Six Day War, and attempted to undermine the hegemony of the dollar.

The assault on conventional 'Europeanism' was as marked as that on conventional Atlanticism. Instead of seeking to strengthen the institutions of the European Community and proclaiming adherence to the quasi-federal 'European idea', de Gaulle pursued a special relationship with West Germany, culminating in a treaty in January 1963, and this seemed to constitute the establishment of a traditional two-power alliance to take charge of Community affairs. Rather than accepting a new stage of supranationalism as envisaged in the Treaty of Rome, he boycotted Community institutions until the right to use a national veto was recognised (June 1965–January 1966). Instead of welcoming enlargement of the Community through British adherence, he twice issued a personal veto on the application (January 1963 and November 1967). And rather than accepting the EEC as the European pillar in the Atlantic Alliance, he advocated a 'European Europe' which would determine its own interests and policies.

To characterise such initiatives as unconventional is not to endorse the view that French foreign policy was changed in its fundamental aspects by the General. In fact France remained both Atlanticist and 'European' with further steps taken in the internationalisation of the economy, and signs of renewed political co-operation with Washington in 1968–69. However, the *domestic* importance of the external initiatives can scarcely be exaggerated, for de Gaulle transformed French political culture by providing a justification for his policies which was both relatively coherent and enormously popular.

De Gaulle's belief, developed over time and stated with conviction, was that the interests of the nation-state were both permanent and paramount. In the French case these necessitated a search for grandeur, the first essential of which was the re-establishment of French national independence. This did not preclude co-operation with other nation-states, and de Gaulle favoured membership of the Atlantic Alliance to ensure security against the Soviet Union, and the EEC to enhance European (and hence French) political and economic power. But since the defence of French interests was of supreme importance, it was absolutely legitimate to contest the pretensions of the USA or the European Commission when these were seen as threatening, to negotiate an alliance with West Germany so that the EEC could be run by those with 'real power', or to veto the British application to forestall competition for political leadership and to prevent any further strengthening of Atlanticist influence. Given the bitter mood of national humiliation, and the latent resentment against the USA and Britain, which had existed in the last years of the Fourth Republic, this kind of legitimation for a policy which was both national and European inevitably exerted a powerful interclass appeal.

How would the Atlanticism and 'Europeanism' of the SFIO be affected when the capitalist state partially redefined the terms of its co-operation in Western Europe and in the Atlantic Alliance, with a powerful reassertion of nationalist rhetoric? How would the Communists react when the nation-state, under right-wing control, appeared to adopt some of their own international objectives? If the hegemony of the right were to be dislodged, the left needed to secure a workable agreement on international as well as domestic problems and this would involve a reevaluation of existing priorities by both Communists and Socialists.

The election of François Mitterrand to the leadership of the new *Parti socialiste* (PS) at its unifying congress at Epinay in June 1971 can be regarded as the end of the first phase in the 'long march of the French left' to find an electoral and political alternative to Gaullism. This chapter therefore considers the evolution of the process up to this point.

The Evolution of the Left, 1958–71[2]

The immediate effects of de Gaulle's takeover were catastrophic for both the Communists and the Socialists. The PCF was severely weakened and, against the wishes of a dissident minority, adopted a sterile and contradictory policy of opposition in which the unity of the left was simultaneously urged and negated by the banality of some communist propaganda. Meanwhile Mollet's support for the recall of the General precipitated yet another party crisis, this time leading to the establishment of a new socialist party (*Parti socialiste autonome* – PSA) by the dissidents. It was only in October 1962 that Mollet announced a real change of front by encouraging limited electoral pacts with the PCF in the forthcoming legislative elections. The new two-ballot voting system made such alliances an urgent necessity for the left, and the 1962 agreements appeared to limit the losses of both parties and ushered in a search for greater unity.[3]

Between 1962 and 1971 there was no dramatic break in PCF policy, but a gradual recognition of the consequences of the existing circumstances. In reality, the Leninist strategy of insurrection had long since been abandoned but this had been masked during the Cold War period. Now Kruschev's attempt to follow a policy of peaceful coexistence through direct negotiations with Washington made Western communist mobilisation of the masses against the United States less important to the Soviet Union, and this necessitated a reevaluation of PCF priorities. Since it was self-evident that only an alliance with socialist forces could bring the PCF to power through electoral means, the party became increasingly committed to this course. The objective was naturally to maintain PCF policies as fully as possible in any such alliance–and hence to dominate it. However, it became clear that the unity of the left could not be established unless concessions were made and this provided an incentive for younger elements in the leadership to moderate the pro-Soviet line.[4] Under these conflicting pressures the PCF had, by 1971, become a unique phenomenon, poised uneasily between the open reformism of the Italian Communist Party (PCI) and continued adherence to the Soviet model. Nevertheless, great changes in policy had occurred, the party was reviving fast after the temporary set-back which it had suffered in the crisis elections of June 1968, and it had some reason to hope that the PCF would become the dominant partner if an alliance with the socialists were eventually agreed.

The evolution of French socialism was still more complex both because a series of organisational changes took place, eventually culminating in the establishment of the *Parti socialiste* in 1969 and its enlargement in June 1971, and because of the ideological heterogeneity of the non-communist left in this period. The PS was thus to contain three broad categories of opinion: SFIO traditionalists whose convictions had scarcely changed since the Fourth Republic; various left-wing groups who sought a 'rupture of capitalism' based on unity with the Communists; and pragmatists who wanted agreement with the PCF in order to strengthen socialist forces and who were prepared to adopt left-wing rhetoric to this end. The differentiation between these categories was not always clear-cut and it was (and is) therefore difficult to assess the balance of forces within the socialist movement in these years. The main stages in the reorganisation of French socialism, and the search for agreement between Socialists and Communists can be outlined briefly.

In 1962, despite the apparent electoral advantages of agreement with the PCF, powerful forces within the SFIO still preferred the prospect of an alliance with the centre and in 1964 the party still seemed to be facing both ways: thus in January it began a dialogue with the PCF, while the next month it endorsed Gaston Defferre as its presidential candidate, although his case had been pressed by centrists outside the SFIO, and was bitterly opposed by the PCF. These two strategies remained in contention for eighteen months, until Mollet managed to thwart Defferre's candidature. However, before this occurred it had become clear that the course of French socialism was no longer solely dependent on the manoeuverings of the SFIO.

In 1960 the PSA had merged with dissident communists and independent left-wing forces to form a more influential *Parti socialiste unifié* (PSU), which constantly sought a revitalisation and radicalisation of socialism.[5] In addition, left-wing clubs had also proliferated outside the SFIO and in 1964 many of these had united under François Mitterrand.[6] Although Mitterrand had not been a Socialist during the Fourth Republic, he had consistently opposed the Gaullist takeover and the institutional make-up of the Fifth Republic and favoured a strategy of opposition based on the unity of the left.[7] With Defferre's withdrawal a new alliance of the non-communist left was formed (Fédération de la gauche démocrate et socialiste – FGDS), whose first task was to promote Mitterrand's candidature. He secured the support of the left as a whole (including the PCF and PSU) and forced de Gaulle to a second ballot in December 1965.

The charter of the FGDS had been moderate but it was subsequently radicalised by a variety of factors, including the search for an alliance with the Communists.[8] Thus in December 1966 the FGDS and PCF reached an agreement for the legislative elections of March 1967, and this again appeared beneficial in electoral terms.[9] Following a further series of meetings, the two organisations then made a common declaration in February 1968, which constituted the highest point of agreement since the Second World War, although continuing differences, particularly over West European integration and the extent of an appropriate nationalisation policy, were publicly acknowledged.

The stage appeared set for the development of a common programme and a strategy for the achievement of power through electoral means when the student–worker uprising of May–June 1968 occurred. This shattered the electoral strategy of the left by reviving the anti-communism of right-wing Socialists and alienating both the SFIO and the PCF from Mitterrand, who had appeared to offer himself as President in the midst of the crisis. The legislative elections which de Gaulle called in June 1968 were thus disastrous for both the PCF and the FGDS, and the Soviet invasion of Czechoslovakia two months later created further difficulties for the proponents of the *union de la gauche*.[10] Nor did the situation appear to improve the next year. Pompidou easily won the presidential elections in June, with the Communists and Socialists unable to agree on a common candidate;[11] and although the PS had been established the previous month to replace the FGDS and SFIO, many Socialists, including Mitterrand and his closest supporters remained outside it and it was dominated by the SFIO. Nevertheless, there were also more encouraging signs: the dialogue with the PCF was soon resumed and both Mitterrand (and his closest associates) and the PS had an incentive to resolve their differences in order to strengthen the non-communist left.

The unifying congress thus took place in June 1971 and was to constitute a major step forward in the progress of the left. It did not, however, resolve the ambiguities in French socialism: Mitterrand's views remained elusive and, although the position of the left was strengthened within the party, the new leader owed his position to both the most eager proponents of unity with the Communists and some of the main opponents of this strategy.

By June 1971 the strength and nature of the response of the left to the electoral/political challenge of Gaullism was therefore still uncertain, but it was evident that great movement and progress had been made since the dismal days of 1958. As will now be shown, however, it was also clear that de Gaulle's ideological challenge over 'Europe' and the nation-state had presented the left with one of its most difficult problems.

The Left, Gaullism and 'Europe', 1958–71

From Rejection to Acquiescence: The Evolution of Communist Policy
From 1958 to 1962 Thorez and the majority of the leadership reacted in traditional style to the party's position of weakness in the new regime. That is, they adopted aggressive and simplistic rhetoric to compensate for their isolation. The new regime was thus likened to fascism and de Gaulle's foreign policy was denounced as antinational and dependent on its foreign capitalist backers.[12] This line, which was always the dominant one, assumed complete ascendancy in 1960–61, with the expulsion of a dissident minority which had argued that there were increasing contradictions between the USA and Western Europe and that de Gaulle's policy of independence represented the national section of monopoly capitalism in a struggle against cosmopolitan capital, dominated by the USA.[13] The dissident viewpoint, it may be recalled, bore a striking resemblance to the appraisal of the EEC, tentatively suggested in the journal *Economie et politique* in 1957 (see p. 49) and, indeed, its editor was one of the exponents of this interpretation of Gaullism. Its defeat enabled the party to take refuge in its well-worn themes about the total subordination of both France and the EEC to the USA, and to cite de Gaulle's warmth to Adenauer as the latest example of the

way in which the bourgeoisie betrayed France to neo-Nazi domination. However, the majority viewpoint was to change once again following a meeting of communist economists from 22 countries in Moscow in August 1962.

Four months earlier a leading member of the PCI had argued that European integration had been an essential element in Italian economic development, and that a distinction should be drawn between the internationalisation of the economy, which was beneficial, and the undemocratic aspects of the institutional structure of the EEC.[14] The French delegates at the Moscow conference sought to refute any such thesis with the argument that the Community only benefited monopoly capitalists, increased the danger of war, and formed the economic basis of NATO. The meeting rejected the PCI's positive evaluation of West European integration and called for a struggle against the EEC and the integrationist and 'European' ideologies of grand capital, but two of its conclusions also differed from the traditional line of the PCF. First, it accepted the fact that the internationalisation of economic life, through the development of productive forces, was an irreversible tendency; and secondly, while giving priority to the national framework, it implicitly recognised an EEC dimension in the working-class struggle against capitalism. Both points were important for they enabled the PCF to seek a *rapprochement* with the Socialists if the latter moved away from uncritical acceptance of the EEC. Finally, the conference also offered the PCF some encouragement again to reverse its totally hostile attitude to de Gaulle's claims that he was seeking national independence from American domination.[15]

In late 1962 PCF policy was therefore in a state of flux and it was in these circumstances that the first electoral pacts with the SFIO took place. This signified the beginning of a complex process in which the PCF constantly sought formulae which might lead to agreements on 'Europe', only to find these undermined by the reality of their continuing differences.

The first step took place immediately after the legislative elections when Waldeck-Rochet, the party's second-in-command, announced that the Communists would not make agreement on French withdrawal from NATO or the EEC a precondition for Socialist–Communist accord.[16] At the beginning of the next year François Billoux followed this up by seeking to define the way in which 'Europe' could be included in a Communist/Socialist *rapprochement*. Having first repeated the characteristic PCF views as evidence against the SFIO's notion that the EEC was a step towards European unity, he noted that the Socialists were also opposed to de Gaulle's conception of Europe.

On this point couldn't we, socialists and communists, agree that that which is underway is the integrated Europe of the trusts under the direction of state monopoly capitalism and that, consequently, it has nothing to do with socialism? Given the existence of the Common Market, as it is now, let us therefore see where the interests of the working class lie and let us search, on this basis, for the points which would allow an agreement to be reached ...[17]

His concrete suggestions for such an agreement did not in fact reveal any major departure from the traditional Communist line. Nevertheless, the attempt to specify policies on which co-operation would be possible – for instance in encouraging EEC trade with Comecon – implied a new degree of flexibility. On the other hand, de Gaulle's European policy constantly exposed the extent of the divergence from the Socialists. Thus although the PCF attempted to derive comfort from the fact that both the SFIO and the Communists opposed de Gaulle's treaty with West Germany, this was tortuous in the extreme since the basis of SFIO opposition lay in its continued 'Europeanism' and not, as with the PCF, in hostility to placing France 'under the dependency of pan-germanists and Hitlerian racists'.[18] Moreover, the Communists supported de Gaulle on the question of British entry into the EEC, on the grounds that this would strengthen the military, economic and political ties between the Community and the USA,[19] while the SFIO vehemently opposed him.

By 1963 party policy was, however, reaching the next stage in its evolution on the theoretical level and this was again facilitated by a continuing softening of the attitude of the international communist movement. In the declaration by the Communist Parties of the Six, who met in Budapest in 1963, emphasis was placed on co-ordinating struggles both within the national frameworks and in the EEC countries as a whole, between communist parties, socialist parties and trade unions; and although the anti-democratic character of the Community institutions was denounced, the antidote was held to lie in the demand that 'elected national assemblies and trade union organisations of the interested countries can exercise, without discrimination, a right of initiative and control'.[20] At an international colloquium in Paris in October 1963 CGT speakers thus put far greater stress than was previously the case on the need for united trade union action within the EEC as a whole, and tried to encourage Socialists to appraise the treaties more critically. Jean Duret asked:

Do you really think that it is possible to introduce constructive solutions [e.g., on control of foreign investment] while respecting the spirit and the letter of the Treaty of Rome? Or to the extent that one is really trying to bring about constructive solutions of a socialist character is it not necessary to go somewhat beyond these conditions?[21]

The logic of this *de facto* recognition of integration was taken still further in Waldeck-Rochet's report to the Central Committee in May 1964 and within a few months the PCF was claiming that it was possible and vital to fight for the nationalisation of the steel industry and that this could be done without contravening, or calling into question, the Coal and Steel Community.[22]

Yet once again the contradictions between theory and reality became apparent. When campaigning to defeat Defferre's presidential candidature in 1965, the Communists maintained that some form of Socialist–PCF unity would be possible if the SFIO's centrist alliance were prevented, and suggested that this might even incorporate West European integration. However, just as Mitterrand replaced Defferre and Socialist–Communist unity was supposedly at its height, de Gaulle was also in the process of boycotting the Community's institutions. Once again the PCF inevitably sympathised with Gaullism and, although this was generally played down in the interests of left-wing unity, one Communist writer could not resist the temptation to suggest that those who wanted France to be dominated abroad were seeking to prevent the introduction of radical domestic reform in precisely the same way as those who had said 'Better Hitler than the Popular Front'.[23] This hardly implied convergence with the Socialists (or tact) since they were attacking de Gaulle for his anti-Europeanism! But if political reality continued to divide them from the Socialists, this did not prevent the Communists from continuing the search for a basis for common positions and this was now reflected in the PCF's role in the international communist movement.

In practice the PCF had already accepted the theory that, in a system of 'state monopoly capitalism', power could be attained peacefully through an anti-monopolist alliance whose major priority would be to build an advanced democracy to remove the control of the monopolies over key sectors of the economy through a policy of nationalisation.[24] It now argued that monopoly integration was the product and servant of the various states in which state monopoly capitalism was dominant. It therefore claimed that West European integration was, in the international sphere, a means through which the system of state monopoly capitalism sought to maintain its own strength and defeat and weaken socialist and anti-imperialist forces. Its domestic purpose was seen as the strengthening of monopoly forces at the expense of the working class and its potential allies. The greater the degree of integration, the more detrimental its effects would be.[25] The policy for the anti-monopoly alliance, sought by the PCF, was then inevitably one of antagonistic opposition to the EEC and the party would not therefore accept the Community in the manner of the Italian Communist Party. However, its new theory did enable it to hold out a further olive branch to the Socialists. If state monopoly capitalism could be transcended domestically through 'advanced democracy', and the EEC was a means of integrating state monopoly capitalism internationally, did it not follow that the Community could also be transcended by an international anti-monopoly alliance in the EEC as a whole? The PCF was cautious about any such conclusions, which could be taken as a negation of its national strategy. Nevertheless, during 1966, when seeking agreement with the Socialists, it did hint at the possibility.[26] Yet when it tried to define the content of the policy little progress was made.

The party continued to give absolute priority to the anti-monopolist campaign within the national framework, while the European dimension was seen, at most, as a terrain for co-ordinating such efforts. To counter the typical argument by the non-communist left that socialism could not be built within France alone, the PCF asserted that a change in France would have a great effect on other countries and would receive help from other working-class and democratic movements.

> Moreover, it is indisputable that the existence of the Soviet Union and other socialist countries, with the possibilities for economic and political co-operation that this opens up, constitutes a major trump card in the event of the transition to socialism in a single West European country.[27]

Such an argument had limited appeal outside Communist circles.

In these circumstances, and despite the extent of convergence on other foreign policy issues, agreement with the Socialists on the EEC proved impossible. Thus in the February 1968 declaration, while the FGDS publicly stressed the importance of the European Community, the PCF called for national independence both in security matters, by non-renewal of the Atlantic Alliance, and with regard to 'Europe':

> [The PCF] believes it necessary that France should not confine itself within the narrow framework of little capitalist Europe – whether six, seven or more – but must develop its economic and technical relations with all the countries of Europe on the basis of mutual advantage ...

The PCF reaffirms its hostility to the establishment of a supranational authority, created and dominated by grand capital, which would accentuate the division of Europe, aggravate the harmful consequences for the workers of the present policy of the Common Market and would put the democratic policy desired by the French poeple at the mercy of foreign governments dominated by reactionary forces.

Little supranational Europe would not be independent, but would be dangerously subordinated to the hegemony of an expansionist and revanchist Germany and simultaneously to American tutelage through the Atlantic Pact.[28]

Yet although this reiterated the traditional themes, a further overture was being made, for the party was arguing that a supranational Europe *would* have harmful consequences and must therefore be opposed. The implication was that, at present, the European Community was not supranational and that a French left-wing government would be able to work within it so long as further integration were opposed.[29] However, this concession was still insufficient to secure agreement with the Socialists.

Between February 1968 and Mitterrand's election to the leadership of the PS in June 1971 the PCF maintained this ambiguous policy. In 1969 it thus produced a major study, entitled *Pour ou contre l'Europe*, which combined the greater flexibility which it had manifested during the 1960s, with strident anti-EEC rhetoric. On the conciliatory side, it called for a united left-wing policy, nationally and internationally, mentioned the possibility of reforming the Treaty of Rome to control capital movements and emphasised the compatibility of nationalisations with existing EEC principles.[30] However, on other fundamental issues there was no movement. British entry into the EEC was still vehemently opposed because it would reinforce the position of the USA in Western Europe and place it 'still more tightly in the "Atlantic" orbit';[31] and since the EEC was the organ of the monopolies which controlled each state, further integration would bring about a 'new reactionary Holy Alliance of the monopolist states of Western Europe', which could not possibly increase European independence from the USA but, on the contrary, would enhance American domination.[32] Finally, the party remained bitterly opposed to the principle of direct elections because the representatives of the other states could impose their decisions on France and this would mean the 'liquidation of national independence'.[33] And, when discussing the probable ideological orientation of the directly elected representatives to Strasbourg, the PCF could not resist its long-accustomed emotive use of the German question: 'One would no doubt even see some West German neo-Nazi representatives of the NPD participating in the elaboration of European legislation.'[34]

No further shift in position was discernible at this stage, so that the December 1970 summary of conversations with the PS merely reiterated the differences over the European question which had been spelled out in the statement of February 1968. It was only after the formation of the enlarged PS under Mitterrand that the PCF was to move further.

Overall, it is clear that, after the initial hardening of its outlook until late 1962, the PCF had become more flexible in its attitudes to the EEC. Recognition of the inevitable internationalisation of the economy and of an EEC dimension to a working-class struggle against monopoly capitalism enabled a dialogue with the Socialists to be undertaken, and *de facto* acceptance of French membership of the EEC made agreement on a common governmental programme conceivable. However, there were also clear limits to the extent to which the party had moved or indeed could move, without a major transformation in its *raison d'être*. These constraints were all rooted in the PCF's conception of, and role in, the French nation-state.

It was argued earlier that, since the Popular Front, the Communists had constantly emphasised the identity of interests between the working class and the nation and that this had been expressed in a policy of national independence against external capitalist domination. In the Gaullist era, as previously, the Communists were often chauvinistic in their rhetoric but their socialist analysis had also become more sophisticated. Chauvinism and socialism combined to impose limits on PCF flexibility on 'Europe'.

The chauvinist aspect is easily explained. The fact that de Gaulle expressed his goal to be the pursuit of national independence inevitably meant that the PCF sought to out-do the General in this respect. Its first inclination was to deny the genuineness of de Gaulle's intentions; later it claimed that, under the pressure of the masses, the state had been forced to adopt a more national policy; and finally, after de Gaulle's resignation, it bemoaned the extent to which his successor was abandoning the positive aspects in his policy (for example by accepting Britain into the EEC and seeking to improve Franco-American relations). Yet however de Gaulle's own policy was interpreted, the PCF ensured that its rhetoric about the national interest (and its use of emotive nationalism) was as strident as his. Given its anxiety to present itself as the national party and its hopes of securing popular support from such an appeal, no other course was to be expected.

What were the *socialist* grounds for resisting 'Europeanism' (and supporting elements of Gaullism)? The first lay in the party's continued belief in the nature of the international struggle between socialism and capitalism. In other words, the French Communists continued to identify strongly with the Soviet bloc and remained

fundamentally hostile to the USA as the centre of world imperialism. Time had not led to any substantial change in its explanation of
the origins of integration and its analysis of the contemporary
situation always emphasised the extent to which American capitalism was dominant within the EEC. Hostility to the Community
therefore still stemmed in part from the conviction that its further
consolidation would help the USA and threaten the Soviet bloc.[35]
Yet the era had passed in which a defence of Soviet interests took
automatic precedence over all other considerations in PCF policy-
making, and opposition also stemmed from the party's view of
French needs. It was, in particular, based on the fear that integration strengthened the monopolies and weakened the forces who
would constitute the 'anti-monopolist alliance'. The greater the
extent to which France was absorbed into an integrated Western
Europe, the greater would be the power of the monopolies and the
more difficult it would be to construct a system of advanced
democracy in France. The language is different but there is, in fact,
an important element of continuity between this policy and the
Communist opposition to internationalisation in the name of
threatened national interests which had been evident throughout the
post-war period. This was equally true of the Communists' favoured
solution. Since further integration would, according to the PCF,
only reinforce the hegemony of the monopolies, the solution lay in a
French left government taking action against American economic,
financial and monetary domination, emancipating itself from the
Atlantic Alliance, loosening the ties between the EEC member
states, and forging a new relationship between the states of Western
Europe and the Soviet Union.

As will be shown later, there are important parallels between
some of these attitudes and those of Labour Party opponents of the
EEC. However, the extent of the continuing divergence from the
position of the majority of French Socialists can be appreciated if we
now turn to the evolution of socialist perspectives in the same
period.

From Uncritical to Critical Acceptance: Socialists and 'Europe'
The disintegration of the SFIO and the proliferation of groups
outside the party meant that Socialist attitudes towards 'Europe'
became increasingly complex, ambivalent and intangible. There
was, moreover, a further complicating factor. Because Gaullist and
Communist language was often so similar, when Socialists eventually became more critical of the USA it was not always clear whether
this constituted a move towards the former or the latter. That is, it
was uncertain whether it implied acceptance of the definition of
national interests now made by the capitalist state, or the break with

capitalism sought by the PCF.

During the first four years of the Fifth Republic the SFIO tended to revert to its traditional European stance.[36] Having been cautious on the issue of supranationalism when in government at the time of the formation of the EEC, it now reasserted its enthusiasm for the eventual creation of a United States of Europe. Similarly, its support for NATO, and its hostility to the Soviet Union remained undiminished. Thus de Gaulle was criticised for his nationalist attitudes to the European Community and defence, and for bringing about the isolation of France from her traditional allies in Europe and the United States. And although the SFIO also expressed a certain amount of dissatisfaction with the liberal economics of the EEC, and the concentration of capital which was occurring, this was by no means a major theme in party propaganda. The July 1960 party congress reflected the general priorities when it stated:

> The Socialist Party continues to believe that the principal objective of France must be the construction of Europe, but a Europe which would be neither that of trusts and capitalism nor that of sovereign states ...
>
> [It] must ... obtain the rapid definition amongst the Six of a common economic policy ... seek, with the agreement of the trade union organisations, the harmonisation of social legislation, and participate in the establishment of democratic political control of the existing institutions by the election of an Assembly by universal suffrage.[37]

If the PCF was still seeking to strengthen international communist condemnation of the EEC at this stage, the SFIO remained in the vanguard of the socialist parties which offered it almost uncritical support.[38] However, as the party moved into opposition to Gaullism, in theory at least, it began to go beyond passive acceptance of both French capitalism and the existing nature of the EEC. In March 1963 Roger Quilliot, who was to handle the ideological dialogue with the PCF the following year, thus asked how it would be possible to carry out revolutionary transformations whilst remaining faithful to the 'law of the majority'. He continued:

> There is no doubt that the international situation constitutes a brake on any transformation ...
>
> We are members of NATO, Europe, and the Common Market, our economic system overlaps with that of our partners [and is] essentially capitalist. How can our structures be radically modified in this context, without shaking the whole construction? ...
>
> The English Labour Party, who intend to keep their hands

free, have kept separate from the Common Market; the German and Dutch socialists have adopted the opposite logic, sacrificing Marxism.

Could we claim to reconcile the irreconcilable? Everything indicates that we would, once again, be revolutionary in words, and reformists in fact.[39]

This recognised a potential contradiction between 'Europe' and socialism, which the SFIO had normally refused to acknowledge. However, Quilliot's conclusion was less of a departure:

The only solution: to push forward in the formation of an integrated Europe, but as independent as possible from American capitalism; such a conception would respond to the secret wishes of the French; it would put us in a better position with the Third World countries; and it would facilitate the socialisation of Europe.[40]

Although he also called for a *rapprochement* with the PCF on the basis of internal policy, the suggestion that the French wished to be as independent as possible from American capitalism, could imply an attempt to harmonise SFIO policy with that of the Gaullist state as well as with the PCF.

In any case, Socialists, like Communists, found that events exposed the reality of their positions even when theoretical formulations sought to mask them. De Gaulle's veto on British membership of the Community and his alliance with Adenauer thus revealed the continuity in SFIO policy. Whereas the party had earlier found British negotiating positions unacceptable, and had not even been able to reach agreement with the Labour Party over the EEC at the November 1962 Congress of EEC (and Applicant) Socialist Parties (see chapter 5 for Labour's attitude), it bitterly opposed de Gaulle's veto. Indeed since European policy had been one of the catalysts for the SFIO's move towards outright opposition to the General, the question of British entry reassumed the ideological importance within French politics that it had had in the late 1940s. Having been adamant in 1961 that the British must accept the Treaty of Rome,[41] the party now claimed that the reasons put forward by de Gaulle were, for the most part

pretexts to attempt to deceive public opinion on the real objectives of Gaullist foreign policy: through the inevitable but surmountable difficulties of a negotiation for the admission of Great Britain to the Common Market, General de Gaulle has seen an opportunity to block the march towards the construction of an integrated Europe, creating a lasting conflict between France and her partners.[42]

Similarly, it condemned de Gaulle's policy towards West Germany, arguing that the Franco-German treaty was inspired 'by out-dated concepts, derived from the will to power and hegemony', and that it harmed the Community by causing an outrage in the Benelux countries and by the risk that it would provoke French and German nationalism.[43]

In fact the visible movement by the SFIO on foreign policy in general and the EEC in particular between 1962 and Mitterrand's presidential campaign was comparatively slight. De Gaulle's policy was continually denounced in fervent terms from a conventional 'European' and Atlanticist perspective,[44] and during the presidential campaign itself when de Gaulle blocked the progress towards supranationalism, the SFIO reaffirmed its complete fidelity to the spirit and the letter of the Treaty of Rome.[45] It is true that more stress was sometimes placed on the need to prevent the EEC from acting as 'the Europe of the trusts'[46] but there was little indication that the party had any concrete plans for its transformation. And while the SFIO called for reforms of NATO to bring about greater equality between the USA and the EEC, American policies were hardly criticised and the necessity for NATO was constantly reaffirmed.

The replacement of Defferre by Mitterrand as presidential candidate had only a very limited impact on such issues for, although Defferre's centrist campaign had stressed the Fourth Republic's themes of modernisation and federalism more openly,[47] Mitterrand was a long-term and committed 'European'. Nor had the organisations which provided his principal backing moved far from SFIO traditions on West European integration. His closest associates thus called for a federal Europe with a directly elected European Parliament, which would be:

> sufficiently socialist ... to be able to enter into a constructive dialogue with the countries of the East, and sufficiently liberal in its intentions and customs to be able to maintain solidarity with the United States.[48]

The FGDS charter reiterated these points, called for a reopening of discussions with Britain and maintained that a democratic socialist Europe was the framework in which the charter was most likely to be achieved. Similarly, the commitment to the Atlantic Alliance was reaffirmed, although it was now argued that this should be progressively converted into an equal partnership.[49]

None of this suggested a major shift from SFIO traditions, although there was perhaps a more marked tendency to perceive 'Europe' as a 'third force' than had been the case since the late 1940s, and the charter did show a greater proximity to PCF positions in its emphasis on peaceful coexistence, the development of relations between Eastern and Western Europe, disarmament and the abandonment of French nuclear weapons. Mitterrand himself also offered rhetorical gestures to the unity of the left: 'the Europe that we desire must be neither *the Europe of technocrats*, nor *the Europe of monopoly capitalists*. It must be *the Europe of democratic peoples*.'[50] Yet his emphasis on West European integration was unshakeable, and quite in line with SFIO traditions:

> I cannot repeat often enough that Europe is our 'great hope'. The world is dominated by ... vast units. France and the other nations of Western Europe cannot remain divided and isolated from each other if they want to participate in technical, economic and social progress.[51]

Communist hopes for a major shift in the Socialists' position on 'Europe' were not, however, entirely misplaced. Given de Gaulle's attitude to the Americans, it was ultimately untenable for the Socialists to maintain total solidarity with the USA, particularly after its actions in the Dominican Republic and Vietnam aroused widespread abhorrence in Europe. Moreover, the development of a critical appraisal of the EEC by elements on the non-communist left, especially in and around the PSU, was bound to exert some influence on Socialists as the search for unity with the PCF continued and as the power of multinational capitalism in the EEC became apparent.

The PSU only succeeded in defining its foreign policy in June 1965. By then leftist influence on its international policy was evident, but on the European Community it sought a synthesis between 'Europeanism' and left-socialism:

> The PSU declares that Gaullism has blocked all progress towards a politically and economically democratic Europe. Gaullism, on the contrary, delivers the Common Market to cartels, whose action is removed from all public control. It is immediately necessary to:
> – democratise the existing European institutions;
> – co-ordinate social struggles at the European level and conclude collective European agreements;
> – establish European planning with continuous participation by the workers' representatives;

– ensure European independence with regard to international trusts, particularly American ones;
– open up current European achievements to all European countries which accept the rules of democratic European construction.[52]

This programme was not purely propagandist, for thinkers, either in the PSU or close to it, had for some years been seriously attempting to analyse a strategy for socialism in an increasingly integrated Western Europe. For example, at an international conference on the subject in Paris in October 1963 highly sophisticated discussions and disputes had taken place between PSU speakers as to whether or not the internationalisation of capital that had already occurred meant that the working-class movement could more successfully seek power on the national or European levels.[53] Even if the result of the discussions was inconclusive, by continuing to devote thought to the means of resolving such problems, and by arranging conferences in which different sectors of the left confronted one another in discussions of concrete issues, the PSU played a role in stimulating the Socialists to consider the EEC in a more critical way. Even so, the SFIO leadership, which remained the dominant force in the FGDS shifted more quickly in criticising American foreign policy than in developing an anti-capitalist strategy within the EEC. For example in May 1966, Gerard Jaquet, a leading force in SFIO 'Europeanism' for almost two decades, condemned de Gaulle's EEC policy from the traditional supranationalist standpoint without any mention of the problem of multinationals. But he maintained that Europeans must have the absolute right to criticise American actions in the strongest possible way, and suggested an intermediary role for Western Europe involving extensive departures from traditional Western policies.[54] The FGDS programme went further still in this direction and, rather than simply denouncing de Gaulle's attitude to NATO as would have been the case earlier, it claimed that a thorough reorganisation of the Atlantic Alliance was necessary. However, on the EEC itself the movement was confined to the statement that

> The left will propose to its Common Market partners that a policy with regard to foreign investments, and particularly American ones, should be founded on the basis of integrating foreign enterprises in the national economy of the host country and of harnessing them fully to its economic progress.[55]

After the failure to reach agreement on the EEC with the PCF in December 1966, a joint communiqué of the FGDS and PSU stated that a common programme for a government of the left would aim at

a synthesis between the imperatives of the indispensable European Construction and the necessity for a real independence of our continent, and the establishment of an international system of collective security.[56]

But how much impact did the viewpoints of left-wing socialists and the PSU have on the European attitudes of the dominant forces in the socialist movement between 1967–71? The evidence is contradictory for there were now different tendencies coexisting within the mainstream of socialist politics and it was not yet clear how the differences would be resolved. Socialist policy cannot, therefore, be ascertained simply by analysis of published statements, which were often uneasy compromises between different viewpoints. The major currents within the socialist movement must themselves be examined.

On the extreme left of the SFIO a new group, CERES (*Centre d'études, de recherches et d'éducation socialists*), was formed in 1966. It regarded itself as Marxist (though eclectic in its sources) and was wholly committed to the creation of a union with the PCF as the sole means of establishing socialism.[57] Its attitudes to 'Europe' clearly revealed this motivation. Its argument (which will be examined further in the next chapter) was essentially twofold: first that the immediate necessity was to combat American economic and political hegemony in Europe, since this threatened to stifle all socialism; and secondly, that the acceptance of the existing Community by a French left-wing government should become conditional upon EEC non-interference in French domestic policy, while support for further integration would depend upon the Community's taking concerted action on aspects of policy beneficial to the realisation of socialism in France.[58] These ideas were later also to receive some support from the confederation of clubs, of which Mitterrand remained President, but which moved sharply to the left after May 1968.[59]

On the other wing of the socialist movement was the large body of SFIO traditionalists whose attitudes to 'Europe' had scarcely shifted since the Fourth Republic. There were, for example, those who confessed that, if forced to choose, they would prefer a liberal–capitalist federal Europe to any move towards autarchy and protectionism, which was associated with PCF policy.[60] And many attempted to demonstrate that the attempt to introduce socialism into France in isolation from the EEC would inevitably end in failure.[61] Sometimes the tone was far more aggressive. Thus in October 1968 *La Revue socialiste* published a long critique of com-

munist and left-socialist positions on Europe.[62] It was argued quite
simply that the PCF's programme of nationalising key industries
and the introduction of obligatory planning would produce a public
sector which, by its size and management, would develop outside all
competition, thus becoming

> an enormous monopoly, an extraordinary instrument of politico-
> social domination in the hands of the best organised party, as the
> example of the Eastern countries shows. This monopoly is clearly
> incompatible with the principles of the Treaty of Rome and the
> development of the Community.

Nor were CERES's suggested bargains between a socialist France
and the rest of the Community acceptable. Either they would lead to
the break-up of the Community or France would be forced to
withdraw from it: 'in either case it would surely remain only for
France to barricade herself behind new protectionist barriers in
order to "construct socialism" and align herself in the camp of the
socialist countries'. This would lead to immense economic difficulties and a lowering of living standards, bringing about violent
reactions in all social classes:

> The FGDS/PC government would therefore face the following
> alternatives: either its own collapse and the return of the right to
> power, or its maintenance by dictatorship and the forced involve-
> ment of the French people in a super Castro-like adventure with
> the exhilarating perspective of a passage into the 'camp of the
> socialist countries', of supposed aid from the USSR, and of world
> upheaval.

The conclusion was that there must never be any incompatibility
between the programme of a left-wing government and the EEC.
The principle of a 'mixed economy' should be accepted and
nationalisations only undertaken to increase profitability and
rationalise the economic structure, and democratic socialists should
seek a new *relance européenne* to press ahead with supranationalism.

During the process of their reformation into the new PS, socialist
statements reflected these contradictory pressures. At the SFIO
National Congress in 1967, for example, the USA was condemned as
bitterly as the USSR and a distinction was drawn between socialist
support for European integration and that of the defenders of
capitalism. Yet full adherence to the Treaty of Rome was
reiterated.[63] Similarly the FGDS statement on the EEC in February
1968, which diverged so sharply from that of the PCF, was both a
powerful reaffirmation of socialist Europeanism, and incorporated a

conditional aspect into its support for further integration.[64] Moreover, although the new PS produced doctrinal statements which were well to the left of most of those of the SFIO, the first leader was Alain Savary, who had, in 1957, recommended ratification of the Treaty of Rome on the grounds that it would modernise the French economy, and who still maintained that one of the greatest achievements of the SFIO had been to take France into the EEC.[65] But the greatest enigma of all, who was subsequently to embody all the contradictions in French socialism, was François Mitterrand himself.

In 1965, when asked to explain how he could act as the common presidential candidate of the left, given the difference between his outlook on 'Europe' and that of the PCF, Mitterrand's reply had typified the way in which he always sought to rally the Communists to traditional socialist positions with slight redefinitions of the issue. Claiming that the communist attitude was perfectly understandable in historical terms because Europe had been an outpost of American power, he maintained that the objective was now to show that Europe was capable of being free and a factor for peace and progress.

> From the moment a man of the left like myself, and other really sincere Europeans – and you know the position of the SFIO and notably Guy Mollet – from the moment when numerous men and women of the left think that Europe is the chance for France, and the chance for the workers, because it provides greater outlets and production, and provides a capacity for new expansion and therefore for wealth and social progress – well! The Communists, who are realists will certainly admit the value of these arguments, and will undoubtedly discuss them ...[66]

Subsequently Mitterrand had shared in the increasingly critical attitude towards the United States and urged greater European autonomy in the realms of economics and security, but his faith in 'Europe' remained an absolute priority in his political creed. Indeed even when he was most anxious to stress his desire to reach agreement with the PCF his basic assumption, explicitly counterposed to that of the Communists, was that national independence was an empty slogan:

> while American capital and management infiltrate the Common Market economy and the Russian Army ... possesses a nuclear force capable of annihilating each of the six countries of 'little Europe' in the first quarter of an hour of a war ...[67]

In fact he claimed that American inaction over the Soviet invasion of

Czechoslovakia showed that the division of Europe was total. If the Americans would not intervene to prevent the crushing of the Czechoslovak 'rebels' in Prague, nor would the Russians do anything to oppose a generals' coup in Paris, aided by the CIA. Thus 'the Czechoslovak drama must make us seek the ways to the independence of France in the independence of Europe'.[68] And he saw the construction of an independent Europe as the sole means of creating the 'synthesis of peace and liberty' which could substitute itself for a Europe divided into spheres of influence.

Mitterrand was, by the end of the decade, highly critical of the USA, but he was always insistent that the left must ensure that any action taken to gain independence from one bloc did not result in delivering her to the other. And although he continued to favour the progressive and simultaneous disintegration of the alliances and the creation of a demilitarised zone in Central Europe, he would not advocate quitting the Atlantic Alliance completely since the USSR could not offer any guarantee of the effects of such an action.[69]

How did Mitterrand reconcile his certainty that West European construction was an essential prerequisite for French independence with socialism? Was Europe to be integrated first and socialised afterwards? And what if further immersion in a capitalist Europe made it more difficult to construct socialism in France? Mitterrand sought to transcend such problems with the assertion that it was not necessary 'to opt for Europe against socialism or for socialism against Europe'.[70] He sought to justify this contention with the argument that industrial specialisation was the prerequisite to economic expansion and that this was possible only on a European scale. Similarly, he attempted to demonstrate the incompatibility between genuine European construction and capitalism, with the argument that integration on a capitalist basis would simply reinforce American domination. An independent or 'European Europe' was possible only with socialism and the task of a left-wing government in France was to further its own domestic programme within a capitalist EEC, while impelling the latter towards 'independence' and socialism by putting the 'industrial spearhead' under public control.

Mitterrand's 'Europeanism' was thus imprecise and contradictory. On the one hand his assertions that Europe could not be 'European' unless it was also socialist, and his claim that a left-wing government in France would both maintain an important margin of manoeuvre within a capitalist Europe, and provide impetus for transforming Europe towards socialism, reflected the influence of the arguments of left-socialists. On the other hand the fact that he sometimes appeared to view anything which heightened the possibility of European independence as, by definition, 'socialist', and vehemently opposed the autarchic tendencies of some of the left implied a form of 'left-Gaullism'.[71]

However, the imprecision and contradiction in Mitterrand's political outlook was not a purely personal matter: it reflected the coexistence of distinct forces within French socialism at the time. And it is because the PS was, from its inception, such a heterogeneous formation that it is difficult precisely to assess its response to the challenge of Gaullism, and its degree of convergence with the PCF by 1971.

It is clear that, during the second half of the 1960s, French Socialists as a whole had become increasingly critical of the USA and more assertive about the need to secure European independence. This in itself appeared to constitute a step towards the communist position but, of course, it also reflected the general shift in outlook that de Gaulle had precipitated throughout French society. That is, if Gaullists commanded widespread support for the notion of independence from the USA, even right-wing Socialists would eventually be expected to adopt this theme and to give it a more socialistic gloss (for example by inveighing against multinationals). However, *in general*, socialist-Europeanism differed from Gaullism because it remained integrationist and supranationalist, and from communism because it maintained a positive commitment to the European Community. What did this continued Europeanism signify?

One contemporary proponent of Socialist–Communist unity claimed that the fact that 'Europe' was a major stumbling block to an agreement by the left revealed the Socialists' continued acceptance of international capitalism:

> The significance of a 'European mystique' is often the acceptance of the lines of dependence between the capitalism of the EEC and that of the USA. The primacy accorded to the European objective over agreement with the [communists] confirms the deep-seated refusal to govern with [them].[72]

This is too stark a judgement for socialist-Europeanism contained many strands. It is true that many on the right of the party (particularly among SFIO traditionalists) remained fully committed to the EEC, at least in part, because they were content to work within the constraints of capitalism, while it was generally the left of the party (particularly CERES) who were the least enthusiastic about the Community. There is, therefore, as we shall see later, a parallel with the British Labour Party, where, in general, the revisionist right-wing was to adopt 'Europeanism' whilst the left remained adamantly opposed to it. However, even left-wing Socialists in France believed that French socialism needed a West European dimension and there were some who felt that the PCF insistence on the 'primacy of the nation' inevitably made it an accomplice in Gaullist nationalism.[73]

In any case, it is true that 'Europeanism' continued to drive a wedge between the Socialists and the Communists. Indeed in 1967 Mitterrand had even believed that the attempt to reach agreement on 'Europe' would undermine the whole search for left-wing unity.[74] Thus although the attempt to ascribe the Communist–Socialist disunity to a single factor is bound to be simplistic, the fact remains that the divergencies on 'Europe' were significant because they still reflected a whole range of differences between the two major sections of the left. Whether agreement would eventually be reached and, if so, whether it would result in a socialist synthesis or the incorporation of the left in the Gaullist perspective would depend upon the resolution of the contradictions within the new *Parti socialiste*, and the evolution of its relations with the Communists.

Notes

1 For analyses of Gaullist foreign policy, see A. Grosser, *La Politique extérieure de la Ve République* (Seuil, 1965); P. Cerny, *The Politicis of Grandeur – Ideological Aspects of de Gaulle's Foreign Policy* (Cambridge University Press, 1980); L. Pattison de Ménil, *Who Speaks for Europe? The Vision of Charles de Gaulle* (Weidenfeld, 1977); and for a full treatment of de Gaulle's European policy, with original texts, see E. Jouve, *Le Général de Gaulle et la construction de l'Europe, 1940–66* (LGDJ, 1967).

2 For full discussion, see R.W. Johnson, *The Long March of the French Left* (Macmillan, 1981); N. Nugent and D. Lowe, *The Left in France* (Macmillan, 1982); J. Poperen, *La Gauche française*, vol. I, *Le Nouvel Age, 1958–65* and vol. II, *L'Unité de la gauche, 1965–73* (Fayard, 1972 and 1975); C. Hurtig, *De la SFIO au nouveau parti socialiste* (Colin, 1970). For a socialist view, see R. Verdier, *PS/PC – une lutte pour l'entente* (Seghers, 1976), and for a communist one, see *Histoire du réformisme en France depuis 1920*, vol.2 (Editions sociales, 1976). For a useful general survey, see H. Machin and V. Wright 'The French Left Under the Fifth Republic: The Search for Identity in Unity', *Comparative Politics*, vol. 10, no. 1, Oct. 1977.

3 In 1958 the PCF had obtained only 10 seats in the national assembly and the SFIO 44. These results were badly distorted by the two-ballot voting system, for the PCF had obtained 3.9 million votes (19.2%) in the first ballot against 3.2 million (15.7%) for the SFIO and, although the Gaullists had only obtained 100,000 more first votes than the PCF (19.5%) they were able to hold 199 seats in the assembly. In the November 1962 elections, co-operation enabled the left to secure more seats on less total votes: 4 million for the PCF (21.7%) resulted in 41 seats and 2.3 million (12.6%) for the SFIO in 66 seats. For full details and analysis, see J. Frears, *Political Parties and Elections in the French Fifth Republic* (Hurst, 1977).

4 Waldeck-Rochet had taken over as leader in 1964 and he himself was effectively replaced by Georges Marchais when he became incurably ill in 1970. Both leaders were less 'instinctively' pro-Soviet than Thorez.

5 See G. Nania, *Le PSU avant Rocard* (Roblot, 1973).

6 The grouping was known as CIR (la Convention des institutions républicaines) For details see D. Loschak, *La Convention des institutions républicaines – François Mitterrand et le Socialisme* (PUF, 1971).

7 For a full discussion, see D. Macshane, *François Mitterrand: A Political Odyssey* (Quartet, 1982).

8 In particular, it had pledged itself to struggle relentlessly against the regime of personal power, to raise living standards, to bring about fairer distribution and economic growth, to provide full employment and to give priority to education and housing. Hurtig, *De la SFIO au nouveau parti socialiste*, pp.47–9.

9 The PCF secured 73 seats (5 million votes (22.5%)) and the FGDS 116 seats (4.2 million votes (19.0%)). The PSU also won 4 seats (0.5 million votes (2.1%)).

10 The PCF lost 600,000 votes and 39 seats, the FGDS lost 500,000 votes and 59 seats, and although the PSU gained 400,000 votes, it lost all its seats.

11 For Gaston Defferre, the Socialist candidate, the result was abysmal for he obtained 1.1 million votes (5.1%) which was only 300,000 more than Michel Rocard, the PSU candidate. Jacques Duclos did far better for the PCF, obtaining 5.2 million votes (21.5%).

12 It was in the early months of the Gaullist takeover that the new regime was likened to fascism (see, for example, the editorial and the article by Garaudy 'De Gaulle et le fascisme', *C du C*, June 1958), whereas by 1959 the regime was seen as the servant of state monopoly capitalism. De Gaulle's anti-national policy was constantly denounced (see, for example 'De Gaulle, ce n'est pas l'indépendence nationale' by P. Villon, *C du C*, Sept. 1958) and this line was confirmed at the 1961 party congress.

13 J. Fauvet, *Histoire du parti communiste français, 1920–76* (Fayard, 1977), pp.491–3; see also Poperen, *Nouvel Age*, pp.202–18.

14 For an informative examination of the European policy of the PCI, see D. Sasson 'The European strategy of the Italian Communist Party' in D. Sasson (ed.), *The Italian Communists Speak for Themselves* (Spokesman, 1978).

15 For the PCF's account of the conference (which is misleading because it claims that its theses were upheld) see H. Jourdain, 'Sur la rencontre de Moscou', *C du C*, Jan.–Feb. 1963; for a corrective, see F. Fejto, *The French Communist Party and the Crisis of International Communism* (Massachusetts Institute of Technology 1967), pp. 140–1.

16 Poperen, *Nouvel Age*, p.312.

17 F. Billoux, 'Le Marché commun et la classe ouvrière', *C du C*, Jan.–Feb. 1963.

18 P. Villon, 'La Politique de l'axe Bonn–Paris à la lumière de l'histoire', *C du C*, April 1963, p.110.

19 Ibid., p.106.

20 Quoted by Waldeck-Rochet in his report of the central committee at the 17th party congress (14–17 May 1964), *C du C*, June–July 1964.

21 'L'Intégration européenne et le mouvement ouvrier', *Les Cahiers du Centre d'Etudes Socialistes*, Sept.–Dec. 1964, nos. 45–51 (*Colloque international*, 4–6 October 1963), p.120.

22 L. Mathey, 'Sur quelques aspects d'un programme démocratique', *C du C*, Dec. 1964.

23 F. Clavaud, 'La crise du Marché commun', *C du C*, Sept. 1965.

24 The emphasis on *démocratie avancée* dates from the manifesto adopted at the Champigny congress in December 1968, but the concept was accepted earlier in the decade. The revised statutes of 1964 stated that, in the short term it sought to establish 'le régime le plus avancé possible dans les conditions du système capitaliste'.

25 The PCF used these arguments at an international communist conference on state monopoly capitalism, held in Paris in May 1966.

26 The furthest it ever went was probably in an article by J. Kahn 'Monopoles, Nations et Marché Commun' (*C du C*, April 1966), where the author stated that 'it isn't unprecedented for an institution appearing in given circumstances and under the influence of given forces to adapt to other ends in different circumstances'.

27 C. Fiterman, 'Les communistes, l'Europe et la nation française', *C du C*, April 1966, p.34.

28 Text as in *Le Populaire de Paris*, 27–28 Feb. 1968, reproduced in Hurtig, *De la SFIO au nouveau parti socialiste*, p.66.

29 This constituted a very slight advance on the 1966 position where it was stated that, 'We think that even within the framework of the Atlantic Alliance or the Common Market the representatives of a democratic France could defend the cause of peaceful coexistence and ensure that the interests of the country were respected there', *C du C*, editorial, April 1966.

30 J. Kanapa and J. Denis, *Pour ou contre l'Europe* (Editions sociales, 1969), pp.132, 136–7, 140–3.

31 Ibid., pp.150–1.

32 Ibid., p.204.

33 Ibid., p.212.

34 Ibid., p.213.

35 Ibid., esp. chs. 2, 7, and 9.

36 See, for example, G., Mollet, *13 mai 1958–13 mai 1962* (Plon 1962); *Les Socialistes et l'Europe*, articles by A. Gazier, G. Jaquet, C. Pineau, with preface by G. Mollet (SFIO, 1962) (Supplément à la documentation socialiste, no. 143).

37 Quoted by J–C. Poulain in 'Le Parti SFIO et "l'intégration européenne"', *C du C*, April 1961, p.737.

38 See the text of the conference of EEC socialist parties of November 1962, and the commentary on it by Gérard Jaquet, who took charge of liaison for it, in 'Le Programme pour une action commune des partis socialistes de la Communauté européenne', *La Revue Socialiste (RS)*, Jan. 1963.

39 'Rénovation et regroupement', *RS*, March 1963, p.281.

40 Ibid.

41 See interview with Mollet in the journal, *Le XXᵉSiècle*, 15 Dec. 1961, reproduced in Mollet, *13 mai 1958–13 mai 1962*, pp. 39–40.

42 'Communiqué du comité directeur 31 Jan. 1963,' *RS*, March 1963, p.328.

43 'Résolution sur le traité franco-allemand', National Congress, 30 May–2 June 1963; *RS*, Sept. 1963, pp.215–16.

44 See, for example, 'Communiqué du comité directeur 28 April 1965', *RS*, June 1965, p.96.

45 'Résolution du Conseil national, 30 October 1965', *RS*, Dec. 1965, p.544.

46 For example in a speech by Mollet at Lille University, quoted by C. Vallin in 'L'Unité d'action et ses perspectives', *C du C*, Sept. 1963, p.20.

47 See, for example, G. Defferre, *Le Nouvel Horizon* (Gallimard, 1965). pp.12–17 and ch.5; and Claude Bruclain (pseudonym), *Le Socialisme et l'Europe* (Club Jean Moulin) (Seuil, 1965).

48 'Charte de la Convention des institutions républicaines', final motion of preparatory conference, Paris 6–7 June 1964, reproduced in Loschak, *La Convention des institutions républicaines*, p.16.

49 *Le Populaire du Paris*, 2–3 October 1965, reproduced in Hurtig, *De la SFIO au nouveau parti socialiste*, pp.51–2.

50 F. Mitterrand, 'Le sens d'un combat', *RS*, Nov. 1965, p.342.

51 Ibid.

52 Reproduced in Nania, *Le PSU avant Rocard*, pp.150–1. (Other parts of the international policy included an active strategy of non-alignment, leading to withdrawal from NATO, recognition of North Vietnam and the Vietcong, a demand for 'aid to the democratic forces of Latin America, Africa and Asia in struggle against imperialism'.)

53 'L'Intégration européenne et le mouvement ouvrier'. See, for example, the disagreements between Pierre Naville and Jean-Marie Vincent.

54 'Perspectives européennes et atlantiques après huit ans de régime gaulliste', *RS*, May 1966.

55 'Le programme de la FGDS', 14 July 1966, reproduced in Hurtig, *De la SFIO au nouveau parti socialiste,* pp.54–7.

56 'Communiqué of 27 January 1967', *RS*, March 1967, pp.269–71.

57 See *Le CERES par lui-même* (Christiane Bourgois, 1979).

58 See, for example, the commentary by G. Malet (secretary of CERES) on the FGDS/PCF agreement of 24 Feb. 1968 in *RS*, March 1968; and R. Mouriaux, 'La Gauche française et l'Europe: l'étape de Cachan, 24–25 fevrier 1968', *Projet*, April 1968.

59 See 'Le contrat socialiste' in F. Mitterrand, *Un Socialisme du possible* (Seuil, 1970), pp.96–9.

60 For example, the ex–SFIO Foreign Minister, Christian Pineau at the Cachan conference, Mouriaux, 'La Gauche française et l'Europe'.

61 For example, J. Taillefer, 'Demain, l'Europe', *RS*, Dec. 1967.

62 A. Ferrat, 'L'Europe et le socialisme'. (The next three quotations are taken from this article.)

63 'Résolution sur la politique internationale', *congrès national*, 29 June–2 July 1967.

64 It thus called for the ceding of powers to European institutions *after* more common policies had been introduced. Text in Hurtig, *De la SFIO au Nouveau parti socialiste,* pp. 64–6.

65 A. Savary, *Pour le Nouveau parti socialiste* (Seuil, 1970), pp. 39, 156–7.

66 Interview on 'France Inter' 25 Nov 1965, reproduced in F. Mitterrand, *Politique* (Fayard, 1977), p. 425.

67 F. Mitterrand, *Ma Part de Vérité* (Fayard, 1969), p.76.

68 Ibid., p.136.

69 Ibid., p.197.

70 Ibid.

71 Press conference, 16 Aug. 1967, quoted in *Politique,* p.450.

72 Mouriaux, 'La gauche française et l'Europe', p.486.

73 This was the view of the PSU. See its theses on 'Capitalisme en Crise' (especially no. 17) adopted in March 1969, and reproduced in M. Rocard, *Le PSU et l'avenir socialiste de la France* (Seuil, 1969).

74 Verbatim record of CERES conference on 'Egalité en France' at Suresnes, *RS*, Sept. 1967, p.250.

3

The Contemporary Left and 'Europe'

Socialist Synthesis or Acceptance of the *Status Quo?*

In the ten years between the unification of the *Parti socialiste* and its overwhelming victory in May–June 1981, relations between the two parties of the left were complex and vacillating.[1] In the latter half of 1971 and the first part of 1972 they appeared strained, but in June 1972 their two leaders were finally able to reach agreement upon a common governmental programme. For the next two years, although each party stressed its independence and made no secret of its intention of dominating the other, the climate improved and they displayed a semblance of unity. However, in autumn 1974 a new deterioration became evident as the PCF launched an attack on the PS for moving to the right. This charge was not wholly unfounded for in the presidential election earlier that year, Mitterrand (who had been only narrowly defeated by Giscard d'Estaing) had treated the Communists in a somewhat cavalier fashion and had placed a new emphasis on the battle against inflation; and in October the PS held a well-publicised conference with socialists outside the party in which all the emphasis was on *autogestion* [self-management] and scant regard was paid to the Common Programme. However, the main reason for the attack was the clear evidence in the by-elections in September that the PS was now becoming the major electoral party and could be expected to dominate any government of the left.[2] For the next three years, although the electoral agreement was upheld, relations between the two parties thus grew increasingly bitter as successive local elections confirmed the lead of the PS, which continued to interpret the Common Programme in its own 'moderate' manner. In September 1977 the break finally came when negotiations for the up-dating of the Programme collapsed amidst mutual recriminations and, largely as a result, the left was narrowly defeated in the legislative elections in March 1978.[3] Relations then grew worse than at any time since 1962 and in the by-elections in

December 1980 the Communist leadership even rejected the electoral agreement.[4] However, after achieving their poorest result for almost fifty years in the presidential and legislative elections of May–June 1981, the Communists again recanted, paid obeisance to the policies of the PS, and entered the new government.

The European question had not prevented agreement being reached between Communists and Socialists either in 1972 or in June 1981 and indeed on both occasions the two parties had included a formulation on 'Europe' in their wider declarations of joint policy. Yet this did not mean that the lasting divergencies on external policy had finally been resolved. Even when relations between them were relatively harmonious (between June 1972 and September 1974) major differences on 'Europe' remained and these became fully apparent as communist/socialist antagonism mounted once more. And any new breaks between the two parties will bring renewed bitter conflict on EEC policy, because the joint statement of June 1981 did no more than paper over disagreements which had once again deepened since 1978 and which can be expected to endure. This chapter will demonstrate these continuing differences between the PS and the PCF by examining the evolution of each. It will then consider a further question (which will be discussed at greater length in the conclusion): has the PS, as the dominant party of the French left, overcome its own contradictions and achieved a synthesis for the socialist transformation of the nation-state and Europe? Or has it become the progressive part of a French national consensus which, since the Gaullist era, has defined its aim as the pursuit of national independence from within the European Community?[5]

The PCF From 'Eurocommunism' to Chauvinism

The PCF tried, unsuccessfully, to pressurise the Socialists into negotiations for a common programme while they remained comparatively weak before their unifying congress in June 1971. Thereafter it abused Mitterrand for his strategy of strengthening the Socialists before signing a common programme, and exerted further pressure by publishing its own programme for a 'democratic government of popular union' in October 1971.[6] This was a reaffirmation of the doctrine of state monopoly capitalism, calling for nationalisation of key sectors of the economy as the first step to advanced democracy, and as the economic basis of national independence. Although it stated that France could not unilaterally break the links created by the EEC without serious inconvenience, the programme again emphasised its vehement opposition to any supranationalism, called for measures to defend national economic interests, and to establish political and economic relations with the rest of Europe. It also maintained that: 'The entry of Great Britain would aggravate all the harmful aspects of the Common Market, accentuate American penetration, and deepen the division of Europe.'[7] But although Pompidou held a referendum on British entry in April 1972 in which the PCF called for a 'No' vote while the PS urged abstention, in June 1972 Marchais signed the Common Programme with Mitterrand, in which the 'European' section was far less negative than in the PCF's own programme.[8]

The section on the EEC began with the bold assertion that the task of a left-wing government would be

> to participate in the construction of the EEC, in its institutions and in its common policies, with the will to liberate it from the domination of large-scale capital, to democratise its institutions, to uphold the demands of the workers, and to orientate community projects in conformity with their interests.[9]

Similarly, other assertions directly or indirectly accepted the legitimacy of Community initiatives in a way that was out of keeping with the normal communist view. For example, it was agreed that the European Parliament must be able to control the execution of the EEC budget, and ought to be more closely associated in the preparation of all kinds of Community decisions; defensive use of the Treaty of Rome was frequently invoked, thereby giving tacit recognition to a treaty whose purpose was to promote the integration to which the PCF had always expressed fundamental hostility; political co-operation between the EEC members to define a foreign policy was urged; and it was stated that a government of the left would call for the Common Market to follow it in controlling foreign investment, and would seek its economic and monetary co-operation to defend the franc.[10]

This shift in the PCF position was not because there had been any real change in its attitude to 'Europe', or indeed in other aspects of policy. As Marchais told the Central Committee:

> We have no intention of exchanging our programme for the Common Programme. On the contrary we consider the latter as a step forward, allowing the establishment of the most favourable conditions for mobilising the masses on *our* ideas, *our* solutions, and *our* objectives.[11]

However, in order to secure the agreement which Marchais hoped would lead to this strengthening of the PCF, it had been necessary to make concessions on the EEC (and the Atlantic Alliance) because Mitterrand had bargained particularly hard on these points.[12]

During the period in which the PCF still believed that it might achieve leadership of the left (approximately until autumn 1974) its attitude to the EEC was, however, influenced by its new commitments in the Common Programme. There were thus signs that the Communists became less preoccupied with the question, and their analysis of it, though negative, was often highly sophisticated and less propagandist than previously.[13] There were also occasional indications that they recognised, at least *de facto*, the importance of an EEC dimension. For example, in September 1973, when faced with American pressure for a reduction in the common external tariff, the PCF Central Committee placed emphasis on the need for a Community response and specified measures which should be adopted at EEC level. Indeed, at this time, the party went so far as to maintain that participation in the EEC, on the basis of the Common Programme, was a major priority.[14] And even when it reiterated its general hostility to 'Europe', great emphasis was placed upon the need for solidarity between working class and progressive forces within the EEC to co-ordinate the anti-capitalist struggle and to elaborate statutes or agreements at West European level.[15]

The turning point came in October 1974 when Socialist successes in the by-elections made it appear increasingly probable that the PS would secure dominance of the left. Once relations with the PS deteriorated, PCF attitudes to West European integration began to re-harden – a process which reached its peak in the nine months preceding the elections to the European Assembly.

By January 1975 the party was claiming that the transfer to the EEC of control over its own budget and the proposal for the Strasbourg assembly to be directly elected indicated that the government was taking the road towards the 'dissolution of France';[16] by December of the same year it asserted that Giscard had abandoned all the 'positive' aspects of de Gaulle's policy; [17] and eighteen months later, suggestions that the EEC should be enlarged were denounced in extreme terms.[18] Moreover, as PS/PCF relations worsened, the Communists increasingly equated the European policy of the Socialists with that of the Giscardien state.[19]

The theoretical and practical concomitant of this hardening of position was a strident reaffirmation of the primacy of the national question. In May 1976 a centrepiece article in *Cahiers du communisme* entitled 'Parler, agir au nom de la France' (To speak and act in the name of France) observed, no doubt correctly (!) that: 'France, the nation, the country – are the words used most often in the document adopted by the 22nd congress.'[20] And the writer maintained that, at a time when social democrats were talking of European socialism, the task of Communists in speaking and acting in the name of France took on a new significance. Victor Hugo's suggestion that national identity was as objective a fact as bread was quoted with approval, while the reformist Socialists' Europeanism was criticised as a means of providing help to anti-national monopolies. Of equal significance, the same issue republished General de Gaulle's victory speech of 8 May 1945, thereby implying that the party now regarded the positive aspects of the General's policy as more important than the negative ones. Moreover, as usual, the renewed emphasis on the national question was combined with an anti-German tone, reminders of the war, and a reaffirmation of the argument that, as in the Resistance era, the working class must battle for the nation, which was being betrayed by the bourgeoisie and let down by the Socialists. Thus in June 1975, Giscard's external policy was said to stem from the French bourgeois tradition of class collaboration with German imperialism and, by abandoning the official celebration of the victory over Nazism, he showed that

> He doesn't even hesitate ... to attempt to erase the Hitlerian crimes ... so great is his will rapidly to attain the creation of 'supranational' political institutions – that is, foreign instruments of intervention and constraint over our people, including the military component of such a policy.[21]

And at the 22nd congress in February 1976 Marchais claimed that Giscard's policy lay 'in making France the stepping stone for West Germany [and it] is a criminal policy, a policy which no Frenchman caring for the interests of the nation could or should accept'.[22]

After the loss of the legislative elections in March 1978 the PCF became most bitter of all in its condemnation of both the government's and the Socialists' European policies and the most vehement in its protestation that the Communists were the sole defenders of the true national interests. The basis for this strategy was reaffirmed in two meetings of the Central Committee in the last quarter of 1978. In the first, on the 27–28 September, the key report argued that:

> The strategy of large-scale capital and of the Giscardien state is to bring about a situation which, by the third millenium, will make France ... a secondary province of an empire whose Charlemagne will be German.[23]

And the subsequent resolution stated that:

> Everything is tied to this essential, lasting fact of national reality:

economic and social problems, political questions and the stance of the different parties, the current conditions for political struggle ... [and] the potentialities and limitations of the process of political change.[24]

The result was a renewed campaign 'Contre le déclin de la France – épanouissement démocratique et national' (Against the decline of France – Démocratic and national blossoming) – in which the EEC was bitterly condemned and, in addition, highly surprising national policy recommendations were sometimes made. For example, the party now took its support for a national defence policy to its logical conclusion by calling for the construction of a sixth nuclear submarine and condemning governmental hesitation on the issue.[25]

The second important stage in the national anti-EEC campaign came with a Central Committee meeting of 12–13 December 1978 and the issuing of the party's statement for the forthcoming European elections. The introductory passage is worth quoting at length for it indicates exactly the tone of the PCF's propaganda in this period:

> More than twenty years ago, those who created the Coal and Steel pool, and then the Common Market, presented it as the chance for the country, the solution to all its problems. They lied. Seven million unemployed, a lethargic economy, agriculture in crisis, the dismantling of industrial sectors like coal and steel, factories closing, regions dying – that is their Europe, the Europe of the right and of social-democracy.
>
> Today they have decided to go further, very much further. They have decided to organise the uncontrolled domination of multinational companies, and the uncontrolled exploitation of the workers and peoples at the level of capitalist Europe. The sole ambition of the Giscardien state and of those who support its projects is to permit a limited number of French trusts to have a place in this feast of giants. Their sole wish is to rely on foreign support to oppose the people of France in the tradition of the emigrés of Coblenz; of Thiers allying himself with Bismarck against the Commune; and of the Pétainist collaboration with Hitler.
>
> For this, they want the fundamental decisions which concern the life of the country and its inhabitants to be taken in Brussels or in Bonn and no longer in Paris. They want the French parliament to be deprived of its prerogatives for the benefit of the European Assembly. They want the flight of capital and enterprises abroad and the exile of workers forced to follow them. They want the dismantling of entire sectors of our economy, the

disorganisation and weakening of public research, and they want foreign control. They want the subordination of the franc to the mark, making ... West Germany the banker of Europe which holds its purse-strings and dictates its law. They want to integrate the French army into a European and Atlantic military force. They want the recoil of national and regional cultures, and standardisation in the American mould. They want France to be fragmented, weakened and integrated, lost in a West European conglomerate placed under West German hegemony and the high protectorship of the United States.[26]

Careful attention to the Communists' concrete proposals for the EEC reveals that, in practical terms, party policy had changed far less since the era of the Common Programme than the impression given by its anti-EEC propaganda.[27] But although this is of importance in the long term, it is of little relevance in considering the communist position on the European question at this time for the PCF clearly wanted to project itself as totally opposed to the EEC and the only loyal defender of the nation. 'No to Euro-unemployment' was actually a Gaullist slogan while 'An independent France in a democratic Europe' was communist. But the reverse could easily have been true.

The effects of this campaign against all aspects of *Europe d'étranger* were unclear. For the first time since the signing of the Common Programme, but on a greatly reduced turn-out, the PCF share of the poll stabilised while that of the PS declined, although still outstripping the PCF.[28] Naturally, the Communists drew confident conclusions from this, but the two groupings who favoured the EEC came first and second, and the overall victor was the list of Simone Veil, whose committed Europeanism served the interests of the Giscardien Government in doing everything that the PCF opposed.

Between the direct elections of 1979 and the presidential campaign the EEC became a less salient issue. Nevertheless, the PCF continued its strident denunciations of both the Giscardien state and the Socialists for their 'anti-national' policies, and condemned any signs of compromise in defending French interests against, for example, British demands. Moreover, the attempt to combine appeals to the working class and the nation dropped to its most abysmal level during the presidential campaign, when the PCF sought to exploit anti-immigrant prejudices, by harrassing North Africans already in the country and demanding an end to new immigration.[29] Yet despite its unprincipled appeal to popular xenophobia, the PCF had not actually rewritten its theory, and the evolution which had taken place during the 1960s and early 1970s meant that the less intransigent attitude was still available for use if required. After the overwhelming victory by the Socialists in June 1981, the PCF was thus able to sign a new common statement on the EEC in order to enter the government (on a more junior basis than would have been necessary in March 1978).[30] Because of the changed power ratio between the PCF and PS (and because of the evolution of the latter) the new statement was less critical than that in the Common Programme nine years earlier (see above page 85) particularly because it made no mention of the aim of liberating the Community 'from the domination of large-scale capital'. It thus simply stated:

> Both parties will actively support the participation of France in the EEC, in its institutions and its common policies, while respecting France's freedom of action and legitimate interests. They will support common policies in the social field, in the defence of agriculture and threatened sectors, and for the strengthening of research and technologically advanced industries.[31]

What accounted for the opportunistic vacillations of the PCF and its strident reaffirmation of the national question?

The root cause of the PCF's intractable dilemmas after 1974 was, of course, the inexorable growth of the PS, and the prospect of its own decline. In general, until early 1977, the PCF tried to counter this by rivalling the PS with a move in the 'Eurocommunist' direction, whilst simultaneously preserving its own status as the true party of the nation and the working class. Until then limited, but real, criticisms of Soviet internal policies were thus expressed and at the 22nd party congress in February 1976 the leadership announced that it no longer adhered to the concept or policy of the 'dictatorship of the proletariat'. Moreover, during this period the French Communists had frequent meetings with the Italian Communist Party and increasingly welcomed commentators' descriptions of itself as Eurocommunist.

Yet there were very serious limits to the extent to which the PCF could evolve in this direction. First, this ground in France was effectively occupied by the PS, whose theoretical commitment to Marxism as a major doctrinal source allowed it to express ideas which often closely resembled those of the Italian and Spanish communist parties. Indeed the PS made every effort to capitalise on this fact, often emphasising its identity of view and close relations with the Italian Communists and contrasting this situation with that of PS/PCF misunderstanding. And, most galling of all for the PCF, no matter how far it went in abandoning Stalinism, it always seemed to be the PS which derived the greater benefit in terms of electoral support. Secondly, the PCF was not, in any case, likely to adopt the tenets of Eurocommunism in the Italian sense. It believed that the PCI had gone too far in the reformist direction, and the leadership was also adamant that central control and discipline should be maintained. Indeed some of the most dramatic changes in policy (including the abandonment of the 'dictatorship of the proletariat' as a professed goal, and the sudden commitment to the maintenance of nuclear weapons) were made without any genuine rank-and-file participation or discussion of the problems. Nor was the PCF prepared to go so far as the other Eurocommunist parties in its criticisms of, or detachment from, the Soviet Union. Thus although criticisms of the Eastern bloc were certainly made, they were normally of limited extent and were never, apart from in the case of the intervention in Czechoslovakia, of Soviet foreign policy.[32] Finally, the Eurocommunist position brought the Italians and Spaniards very close to the PS position on 'Europe' and emulation of this policy would, of course, have meant a total reorientation of the theory and practice followed by the PCF since the 1930s.[33]

When the PCF adopted Eurocommunism it therefore did so in a very attenuated form. Certainly, it wished to derive what benefit it could from association with the Italian and Spanish parties and, to this end, Marchais again proclaimed that the party was Eurocommunist at the 23rd congress in May 1979. However, the differences from the other two parties remained very real. Yet the PCF would not revert to a potentially insurrectionary or Leninist form of revolution or abandon the pursuit of the anti-monopoly alliance.

In this impasse, the leadership seems to have concluded that traditional values must be reasserted and the traditional faithful rallied.[34] The party thus resumed a sensationalist and chauvinist stance for the 'European' elections of June 1979 (without really altering its fundamental policy) and at the party congress that year Marchais proclaimed that the record in Eastern Europe was 'positive overall' (while maintaining the Eurocommunist tag). In the run-up to the presidential elections of 1981 the Communists became so desperate to maintain the support of 20 per cent of the electorate that the party's tone became more strident than ever. Diatribes against Mitterrand exceeded those against Giscard, pro-Sovietism increased with a vigorous defence of the invasion of Afghanistan, and, as we have seen, the attempt to combine the appeals to the working class and the nation reached a new low, with chauvinism clearly prevailing over socialism. When all this failed, the party made a new volte-face on the calculation that it would benefit from a share in governmental office (at least temporarily).

To describe PCF policy in this way is not to dismiss its underlying arguments against the EEC. The beliefs that the Community is dominated by monopolies and is harmful to small businesses, peasants and the working class, and that greater supranationalism would weaken a left-wing government are partially valid (and, as we shall see, are echoed in different terms by the Labour Party). But the PCF had compromised its views so much to achieve office, had varied so much in the emphasis it chose to place on those views, and had promulgated them with such sensationalism that it was difficult for any but the party faithful to take them seriously. By 1981 the PCF fulfilled the function of exerting pressure on the PS to ensure that it defended the interests of workers and threatened sectors in the national economy, and it still maintained the ability to provide a cogent analysis and critique of the processes at work in international capitalism. But it had not succeeded in elaborating a strategy for transcending capitalism and, rather than providing a synthesis between socialism, the nation and internationalism, the attempt to combine the appeal to the nation and the working class had degenerated into chauvinism; and the main element in the party's socialist internationalism once again appeared to be pro-Sovietism.

Mitterrand, the Socialists and 'Europe': the Success of an Ambiguous Compromise

When Mitterrand and the Socialists finally achieved power in 1981, the contradictions in their European policy had not been fully resolved. They had, however, been contained and the PS *appeared* to combine a socialist and a national appeal. Mitterrand's 'brokerage' between the factions had been as important on this as on any other question. How had he achieved his goal?

The PS programme of March 1972 had incorporated all the potential contradictions on 'Europe' which existed within the party.[35] When it sought to explain why France could no longer isolate herself from her neighbours in outdated nationalism and claimed that European construction, oriented towards socialism, was desirable, its argument was not markedly different from that of numerous SFIO documents since the war. However this was prefaced by a statement of principle and an assertion which had not been characteristic of such pronouncements. For it was declared that

> The reinforcement ... of ... European construction ... will be followed, but only on condition that it cannot ... constitute an obstacle to the march towards socialism.[36]

And that:

> The situation of interdependence which flows in particular from

our insertion in the Common Market, still leaves us a sufficient margin of initiative to set off the process of an advance towards socialism.[37]

The purpose of the rest of the chapter was to provide solid support for the affirmation that there need be no contradiction between the pursuit of West European integration on the one hand and the rupture of capitalism on the other.

The judgement on the social and economic effects of integration was far more negative than ever before in a Socialist Party document, but it still contrasted sharply with that of the PCF, for the PS claimed that the problems stemmed from the free trade policy which had been pursued for the previous twenty years rather than from the EEC itself. Moreover, it was argued that the only means of eliminating American control of the European economies was by: 'The coherent organisation of Europe, initially by the reinforcement of common policies and leading to increasing transfers of sovereignty on the part of member states...'[38]

If this implied a firm commitment to West European integration, the programme sought to dispel the impression that its support would be unconditional for it argued that, at present, the EEC institutions served the interests of capital, but that: 'The socialists would not stand for a European policy whose principal objective was to help capitalism out of a difficult situation.'[39] The programme therefore sought to define a range of policies which would protect an advance towards socialism in France and strengthen 'Europe' without reinforcing the power of European capitalism.

It is questionable whether all of the proposals for consolidating 'Europe' were in fact compatible with the first objective of maintaining the margin of manoeuvre for the construction of socialism in France.[40] But its attitude to the institutional development of the EEC made its position still more ambiguous, for whereas both the PCF and the British Labour Party were convinced that the nation-state was the most favourable terrain for a socialist advance – and were therefore very cautious about any proposals which might strengthen European institutions – the PS was much less certain. In this respect too its programme was an amalgam of the viewpoints of the traditionalists who favoured a strengthening of the Community institutions and of the CERES left, which inclined towards the perspective of the PCF and the Labour Party. On the one hand it was argued that the European construction sought by the PS implied a power of collective decision-making which exceeded that of intergovernmental co-operation between sovereign states. On the other hand it was stated that a left government would announce its readiness to delegate the necessary powers and means to a common political authority only when agreement was reached that the measures suggested by the left government 'would be seriously considered by all'. This condition was vague (what was meant by serious consideration?), and was further diluted with the claim that the powers of control of the European Parliament should immediately be reinforced by securing the right to vote the budget and that, in the longer term, the Parliament should itself be involved in discussions concerning the further extension of its powers. In addition it was argued that the enlargement of the EEC should bring about the reinforcement of its functions and powers of decision-making and the progressive realisation of a common foreign policy.[41] Finally, and most ambiguously of all, it was stated:

> As soon as the propositions of a government of the left enumerated in the preceding paragraphs receive, in their essentials, the agreement of the other member countries, the European Assembly must be elected by universal suffrage and dispose of powers comparable to those of a sovereign parliament.[42]

The intention of the left of the party in this was to tie French acceptance of institutional supranationalism to acceptance by the other member states of a progressive ingredient of socialism in the community structures, but the statement was so unspecific that it could also be interpreted as a more cautious version of the traditional SFIO support for a federal Western Europe. Moreover, while earlier socialist proposals for the progressive dissolution of both blocs and the particular means to this end were reiterated, it was also maintained that the objective of a French left government should be 'to participate, with the European partners of France, in the construction of a system of collective security'.[43] This held open the possibility of a reconstituted European Defence Community – an idea which was anathema to the PCF, and much of the left.

In general, despite its sophistication, *Changer la vie* revealed the underlying tensions within the new PS. Certainly the influence of genuine left-socialist analysis (rather than the Marxist-style rationalisations of the Mollet era) was marked so that it was possible to read the text as a commitment to the overthrow of capitalism to which all else was subordinate. On this reading (the CERES view) the relationship between a left government and the EEC would be based upon bargaining, in which the need of the other states to maintain full French participation would be traded off against their acquiescence in, and even support for, the progressive attainment of socialism in France. But it was equally possible to interpret the programme as an updated version of the traditional viewpoint: a version in which suspicion of the USA had deepened, and recognition of the potential contradiction between socialism and the EEC had grown, but which, nevertheless maintained the commitment to the speedy construction of an integrated Western Europe.

Moreover, Mitterrand who had already rejected the earlier draft by CERES because it was too critical of the EEC and the Atlantic Alliance, shifted the balance towards the traditionalist reading in his short introduction. For his emphasis upon involvement in the EEC – described as the 'primordial choice' of the Socialists – immediately implied a more pro-European nuance than the programme as a whole, as did his assertion that socialism in France would fail and superpower domination would continue unless Western Europe overcame the centrifugal forces of nationalism.[44] Once again he maintained that there must be no contradiction between the pursuit of European construction on the one hand and socialism on the other, but some of his statements appeared still less conditional in this respect than the programme.

Mitterrand was clearly striving to combine the traditional Europeanism of the SFIO with the left-socialist view that the EEC could impede the march to socialism, and simultaneously to convince the electorate that national independence was possible only with European independence. The message was highly plausible in rhetorical terms but in practice he helped the social-democratic wing of the party (though not the unconditional supranationalists).

Yet if Mitterrand tended to strengthen the social-democratic wing of the party on the European question, he also threw in his weight with the left in urging the vital necessity of early union with the Communists. Nor was he seriously deterred from this aim by the continued difference between the two parties manifested in the referendum over British entry. Mitterrand was thus prepared to negotiate a common programme in full knowledge that the Communists' attitude to West European integration was more hostile even than that of CERES whose proposals he had so recently rejected.

We have already seen that the PCF made some concessions to the PS in the Common Programme. Nevertheless, its tone was far more hostile to the EEC than that of the Socialist programme. The Communists had refused the Socialist leader's wish to proclaim that West European integration was a principle of foreign policy, essential for the fulfilment of socialism in France and the independence of Europe, or that a directly elected European Parliament was an eventual goal. The intermediate aims of the Socialists, notably the development of monetary co-operation and general planning at community level, were greatly diluted in the Common Programme, which also reflected PCF determination to enhance French power at state level.[45] Finally, whereas Mitterrand had always maintained that European independence and the ending of blocs depended upon West European construction, the Common Programme adopted a cautious and defensive attitude to the EEC while seeking to hasten the dissolution of blocs and the independence of France.

Given Mitterrand's belief that the grand themes were more important than precise programmes, it is unlikely that he was satisfied with the tone of the EEC chapter in the Common Programme. But nor did it imply any change in his own views. Rather it meant in practice that when the European issue was dormant he scarcely mentioned it,[46] but that when it revived in importance he continued to express his own long-term convictions. For example, in February 1973 he wrote an article in *La Revue socialiste* in which he stressed that the proposed 'Nixon round' was a symptom of the crisis in the economic relations between the USA and Europe, in which the US wished to complete its domination of Europe by effectively 'killing the EEC'. And he prophesied that if the American proposals were implemented, within ten years Europe would be forced to cease further production of civil aviation, would depend on the USA for agricultural and energy supplies, and would have lost the majority of its overseas markets. He argued that the crisis was capitalist and that the solution was socialist, but he stressed the crucial importance of the European dimension rather than specifically socialist measures. His suggestion that there should be thorough-going economic and monetary union, a common policy against inflation, and a European political authority was far removed from the strategy of the Common Programme.[47] Indeed throughout much of 1973 Mitterrand appeared more concerned to strengthen 'Europe' against the USA than to establish socialism in France.[48]

This is not to accuse Mitterrand of insincerity. In his own mind, independence from the USA, the strengthening of the European Community, and the establishment of socialism in France were probably all interconnected. However, the nature of these linkages was somewhat nebulous, and more plausible in terms of rhetoric than analysis. Thus when he called for 'national independence' he (like de Gaulle) sought greater equality within the Atlantic Alliance rather than a total break from the system of international capitalism and the Western bloc; when he called for the establishment of socialism, he tended to regard this as synonymous with the election of a socialist government to office; and when he proclaimed the need for strengthening the European Community, he aspired to diplomatic unity and agreement on common policies rather than a wholly distinct social, economic and political system. The problem was that, when confronted with concrete issues, political and economic interests, rather than vague goals, tended to determine policy. This was apparent not only in Mitterrand's reaction to American pressure, but in his initiative later in the year to seek the adoption of a common policy stance by the Community socialist parties.

This idea made perfect sense from Mitterrand's perspective for it appeared that socialist unity would hasten the advance towards adoption of common policies by the Community and could provide valuable support for the ideas of the PS. However, when one of those parties – the Labour Party – took a fundamentally different line, Mitterrand's 'Europeanism' and a French national perspective appeared to transcend socialist solidarity. For in August 1973 the Labour Party, which was seeking support for its aim of renegotiating British terms of entry, held a bilateral meeting in London with a delegation of the PS and received neither sympathy nor understanding from Mitterrand who brushed aside the British party's complaints against the Community in a way which hardly differed from that of the French government the next year. (For a full discussion of this episode, see chapter 7).

In any case, Mitterrand's wish to strengthen the connections between the socialist parties of the Community precipitated a crisis within the party which was of major importance in the evolution of the PS and revealed the terms of Mitterrand's brokerage between the factions. His idea of sending PS emissaries to all EEC member states was, in itself, potentially contentious. First, the implicit recognition of the EEC as an entity of central importance in socialist strategy contrasted with the cautious attitude of the Common Programme. Secondly, the fact that CERES regarded the two largest parties – the SPD and Labour Party – as centrist reinforced left-socialist hostility to any elevation of the EEC's importance as the framework for socialist solidarity. But Mitterrand then exacerbated the potential conflict by nominating known 'pro-Europeans' as the PS emissaries. The result, on 14 November 1973, was that only ten members of the bureau executive supported the leader's proposal, while eight others abstained, and Mitterrand offered his resignation, arguing that it was vital for the PS to define its attitude to European construction unambiguously. The threat was effective and the *comité directeur* subsequently expressed full confidence in his leadership.[49]

This episode was of great significance in two respects. First, because its immediate result was the holding of an extraordinary congress on Europe at Bagnolet in December 1973 which gave Mitterrand what he wanted; and secondly, because the European question was the focal point of a more classical confrontation between the Socialist right and left and the outcome therefore inevitably affected the whole orientation of the party.

Although obscured by the fact that Mollet's supporters from the SFIO put forward their own unconditional European resolution, the

97

major conflict at the Bagnolet conference was between the European line represented by Mitterrand and that propounded by CERES.[50] The motion of Mitterrand's supporters (*Pour une Europe en marche vers le socialisme*) reflected the familiar amalgam of leftist analysis and broadly traditionalist conclusions. Its starting point was again to emphasise the dominance of the superpowers and the particular role of US multinationals which, it claimed, was so extensive that no European state could exercise a genuinely autonomous policy. The federalist solution was rejected on Marxist-style lines close to that of CERES.[51] But, having thus preempted some of the potential criticisms of the left, the motion argued that each state individually was dominated by the USA and that, despite its Cold War origins and current imperfections, the EEC was a zone of economic growth and increased living standards, feared by the USA as a competitor. Nor could the multinationals be repelled without 'the organisation of a political power of the same dimensions ... capable of confronting [them] on [their] terrain'. Europe was therefore believed to be necessary both to escape the domination of the great powers and to combat American imperialism, as manifested in the multinationals.

The task of Socialists was to strive for socialism within the state and for a Europe which would permit the fulfilment of their eventual goals. It was thus argued that the construction of socialism could begin in France (and it was claimed that the EEC was no barrier to nationalisations), but it was also stressed that:

> we must remain conscious of the fact that decisive steps on the road to socialism cannot be accomplished by limiting our action to the national framework alone.

And that:

> the dismemberment of the Common Market, by impoverishing and isolating our country, would render the march to socialism more difficult, or impossible.

The conclusions of the motion were fully 'European': it thus called for more planning, common European action against inflation, a common monetary system free from domination by the dollar, and a search for Europeans' scientific and technological independence. All this was seen to depend upon thoroughgoing political agreement emanating from a democratised European central authority.

If this positive approach to European construction was difficult to reconcile with the tone of the Common Programme, the balance was also tipped further in favour of an SFIO reading of the party's own programme. The conditional element in support of European construction was virtually eliminated and the motion now called, without prior conditions, for the European Parliament to be elected by universal suffrage and stipulated that it should possess powers of control and initiation.

CERES's analysis was well to the left of this. First, it attached considerable importance to distinguishing between American imperialism and Soviet dominance of a 'limited geographical sphere', not because of sympathy with the East European model of socialism, but because of an insistence that it was American imperialism based on the export of capital, which constituted the principal barrier to the march towards socialism in France and Western Europe as a whole. In contrast, the Soviet Union, seen to be concerned principally with policing its own sphere and with the Chinese problem, was said to constitute only a 'semi-threat'. Whereas Mitterrand's supporters maintained that European construction was vital if the dominance of both superpowers was to be eliminated (and, in reality, remained far more anti-Soviet than anti-American), CERES maintained that the expulsion of American imperialism from Western Europe was the supreme priority.[53] Secondly, the rejection of SFIO traditionalism was far more complete, and it was asserted that, amongst socialist circles: 'The extent of European sentiment has generally varied as a direct function of the tendency to class collaboration.'[54]

Thirdly, in contrast to the majority motion which stressed the compatibility of the EEC treaty with socialist policies, CERES argued that the Treaty of Rome viewed competition as the unique motor of the economy and that this perspective was irreconcilable with socialist aspirations. It therefore argued that the left would want to put the fundamental law of the EEC more closely in accordance with its objectives once it had attained power, and that the PS should immediately propose a study by the European left of the ways in which the treaty should be revised so as to create a real federal state on the basis of democratic planning.[55] Finally, although CERES agreed that the struggle against capitalism must contain an international dimension in which the quest for solidarity with other socialist parties was of preeminent importance, it also stressed the need for a wider *entente* with all anti-capitalist forces and, in the first instance, with the Italian and French communists.[56]

Yet CERES shared many of the views of the main body of the PS. It agreed that the major external constraints on the socialisation of France stemmed from the free exchange system of international capitalism rather than from the EEC itself and it therefore fully supported the notion that Western Europe should confront the USA in tariff and monetary policies and assert its independence.[57] It accepted the argument that the Treaty of Rome was flexible in the short term and imposed no constraint upon the policies outlined in the Common Programme.[58] Moreover, CERES also stressed the belief that a French left government could gain the co-operation of the rest of the EEC and that such co-operation could strengthen it greatly in the task of domestic socialisation.[59]

Moreover, CERES's line on Europe became less intransigent during the course of the party crisis and its whole strategy at Bagnolet indicated a climb-down.[60] The final resolution, which incorporated enough elements of CERES's view to secure its support was thus in some respects, even more 'European' than the original majority motion, and was certainly less conditional in its attitude than the party programme of 1972.[61] However, it also satisfied the left by defeating the overt supranationalism of the ex-SFIO right, and it enabled the pragmatists to appeal to the nation as the party whose 'Europeanism' would further the goal of national independence.

The repercussions of this general victory for Mitterrand surpassed the European issue on which it was focused. Since the Grenoble conference in June of the same year, Mitterrand had had a coherent majority and was no longer dependent upon the support of CERES whose general leftism had brought it into conflict with the main part of the leadership group on a number of questions.[62] The conflict over Europe was, therefore, also a trial of strength between the different tendencies in the party, and the general significance of the episode was that the relative defeat of CERES meant that the centre of gravity shifted towards the right.

Yet, far from being resolved, the contradictions within the party were actually exacerbated throughout 1974 as it rapidly grew in strength and prominence. On the one hand the proportion of CERES members increased while, on the other, Mitterrand's position as close contender in the presidential elections reinforced his general dominance. And during the campaign he and his main associates put forward views, on Europe in particular and foreign policy in general, which were closer in spirit to the SFIO than to the Common Programme.[63] Moreover, the influx of approximately 3,000 new recruits from the largest non-communist union confederation, the *Confédération française démocratique du travail* (CFDT), and the PSU following the *assises nationales, pour le socialisme* in the autumn of 1974 meant that the party's ideology became more ambiguous than ever. The new members were theoretically united by a commitment to *autogestion*, but the term covered a variety of divergent positions. Michel Rocard, the ex-PSU leader and most prominent figure amongst the new recruits to the PS, symbolised this ideological *mélange*.

Even when Rocard had sounded left-revolutionary in much of his analysis and rhetoric when leader of the PSU, he had diverged fundamentally from the PCF and CERES and stressed that democratic socialism could be established only in a region large enough to introduce the most modern industries and techniques.[64] Once he had joined the PS he was increasingly to emphasise the importance of economic modernisation, as had the SFIO in the mid 1950s.

In this situation CERES tried to reinforce the leftist pressures only to find itself totally isolated, as was revealed at the Pau congress (31 January–2 February 1975) when the other major factions united against it and a theoretically homogeneous party directorate, in which Rocard was included, was established. And although all the previous commitments of the party were maintained in theory during the subsequent two years, its political practice often appeared closely aligned to that of social-democratic reformism.

The effect of this was evident on EEC policy. For example, while the party sought to balance the dominance of north European social democracy within the EEC by taking the initiative to co-ordinate southern European socialists, Mitterrand also brought the party into a far closer relationship with the SPD and, in March 1976, he and Willy Brandt established three joint working parties on 'Europe'.[65] Similarly, when the question of direct elections to the European Parliament became actual, Mitterrand cut short any renewed debate within the party with the traditionalist arguments.[66] It would be an exaggeration to suggest that, during this period, the PS expressed unconditional Europeanism,[67] but its arguments in favour of 'Europe' increasingly often resembled those of the former SFIO.

This was, for example, evident in 1977 when the party's theoretical journal, *La Nouvelle Revue socialiste* held a debate on the subject in which every contributor combined pragmatic reformism with 'Europeanism'.[68] True, there was much ritualistic incantation of the sanctity of the Common Programme as the basis of socialist positions on the EEC, but the emphasis was quite different. Stress was placed upon the limited impact that could be made upon the problems of inflation and unemployment within a single state and the disasters that would follow any attempt to reorientate the external relations of France; the attitudes of CERES were identified by one contributor with 'neo-Gaullism' and South American military dictatorship; and it was maintained that the multinationals could be controlled only by a European political authority. In general, 'Europeanism' was affirmed as the sole way forward in a situation in which only limited progress was possible and it was often implicit, and sometimes explicit, that the PS would maintain this European orientation whatever the reaction of the PCF.[69] This general tendency was further reinforced at the party congress at Nantes (17–19 June 1977) when the majority once again closed ranks on CERES, and Rocard openly expressed positions which were clearly incompatible with the spirit of the Common Programme.[70]

In this situation, Mitterrand's role was again essential in maintaining apparent party unity and stemming any sharp move to the right. Thus Chevènement, the most prominent leader of CERES, reiterated the assurance he had already given at Pau two years earlier that, in all the major issues, CERES would always support the present leader,[71] while Mitterrand himself wooed the left with the assertion that the PS was situated ideologically between the PCF and the Italian Communist Party.[72] Nevertheless, the degree of 'leftism' implicit in this assertion was coupled with a fervent and emotional statement of 'Europeanism', clearly aimed against the viewpoints of CERES and the PCF which, he claimed, would begin 'by the defence of socialism and ... end with nationalism'.[73]

Once again Mitterrand was thus playing a pivotal role by simultaneously reassuring CERES that the PS was intent upon the rupture of capitalism and the union of the left and expressing a European policy which was pragmatic rather than leftist.[74] However, during the year between the electoral set-back in March 1978 and the next party congress at Metz (6–8 April 1979) Mitterrand was subject to a mounting challenge from a new *de facto* alliance between traditional social-democratic reformism, centred on Pierre Mauroy, and the ideological *mèlange* of *autogestion* and modernism, represented by Rocard. The underlying basis of the threat was the assumption that association with the PCF had been electorally harmful and that union of the left need not be a permanent strategy. This viewpoint represented an incipient attack on the founding doctrines of the PS and the general strategy pursued by Mitterrand, and it coupled modernist conceptions of the economy with traditional 'Europeanism'. On the other side, CERES's stance on 'Europe' had hardened still further (perhaps in order to keep in step with the PCF) so that it now opposed direct elections and the establishment of a European monetary system, and was very cautious about 'enlargement to the South'.[75] Moreover in July 1978, it had called for the total rejection by the PS of a common platform of EEC socialist parties,[76] which had stemmed from Mitterrand's own initiatives with Brandt two years earlier, and it now claimed that 'the balance-sheet of neo-liberal Europe' was totally negative from the point of view of the masses.[77]

In these circumstances Mitterrand was exposed to the most difficult challenge of all. Victory or compromise with Rocard–Mauroy would almost certainly prevent any early agreement with the PCF and could set the PS towards the centrist orientation which had destroyed the SFIO. However, although Mitterrand could seek a new alliance with CERES to defeat his challengers, it was inconceivable that he would adopt CERES' position on the European question.

His strategy in this situation was to make clear overtures to the left and implicitly to attack every major feature in his challengers' case.[78] This inevitably led him to moderate his enthusiasm for the European cause during the course of the winter of 1978–79.[79]. Nevertheless, he continued to make it clear that West European construction was absolutely necessary in order to secure European independence *vis-à-vis* American imperialism and Soviet expansionism. And he maintained that both nationalist dreams (by implication CERES and the PCF) and confused supranationalism (the PS right) must be rejected. Moreover, at the Metz congress he stated that, while a synthesis with Rocard or Mauroy was impossible, he could not reach agreement with CERES unless their line on Europe was softened.[80]

Once again, as in December 1973, CERES's need of Mitterrand was revealed. It was quick to respond to the leader's overtures, with a clear moderation of its European outlook and a statement by one of its leaders that 'on the subject of Europe no serious divergence is worthy of compromising the synthesis'.[81] Mitterrand then bargained skilfully, realising that CERES was extremely anxious for an agreement which would reaffirm the commitment to 'union of the left' and the 'rupture of capitalism'. Once he had declared that no agreement with CERES would be possible until after the European elections on 10 June, CERES effectively handed him control of the European campaign and, as a result of its agreement to keep relatively silent on the issue, re-entered the party secretariat on 22 April.[82] A new political declaration reaffirmed the general strategy adopted eight years earlier at the Epinay congress, but contained a European section which was almost entirely in line with Mitterrand's own conceptions.[83]

The result of all this in national electoral terms was that the PS campaign for the EEC elections was difficult and not wholly successful. An attempt was made simultaneously to further West European construction while condemning its present social, economic and political content; and to oppose the government's domestic and international policy, without appearing to share the 'nationalistic' stance adopted by the Gaullists and Communists. It was doubtless the difficulty in presenting any clear-cut viewpoint in these circumstances, rather than any decline in the PS's electoral base, which accounted for the slight weakening in socialist support in the European elections; and the appeal of 'Europeanism' appeared to be confirmed by the success of Simone Veil and the failure of the Gaullists.

The European orientation of the party following the Metz congress is of more long-term significance than its performance in the June 1979 elections for the Strasbourg Parliament. For once he had effectively muzzled the anti-EEC CERES left, Mitterrand increasingly resumed the attitude of outright 'Europeanism' that he had expressed before he had faced the challenge from the Mauroy–Rocard right. He did not renege on any commitments he had made and continued, for example, to maintain that the powers of the European Parliament must not be extended. But he resumed a more open affirmation of his long-term view that West European construction and the harmonisation of policies must be pursued if superpower domination was to be ended.[84] Of still greater significance, he once again pursued, as a priority matter, the task of deepening the ties between the socialist parties of the EEC, constantly expressing his belief that the issues which united them far outweighed those that divided them.[85] Such assertions stemmed from Mitterrand's argument that the EEC could be changed only if reforming movements of the left took power, but his overtures to social democracy in other EEC countries provide an eloquent testimony to CERES's submission to the leader's 'European' policy by the summer of 1979. When Rocard again challenged him by declaring himself a presidential candidate in 1980, it was thus quite clear that CERES would support Mitterrand however much they differed on 'Europe' in order to preserve the possibility of a 'union of the left'.

It was in these circumstances that Mitterrand and the Socialists were elected to government with a 'European' commitment which was contradictory in its underlying theory, but able to satisfy both the left and the centre of the political spectrum. The party was thus critical of the operation of almost every EEC institution and policy, and urged thoroughgoing reform to create a 'Europe of the workers'. Yet it still maintained that the construction of 'Europe' was essential for the workers and peoples of France and Europe. Similarly it was cautious about supranationalism and yet sought further integration through the creation of more common policies.[86] It bitterly condemned Gaullist and Communist nationalism, but when faced with concrete issues, its rhetoric about 'Europe' now prefaced a vigorous defence of national interests and national independence, particularly against British demands.[87] The same contradictions were apparent in the wider international context. Thus the party which had for the past decade condemned the subordination of the French state to the USA now appeared to accept the viewpoint of an extreme right-wing regime in Washington on the 'Soviet threat' and the appropriate Western defence response.[88] At the same time, the new government was to oppose American views on Latin-American revolutionary movements and to contest the prevailing orthodoxy on monetary policy.

The fact is that the PS remains a contradictory phenomenon in terms of its personnel, its underlying ideology and its electoral support.[89] In 1981, as in 1972, its programme was a compromise between the different tendencies within the party.[90] The professed aim was to transform French society through democratic reform, nationalisation, planning, greater social and economic equality, and reflation through state spending. The European dimension of this policy was supposed to harmonise with the domestic priorities. In other words the general objective was to use the EEC, wherever possible, to facilitate the implementation of the domestic programme. For example, it hoped to help small farmers through a reform of the common agricultural policy (CAP), and to ameliorate unemployment through social and economic measures at Community level. But if this proved impossible – and the prevailing climate in London and Bonn was hardly propitious for such reforms – or if EEC policies appeared to threaten domestic concerns, the idea was to ensure that French interests prevailed. Meanwhile it could continue to make the EEC the lynch-pin of its foreign policy and international consciousness and would try to induce its partners to follow its lead on European and world issues.

This was a programme which could secure support both inside and outside the party and in the months following the electoral victory the government appeared to try to implement it. It thus announced a major programme of nationalisation and decentralisation at home and urged its partners to consider the adoption of Community-wide measures to bring about increased employment by a variety of means including industrial regeneration, early retirement and selective import controls.[91] When this inevitably received a cool response from the orthodox deflationary governments in London and Bonn the French Government seemed committed to go ahead with unilateral measures, risking opposition from its EEC partners, the capitalist world as a whole, and the European Commission.[92] However, it was not clear how determined the government would really prove in the attempt to implement an economic policy which ran counter to the strategy of all the other major capitalist powers. And there was an additional factor of ambiguity in the stance of the Socialist-led administration: while it announced bold plans for social and economic reform it studiously avoided discussion of two immediate controversies within the EEC – the redistribution of the Community budget so as to reduce the outlay on agriculture to the benefit of the social and regional funds, and the adjustment in Britain's contribution which the Thatcher Government was demanding.[93] Such omissions immediately provoked the suspicion that, whatever its hopes for the eventual transformation of the Community, on concrete issues, the new government would act in a similar manner to its predecessors.

It may thus be asked: had the PS achieved a synthesis between 'Europeanism', socialism and the nation-state, or had it simply provided a plausible rationale for continuing with policies which had been favoured by the previous administration? In other words, had the PS simply become the progressive wing of the consensus whose conception of the national interest now accorded with that defined by established capitalist forces? In the difficult situation in which they were placed the indications were that Mitterrand and his ministers would tend towards the former position: that is, the government would act as a progressive force within a French national consensus. It would not preserve the *status quo* in its entirety, but nor would it transform France or the European Community, and it would defend established French 'national interests' as stubbornly as any government of the right.

There was little doubt that if, for example, established French interests clashed with British demands, French Socialist negotiators would prove as firm as their right-wing predecessors. For in these circumstances, there would be little internal conflict on the matter. What was much less clear was the course which the French Government would take if its programme for radical reform ran into the opposition of the European Commission or other member states. In other words, while it was comparatively easy for the government of the left (like its predecessors) to risk incurring unpopularity in 'Europe' in defence of interests on which there was a national consensus, it would naturally be far more difficult to do so if it was also facing opposition from capitalist interests (and their political allies) both inside and outside France. The determination of the government in these circumstances would prove the only real test of its professed belief that socialism could be established while France remained a member of the EEC. It would be far more tempting to court internal popularity by overriding the British demands in the name of 'Europeanism' than to confront the right at home and abroad in pursuit of socialism. However, if the views of Mitterrand and his ministers suggested that this was the most probable course for his government, the situation remained fluid.

The Communist Party and left-wing Socialists within the government would tend to strengthen its determination to fight against capitalist priorities both within France and the European community as would any solidarity shown by other left-wing parties within the EEC. In the course of his electoral strategy, Mitterrand had steered the PS away from Marxism and towards the national consensus. But the party's 'Europeanism' was no longer uncritical and, in appropriate domestic and international circumstances, it might still risk confrontation with the forces of capitalism within France and the European Community.

Notes

1 For full accounts see N. Nugent and D. Lowe, *The Left in France* (Macmillan, 1982), and R. W. Johnson, *The Long March of the French Left* (Macmillan, 1981). The results of the 1981 elections were:

Presidentials: first ballot: Giscard 28.3%, Mitterrand 25.8%, Chirac 18.0%, Marchais 15.3%; second ballot: Giscard 48.2%, Mitterrand 51.8%.

Legislatives: PS/MRG 37.5% (285 seats), PCF 16.2% (44 seats), RPR 20.8% (88 seats), UDF 19.2% (62 seats).

2 In terms of membership the PCF was still strong (450,000 in March 1973 against 150,000 for the PS in 1976) and in March 1973 it still obtained more votes than the PS (21.4% against 20.8% for the PS/MRG). Because the two-ballot system was a disadvantage for the PCF this resulted in only 73 seats as against 101 for the Socialists and the relative decline was confirmed in the by-elections of September 1974 when the PCF share of the vote declined in five out of the six contests while that of the PS increased.

3 On the first ballot the left as a whole obtained 45.26% of the vote (20.56 PCF, 22.59% PS, 2.11 MRG) as against 46.44% for the governmental forces. After the second ballot the left returned 201 deputies (86 PCF, 114 PS and MRG) against 290 on the governmental side. The PCF had published its own suggestions for the *actualisation* of the Programme, without prior consultation with the PS, in March 1977. The most controversial element was its proposal to extend the scope of the nationalisation policy by taking over the subsidiaries of foreign companies, whose future had been left vague in the original version. In May 1977 the PCF also suddenly reversed its defence policy by declaring its support for the French nuclear deterrent which should be fully independent and face in all directions. The PS had also effectively accepted the continuation of French nuclear weapons (as it had modified its interpretation of other aspects of the Common Programme), but without any dramatic shift in its stance.

4 Mitterrand's task was exacerbated by the fact that between 1978–80 he also faced a challenge from within the PS, led by Michel Rocard, who had joined the PS in 1974 after leading the PSU, and combined a commitment to the modernisation of the economy with professed support for the aim of *autogestion*. In late 1978 and early 1979 he had formed a *de facto* alliance with Pierre Mauroy, a more traditionalist SFIO figure who managed the powerful 'Nord' federation of the party. But Mitterrand made his peace with Mauroy so that when, in 1980, Rocard announced his willingness to act as presidential candidate for the PS, Mauroy's support for Mitterrand was assured.

5 Under both Pompidou and Giscard d'Estaing there were signs of increased Atlanticism and Europeanism in both economic and military spheres, although conflicts with the USA, particularly over commercial relations and the Middle East continued (1973–74, 1978–79), and France remained vehement against British demands within the EEC (1970–72, 1974–75, 1979–80). However, adherence to the goal of national independence was proclaimed on all occasions for internal consumption. For recent discussions, see J. Frears, *France in the Giscard Presidency* (Allen and Unwin, 1981), chs. 5 and 6; D. Pickles, *Problems of Contemporary France* (Methuen, 1982), chs. 6 and 7.

6 *Changer de Cap: programme pour un gouvernement démocratique d'union populaire* (Editions sociales, 1971).

7 Ibid., p.223.

8 The results of the referendum were inconclusive mainly because it was justifiably regarded as a manoeuvre by the government to secure general support and to divide the left. 40% abstained and a further 7% spoiled their ballot papers. Of the remainder, 68% favoured entry and 32% voted against. The PCF was the only

major party to campaign for a 'no' vote. Even before de Gaulle's resignation, French governmental opinion had become more prepared to accept British entry, at least until the Soames affair of February 1969 (For a full discussion of this event see, A. Campbell, 'Anglo-French Relations a Decade Ago', *International Affairs*, vol.58, no.2, 1982.) Much elite opinion favoured British entry as a means of widening the French export market for both manufacturers and agriculture, helping to finance the Community, and perhaps offsetting German dominance. For a discussion of French attitudes, see U. Kitzinger, *Diplomacy and Persuasion: How Britain Joined the Common Market*, Thames & Hudson, 1973), Part I.

 9 *Programme commun de gouvernement* (Editions sociales, 1972), p.177. The other part of the dual objective was 'to preserve in the heart of the Common Market [the French government's] freedom of action for the realisation of its political, economic and social programme'.

10 Ibid., pp.177–81

11 Report to the Central Committee, 29 June 1972, reproduced in E. Fajon, *L'Union est un Combat* (Editions sociales), 1975, p.89.

12 Marchais told the Central Committee: 'The definition of the foreign policy of a democratic government ... posed particularly difficult problems. To summarise, it concerned in essence French membership of both the Atlantic Alliance and the European Economic Community. Both impose a constraint on the independence of France. Both constitute class alliances, having as their nature and function, the chaining of our country to the imperialist system, under the direction of the United States.

   It is for this fundamental reason that the Parti socialiste is profoundly attached BOTH to the Atlantic Alliance AND to the integration of little Western Europe.' (Fajon, *L'Union est un Combat*, p.95).

13 See, for example, P. Boccara, 'La Crise monétaire et l'approfondisement de la crise du C.M.E.', *C du C*, April 1973; Boccara, 'La crise des relations économiques internationales et les moyens d'en sortir', *C du C*, Oct. 1973; and the articles by G. Julis and G. Bordu in *C du C*, Feb. 1974.

14 This followed the agreement of a common statement by the union of the left after a deterioration in relations caused partly by PCF objections to a letter sent by Mitterrand to the Prime Minister in July concerning US/EEC relations.

15 Julis, *C du C* Feb. 1974. An important stage was the meeting of the communist parties of capitalist Europe, 26–28 Jan. 1974, in which the PCF appears to have accepted the view of the PCI on the EEC to a greater extent than normal. For the text of the resolution, see *C du C*, March 1974.

16 G. Bordu, 'Relance européenne – de nouveaux abandons au détriment de la France', *C du C*, Jan. 1975.

17 Statement by the *bureau politique*, 'Une politique d'abandon national', 23 Dec. 1975, in *C du C*, April 1976.

18 PCF statement 'L'Elargissement du marché commun: de graves conséquences pour notre agriculture', 26 July 1977, in *C du C*, Sept. 1977.

19 P. Promonteil, 'Après le Congres de Pau où en est le Parti socialiste?', *C du C*, April 1975.

20 P. Roubaud, p.64.

21 L. Odru, 'La politique extérieure sous Giscard d'Estaing', *C du C*, June 1975.

22 *C du C*, Feb. 1976, p.30. The shift in policy was not fully uniform. Between late 1974 and the 22nd congress sophisticated analyses continued to coexist with the more emotive viewpoints quoted above. After early 1976 the tone became more generally propagandist, although there were further discernible shifts following the breakdown in relations in October 1977, the loss of the elections and the start of the campaign for the Strasbourg assembly.

23 Quoted by A. Rouy and C. Montaguy, 'Vers une Europe allemande sous tutelle américaine', *C du C*, Nov. 1978, p.76.

24 Editorial, *C du C*, November 1978.
25 L. Baillot, 'Intégration européenne et atlantique ou véritable défense nationale', *C du C*, Nov. 1978, pp.40–1. From the last quarter of 1978 the party press was preoccupied with West European integration and probably devoted more articles to it even than at the time of the EDC. In 1979 it also published two books on the subject: D. Débatisse *et al.*, *L'Europe – La France en jeu* (Editions sociales); R. Martelli, *La Nation* (Editions sociales).
26 'Pour une France indépendante – une Europe démocratique', Central Committee document of 12–13 December 1978, *C du C*, Jan. 1979.
27 See, for example, 'Vingt propositions pour l'Europe' in ibid.
28 On a poll of 57.66% of the population, Mitterrand's list secured 4,764,341 votes (23.53%), Simone Veil's list obtained 5,588,026 (27.60%), Marchais's 4,154,512 (20.52%) and Chirac's 3,302,131 (16.31%).
29 The most notorious of a series of incidents was the demolition of an immigrant hostel by the Communist Mayor of Vitry in January 1981.
30 There were four PCF ministers in the government, the most important being Charles Fiterman, as Minister of Transport.
31 Statement of 24 June 1981, reproduced in the Appendix in Nugent and Lowe, *The Left in France*.
32 In *Le Défi Démocratique* (Grasset, 1973), often regarded as a Eurocommunist work, Marchais states the following principle: *'Everything which tends to tone down or deny the achievements of socialism actually contributes to the maintenance of the domination of the power of the monopolies over our people.* On the other hand, to tell the truth about the socialist countries is to strike a hard blow against this domination' (p.152). He then proceeded to 'tell the truth' by giving a totally uncritical account of the triumphs of the Soviet Union (pp. 153–180)!
33 In the Eurocommunist charter of 3 March 1977 (*C du C*, April 1977) an attempt was made to mask the differences of attitude to the EEC, but the communiqués of the PCI and PCF of 3 May 1977 (*C du C*, June 1977), 4–5 Oct. 1978 (*C du C*, Nov. 1978), and 15 Dec. 1978 (*C du C*, Jan. 1979), made these clear. Marchais tried to claim that the differences, which were still more acute between the Spanish and French parties on the question of enlargement, were peripheral and evidence of the absolute independence of each party. See, for example, the interview in *Le Monde*, 31 May 1979.
34 Yet the failure of the policy is hardly surprising. Two-thirds of PCF members in 1980 had joined the party since 1968 so that traditional and unquestioning cadres were in the minority (Nugent and Lowe, *The Left in France*, p.118). In fact the breakdown in party discipline – and the clear intention of many members to support Mitterrand in 1981 whatever the leadership's line – was no doubt partly responsible for the volte-face. Nor was the traditional electoral support maintained, for in 1976 only 4% of the PCF electorate were employed in agriculture (cf. 13% in 1952) while working-class support had increased in the same years from 38% to 52% of the party's total electoral support. Some of this change can be explained by the reclassification of social class as a result of the drift from the land, but this raises the question (which the leadership did not seem to consider) of whether the traditional national appeal would still be effective in these circumstances
35 *Changer la vie: programme de gouvernement du Parti socialiste* (Flammarion, 1972). For a detailed analysis of the programme, see R. Pinto-Lyra, *La Gauche en France et la construction européene* (LGDJ, 1978). p.189 *et seq.*
36 *Changer la Vie*, p.183.
37 Ibid., p.184.
38 Ibid., p.185.
39 Ibid., pp.185–6.
40 In particular, the co-ordination of the rates of interest between the various EEC

countries, called for in the programme (ibid., p.190) could naturally impose a constraint on a left-wing government.

41 Ibid., pp.192–3.

42 Ibid., p.193.

43 Ibid., pp.203–7.

44 Ibid., pp.14, 27–8. Mitterrand was also less tentative about the advantages of British entry and the need to increase the range of common Community policies than the programme (cf. pp. 28 and 187).

45 *Programme Commun*, p.177.

46 In his book *La Rose au poing* (Flammarion, 1973), written largely to justify signing the Common Programme, he mentioned it only once, and then solely by implication (pp. 212–16).

47 'L'Europe et les Etats-Unis', *RS*, Feb. 1973

48 See the letter from Mitterrand to Pierre Messmer, the Prime Minister, of 9 July, published in *Le Monde* three days later.

49 See the articles by Thierry Pfister in *Le Monde*, 17 and 20 November 1973 and also his article 'L'Europe dans le programme commun' in *30 Jours en Europe*, Feb. 1974.

50 This was not obvious on the surface since CERES did not put forward a resolution of its own, whereas SFIO federalists close to Mollet did so. However, this may have been mainly tactical. The text of the resolutions is given in the party journal *Le Poing et la rose;* no.22 special edn, Nov. 1973, 'Congrès extraordinaire sur les problèmes européens'.

51 'Analysing here what could be the future European state, let us remember that, in a socialist analysis, the State expresses "the relations of class ... the relations of their power" (Jean Jaures). It is clear that, if one applies this analysis to Europe, the introduction of the subsidiaries of multinational companies, their most frequent role as "leader" enterprises, the introduction of the American ideology and the inevitable solidarity of the European bourgeoisies with the American bourgeoisie, mean that an eventual European supranational state founded on the present basis would take responsibility for the interests of the growing fraction of the European bourgeoisie, economically dominated by, and in ideological solidarity with, that of the USA.' ('Pour une Europe en marche vers le socialisme', ibid., p.10).

52 Ibid., pp.10–11. (The next three quotations are from the same resolution.)

53 See, for example, 'La gauche et l'Europe' in CERES's journal *Frontière*, Nov. 1973; and theses 1–3 in CERES's contribution at Bagnolet 'Pour donner une dimension européenne à notre strategie de rupture avec le capitalisme' in *Le Poing et la rose* no.22, Nov. 1973, pp. 15–21.

54 *Frontière*, Nov. 1973, p.46.

55 Thesis 13 of CERES's contribution, p.21.

56 Thesis 11, in ibid.

57 Thesis 5, in ibid.

58 Thesis 13, in ibid.

59 Thesis 10, in ibid; amendments to motion 1, in ibid.

60 Before Mitterrand's resignation threat it had opposed the suggestion that the European Parliament should be directly elected (*Frontière*, Nov. 1973 p.55) but at Bagnolet CERES simply claimed that universal suffrage was 'doubtless necessary' but insufficient for the democratisation of the EEC. Similarly even a forceful critique of supranationalism, which was presented to the congress, ended with the concession that some transfers of powers to the EEC would be acceptable so long as they conformed to the Common Programme (Thesis 6).

61 For the final resolution, see 'Congres extraordinaire de Bagnolet – Oui à l'Europe', *Le Poing et la rose*, supplement to no.23, Dec. 1973, pp. 7–11.

62 The most recent issue was the Middle East, where CERES took a strongly anti-Israeli line while Mitterrand sought a balanced judgement. In his resignation letter Mitterrand had stated that the dispute was not confined to the European question, but that he was exasperated that the party directorate risked being split over every issue. T. Pfister, *Le Monde*, 17 Nov. 1973.

63 See, for example, Mitterrand's statements on 11 April 1974 (quoted in R. Verdier, *PS/PC – Une lutte pour l'entente* (Seghers, 1976), p. 284) which appeared to support continued membership of the Atlantic Alliance. His Commission de la défense nationale also supported the maintenance of French nuclear weapons (*La Nouvelle Revue socialiste* (henceforth *NRS*) no.6, 1974, p.10.)

64 M. Rocard, *Le PSU et l'avenir socialiste de la France* (Seuil, 1969) pp. 52–117; and the collective PSU work B. Jaumont, D. Lenegre, and M. Rocard, *Le Marché commun contre l'Europe* (Seuil, 1973), pp.136–7, 146–58.

65 Two congresses of southern European socialist parties were held in May 1975 and January 1976. But despite CERES's enthusiasm for the idea, the congresses only demonstrated that there was no clear north/south ideological division. Mitterrand had been forging a closer relationship with the SPD since he met Brandt in February 1974.

66 *L'Unité*, Jan. 1976, quoted by J. Huntzinger in W.J. Feld (ed.), *The Foreign Policies of West European Socialist Parties* (Praeger, 1978), p.77.

67 For example, it opposed the Tindemans's report on political union on the grounds that it was Atlanticist, helpful to multinationals, implicitly repressive in its foreign policy orientation, and restrictive in its monetary and budgetary ideas. J-P. Cot and J-P. Sebord, 'L'Inacceptable Rapport Tindemans', *L'Unité*, no. 193, 20–26 Feb. 1976.

68 'Débat – L'Europe', *NRS*, no.23. The contributors were G. Fuchs, J-P. Cot, R. Pontillon, A. Salomon, G. Jaquet and J. Delors.

69 For example, in the article by Jaquet, 'L'Europe Unie: Hier et Aujourd'Hui', *NRS*, no.23. Jaquet, who had been a key member of the *Mouvement socialiste pour les Etats-Unis de l'Europe* with André Philip in the 1940s, was a symbol of the continuity in the European policy of the SFIO and the PS. For he was still President of the *Organisation française de la gauche européenne* and special attaché to Mitterrand on external affairs.

70 He now affirmed the primacy of the market and argued that the main priorities of a left-wing government must be to ensure low-cost production and increased exports. He also implied that nationalisations were only justifiable if they enhanced productivity and appeared to wish to limit the safeguard measures against external forces which had been envisaged under the Common Programme and which he now criticised as leading to *étatiste* socialism (text of Nantes Congress, *NRS*, no.27, 1977, pp.69–76).

71 *NRS*, no.28, p.23. For his speech at Pau, see *L'Unité*, no.144, 7–13 Feb. 1975, p.3.

72 *NRS*, no. 28, pp.63–83. The PS often tried to make a virtue of its ideological heterogeneity. See A. Meyer *et al.*, 'Reflexions sur l'originalité du PS', *NRS*, nos. 12–13, 1975, also sold as a pamphlet.

73 *NRS*, no. 28, p.79.

74 Although Mitterrand insisted on the continued exclusion of CERES from the secretariat on the grounds that it could act as a 'stalking horse' for the PCF when the final breakdown in relations was very near. D. Macshane, *François Mitterrand: A Political Odyssey* (Quartet, 1982), p.202.

75 For details see the collection of articles in CERES, *L'Enlèvement de l'Europe* (Editions entente, 1979).

76 Text presented by CERES to *comité directeur*, 8 July 1978 in *Le CERES par lui-même* (Christian Bourgois, 1979), pp.170–2.

77 D. Motchane, Introduction to *L'Enlèvement*. CERES now went even further than the PCF and seemed to oppose harmonisation of social benefits at the highest level within the EEC on the grounds that this could be a trap by the right to incorporate the left in the integrationist mechanism. 'Le sens caché', *Repères* nos. 55–6 in *L'Enlèvement*.

78 See, for example, his speech to the *comité directeur* of the party on 11 Feb. 1979, *Le Monde*, 13 Feb. 1979.

79 On 6 December 1978 he supported a Bureau executive statement which condemned the new European monetary system for bringing about austerity and servitude to the mark and declared opposition to the ratification of the Bremen Agreement, whereas Rocard had urged support for it. ('Sur le systeme monétaire européen', 6 Dec. 1978, *NRS*, no. 36; for Rocard's attitude, see *Le Monde*, 24 Oct. 1978); at a Brussels meeting of EEC socialists on 12 January 1979 he opposed the demand of the Dutch, Italian and German parties for an increase in the powers of a directly elected Strasbourg Parliament (*Le Monde*, 13 Jan 1979); and in his speech to the *comité directeur* on 11 February, his propositions on the EEC were all acceptable to the left of the party: a return to full employment, control of the multinationals by European institutions, European-wide collective bargaining, EEC recognition of leave for further education, equality of rights for the sexes, and a European charter of basic social rights (*Le Monde*, 13 Feb. 1979).

80 *Le Monde*, 10 April 1979.

81 Statement by Motchane, *L'Unité*, 13–19 April 1979, p.13.

82 *Le Monde*, 24 April 1979.

83 *L'Unité*, 27 April–3 May 1979.

84 Interview in *Le Monde*, 1 June 1979 and speech of 8 June. *Le Monde*, 10–11 June 1979.

85 *Le Monde*, 23 May, 27 May, 1 June, 7 June 1979.

86 In 1980 the party finally issued the long-awaited *Projet socialiste*, drafted mainly by Chevènement of the CERES group. With regard to 'Europe' this built on the PS programme of 1972 and the party's 'Manifeste socialiste pour l'election européenne' (For the full text of this latter document, see *NRS*, no. 36, Dec. 1978), and tried to specify the socioeconomic reforms at Community level which it believed necessary. *(Projet socialiste*, Club socialiste du livre, 1980), pp. 351–4). These were further pared down in Mitterrand's own presidential campaign and given the significant *Gaullien* slogan of 'A strong France within an Independent Europe'. In this he emphasised the importance of defending European employment by common policies and mentioned the possibility of import controls against Japanese and American products. The CAP was also to be reformed to provide greater equity for small farmers. (Mitterrand's 110 propositions are reproduced as an appendix in Macshane, *François Mitterrand*).

87 In Mitterrand's television confrontation with Giscard d'Estaing he accused him of being too yielding to the British over the budget (*Le Monde*, 7 May 1981).

88 In the same confrontation, Mitterrand condemned Giscard for meeting Brezhnev after the Soviet invasion of Afghanistan; and at the time of the election the PS called for parity with the USSR before disarmament by the West. Nugent and Lowe, *The Left in France*, p.83.

89 Before the 1981 elections the PS had become the most representative party in terms of electoral support, regionally, socially and as between the sexes. *(Le Nouvel Observateur*, 10 November 1980). In those elections it received both 44% of the working-class vote (20% more than the PCF) and 38% of the votes of the top social category (Nugent and Lowe, p.92). One third of its members had working-class origins, but only 20% were now in working-class jobs, whereas in 1951 44% of SFIO members had been (Nugent and Lowe, p.87). Only two socialist deputies were manual workers and an overwhelming proportion were teachers.

90 Moreover, while the *Projet socialiste* had been drafted by the left, the key ministers in charge of implementation were on the social-democratic or pro-EEC right-wing of the party. This included Pierre Mauroy, the Prime Minister, Jacques Delors, the Economics Minister, Michel Rocard, the Minister for Planning,

Claude Cheysson the Minister for External Relations (and his Minister for European Affairs, André Chandernagor) and Michel Jobert, the Foreign Trade Minister.

91 Memorandum handed by Chandernagor to EEC ministers, *Le Monde*, 9 October 1981.

92 The French strategy was proclaimed as 'reconquering the French market' (*Guardian*, 27 Jan. 1982). However, following a sharp reaction from other EEC countries, the French government almost immediately gave an assurance that it did not intend to act against imports from elsewhere within the Community. (*Financial Times*, 2 Feb. 1982). It was still not clear whether or not the government would use non-tariff controls against its partners.

93 Immediately after his election Mitterrand asked for a delay of three months on such issues (*Le Monde*, 26 May 1981). Subsequently the French government stalled on negotiations, continuously opposed the British notion of 'just return' (e.g., Chandernagor, *Le Monde*, 11 Aug. 1981), criticised the reduction agreed in May 1980 (e.g., Chandernagor, quoted in *Financial Times*, 4 Oct. 1981) and, of course, ultimately disregarded the British veto on increased farm prices in May 1982.

Summary of Part One

In France, after the Second World War, there was no consensus over the country's fundamental national orientation – whether to look to the West or East, whether to dismember Germany or seek a reconciliation with her – and there was bitter disagreement between Socialists and Communists. For the PCF the interests of the 'true nation' were seen to lie in the pursuit of independence from the capitalist West in alliance with the Soviet Union, and all moves towards integration, whether with the USA or Western Europe, were denounced in a totally uncompromising way. Even though valid socialist arguments were produced, the overwhelming impression given was of anti-Germanism utilised in support of policies determined by other considerations. No reconciliation between socialism and the nation-state could be realised, for the chauvinism negated the socialist vision which was, in any case, subordinated to unconditional support for Stalinist Russia. During the same period, however, the outlook of the SFIO was equally unpromising. Equating socialism and internationalism in a highly idealised fashion, the socialists provided rationalisations for the incorporation of France into a capitalist bloc with military, political and economic dimensions. When the European Defence Community provoked a sharp reaction, the PCF and a large Socialist minority were able to come together with the nationalist right to defeat the proposal, but no synthesis between the nation and socialism was achieved and the unity was only temporary. Thereafter the PCF relapsed into its former stance – though with less conviction and vehemence – and the SFIO continued to mouth internationalist slogans, whilst pursuing policies in Suez, Algeria and Western Europe which were fully in accord with the dominant interests in the nation-state. Paradoxically, it was General de Gaulle who created the conditions for more fruitful developments on the left. He did so both through the domestic impact of his external policy and the political logic with which the left was confronted in the Gaullist regime.

Once de Gaulle adopted a stance of relative independence *vis-à-vis* the USA, the PCF could modify its insistence that it was the sole representative of the 'true nation' and seek instead an alliance strategy to reinforce the trend that was already emerging. But Gaullism also provided a salutary lesson for the Socialists for, if the French bourgeoisie now believed that *national* interests needed to be defended against total incorporation in an American-led supranational bloc, Socialists could hardly maintain the stance which ceded power to international capitalism while indulging in socialist rhetoric. The seeds were thus sown for convergence between the communist emphasis on national independence and socialist 'Europeanism' – a convergence which could also mean the establishment of a new consensus over national goals. It was, however, political logic which dictated the eventual attainment of a *modus vivendi* on the left.

The outlook of the two parties of the left on Europe, as on other important issues, remained quite distinct throughout the years of *rapprochement* which began in 1962. Yet both sought governmental office primarily through electoral means and, at least until the unprecedented triumph of the Socialists in June 1981, it seemed clear that neither could succeed without some form of alliance. If international policy in general and the European Community in particular were to prove among the most difficult areas on which to reach agreement, they were also essential if any pact was to be credible. The desired *entente* was therefore secured in the Common Programme in 1972 and again, when the Communists entered the government, nine years later. By then, of course, the Socialists had become the dominant force on the French left and the Communists were prepared to pay obeisance to Mitterrand's policy in return for the award of some governmental posts. Nevertheless, the concessions were not all in one direction. The Socialists had adopted an increasingly national emphasis in their pronouncements and Mitterrand emphasised that his 'Europeanism' was not unconditional in the manner of the SFIO.

It was therefore possible for the left to take office in 1981 pledged to introduce radical reforms for the revival of the economy and apparently confident that the domestic programme could be implemented from within the European Community and would even be aided by it. By then it was clear that, if the established French national interests clashed with Community demands, Mitterrand intended to be as intransigent as his right-wing forerunners. There was no mystery in this for although the French Socialists retained a form of European consciousness they also shared the national conviction that, in the event of conflict between Europeanism as

115

defined by the Community institutions and by the French state, the latter version must prevail. And if the Communists did not share the European consciousness they had no qualms about supporting the supremacy of the French state. In this respect a rudimentary consensus over the nation and its primary international orientation had been built.

However, it was always much less certain that the Socialist-led government would really be prepared to confront the forces of capitalism in 'Europe' or France. For Mitterrand and the dominant wing of the *Parti socialiste* (which was also the major force in the left as a whole by 1981) commitment to 'Europeanism' and a form of social democracy have always appeared stronger than intransigent anti-capitalism. During the 1960s the majority of socialists had become more critical of the EEC but there had always been a tendency to fudge the distinction between a capitalist and a socialist Europe with attractive but theoretically inadequate assertions about the compatibility between socialism and the European community. Such ambiguity on this issue and others was no doubt part of the reason for the evolution of the PS into a governmental party, for it could stress different aspects of its policy and ideology to different audiences. Yet it also suggested the likelihood that a Mitterrand-led Government would compromise on its programme and, indeed, within a year it had retreated on the issues of import controls, state subsidies, aspects of the nationalisation programme, and ultimately even on the reflationary policy itself.

However, if the government diluted its programme of reform, and if it tended to follow a French national policy rather than a specifically socialist one, this did not necessarily invalidate the strategy to which the PS was theoretically committed. The PS left had worked on two assumptions: first that EEC membership would allow a left-wing government a margin of manoeuvre for the socialist transformation in France; and secondly that, in certain circumstances, the European Community could aid this process by ensuring that a socialist government would not be forced to confront the full pressures of international capitalism in isolation. On the first point the actual experience of the government was inconclusive. The European Commission certainly opposed some French initiatives as an infringement of both the competition and tariff policies.[1] On the other hand it supported the nationalisation measures as compatible with the Treaty of Rome (against the wishes of the French right);[2] it followed the lead given by the Community governments rather than initiating confrontation with the French state;[3] and its opposition was probably far less worrying for the Mitterrand–Mauroy government than that emanating more generally from capitalist forces both inside and outside the Community. And this leads to the second PS assumption. For the fact was that in the early 1980s the circumst-ances in which the European Community would provide support for a socialist government simply did not exist because the two other major powers in Western Europe were fundamentally opposed to the reforms which the French administration was seeking to imple-ment, and the international recession was deepening.

In other words, although the European Community is still a vehicle for anti-socialist forces, it would be simplistic to conclude that the Mitterrand Government was giving way to EEC pressure. In fact the major constraints on the administration during its first year of office would have been experienced whether or not France was a member of the EEC.[4]

It must therefore be concluded that the argument of much of the French left that socialism cannot be established within a single European state, and that membership of the European Community could under certain circumstances be beneficial, remains unproven. This may not be a highly positive conclusion, but it is worth bearing in mind as we consider the evolution of the more negative attitudes of the left in Britain towards West European integration.

Notes

1 Brussels opened investigations on the possible import controls shortly before Christmas 1981 and the industrial commissioner visited Mauroy in Paris on 20 January 1982 to discuss the matter (*Financial Times*, 27 Jan. 1982). In February 1982 the Commission also began investigations into governmental subsidies to the textile and steel industries to ascertain whether or not they infringed competition policy (*Le Monde*, 6 Feb. 1982), and had not reached a decision by June 1982.

2 *Le Monde*, 16 October 1981. It also ruled that plans to restructure several industries and reduce import penetration did *not* conflict with EEC regulations (*International Herald Tribune*, 5 Feb. 1982).

3 It was to the EEC *governments* rather than the Commission that the French were forced to give informal assurances about import controls, and it was German capital interests rather than the EEC which led to the abandonment of plans to nationalise the French pharmaceutical firm, Roussel-Uclaf.

4 The OECD complained about French import controls (*Financial Times*, 2 Feb. 1982), and the pressure by multinationals to prevent nationalisation would have been the same inside or outside the EEC (something still more true in Britain where there is a greater proportion of American ownership). This is not to minimise the constraints emanating from the EEC for, apart from the Commis-sion's role, it was of still greater significance that the French Government had to obtain permission from its partners in the EMS for devaluation on 12 June 1982, and were forced to agree to severe deflation in return. (*Guardian*, 14 June 1982). However, the Labour Government had acted in precisely the same way in 1976 following IMF pressure; and in June 1982 the American Government threatened retaliation against British steel imports because of governmental subsidies; this could have happened whether or not Britain had been a member of the Community.

Part Two

4
Labour, Europe and the World

The Post-War Labour Government and
West European Integration

In July 1945, for the first time in history, the Labour Party was elected to government with a total majority (of 146 seats) over all other parties in the House of Commons. Not only was it dominant over the forces of the right, but it had secured complete ascendancy over the labour movement, with its nearest rival, the Communist Party having won only 0.4 per cent of the poll, and all other left-wing movements in sharp decline. In the general election of February 1950 its governmental majority over all other parties was reduced to five (although its share of the vote increased and its predominance in the labour movement was more complete than ever), but it retained power until October 1951 when Clement Attlee called, and lost, an unnecessary General Election.[1] A Labour Government was thus in charge of the nation's affairs throughout the formative stages of the movement towards the integration of Western Europe and, as is well known, it adopted a highly negative attitude to the process as soon as it threatened to assume a supranational form in the late 1940s.[2]

Marshall Aid was seen as vital to prevent economic collapse and political destabilisation in Western Europe and Ernest Bevin, the Foreign Secretary, therefore played a pivotal role in its support, not only at diplomatic level, but also through the Labour Party, by holding an international socialist conference at Selsdon in March 1948 to rally socialist parties in its favour. Its propaganda at the conference about the progressive and disinterested character of the Aid was as enthusiastic as that of Leon Blum in France.[3] But when the Organisation for European Economic Co-operation (OEEC) considered the introduction of supranational powers to plan the distribution of aid, the British Government immediately declared its opposition to any moves that might thwart its domestic economic policy or its commercial and financial dealings with the sterling area. Simultaneously Bevin initiated and welcomed the defence

121

agreements with France and the Benelux countries which led to the Brussels Pact of 1948, but sought to prevent any accretion of power in the parliamentary assembly that was established with it. The same pattern was repeated the next year. Bevin was thus effusive in his support for the NATO alliance, which he saw as his crowning achievement, but was reserved about the whole notion of a Council of Europe, and insisted that the Assembly should be powerless. Nor would the British Government seriously consider joint economic planning with the French, which might have impeded its domestic economic control, or the easing of currency controls within the OEEC if this threatened its control over the sterling area. Finally, when in 1950 the Schuman proposal sidestepped British delaying tactics, by insisting on acceptance of supranationalism as a precondition for participation, the British Government refused the invitation to enter the Community. Yet within a few months its support for Western defence arrangements was taken a stage further when it accepted the principle of West German rearmament within NATO.[4]

The Labour Government had thus sought the political, economic and military strengthening of Western Europe on a liberal–democratic basis in a firm alliance with the United States, but had simultaneously tried to impede the process of supranational integration. When its strategy proved abortive in the case of the Schuman Plan it had chosen to remain aloof in the hope and expectation that the embryonic Community would fail without British participation.[5] Why had the Labour Government approached the question of integration in a manner which diverged so sharply from that of the French Government, and the SFLO, in the same period?

The National Context

For the French the military collapse in 1940 and the subsequent Nazi occupation had reinforced the sense of relative weakness which had existed since the defeat by Germany (Prussia) in 1870. For the British the position seemed quite different. Despite the objective trend of long-term relative decline and an acute awareness of the material losses resulting from the war, the fact that Britain had fought alone for a year, and in the Grand Alliance from 1941 onwards, induced a belief in her continued 'greatness'.[6] This conviction was held just as strongly by the Labour leadership as by the rest of the political elite. Ernest Bevin, the Foreign Secretary, told the House of Commons in 1947:

His Majesty's Government do not accept the view ... that we have ceased to be a great power, or the contention that we have ceased to play that role. We regard ourselves as one of the powers most vital to the peace of the world and we still have our historic role to play. The very fact that we have fought so hard for liberty, and paid such a price, warrants our retaining this position; and indeed it places a duty upon us to continue to retain it ...[7]

Almost every policy statement, public and private, produced by the post-war Labour Government was predicated on the supposition of Britain's enduring grandeur. Whilst the French state thus came to see West European integration as a means of overcoming relative weakness, British policy-makers naturally viewed it as a threat: that is as a means of *reducing* Britain to the same level as the other West European states.

This objection to involvement in supranational integration was reinforced by a second difference between French and British historical development. In 1947 it was extremely difficult for French liberal-democrats to retain any real confidence in their political institutions, as the instability and polarisation which had characterised the pre-war period appeared to be recurring. Incorporation in a wider European grouping based on the forces of political centrism was therefore a relatively attractive prospect. In Britain the situation was again totally different.

The war, particularly from 1941 onwards, had led to a far deeper form of consensus than had existed in the 1930s and this endured in the post-war era. Rather than leading to any loss of confidence in the nation-state, there was thus a heightened popular patriotism and a conviction that the British political system was uniquely resilient. Once again, such sentiments were fully shared by the Labour leadership, whose deep-seated faith in the British constitutional system was reinforced not only by the war but, above all, by Labour's resounding electoral success in 1945. Labour leaders therefore constantly contrasted the triumphant characteristics of British democratic socialism with pessimism about continental nation-states and their political systems, and such convictions underlay the refusal to entertain any notion of incorporation in a supranational organisation with them. Shortly after the Schuman proposal was made, Hugh Dalton wrote:

No doubt ... the experiences of war, including the experience of being occupied by the enemy has broken the back of nationalist pride in many of these countries and this helps to popularise the federalist myth.[8]

It would be quite out of the question for us to hand over our coal and iron and steel industries to a 'High Authority' of European

> dictators, entirely out of reach of any control by the British government or the British House of Commons ...[9]

A third, and still more fundamental, difference between the two nation-states concerned their central foreign policy preoccupations. For France the overriding concerns were with European issues and, as was argued earlier, a principal attraction of integration was the fact that it apparently offered a solution to the 'German problem' when American and British objections precluded dismemberment. During the war itself British policy-makers had naturally viewed the defeat and weakening of Germany as the major priority, but even then their outlook had remained imperial rather than simply European. It was *on* the Empire that the Government had relied for material and military support and it was *in* the Empire that the British had primarily fought the war. The popular image in 1945, undoubtedly shared by the elite, was of the Commonwealth having valiantly fought with Britain and her American and Soviet allies for the defeat of Nazi Germany. If, in reality, the war had loosened the British hold on her imperial possessions this was not generally recognised, and the world-wide role remained central not only to Britain's material position but to her rulers' mental outlook.

After the war, policy-makers were acutely conscious of the impossibility of full disengagement from the continent, and the problems of West European security and stabilisation were a constant preoccupation. Yet the perspective was always global as well as 'European': the continent was perceived as only one area in which Britain was concerned, and Germany again came to assume significance within the general constellation of problems rather than as the preeminent issue. This did not mean that there was an immediate shift in the goal of weakening and controlling Germany. Indeed even the agreement in December 1946 to merge the British and American occupation zones did not imply that Bevin now favoured the conciliation of a Western Germany as an anti-Soviet bastion for, although the move was certainly seen partly as a means of pressurising the Soviet Union, it was also brought about by strictly economic motives; and months after the decision had been taken Bevin and Dalton, the Chancellor of the Exchequer, both made speeches in which an anti-German tone remained dominant.[10] Moreover, at this stage Bevin still reaffirmed the commitment, to which the SFLO attached such importance, of the March 1945 Anglo-French socialist agreement, to nationalise the Ruhr industries.[11] However, the *de facto* alliance with the immensely more powerful USA was quickly to lead to the abandonment of the earlier Labour position. In particular, while Bevin initially sought to prevent the inclusion of the Western zones of Germany in the

Marshall Aid programme his opposition evaporated when it became clear that the establishment of a strong West Germany was a major American priority and was seen as a crucial element in the European recovery programme. Similarly, American determination to ensure that the new West Germany was solidly capitalist led to a progressive emasculation of the commitment to nationalise the Ruhr industry. In fact after 1947 the Labour Government supported each stage in the creation of a capitalist state in West Germany and the elimination of the restrictions on its sovereignty.

Alignment with the USA thus expedited the shift in the Labour leadership's German policy in a way which resembled the processes which occurred in France under American pressure in the same period. Yet because the leadership identified itself so totally with the American perception of the international situation, the change in attitude towards Germany could still be felt to be autonomous – an evolution which had occurred because of changing circumstances, rather than as an imposition by the USA. Whereas the French Government and the SFLO came to see Franco-West German co-operation in an integrated Western Europe as a solution to the problem of relative weakness, the German question therefore had no such effect upon the attitudes of the British Establishment or the Labour Government.

The Labour leadership also shared the outlook of the elite with regard to the Commonwealth and world-wide roles, and the con-comitant perception of European issues.[12] Indeed, as will be seen, material factors, and a less tangible political consciousness emanating from the Commonwealth role, constituted a decisive factor in the refusal to countenance close involvement in an integrated Western Europe.

These differences from the French situation, and the consequent hostility to supranational integration, do not mean that the British Establishment never considered close political involvement in Western Europe. Such notions were entertained in the early stages of the war, and Churchill in particular favoured the idea in 1942–43 (as well as in 1946–47 in a more explicitly anti-Soviet context).[13] However, not only were such conceptions schematic and ephemeral, but there was never any suggestion in governmental circles that Britain's world role should be restricted by participation in a European grouping. On the contrary, the assumption was always that Britain would lead any such organisation which would also strengthen her influence in the world as a whole. Here again the outlook of the Labour leadership was fully in accord with that of the Establishment as a whole. Thus, for example, Ernest Bevin aspired to the amalgamation of the British Commonwealth with the European nations into 'One Great European Commonwealth' where

Britain could provide leadership 'of the inarticulate masses of Europe',[14] while Dalton recorded the results of conversations with Stalin as follows:

> Stalin agrees to *our* being the dominant power in Western Europe – which he as good as says might be federated under our direction and control – and thinks very wisely, that Germany should be broken up ... It is quite true (to continue talking in terms of Power Politics and not in those of waffle) that the USA would not like our being in control of a federated Western Europe and that we might, in the long run, have to 'buy her off', by abandoning, say our South American or Far Eastern positions ...
>
> P.S. Essentially, the situation is that we can maintain our position as a World Power *either* by being the centre (economic and political) of the British Empire, including the Dominions, *or* by leading some European bloc.[15]

Although the Labour leadership, like the government as a whole, had come by 1945 to believe that the Empire rather than Western Europe would provide the main basis of British power in the post-war period, Bevin sometimes continued to hope that it might be possible to combine the two.[16] Indeed, Avi Schlaim has argued, very convincingly, that Bevin even had a 'grand design' of this kind at the time of the Marshall Aid offer. His aspiration was thus to unite with the other West European imperial powers in collaborative development (or exploitation) of the overseas territories in the belief that this could provide Britain with a basis for economic independence from the United States, and a continued role as a first-class power. Once again a prerequisite of this impracticable hankering after the imperial past was that Britain should not be subordinated to the European grouping, but should remain a fully independent power, supplemented by the grouping in Western Europe, the Commonwealth, and the special relationship with the United States.[17]

If such assumptions underlay the European outlook of the post-war government it seems almost unnecessary to ask whether there was a socialist element in the policy. Not only do analysts of the period show a rare unanimity in rejecting any such claim, but even the participants themselves were anxious to deny it. In 1945 Bevin thus suggested that foreign and defence policy should be put on a special footing outside party conflict;[18] and in November 1946 Attlee told back-bench rebels: 'We are not acting as representatives of an ideological abstraction but as the representatives of the people of this country.'[19]

In 1947 Hugh Dalton and Denis Healey (then Head of the International Department) even provided a rationale for the Labour

Government to pursue power untainted by socialism:

> Until International Relations can be conducted entirely under a guaranteed rule of law, the effectiveness of Britain's part depends on her power, whether her policy is capitalist, socialist, communist or fascist ...[20]

Yet despite all this it would seem that there were some distinctly 'Labourist' elements in the government's European strategy, even if these were overlaid by national ones. The following section examines the evolving policy with reference to the leadership's justifications for it. As we shall see later, these formed part of the ideology of the Labour Party and were to remain important even after Britain's material circumstances, and the policy of the centre and right, had changed.

The Labour Leadership and 'Europe': From Marshall Aid to the Schuman Plan

The leadership's reservations about the form of European integration sought by the USA under the Marshall Aid proposal were made evident almost immediately. Whilst accepting the conventional argument that the productivity of Western Europe would be enhanced by its conversion into a single economic unit, it urged caution as to the speed with which this could be achieved, and stipulated that the importance of Britain's overseas connections must be taken into account in any proposed changes. Moreover, it was unwilling to specify any model on which such unification could be based, reiterating the vague pronouncements of Bevin who had called for a union based on a common heritage reflecting 'our sacrifices in the war, our hatred of injustice and oppression, our Parliamentary democracy, our strivings for economic rights, and our conception and love of liberty'.[21]

If Labour was following the policy of the Establishment as a whole in thus seeking a loose form of co-operation which would neither impede British economic relations with the Commonwealth nor restrict the government's domestic freedom of action, there were nevertheless some respects in which the government's perceptions of the European issue were specific to the labour movement.

The leadership shared the general tendency of the party to associate the movement towards West European unification with the political right, particularly in view of Churchill's early involvement in it. The Conservative leader's attempt to mobilise support for the 'United States of Europe' as an anti-Soviet bloc in 1946 had alienated the Labour leadership because the government had still claimed to believe that agreement with the Russians was possible. It now also maintained that the object of Conservative propaganda was not only to consolidate Western Europe on an anti-communist basis, but also to strengthen free enterprise in Britain by mobilising the nascent European Movement against the Labour Government.[22] At the Selsdon conference the Labour Party thus tried to dissuade other socialist parties from participating in the forthcoming Hague congress, where British right-wingers were expected to play a leading role:

> The survival of democratic socialism as a separate political form is closely bound up with the survival of Western Europe as a spiritual union. This in itself imposes an obligation on Socialist Parties to work for a closer association of the free countries of Western Europe. And the obligation is greatly strengthened by the danger that the concept of European Unity may be corrupted in the hands of reaction. Socialists everywhere must guard against the prostitution of this great constructive ideal into the vulgar instrument of anti-soviet propaganda, by discredited politicians who hope to rebuild their shattered fortunes under the protection of its popular appeal. This is not to say that socialists alone are capable of disinterested passion for European unity. But the danger exists, and it can best be reduced if socialists themselves take the initiative in promoting the ideal on the plane of constructive realism.[23]

In fact the leadership was well aware of the differences between its views and those of the SFIO, which had already sought to obtain a united front with Labour to promote the establishment of a federal Europe. These efforts had been repelled by Labour which had privately described its own policy in the following significant terms:

> (a) The achievement of general economic stability in Western Europe must precede any political union. (Socialists particularly must insist on this order of priority, since at the moment the economic stability of the various countries in Western Europe is almost directly proportional to the degree in which Socialists control their governments. So, for example, the Scandinavian socialist democracies are unwilling to jeopardise their own economic wellbeing by committing themselves politically to permanent union with countries like France and Italy, whose economic and social policies at the moment are laissez-faire, and whose administrative apparatus is too corrupt and inefficient to take the strain of a state-planned economy.)

(b) Economic stability in Western Europe depends on efficient national economies and on a vast extension of mutual co-operation in which the main instrument should be the continuing organisation set up under the European Recovery Programme. The decisions of this continuing organisation should depend on mutual agreement for the time being, since any attempt to give it supranational powers would prevent many countries from participating at all.[24]

The belief that Labour's economic policy was more planned than that in France was only partially valid in view of the existence of Monnet's *commissariat du plan*. Yet it was probably sincerely held. In any case, though confident that it had been triumphant in securing its aims at Selsdon, the Labour leadership was soon to find that this was a pyrrhic victory.[25] For at the Socialist Conference on European Unity in Paris the next month a federalist resolution was passed, and continental socialists were to be well represented at the Hague Congress in May.

Having failed to carry the socialists of France or the Benelux countries, the leadership now sought a riposte which would at least rally the Labour Party. At the annual conference, held less than a week after the Hague congress Dalton explained the governmental position, in response to a resolution by Fenner Brockway in favour of support for a United Socialist States of Europe (see below).[26] Characteristically, he combined some arguments which would equally well have suited any Conservative politician, with others which were specific to the Labour Party. He thus asserted that the government believed West European union to be vital and that no one had done more to achieve this than Bevin, but repeated the claim that federation, if ever possible, must wait until functional co-operation had progressed. The means to this end was, he claimed, through governmental meetings rather than through 'conclaves of chatterboxes' (i.e., the Hague). He also made two further conditions before launching into his full polemic: first that the NEC would accept the resolution only on the understanding that it did not preclude military obligations either to the UN or within regional or group arrangements (i.e., the Brussels Pact); secondly, that Western Europe would be much 'less interesting' to Britain if some of the countries did not have colonies, for the mainland could not supply the foodstuffs and raw materials in the way that Eastern Europe, the Commonwealth and Latin America could. The position would change if the colonies were included: 'But, even so, you cannot focus yourself too completely on the countries of Western Europe, without having regard to other areas of the world.'

This opened the way for a hymn of praise to the Commonwealth

and an assertion of a determination to develop and strengthen the
British relationship with it:

> It is no good denying that we are very much closer, in all respects
> except distance to Australia and New Zealand than we are to
> Western Europe. Australia and New Zealand are populated by
> our kinsmen. They live under Labour governments, they are
> democracies, they speak our language, they have high standards
> of life and have the same political ideals as we have. If you go to
> those countries you find yourself at once completely at home in a
> way that you do not if you go to a foreign country as distinct from
> a British community overseas ... I am quite sure if the choice
> were put to us: 'Will you move closer to Western Europe at the
> cost of moving further away from the countries of the Common-
> wealth?' for my part I would answer 'No'.

This type of argument represented the stock-in-trade of any
Conservative politician and, apart from the brief reference to
Commonwealth Labour governments, it contained no element of
socialist thought. Yet he ended on a different note:

> We in Britain have fought through long years to win power for
> Socialism, and as a result today we have full employment, which
> we should not have except for the Socialist Government. We are
> not going to throw away the solid gains brought to us by a whole
> generation of political agitation and by the votes of our people
> and by three years of solid work in Parliament, in the Trade
> Unions and in the Government, upon any doctrinal altar of a
> federal Western Europe. When it comes to clever lawyers drafting
> a federal Constitution, it must be made quite clear ... that we are
> not going to have chance majorities of reactionaries who might be
> thrown up from any part of Western Europe having the power to
> decree that we in Britain shall go back to the inter-war years of
> trade depression and all the rest of it ...
> ... We are quite confident that the success of any scheme for a
> United States of Europe ... is going to depend upon the success of
> ... democratic Socialist Parties ... If we could assure an equal
> strength for our Socialist comrades in all these countries as we
> command here, then indeed it would not be difficult to make a
> triumphant success of a United States of Western Europe. If, on
> the other hand, we are to find a group of reactionaries riding to
> power in some of these Western countries of Europe, then we
> shall do well to look once and twice at the extent of our proposals
> to collaborate with them and put our fate in their hands ...
> If this great vision is to come true and is to carry blessings to all

the peoples of Western Europe and wider areas of the world, it can only do so if we here hold the Socialist advances we have made and if others in these other countries advance with us along the road towards Socialist triumph all along the Western European line.

In the very same speech Dalton was thus able to eulogise the Commonwealth, emphasising the 'kith-and-kin' argument for imperial unity, and to mobilise the rank and file for the defence of British Socialism against continental reaction. It is scarcely surprising that French Socialists were baffled and, in some cases, outraged. Yet this combination of arguments was by no means peculiar to Dalton. It was indeed common to the leadership as a whole and with a greater or lesser emphasis, was reiterated in almost every subsequent statement on Western European integration. Of course it may simply have been a cynical device to bind the rank and file to the government, but it seems more likely that such convictions were deep in the consciousness of Labour leaders.

Despite the arguments and delaying tactics Labour ministers could not hold back the impetus for a semi-federal political union rather than one based on intergovernmental co-operation and, although they were able to emasculate the proposals to such an extent that the powers of the Assembly of the Council of Europe were minimal, the Labour delegation still found itself in an uncomfortable position at its first session in August 1949.[27] It also encountered, and reciprocated, hostility from the SFIO and other continental socialists who supported the quasi-federalist impetus in the Assembly's debates.[28]

The result was a new effort to resolve the deadlock between functional and federal integration by passing the matter to the General Affairs Committee on which Mollet was *rapporteur* and Dalton the chief Labour delegate. The first attempt to define Labour's position for the committee was by Denis Healey in a memorandum, entitled 'The Labour Party and European Unity'.[29] Written at the height of the Cold War in October 1949, this sought to combine absolute solidarity with the anti-communist mission of the United States, with a total rejection of the supranational integration favoured by the American Government. Its major premise was that, if any Federal Western Europe were created, British isolation from it would be the most effective anti-communist strategy. This was justified with the argument that purely regional solutions would be inadequate to the task of uniting the whole non-communist world against Stalinism, while the Commonwealth could play a 'central role in building a world system' based upon its members' economic connections and the 'spiritual factors' which

131

united them. All this meant that:

> Europe would gain little and lose all if Britain's membership of the European community cost her freedom of initiative in the wider sphere. For Britain a United Europe must, like the Commonwealth itself, remain essentially an open system. It cannot be a closed society, membership of which excludes active and independent association with other groupings.

The political arguments for European unity were introduced from a similar perspective:

> European unity is needed and desired today primarily because no country in Western Europe wishes to see Soviet power extending further westward through the military, political or economic collapse of any other – and some countries feel unable to survive themselves without help ... Political defence against Communist penetration is a problem which various countries have tried to solve in various ways. The Labour Party is convinced that the best defence, if possible, is democratic socialism; for democratic socialism destroys the social and economic conditions which Communism needs to develop mass support.

The argument for democratic socialism was thus raised in a specifically anti-communist context and, in precisely the same way as Leon Blum had argued in Washington in 1946, Healey asserted that the controls which had been introduced by the Labour Government had been economic rather than ideological in origin – that is, as a means of stimulating exports and reinvestment in order to revive the economy and reduce the dollar gap. However, Healey, then took the offensive with the assertion that, while democratic socialism offered the best defence against communism, the preconditions for it did not exist 'in certain large European States' (and he clearly meant France and Italy):

> Democratic planning and control can function only in a state where the citizens feel social responsibility and respect for law and where the civil service is both honest and efficient. In some countries where it was sought to apply the methods of planning to solve the post-war problems, the attempt was wrecked on the twin obstacles of civic irresponsibility and administrative inefficiency.

In such cases the classical methods of deflation were more successful, although 'the scale of suffering they impose on the working-class has favoured the growth of large communist parties'. In any case, it followed that proposals for European co-operation which involved uniformity in internal policies must be excluded because: 'Britain could not afford the economic and social consequences of laissez-faire, while other countries are either unwilling or unable to apply policies which demand control and planning by the State.'

Finally, after two years' experience of American-led efforts to bring about free trade and currency convertibility within Western Europe, thereby threatening Britain's sterling balances, Healey disputed the most fundamental economic assumption of the proponents of full integration: that the establishment of a single large market would stimulate productivity. He claimed instead that the solution lay in limited co-operation, limited encouragement to intra-European trade, co-operation in colonial development, and Labour-style domestic planning.

Healey's arguments against federalism and the economic assumptions of the market contained a socialistic element, forcefully stated; but the striking feature of his memorandum was the way in which these points were overlaid by the implicit suggestion of British and Commonwealth superiority, Atlanticism and anti-communism. It is not known whether the NEC found any of this objectionable for the minutes only record an agreement to publish a shortened version at an appropriate time, but it is unlikely that any objections which were raised related to matters of principle, for the next month Dalton and the whole Labour delegation to Strasbourg (apart from Mackay, the sole federalist)–(see below)–submitted a shorter memorandum which reiterated Healey's arguments. Indeed Dalton went still further in Atlanticism by suggesting that if federalism were held to be a practical proposition, it might be preferable to found it on the Atlantic Pact, rather than Western Europe![30]

The campaign for the General Election of February 1950 intervened to prevent further developments in the definition of the leadership's 'European' attitudes, but almost immediately afterwards an attempt was made to put the democratic socialist argument at the centre of the campaign against supranational integration. In April Bevin's Parliamentary Private Secretary (Ernest Davies) wrote a new memorandum, 'The Labour Party and European Co-operation', which the Foreign Secretary had asked for because he feared that some party members might be too favourably disposed towards the Council of Europe. It began:

In its approach to European co-operation the Labour Party must above all else have regard for the preservation of democratic socialism in Britain. No policy should be pursued which is in any way inconsistent with the maintenance or extension of political

133

and social democracy in Britain on a socialist basis. There can be
no surrender of the Government's power to control the economic
policy of the nation and thereby to carry through its programme;
this requires retention by the Government of final control over
the economic power of the State ... Maintenance of the welfare
state and a planned economy to ensure maximum production,
full employment and a fairer distribution of the national income
are among the chief aims of Labour's economic policy. There
must therefore be complete freedom to plan, and power to control
production, investment, prices and distribution of goods in short
supply, all of which means that the preservation of Socialist
democracy necessitates a closed economy.[31]

The Commonwealth and world-wide network was presented,
without sentimentality, in an economic context. It was argued that
interference in the use of sterling would undermine Britain's financial strength and that any curb on her freedom to purchase within
the Commonwealth, or to undertake bulk buying elsewhere, would
threaten the price structure on which wages policy and the control of
inflation rested. Such considerations reinforced the general argument that:

The extension of European co-operation to the point where this
[internal freedom for Socialist planning] might be jeopardised or
where there would be any surrender of sovereignty would clearly
be of potential danger to Britain's closed socialist economy.

Nor were intermediate steps between governmental co-operation
and full federation–for example by an increase in the power of the
European Assembly–any more acceptable. Intergovernmental co-
operation, as in the OEEC, was as far as it was possible to go
without endangering the planned economy and even here serious
difficulties had been encountered. Britain could therefore never
commit herself so far as to be unable to contract out of any European
organisation on specific issues if its policy conflicted with British
responsibilities abroad or policies at home.[32] Davies's conclusion
was that the NEC should approach all proposals for increased
co-operation in the Council of Europe with caution and that the
Labour Government's positive strategy should be to extend co-
operation as widely as possible in those fields which would not entail
a conflict with British interests: for example, harmonisation in
economic development and the co-ordination of investment, the
formulation of schemes for European civil aviation or hydro-electric
development, freedom of travel, social security and cultural conven-
tions, and perhaps human rights policy. A major advantage of

concrete achievements in these fields was that they 'might well assist in relieving the pressure for undesirable and unacceptable powers to be conferred upon the Consultative Assembly'.

This memorandum was clearly based on illusions as to the extent to which Britain had a closed economy or a socialist one. Nevertheless it did provide the germs of a *socialist* argument against 'Europe' rather than one in which this element was subordinate to Atlanticist, Commonwealth and anti-communist invective. Moreover, its ideas were taken up by Healey who suggested to Dalton that the Labour delegation should undertake a more attacking strategy in the Council of Europe:

> I think that if we try to rub their noses in full employment and fair shares we could, as a Labour delegation, completely capture the initiative from the Tories and Right-Wing groups in the Assembly.[33]

Dalton accepted this argument and fully intended to take the offensive when the Assembly reassembled in August. However, the main battle was now carried outside the Council for in May, Schuman announced the proposal for a coal and steel community and insisted that the supranational principle must be accepted before negotiations began. It was thus the British who were under attack and in this situation Labour ministers resumed their hybrid national and socialistic policy.

Given their general foreign policy aims, the British could not totally condemn a proposal which appeared to constitute a major step towards overcoming Franco-German tension and integrating West Germany into the Western bloc. On 11 May Attlee therefore welcomed the French initiative and said that Britain would approach the problem in a sympathetic spirit. On the other hand the French stipulation of acquiescence in supranationalism as a prerequisite to negotiation meant that there was no possibility of British adherence unless the plan was altered, almost beyond recognition. Apart from working on the diplomatic level to seek clarification of the proposal, the leadership therefore decided to resume its offensive at an international socialist conference due to take place on 17 June. Both at this meeting, and in the final draft of the controversial Healey–Dalton manifesto, *European Unity*, which was published just previously, Labour sought to muster the British democratic socialist argument against supranational integration. It argued that the iron and steel planning envisaged in the Schuman Plan would be in the public interest only if production were expanded, and that this could be guaranteed solely through public ownership. But:

There is no doubt that at present Europe's private industrialists fear overproduction and will try to reorganise restrictive cartels as in the past. They will seek to pervert the Schuman proposals for their own selfish and monopolistic ends. A co-ordinated perversion of this type would be far worse than our present unco-ordinated competition.[34]

It argued that parliamentary democracy was being undermined by extremism in Germany, France and Italy arising from the failure to provide full employment, social justice and economic stability, and that this threat to democracy presented a major problem for European unity itself. Following the suggestion originally made by Davies, it thus claimed that the Assembly would be performing a really useful function if it turned its attention to these problems.

It is very unlikely that the adoption of an anti-supranationalist policy would by now have made any great impact on the French Socialists who were, as has been seen, determined to support the Schuman Plan. But in any case the Labour leadership never justified its case with arguments that were primarily socialist. While the Healey–Dalton manifesto certainly gave more emphasis to democratic socialism than the authors' earlier drafts, it still placed enormous stress on the battle against communism – including a commitment to the aim of returning the peoples of Eastern Europe to 'the world of freedom' – and to the spiritual unity of the British with their 'kinsmen' in New Zealand and Australia. Moreover, a tone of haughty British superiority was again evident in the argument that Western Europe was just one part of the desired unity of all the non-communist peoples, while the Commonwealth represented 'the nucleus of a potential world society based on free competition'. Similarly, the stress on democratic socialism was incongruous alongside a total idealisation of the USA which was now seen as a bastion of progressive policies:

> in its social and economic policy, Western Europe as a whole would stand to the right of the USA, not between America and Russia. Outside Britain and Scandinavia there is no government with a more progressive domestic or foreign policy than the present American administration.[35]

The Labour Government was, of course, unable either to impede progress towards the Coal and Steel Community or to dissuade the SFIO from supporting it. And by the time the Labour delegation was granted the right opportunity to take the offensive which it had planned at the second session of the Assembly of the Council of Europe in August 1950, the Korean War crisis dominated international relations. In these circumstances, any impact that the socialistic element in the British proposals might have had was again negated by the extreme Atlanticist, anti-communist and pro-Commonwealth emphasis in Dalton's speech and in his behind-the-scenes activities.[36] Moreover, when the Minister of War, John Strachey, denounced the Schuman proposal as a 'capitalist plot', Attlee (and then Strachey himself) disavowed this language and denied that the government response had been based upon such assumptions.[37] Even if Strachey's original sentiments had been sincere, they did not represent the private thoughts of other ministers. Thus, for example, in July Dalton had informed a New Zealand journalist that:

> I am quite sure ... we must think first of all of our own Commonwealth and of the development of its boundless resources ... The Labour Party and the Labour Government ... are determined that our ties with our kinsmen in other parts of the Commonwealth shall be strengthened and not weakened in the years to come.[38]

And his original notes for his Strasbourg speech in August had been blatantly chauvinistic, emphasising that the Korean crisis demonstrated that Britain was no mere province of Europe for she alone amongst the members of the Council possessed a fleet which had gone into action, while Commonwealth solidarity had been shown by the fact that Australia had sent in her fighter aircraft.[39] Overall, the combination of national and socialistic arguments deployed in the statement *European Unity* was therefore probably an accurate reflection of the Cabinet's attitudes.

During the Labour Government's remaining year in office some of the negative effects of the Atlantic solidarity, to which the leadership attached such importance, became apparent. In a situation of unprecedented American pressure Labour ministers thus not only accepted the principle of West German rearmament but even offered diplomatic support for the European Defence Community (while making clear Britain's refusal to participate).[40] Still more significantly, as is well known, American pressure for rearmament led to a reduction in social welfare expenditure and the notorious imposition of charges within the newly established National Health Service.

These events highlighted three fundamental contradictions in the policy (and policy justifications) of the Labour Government, which had existed for the previous four years. First, the leadership claimed that West European integration could threaten Britain's socialist programme, although the United States was already far more of a constraining influence than Western Europe could be for years to come. Because alignment with the United States was seen as essential, the Atlantic Alliance was held in reverence whilst supra-national integration in Western Europe was pilloried as the major threat to democratic socialism.[41] Secondly, the Labour leadership condemned the reactionary nature of the continental governments but it shared a responsibility for their existence as it had joined with the United States in seeking to weaken communism and left-wing socialism in France, Belgium, Italy and West Germany. Finally, the government (like the Establishment as a whole) had originally adopted the negative attitude to integration largely because of the conviction that Britain remained a great power with world-wide responsibilities. Yet its relative decline was ever more apparent, and was manifested in its inability to prevent the Six from going their own way.

Before any comparison with the French left is made, or any overall evaluation is attempted, it is necessary to consider whether there was any opposition to leadership policies on 'Europe' within the labour movement at this stage and, if so, why it was ineffective.

The Labour 'Europeans'

In the early post-war period, the main source of opposition to the leadership's overall foreign policy strategies came from the Communist Party and pro-communist forces within the Labour Party.[42] Since their policy followed the same trajectory as that of the PCF (and the Soviet Union) they were not opposed to the 'European' policy of the government although they were, of course, bitterly condemnatory of its Atlanticism particularly after the formation of the Cominform.[43] However, if the majority of the dissidence within the labour movement concerned the government's stance in the East–West conflict, for a short period in 1947 and the beginning of 1948, it did seem that an organised, and potentially influential, pro-'European' pressure group might arise within the Labour Party from the convergence of three distinct forces.

The first, and easily the most significant in terms of political weight, was the so-called Keep Left group, comprising a number of dissident backbench Labour MPs of whom the most prominent were Richard Crossman, Ian Mikardo and Michael Foot. The name was derived from a manifesto, by MPs who were members of the editorial staff of the *New Statesman* and *Tribune*, published at the end of April 1947;[44] and the immediate origins of this publication was a backbench rebellion, led by Richard Crossman, against the government's foreign policy the previous November.[45]

There had been sympathy for the notion of European unification amongst some sections of the parliamentary Labour left during the war, but by 1945 this had given way to a preoccupation with the relationship between the great powers.[46] There had then followed a period in which the non-communist parliamentary left had tended to align itself with the 'fellow-travellers' in condemning Britain and the United States for the deterioration in relations with the Soviet Union; but their ideological position was really quite different from that of the Communist Party and, by the middle of 1946, this was becoming apparent. As Anglo-Soviet differences accumulated, the parliamentary Labour left thus turned towards the idea of a 'third force' which would assume independence from both the Soviet Union and the United States.[47] From this was to come a new commitment to the goal of a United Europe, expressed most clearly in the *Keep Left* manifesto.

Keep Left was quite different in tone from pro-communist publications. It argued that the anti-British policy of the Soviet Government had been a 'disastrous mistake' but that, by relying on American support to counter it, Britain had endangered its relations with democratic forces, permitting them to be squeezed out by the division of every country into communist and anti-communist. The recent signature of the alliance with France was seen as a welcome sign that the government might now be trying to redress the balance, and, as the French were bound to the Soviet Union as closely as Britain was bound to the United States, *Keep Left* argued that France and Britain could determine whether Europe would be divided into two parts or united through the Anglo-French alliance as the keystone of the arch of world peace. The British, it argued, had now become Europeans whose prosperity and security was dependent on that of the rest of Europe:

> Working together, we are still strong enough to hold the balance of world power, to halt the division into a Western and Eastern bloc, and so to make the United Nations a reality. But if we permit ourselves to be separated from France, and so from the rest of Europe, and if we take cover under the mantle of America, we shall not only destroy our own and Europe's chances of recovery, but also make a third world war inevitable ...
>
> A Socialist Britain cannot prosper so long as Europe is divided. The goal we should work for is a federation which binds together the nations now under Eastern domination with the peoples of Western Europe. But this is a long way off. For the present it would be wise to concentrate on less spectacular forms of European collaboration designed gradually to remove the Iron

Curtain.[48]

It went on to assert that the European collaborative effort could be enhanced through the development of intra-European trade which would be facilitated by the fact that almost every European country was now planning its economy on socialist lines. Furthermore, it maintained that a united Germany could safely be absorbed into this system, which could also bring about a European regional security organisation within the terms of the United Nations Charter.

Much could be said about the practicability of this scheme: it was, for example, probably based on an exaggerated estimate of the power of France and Britain, and it was also naively optimistic about the prospects of alleviating Soviet hostility to such a bloc. Nor – as will be discussed later – was the ideological impetus of *Keep Left* so clearly distinct from that of the government as it appeared. Nevertheless, the rebellion seemed to mean that the dissident left was now prepared to champion the involvement of Britain in the movement towards West European integration.

Such possibilities were enhanced by the fact that a second strand of pro-European opinion in the Labour Party immediately joined forces with *Keep Left*. This was the small band of Federalists, personified by their most active and consistent spokesman, R.W.G. Mackay.[49] Mackay had been a leading figure in the Federal Union movement, which had secured some prominence in the early stages of the war, and in 1942 he had even stood as a Federal Union candidate in a by-election.[50] From the start he had been particularly interested in the notion of federalism in Europe and, although this prospect had appeared to fade as a practical possibility at the end of the war, he had maintained contact with pro-European circles, including Richard Coudenhove-Kalergi, who had originated the Pan-Europe movement after the First World War.[51] In 1946–47, he actively dissuaded the latter from basing a movement for European unity on Churchill and Duncan Sandys, arguing that they were discredited with the working classes, and sought a wider grouping in which the Labour Party could play a major role. Yet Mackay was not on the left of the party, for his ideas resembled those of André Philip and the SFIO right-wing. He was insistent that the unification of Western Europe was essential because the whole area faced the prospect of a long-term decline unless it could secure economies of scale through its conversion into a single market on the American pattern, and he accepted the capitalist argument that open competition would then be beneficial since it would bring about modernisation. Likewise he was convinced that the economic prerequisites for development were dependent upon the yielding of sovereignty to federal institutions at European level and that these institutions were neutral so that they could be converted to socialism at a later date.[52] His difference from the Labour leadership was less in the sphere of socialist ideology than in his fervent belief that Britain was part of Europe, and that its future depended on recognition of this fact rather than remaining in isolation or in association with the Commonwealth alone.

Nevertheless, while the underlying basis of Mackay's objections to the leadership's policy differed from that of the PLP left, Crossman's rebellion of November 1946 provided him with the opportunity which he sought. He thus joined the group which produced the *Keep Left* manifesto, no doubt contributing to its 'European' emphasis. Moreover, late in 1947, after further correspondence with Coudenhove-Kalergi, he established two parliamentary groups to campaign for European union: an all-party committee and the Labour Europe Group, to which he secured the adherence of the major signatories of *Keep Left*, and which was to claim the support of 80 Labour MPs (although attendance was far lower).

The convergence of *Keep Left* with Federalist opinion in the Labour Europe Group constituted the main potential power base for Labour 'Europeans', but their ranks were strengthened by an alliance with a third force: the British section of the Committee of Study and Action for a United Socialist States of Europe (hereafter, Committee for a United Socialist States of Europe). This had also been formed in 1947 and was centred on the Independent Labour Party (ILP) and ex-ILP members who had now joined the Labour Party. Throughout the war (which it had opposed) the ILP had campaigned for the establishment of a United Socialist States of Europe which would provide a synthesis between the politial freedoms of liberal democracy and the economic equality and organisation of the Soviet Union. It had pinned its hopes on the development of a European-wide anti-fascist revolution as its basis and it was always adamant that 'the future of British socialism [was] indissolubly bound up with the United Socialist States of Europe'.[53]

Although the ILP was no longer a major independent force in British politics at the end of the war it had resumed its contacts with like-minded socialists on the continent as soon as possible, and had provided much of the impetus for the establishment of the Committee for a United Socialist States of Europe and Bob Edwards, one of its leading figures, became its first Chairman.[54] The ideological outlook of the ILP closely resembled that of Marceau Pivert in France, who became President of the International Committee at its first congress, while Edwards took charge of the British section. The similarity also applied to political practice: Pivert entered the SFIO while Fenner Brockway, the former leader of the ILP, joined the Labour Party.

Both sought to convert the majority socialist party in their respective countries to their versions of libertarian, internationalist socialism and both saw the necessity for Labour Party/SFIO understanding as the nucleus for the united Europe which they envisaged.[55] As soon as the Labour Europe Group was formed, those associated with the committee thus made contact with it and sought a close harmonisation of policy.[56]

At the end of 1947 the Labour 'Europeans' were ready to launch a campaign whose major immediate purposes were to convert the Labour Party into active support for the goal of the unification of Europe, and to bring about a reconciliation between the views of the British and French socialists. Why was their failure so total?

Once the Labour Europe Group sought to clarify its objectives, serious divisions became evident. One problem, to which it was forced to devote considerable time, was that of whether it was prepared to work for European unity on a capitalist basis in the first instance, or whether only a socialist Europe could be supported. Christopher Shawcross, the Group's secretary, undoubtedly spoke for the overwhelming majority when he put his view to Mackay just after the inaugural meeting:

> although Socialism is essential for the success of a United Europe, our immediate task must be to save Socialism in Europe and the only possible way of doing this is by creating that unity. Without that, Socialist governments wherever they may be, including our own, will fail to deliver the goods to their own people and will thus fail politically, and at the same time of course, Socialism as an economic policy will also fail.[57]

This line was also taken by the ILP–led committee for, like Pivert in France, hatred of Stalinism and a genuine internationalism led it to support non-socialist integration. Brockway thus told Shawcross in January 1948:

> I think it will be quite good if you also have representatives with the Federalists or any other crowd who are doing effective work for the 'economic and political integration of Europe' in a way consistent with socialism.[58]

This position was maintained in 1948–49 in that the British section, like the *Pivertistes*, were prepared to participate in the Hague congress and become associated with the European Movement.[59] The only consistent opponent to this stance within the Labour Europe Group, whose persistence ensured that the problem was considered at length, was William Warbey, on the extreme left of the

Parliamentary Party.[60] The essence of his argument was that, in the prevailing political conditions, West European integration could be achieved only in alliance with 'a nondescript collection of anti-communist forces and against the will of the majority of the European working-classes'; and that the Group should therefore delay any major European socialist initiative until circumstances had changed.[61] This viewpoint was decisively rejected at a special Group meeting on 2 March 1948, but Warbey[62] continued to advocate it, openly attacking Mackay at the 1948 Labour Party Conference,[63] and forming his own faction, the Parliamentary Socialist Europe Group, that autumn.[64] From a socialist perspective, Warbey's arguments were highly cogent (though often close to those of 'fellow-travellers') but, given the comparative isolation of the Labour 'Europeans' in any case, his actions probably further weakened them. However, this division was far less important than another: that which concerned the extent of the 'European' commitment itself.

Both Mackay and the Federalists, and the Committee for the United Socialist States of Europe, actively sought West European integration in ways which closely resembled those of pro-'European' forces on the Continent. The aims of the Keep Left group were much less certain, and this became clear in March 1948, when Mackay failed in an attempt to secure the Europe Group's support for the goal of European federation. Instead it voted in favour of a proposal for functional integration (presented by Aidan Crawley, with Cross-man's support).[65] This was designed to counter the immediate threat of economic collapse and political destabilisation and closely resembled the strategy and priorities of the government. And although the Group then expressed the aspiration of attaining a synthesis between the federalist and functionalist positions, this was to prove just as illusive within the ranks of the Labour 'Europeans' as it was between the British Government and the continental 'Europeans'.

This fundamental division of purpose – though masked until March – reduced the impact, even of limited initiatives by the Group. Thus considerable importance had been attached to a meeting with representatives of the SFIO and the French section of the Committee for a United Socialist States of Europe which was held in February 1948. The initiative for this had come from the French, who clearly hoped that the Keep Left members of the Labour Europe Group could act as intermediaries with the Labour leadership in order to bring about a convergence with the position of the SFIO.[66] In the event, however, the British delegation comprised only the Federalists – shortly to be revealed as the minority – and they were unable even to inform the SFIO as to the policy of the

Labour Europe Group, let alone that of the party as a whole. [67] Internal differences were also revealed over the question of attendance at the Hague congress for, when the leadership made its views clear, only a minority of the original group, led by the committed Federalists, risked disapproval.[68] Moreover, while Fenner Brockway's resolution at the 1948 Party Conference in favour of 'practical steps to achieve the United Socialist States of Europe' should have provided an opportunity to secure the maximum publicity for the Group's aims, it revealed further division, as Labour's 'Europeans' publicly opposed one another, and the most prominent Keep Lefters remained silent.[69]

The Group continued to function until 1949 but it never really acted as a pressure group after early 1948. Mackay was included within the Labour delegation in the Assembly of the Council of Europe because of his specialist knowledge, and there he remained indefatigable in countering leadership policy, and influenced the continental 'Europeans'.[70] He also maintained contact with Crossman and co-operated with Brockway in what had now become the British Centre of the Socialist Movement for a United States of Europe (and a part of the European Movement).[71] But the alliance which had looked so promising in late 1947 never revived. The main reason for this was that the Keep Left group, on which the political influence of 'Europeanism' within the Labour Party had always depended, diverged ever more sharply from the attitudes of the European Movement.

In November 1949 *Tribune* declared that 'to plunge into European integration was to fall in with the methods of ruthless deflation and laissez-faire now prevalent on the Continent'.[72] True, *Keeping Left* (published in January 1950) still contained criticisms of the government's stance and argued that Western European integration remained the right policy. However, its positive suggestions were very similar to those that Healey and Dalton were to put forward in *European Unity*. *Keeping Left* thus shared the view that it would be quite impossible for a planned British economy to be integrated with those of free enterprise countries. Instead it urged co-operation in less threatening areas and maintained, just as the leadership was to do, that the Labour Party should use the Strasbourg Parliament as a sounding board for socialist plans for Western union, based on full employment and 'fair shares'.[73]

Neither *Keeping Left* nor Tribune's rallying call in 1950, *Full Speed Ahead*, urged a European policy which differed significantly from that of the government; and both *Tribune* and the *New Statesman* supported the Dalton–Healey manifesto *European Unity* and the leadership's attitude to the Schuman Plan.[74] Moreover, the volatile and changeable Crossman now denounced the whole conception of a neutral 'third force' Europe as signifying spiritual defeat and an acceptance of capitalism. The only viable policy, he maintained, was for the Labour Party to support the alliance with the USA, which was quite natural because America was progressive, while communism was repressive everywhere beyond Russia's western frontiers.[75] If this defection of the Keep Left group from the pro-European camp is to be understood, its original motivations in supporting the goal of a European federation must be recalled.

In 1947 the parliamentary left had ceased to believe in the good intentions of the Soviet Union, but still believed close alignment with the United States dangerous. Konni Zilliacus, an extreme left dissident in the Labour Party described their position in a crushing contemporary comment:

> Unhappily these alternatives [of American capitalism and Soviet communism] appear so distasteful and alarming to most of the Left in the Parliamentary Labour Party that they could not bring themselves to choose between them and clung desperately to a phantom third alternative, the illusion of a Western Union run by Social Democrats and independent of both the USA and the USSR – what I call the policy of a little grey home in the West for pinks scared white by the reds.[76]

This pinpoints a key element in the Keep Left group's motivation. Crossman and his associates had been neither Federalists, nor theoreticians who had concluded that a European dimension was necessary for the construction of socialism. Their impulse was the far more immediate one of stabilising West European parliamentary democracy and simultaneously avoiding subordination to the United States. These motivations were clearly evident early in January 1948 when the key Keep Left leaders signed a letter to Bevin, on behalf of the Labour Europe Group, urging him to take the lead in proposing an effective overall plan for Western Europe:

> We are convinced that the Communists will launch a new offensive in the not too distant future. Unless the French Republicans, and in particular the Socialists, can be given some backbone, this might well result in the installation of a Gaullist dictatorship which would obstruct Anglo-French collaboration and render almost impossible any socialist plan for Western European reconstruction. The situation in Italy is almost equally precarious.[77]

At this stage, the Keep Left group were thus supporting the SFIO in the attempt to construct a 'third force' in Western Europe and believed that a British diplomatic initiative would be of decisive importance in this respect. But it is not clear that they differed significantly from the leadership on the fundamental issues which would be involved in British participation in a supranational Europe. Thus, for example, the original *Keep Left* manifesto had made it clear that the group attached great importance to the Commonwealth, and this was emphasised in the letter to Bevin.[78] Moreover, as has been shown, the majority supported functional rather than federal integration. It is therefore probable that Bevin's proposal for Western Union – vague though it was – satisfied many of the original Keep Lefters. However, there was a further equally important factor which led to the erosion of support for 'Europe' amongst this sector of opinion: the change in the evaluation of the USA.

Although the original impetus for the Keep Left revolt had been distaste for the United States as well as the Soviet Union, once the Cold War polarisation increased, this attitude was abandoned with remarkable speed. On 17 June 1947 *Tribune's* view on Marshall Aid was revealed by the title of its editorial 'Dollars from Heaven'; by 17 October the formation of the Cominform was condemned in the most bitter terms, whilst support for the intentions of the American Government was offered; and by 30 January 1948 *Tribune* asserted that a decisive battle was being fought in the USA between the government and the isolationists and that the British left must align itself with the American labour movement behind the Truman administration. Leading spokesman of Keep Left had thus already shed much of the commitment to semi-neutralist mediation and were in the process of rallying to the American side in the Cold War polarity before the major international crises of 1948–49 greatly accentuated this trend.

'Third forcist' thinking had sprung from a desire to find a middle way between the USA and the USSR. The Prague coup and the Berlin blockade convinced the majority of Keep Lefters that no such possibility existed. Not only did they now argue that Soviet Communism was the greater enemy but also sought to legitimise the Anglo-American alliance as a contribution to world democracy and socialism. President Truman was seen as an incipient socialist, and an Atlantic military alliance, which had been denounced as a step towards World War Three in 1947, was now viewed as an essential means of curbing Soviet expansionism.[79] This reorientation inevitably also affected the attitudes of the former Keep Lefters to the question of West European integration.

Once Keep Left accepted the justification for alignment with the United States, the basis for its alternative foreign policy was removed. Its Europeanism had never been well defined or rooted in a clear framework of socialist theory. As it came to share the general perceptions of the leadership and Western Europe appeared to be stabilised by American military and economic power, there remained no particular reason for the goal of integration to be supported.

It thus follows that Ian Mikardo, who was the only prominent member of Keep Left to reject the American alignment and NATO, was also the only one to retain his full support for West European integration as the mainstay in a 'third force' policy, and, late in 1950 he was still distributing propaganda on behalf of the Council of Europe.[80] The rest accepted Foot's tortuous argument that, in the present circumstances, the 'third force' lay in understanding the totality of the conflict with Soviet ideology, and in maintaining the closest possible ties with the American labour movement.[81]

Once the Keep Lefters had regained their faith in the USA, their support for 'Europe' thus disappeared. But without their support, the other dissident Labour Europeans could make no impact at all. Their voice was drowned in the general consensus in favour of Atlanticism and the Commonwealth.

Labour and 'Europe' in the Early Post-War Period: Comparisons with the French Left

The early post-war period was of crucial importance in the formation of attitudes towards West European integration: how then can the outlook of the British labour movement be compared with that in France?

It is first necessary to make the obvious, but important, point that the organisational, institutional and ideological characteristics of the left in each country were quite distinct. In France the division of the left was not only institutionalised, but was heightened by the domestic and international conflicts of the period, particularly after 1947. Thereafter, the SFIO was acting as a junior partner in a centrist coalition while the PCF was not only operating outside the governmental framework, but defined its policy primarily in accordance with the needs of the Soviet Union, and a particular interpretation of Marxism. Nor was either party seriously constrained by the organised working classes in a trade union movement. In Britain, by contrast, the Labour Party dominated the left, held governmental office alone, was closely associated with the trade union movement, and was working within a framework of consensus politics. Labour cannot, therefore, be regarded as the exact equivalent of either the SFIO or the PCF. However, it is clear that, in the period in question (and particularly after 1947) its function within the political and economic system was far closer to that of the former than the latter: that is, the Labour Government, with the support or acquiescence of the party, was attempting to work the existing system (though with important reforms) rather than to effect a fundamental transformation in its direction and priorities.

It appears paradoxical to argue against the primary comparison being made with the PCF because, on the specific question of West European integration, there appeared to be important elements of similarity between the positions of the Labour Party and the French Communists. This was the case not only in the obvious sense that both opposed the process of integration but, more particularly in their professed fears about the nature of the economic system that would be established in any West European federation, and in their continuing confidence about the nation-state as a framework for the construction of socialism. Such similarities were to develop further in later years, particularly in the 1970s, when the Labour Party's view of the weakness of the British economy, and its vulnerability to foreign competition in an open market, resembled the fears expressed by the PCF about the French economy in the immediate post-war era. However, the resemblances between the reasons for PCF and Labour Party opposition to integration in the period up to 1951 were more apparent than real. The primary determinant of the attitude of the French Communists was the security of the Soviet Union, while the major consideration of the Labour Party (at leadership level, at least) was the wish to continue the world role.

If the Labour Party is compared with the SFIO, it is evident that the contrasting positions of France and Britain largely account for the differences in the outlook of their leaders on West European integration, for their general perspectives were similar. By the late 1940s both had thus come to accept the American Cold War perspective and sought the strengthening of Western Europe in alliance with the USA; and both wished to combine their notions of domestic social and economic reform with the defence of international policies, which were supported by non-socialist forces, and which primarily favoured the established interests in each state. However, while the French saw economic advantages in controlling, and sharing in, West Germany's potential wealth, and political benefits in leading an integrated West European bloc, the British wished to maintain control of their own resources, and to continue the pursuit of a world-wide role, without experiencing new constraints through membership of a new European Community. Instead of considering *modernisation*, as did the SFIO and much of the French elite in a state which was still relatively weak, the Labour leadership favoured *retention* of Britain's existing power base; and whereas the SFIO had lost confidence in the nation-state as a vehicle for moderate reform, the Labour leadership assumed its continuation as the primary framework for political and economic development.

Because so much in the policies of the leadership in each country accorded with those favoured by non-socialist forces, their socialistic justifications were, in a sense, rationalisations for strategies supported by pro-capitalist interests. Yet this perspective on the problem of policy-making by reforming socialist parties, fails to do justice to the realm of consciousness at both leadership and rank-and-file levels. The SFIO believed that a quasi-federalist Europe could eventually be transformed by socialists, even if capitalist forces also favoured the creation of an integrated Western Europe. Similarly, Labour's opposition to a 'Europe' which would be dominated by capitalism appeared to make perfect sense even if the British Establishment was also against it. If in France the majority of the SFIO were probably sincere in perceiving integration as a step towards socialism, the majority of the Labour Party were doubtless equally genuine in the belief that they were defending British democratic socialism against continental reactionaries. However, in both countries such convictions also served intangible but important political functions.

The SFIO's support for integration was strengthened by the fact that it projected its aspirations onto a higher, and idealised, European plane because of its failure to achieve them in the domestic sphere. In this way, the discouraging domestic circumstances became easier to tolerate. In Labour's case, the idealisation worked in the opposite direction: that is, in the belief that there was something special about British democratic socialism which would be threatened by involvement in a capitalist supranational Europe, when, in reality, the government's reforming achievements had effectively come to an end by 1948 when the impetus for integration developed. By the time the Labour Government left office, 'Europe' had not yet become a salient issue amongst the mass movement or the electorate, but the impulses behind the hostile stance were so deep-seated that the Labour leadership (like the *Parti communiste française*) would find it exceedingly difficult to relinquish the policy when material circumstances changed. In this sense the impact of the early post-war period was to reverberate throughout the subsequent decades.

Notes

1 For a recent study of the post-war Labour Government, see R. Eatwell, *The 1945–51*

Labour Government (Batsford, 1979). Other useful works which cover the period and deal more generally with the British labour movement are: D. Coates, *The Labour Party and the Struggle for Socialism* (Cambridge University Press, 1975); B. Donoghue and G. Jones. *Herbert Morrison* (Weidenfeld, 1973); M. Foot, *Aneurin Bevan*, vol.II (Paladin, 1975); D. Howell, *British Social Democracy* (Croom Helm, 1976); M. Jenkins, *Bevanism* (Spokesman, 1979); R. Miliband, *Parliamentary Socialism* (Merlin, 1961). For a pro-communist view, see D. Pritt. *The Labour Government, 1945–51* (Lawrence and Wishart, 1963).

2 The following are useful sources on the policy of the post-war Labour Government: A. Shlaim, *Britain and the Origins of European Unity* (University of Reading, 1978); H. Dalton, *Memoirs 1945–60, High Tide and After* (Frederick Muller, 1962); F.S. Northedge, *British Foreign Policy, 1945–61* (Allen & Unwin, 1962); E. Barker, *Britain in a Divided Europe, 1945–70* (Weidenfeld, 1971); R.B. Manderson-Jones, *The Special Relationship: Anglo-American Relations and West European Unity, 1947–56* (Weidenfeld, 1972); J. Frankel, *British Foreign Policy, 1945–73* (Oxford University Press 1975); M. Gordon, *Conflict and Consensus in Labour's Foreign Policy, 1914–65* (Stanford University, 1969); C.R. Rose, 'The Relation of Socialist Principles to British Labour Foreign Policy, 1945–51' (unpublished D. Phil. thesis, Oxford University 1959); J. Grantham, 'The Labour Party and European Unity, 1939–51' (unpublished Phd thesis, Cambridge University, 1977); G. Warner, 'The Reconstruction and Defence of Western Europe after 1945', in N. Waites (ed.) *Troubled Neighbours: Anglo-French Relations in the Twentieth Century* (Weidenfeld, 1971).

3 'European Co-Operation within the framework of the Recovery Programme', The Labour Party, 24 Feb. 1948, memorandum submitted to the conference of socialist parties, Selsdon, 21–22 March 1948 (*Britain and Europe Since 1945*, Harvester Primary Social Sources, Harvester Press, 1973 hereafter, Harvester Microfilm)).

4 The reorientation of German policy is outlined in D.C. Watt, *Britain Looks to Germany* (Wolff, 1965). In March 1950 the government had declared its opposition to German rearmament and in September Bevin had repeated this position when arriving in New York for negotiations, but had recanted while there, leading Attlee to announce support for the principle, under various conditions (see chapter 5) in February 1951. On 14 September 1951, Morrison, as Foreign Secretary, made a joint statement with Acheson and Schuman which was very sympathetic to the European Defence Community, towards which the Labour leadership had previously been hostile. Warner, 'Reconstruction and Defence of Western Europe', pp. 269–80.

5 See U. Sahm, 'Britain and Europe, 1950' and the Comment by K. Younger, in *International Affairs*, vol. 43, no. 1, January 1967.

6 For an interesting discussion of the long-term relative decline, see A. Gamble, *Britain in Decline* (Macmillan, 1981). Shlaim summarises the immediate material losses resulting from the war as follows: 'According to official estimates about one quarter (£7,300 million) of Britain's pre-war national wealth had been lost in fighting the war. The main factors were physical destruction (£1,500 million); shipping losses (£700 million); internal disinvestment (£900 million); and external disinvestment (£4,200 million). The liquidation of a sizeable proportion of Britain's overseas investments in order to defray the cost of the war; the accumulation of a vast national debt of over £3,000 million and the running down of gold and dollar reserves helped to shift Britain from being the world's greatest creditor to the world's greatest debtor. Her exports stood at 42% of the 1938 level and to achieve solvency Britain was faced with the task of raising her exports to 175% of the pre-war total ... at a time when certain sectors of British industry were in a rundown condition and many of Britain's traditional markets were disrupted and impoverished' (*Britain and Origins of European Unity*, p. 98). The problems were then greatly exacerbated by the abrupt cancellation of lend-lease in August 1945.

7 House of Commons Debates, vol. 437, col. 1965, 16 May 1947, quoted in Shlaim,

Britain and Origins of European Unity, p. 101.

8 Dalton to Bevin, 18 August 1950, quoted in Warner, 'Reconstruction and Defence of Western Europe', p. 280

9 Dalton to a New Zealand journalist, 3 July 1950, Dalton Papers, British Library of Political and Economic Science, Part II, C file 9/9.

10 Bevin's speech to the Commons, 22 October 1946, published by the Labour Party as *Britain's Foreign Policy* (1946); and Dalton's speech at the Mansion House, 16 October 1946 in *High Tide and After*, p. 166. However, it may be that Bevin was more inclined to favour a reorientation of Germany policy: his speech at the Labour Party Conference on 12 June 1946 had been implicitly more anti-Soviet and less anti-German than his Commons speech and Bill Jones (citing R. Stephens, 'What Stalin told Ernest Bevin', *The Observer*, 2 Jan. 1977) claims that on 7 May 1946 Dalton and Bevan resisted Bevin's assessment in Cabinet that the 'danger of Russia has become certainly as great as, and possibly even greater than, that of a revived Germany' (*The Russia Complex* (Manchester University Press, 1977), p. 131). Considerable controversy remains as to the timing of Bevin's adoption of a Cold War strategy. For example, Shlaim and Jones suggest that his anti-communism became dominant almost as soon as the war ended and that, thereafter, his professions of friendship for the Soviet Union were largely propagandist, while Rothwell seeks to refute this view, arguing that he only accepted the notion of an anti-Soviet alignment late in 1947 (V. Rothwell, *Britain and the Cold War, 1941–47* (Cape, 1982)).

11 As late as 24 September 1947 the NEC, at the government's request, declared that 'it strongly supported the government in its view that in no circumstances should German heavy industry in the British zone be returned to private ownership in any form' (NEC Minutes, Labour Party Library).

12 For some members of the government there was a genuine belief in a multiracial Commonwealth, particularly after the granting of independence to India. Others retained imperialist attitudes and a willingness to continue the economic exploitation of Third World countries. For a full discussion, see P.S. Gupta, *Imperialism and the British Labour Movement, 1914–64* (Macmillan, 1975).

13 For an informative and interesting analysis of the wartime discussions, see Shlaim, *Britain and Origins of European Unity*, pp. 20–85. For a sympathetic treatment of Churchill's ideas, see also N. Forman, 'The European Movement in Britain, 1945–54' (unpublished Phd thesis, Sussex University, 1973), especially pp. 6–31.

14 N. Diamond, 'Labour and the International Post-War Settlement' (unpublished M. Phil. thesis, Leeds University, 1974), pp. 114–15.

15 Minute by Dalton, 10 Jan. 1942, reproduced as Appendix 2 in ibid.

16 Rothwell, *Britain and the Cold War*, ch. 8, provides evidence of Bevin's aspirations.

17 Shlaim, *Britain and Origins of European Unity*, pp. 134–42. Both Rothwell and Manderson-Jones present further evidence compatible with this interpretation and, as this chapter will demonstrate, statements by other Labour leaders, and internal party memoranda, show that Bevin was not alone in his 'vision'.

18 Speech of 7 April 1945, quoted in ibid., p. 96.

19 House of Commons Debates, vol. 430, col. 581, 18 November 1946. Attlee was answering the critics of the government, led by Richard Crossman, whose ideas are discussed later in the chapter.

20 *Cards on the Table: An Interpretation of Labour's Foreign Policy* (The Labour Party, 1947).

21 House of Commons, 22 January 1948, reproduced in memorandum presented to Selsdon Conference.

22 The NEC officially discouraged association with Churchill's committee in January 1947 (Labour Party Conference Report (hereafter, LPCR) 1947, p. 19) and this was reaffirmed the following year. It also exerted pressure on Labour MPs who sympathised with the aim of a united Europe to dissociate themselves from

Churchill, and persisted in regarding the European Movement as reactionary and in sympathy with the Conservative Party.

23 Memorandum to Selsdon Conference.

24 'Notes on European Unity', International Department memorandum for NEC meeting of 20 April 1948, NEC Minutes.

25 Morgan Phillips, the Labour Party Secretary, reported that delegates had supported the NEC view with regard to the United Europe Committee and had registered their own decisions not to have official association with the Hague Congress, NEC Minutes, 23 March 1948.

26 LPCR 1948, pp. 177–79.

27 For two bitter reports on the proceedings, see Healey, 'Report on the Consultative Assembly of the Council of Europe, 10–23 August 1949' for the International Sub-Committee of the NEC, and Dalton to Attlee, 10 September 1949, Dalton Papers, Part II, C file 9/7.

28 See references in previous note, also Dalton, *High Tide and After*, p. 316 and 'Notes for the Labour Party on the Council of Europe', 12 Aug. 1949, Dalton Papers, Part II, C file 9/7.

29 Denis Healey, 'The Labour Party and European Unity', October 1949, for consideration by the International Sub-Committee and NEC, NEC Minutes, 26 Oct. 1949.

30 'Paper transmitted to Rapporteur of the General Affairs Committee of the Consultative Assembly by some British Members of the Consultative Assembly' (undated), autumn 1949, R.W.G. Mackay Papers, file 22/2. British Library of Political and Economic Science.

31 The memorandum is in Dalton Papers, Part II, C file 9/9, and Dalton expressed his agreement with it.

32 Davies also expressed a real fear, but one which the government would not avow in public: 'A further and perhaps less obvious danger is that if there is any surrender of sovereignty to Europe an avenue of pressure through which the United States could influence Britain, through Europe, to accept its policies is thereby created. The Labour Party in particular is fearful of encroachment upon Britain's independence by the economic and financial power of the United States. All accept the necessity to co-operate with them, but do not wish to place themselves in a position to be dominated. If Britain had to accept the majority decisions made in the Council of Europe all the United States need do to impose its will on Britain would be to influence a majority of the European States there represented '

33 Healey to Dalton, 3 May 1950, Dalton Papers, Part II, C file 9/14.

34 *European Unity*, The Labour Party, May 1950—(Harvester Microfilm). The publication of this pamphlet provoked a major reaction both at home and abroad. In France, as has been seen, it led André Philip to write a reply ('Le Socialisme et l'unité européenne: résponse à l'éxecutif du Labour Party'), while the American commissioner for Marshall Aid was reported to have denounced it as a deplorable example of isolationism, and to have threatened the withdrawal of American aid. Rumours of a Cabinet split between Attlee and Dalton were circulated in the British press. (For press cuttings on the reactions see Dalton Papers, Part II, C file 9/15.) The pamphlet said nothing new, but the timing and tone were thought to have been designed to sabotage the Schuman proposal.

35 *European Unity*, p. 9.

36 Dalton's speech is in *Consultative Assembly Reports* (Council of Europe, 1950), pp. 172–82, and he summarises it in *High Tide and After*, p. 329. Dalton had privately repeated in May his suggestion to Mollet that the Atlantic Pact should form the basis for any federal organisation (Dalton Papers Part II, C file 9/8) and again in August, when persuading Mollet not to resign as *rapporteur* of the General Affairs Committee. In this context, he wrote: 'I am confident that you will do nothing in these difficult days, when all our hopes are threatened by the Communist barbarians, to help those [i.e. the British Conservatives] who ... desire to make impossible the full achievement of those social ideas for which both you and I stand' (Dalton Papers, 21 August 1950 Part II, C file 9/14.) Although Mollet eventually resigned, Dalton had attempted to secure some concessions from the British Government to prevent this occurrence because it would exacerbate the difficulties in Labour's position and the strains in Labour Party/SFIO relations (see Dalton to Bevin, 21 Aug. 1950, and Dalton to Attlee, 1 Sept. 1950, in Dalton Papers Part II, C file 9/9.) In his letter to Bevin, he also made the point that 'whatever may be said of Mollet, he is, anyhow better than André Philip'.

37 Grantham, 'The Labour Party and European Unity', p. 316.

38 Dalton Papers, 3 July 1950, Part II, C file 9/9.

39 Notes for speech at Strasbourg, Dalton Papers Part II C file 9/8.

40 For the leadership's attitude to the EDC, see chapter 5.

41 For an interesting discussion of the effects of American pressure on Labour's policy, see T. Brett, S. Gilliat, and A. Pople, 'Planned Trade, Labour Party Policy and US Intervention: The Successes and Failures of Post-War Reconstruction', *History Workshop Journal* no. 13, spring 1982. For Labour Party evaluations of the USA, see D. Watt, 'American Aid to Britain and the Problem of Socialism, 1945–51', in *Personalities and Politics* (Longmans, 1965).

42 At the end of 1946 membership stood at 42,123 and by June 1947 had declined to 38,579. However, in May 1948 it had risen to 43,000 before declining steadily until the end of 1952, when it was less than 36,000. These figures are given in H. Pelling, *The British Communist Party* (Adam and Charles Black, 1975).

43 The Communist view, and contemporary statements can be found in Pritt, *The Labour Government* and J. Mahon, *Harry Pollitt* (Lawrence & Wishart, 1976). The party's interpretation of 'European Unity' during the war is discussed briefly in M. Newman, 'British Socialists and the Question of European Unity', *European Studies Review*, vol. 10, no. 1, January 1980. Relevant post-war statements can be found in *Labour Monthly*, Nov. 1945, June 1946, July 1947, Oct. 1947, Sept. 1948, May 1949, June 1950 and Feb. 1951. (Although Konni Zilliacus was accused of giving a pro-communist view and was expelled from the Labour Party in 1949, his viewpoint was quite different, for he favoured the economic and political unification of Europe so long as it was based on communist forces in Eastern Europe and was formed with the agreement of the Soviet Union. See, for example, K. Zilliacus, *I Choose Peace* (Penguin, 1949), pp. 445-57.)

44 *Keep Left*, New Statesman pamphlet, 1947. The signatories were Richard Crossman, Michael Foot, Ian Mikardo, Geoffrey Bing, Donald Bruce, Harold Davies, Leslie Hale, Fred Lee, Benn Levy, R.W.G. Mackay, J.P.W. Mallalieu, E.R. Millington, Stephen Swingler, George Wigg and Woodrow Wyatt.

45 House of Commons Debates, vol. 430, cols. 526–30, 18 Nov. 1946.

46 See Newman, 'British Socialists and the Question of European Unity'.

47 For further discussion of the Keep Left rebellion, see Gordon, *Conflict and Consensus*, esp. pp. 156–71 and 183–90.

48 *Keep Left*, p. 38.

49 Apart from Mackay, who was completely consistent in his support for it, there were very few British socialists who were committed to federalism in a strict sense. In March 1945, John Hynd had attended a meeting organised by Italian federalists and he was to join Mackay as a federalist in the Labour Europe Committee, as was Leslie Hale. However, while others, including Christopher Shawcross and Sidney Silverman, sometimes supported federalism, they did not do so consistently.

50 He polled 14,000 at Llandaff and Barry (and the fact that he had stood against the Labour Party was to cause him some difficulty when he sought endorsement from the NEC in 1945). For an evaluation of Federal Union, see R. Wilford, 'The

Federal Union Campaign', *European Studies Review*, vol. 10, no. 1, January 1980.

51 He had outlined his ideas in *Federal Europe* (Michael Joseph, 1940). Forman argues that Mackay influenced Federal Union's priorities towards Europe ('The European Movement in Britain', pp. 76–7.)

52 For Mackay's views at this time, see *Heads in the Sand: A Criticism of the Official Labour Party Attitude to Unity* (Gollancz, 1950); *Britain in Wonderland* (Gollancz, 1948); and *Western Union in Crisis* (Blackwell, 1949). See also, 'Let the Argument Proceed: A Reply by Labour Members of Federal Union to the Policy Statement "European Unity" Issued by the NEC of the Labour Party', 1950 (Harvester Microfilm).

53 Frank Ridley in *The New Leader*, 19 June 1943. For a full statement of the party's attitude, see F. Ridley and B. Edwards, *The United Socialist States of Europe* (International Labour Party, 1944). See also Newman, 'British Socialists and the Question of European Unity'.

54 Information given by Bob Edwards in interview, 26 June 1980. (Edwards joined the Labour Party in 1948.)

55 For details of the way in which such reconciliation was sought, see Mackay Papers, especially letter and memorandum by Jacques Robin, 14 Feb. 1948, file 13/4; letter from Pivert to Edwards, Brockway and McNair, 12 Feb. 1948, file 14/3.

56 See the correspondence between members of the committee and the Labour Europe Group in Mackay Papers, particularly file 14/3, correspondence between McNair and Shawcross, Dec. 1947–January 1948.

57 Shawcross to Mackay, 12 December 1947, Mackay Papers, file 8/3.

58 Brockway to Shawcross, 16 January 1948, Mackay Papers, file 13/4.

59 For evidence of the way in which left-wing socialist analysis on some crucial aspects of West European integration could coexist with silence on others, see the papers for the meeting of the British centre of the Socialist Movement for a United States of Europe, 22–23 Oct. 1949, Mackay Papers, file 14/1. In fact many of the prime movers of the committee, including Edwards, opposed NATO, but this gave rise to no crisis in the European Movement since this body excluded defence from its terms of reference.

60 Warbey seemed so negative about the possibilities of European unification that it might have been suspected that his intention was to disrupt the group. However, this is highly unlikely as his commitment was long standing. See, for example, Warbey, 'Monopoly Nationalism and World Peace', *Tribune*, 27 October 1944.

61 Comments by Warbey on first draft statement of Labour Europe group's policy, Minutes of Meeting of 10 February 1948, Mackay Papers, file 13/4.

62 Warbey had prepared a paper with Leah Manning for this meeting entitled 'Britain and Europe', but it was decisively rejected, with only the two authors voting against West German inclusion in any unit that was eventually created (Mackay Papers, file 9/1). Voting numbers are marked on a copy of a memorandum on the 'crucial questions for decision', prepared by Mackay (file 9/1) and a record of the meeting of the 2 March is in file 8/3.

63 LPCR 1948, pp. 174–5.

64 Sidney Silverman, who also broke with Mackay, became Secretary of the new group, which claimed 35 members. For statements of its ideas, see 'Letter to Labour Party members of the Strasbourg Assembly from the Parliamentary Socialist Europe Group', 28 July 1949, Mackay Papers, file 8/1; and its submission to the General Purposes Committee of the Strasbourg Assembly, 23 January 1950, Mackay Papers, file 22/2. See also the group's, 'A Socialist Plan for European Union', Appendix 3 in Mackay, *Western Union in Crisis*.

65 Crawley's paper was entitled 'Western Union: The Functional Approach' and its suggestions were supported by 12 to 6.

66 They had originally invited Mackay, Hynd, Shawcross, Crossman and Mikardo,

Minutes of Labour Europe Group Meeting, 3 Feb. 1948, Mackay Papers, file 8/3.

67 The delegation had consisted of Mackay, Shawcross, Hynd and Hale. For the French account of the visit to Paris of 27–29 Feb. 1948, see Minutes of Labour Europe Group Meeting, 2 March 1948, Mackay Papers, file 8/3.

68 For the correspondence between Hale and Phillips, see Mackay Papers, file 9/1.

69 LPCR 1948, pp. 174–7.

70 See Mackay's correspondence with Dalton, Morrison and Noel-Baker in late 1949 and early 1950 in which he tried to suggest compromises between the federalist position and that of the leadership (Mackay Papers, files 13/7B and 8/1). In his memoirs, Dalton was complimentary about Mackay (*High Tide and After*, p. 326) but in reality he undoubtedly found him irritating. When making his suggestions for the composition of the Labour delegation to Strasbourg in August 1951 he said that Mackay could not be left out since this would be viewed as victimisation, but that he must remain isolated (Dalton Papers Part II, C file 9/23.)

71 See, for example, Crossman, *The Listener*, 13 January 1949, quoted in Mackay *Western Union in Crisis*, p. 66; Mackay also attempted to enlist Crossman's support against Dalton and the leadership (Mackay to Crossman, 10 September 1949, Mackay Papers, file 8/1).

72 *Tribune*, 25 November 1949 (also quoted in Gordon, *Conflict and Consensus*, pp. 189–90).

73 *Keeping Left*, New Statesman pamphlet, January 1950. The signatories were Sir Richard Acland, Donald Bruce, Barbara Castle, Richard Crossman, Harold Davies, Leslie Hale, Tom Horrabin, Marcus Lipton, Ian Mikardo, Stephen Swingler, George Wigg and Tom Williams.

74 *Tribune* fully supported the NEC statement (Editorial, 23 June 1950) and the *New Stateman* also opposed the Schuman Plan, although it argued that it was not necessary to be so 'Palmerstonian' about it (17 June 1950).

75 Richard Crossman and Kenneth Younger, *Socialist Foreign Policy* (Fabian Tract 287, 1951).

76 K. Zilliacus, *Why I Was Expelled* (Collets, August 1949).

77 Letter to Bevin, 9 January 1948, signed by Richard Acland, S.S. Awberry, D. Bruce, Aidan Crawley, Richard Crossman, Michael Foot, M. Hewitson, John Hynd, Fred Lee, Benn Levy, R.W.G. Mackay, Ian Mikardo, W.T. Proctor, Christopher Shawcross, T.C. Skeffington-Lodge, A. Ungoed-Thomas and Leah Manning. Mackay Papers, file 8/3. See also the group's letter to Emmanuel Shinwell, Mackay Papers, file 8/3.

78 *Keep left* had believed in the continuation of imperial preference (as a bargaining counter in dealings with the USA) and had argued: 'if the dependencies of Western Europe and the Dominions are taken as a whole they would form the largest production and trading unit in the world which, once it is treated as a unit, will have a much larger exportable surplus. Whilst Empire unity is essential to our survival, we believe that unless Britain does throw in her lot with Western Europe and thus make full use of the larger economic area thus created, her inevitable decline will itself imperil her position as centre of the British Commonwealth.'

79 See, for example, *Tribune*, 25 March 1949.

80 Ian Mikardo 'Why I Disagree', *Tribune*, 20 May 1949 and 'The European Revolution' (undated, late 1950), Mackay Papers, file 7/2.

81 *Tribune*, 20 May 1949.

5

From 'Splendid Isolation' to de Gaulle's Veto, 1951–63

The Conservative Government and West European Integration

In January 1952, the new Foreign Secretary, Sir Anthony Eden, made the following plea to an American audience at the University of Columbia:

> The American and British peoples should each understand the strong points in the other's national character. If you drive a nation to adopt procedures which run counter to its instincts, you weaken and may destroy the motive force of its action. This is something you would not wish to do ... to an ally on whose effective co-operation we depend. You will realise that I am speaking of the frequent suggestions that the United Kingdom should join a federation on the continent of Europe ... We know that if we were to attempt it we should relax the springs of our action in the Western Democratic cause and in the Atlantic association which is the expression of that cause.[1]

In July 1961, during the third period of office of the Conservative Government, and with strong American encouragement, Britain finally applied to join the European Community.[2] The fundamental causes of this major change in policy were twofold: first, Britain's failure, during the intervening decade, to impede the process of close political and economic integration which appeared to be strengthening Britain's continental competitors; secondly, and closely connected, her own relative decline in economic and political power.

Even though the 'European' policy of the Conservative Government during the 1950s is explicable in terms of the interests and world outlook examined in chapter 4, in retrospect it appears to have been based on a prolonged series of miscalculations. In 1952 Britain sought to limit the importance of the Six with a plan to subsume the Coal and Steel Community, and any others that might

156

be created, under the Council of Europe which would act as an umbrella organisation. In this way Britain could secure influence over the Six without participating in any supranational institutions. The proposal was hardly considered by the embryonic European Community. At the end of 1954, the British Government believed that the abandonment of the European Defence Community marked the end of the movement towards close integration and, for this reason, it underestimated the importance of the Messina Conference the next year. On the assumption that nothing significant could be established without British participation, the Board of Trade official who represented the government was therefore recalled when discussions focused on the establishment of a customs union, with political direction, rather than a free-trade area. When this misinterpretation of the situation became apparent with the subsequent establishment of the EEC, the Conservative administration attempted to persuade and cajole the Six into compromise. The final stage in this strategy was the creation of the European Free Trade Association (EFTA), with Sweden, Denmark, Norway, Austria, Switzerland and Portugal, in the hope that this would prove an effective bargaining counter. However, by the time EFTA became operational in 1960 it was already clear that it could not serve this purpose, and a high-powered interdepartmental committee recommended a British application to the EEC.[3] The decision had not yet been made but, when it subsequently appeared that association agreements with the Community were impractical and would not, in any case, bring about the political influence which Britain was seeking, the Cabinet 'Europeans' provided the impetus which led to the application.

If Harold Macmillan's attempt to enter the European Community followed a decade of failures in Britain's relations with the Six, it also resulted from still more fundamental problems associated with the continuing relative decline in British power. Until 1955 the Conservative Government attempted to pursue a foreign policy which fully reflected the traditional preoccupations with the Commonwealth and world roles. Indeed in that year the Defence White Paper indicated an effort to keep pace with the superpowers by developing the vastly expensive H-bomb. However, in November 1956 the abortive Suez invasion, and the clear lesson that Britain was unable to exercise a military adventure against the wishes of the Americans, began a process in which some of the illusions of grandeur were stripped away.

Suez indicated that the new Commonwealth would not offer loyal support to the 'mother country' in all situations, and the granting of independence to Black African states (beginning with Ghana in 1957) increased the pressures on the Conservatives, particularly in regard to their friendly relations with South Africa. By 1960 it was thus becoming clear that, rather than simply acting as a powerbase for Britain, the Commonwealth also contained a potential for conflict around the north/south axis. It was also evident that Commonwealth trade and investment were no longer directed to British needs to the extent that had been the case in the imperial past, and that a trend decline in its importance was underway.[4] Meanwhile, Britain was also experiencing difficulties in other spheres. The United States clearly attached diminishing importance to the 'special relationship' while Britain remained outside the Community, and supported the Six rather than the British in the various trade negotiations after 1956. Macmillan's attempt to play an independent role by sponsoring East–West talks was torpedoed by both superpowers in the abortive Paris Conference of May 1960, and the government was forced to abandon its independent nuclear weapon delivery system in the same year.[5] Finally, the severe structural problems in the British economy were also becoming manifest – with the introduction of deflationary measures in 1960 and a weakening of sterling in the next year – while the countries of the European Community remained in a phase of fast economic growth.

In essence the Conservative Government's application to join the EEC in July 1961 thus stemmed from a loss of confidence in Britain's ability to remain a major power outside it. The hope was that membership of the Community would enhance her political influence, by bringing about the leadership of Western Europe, and modernise the economy through tariff-free access to European markets, and by the effects of sharper competition at home. In other words, the government, supported in general by the political and economic elite, had made what it considered to be a pragmatic decision, necessitated by Britain's changed situation.

In the early post-war period the labour movement had rejected such involvement in 'Europe' with a combination of national and socialistic arguments. Would it now make the same pragmatic adjustment as the Conservative Government and, if not, what would be the basis of its objections?

The Labour Party and 'Europe', 1951–60

The decade which began in autumn 1951 was a traumatic one for the Labour Party.[6] Almost immediately after the loss of the election the so-called Bevanite movement developed in opposition to the leadership, both in Parliament and as an extra-parliamentary movement; and a major crisis was only narrowly averted when the leadership drew back from expelling Aneurin Bevan from the party in 1955. During the next two years a reconciliation took place, and this was consecrated with the entry of Bevan into Hugh Gaitskell's Shadow Cabinet as Shadow Foreign Minister in 1957. However, as Labour lost its third successive General Election in October 1959 internal conflict erupted once again. Gaitskell and the revisionist right now sought to abandon the Labour Party's socialist commitment by jettisoning nationalisation as a goal, and converting the party into an organisation explicitly pledged to moderate reform within capitalism. This rejection of party tradition proved too much for the rank and file; the attempt was defeated and a new compromise position defined. However, in 1960 the left captured the initiative by securing a conference majority – against the vehemently expressed wishes of the parliamentary leadership – for a commitment by a Labour government for the unilateral renunciation of nuclear weapons. This decision was overturned at the next conference, but considerable bitterness remained and further battles appeared probable.

Foreign and defence policy had been amongst the most divisive questions within the party during its decade of internal conflict. However, this hardly affected the specific issue of West European integration until it became salient in 1961. It is therefore possible briefly to consider Labour's policy during this decade by concentrating on the leadership.

Throughout the 1950s the Labour leadership retained the same general policy towards West European integration which it had followed when in government. In 1952 it thus supported Eden's attempt to diminish the importance of the emergent supranational unit by calling for a reorganised Council of Europe,[7] and also the government's policy of seeking association with the Coal and Steel Community and any other such organisations that might be formed. In addition it shared – indeed probably surpassed – the government's deep scepticism about the possibility of the Six achieving any meaningful integration without British participation and its opposition to all vestiges of supranationalism or quasi-federalism. Two episodes during the first half of the decade are worth mentioning since they epitomise the attitudes of the leadership: the policy towards the EDC, and a contemplated Labour initiative after its failure.

Whilst in office, the leadership had been highly sceptical of the proposal for a defence community, but had accepted the demand for a rearmed West Germany within the Western bloc, and the EDC as the most probable means of securing the requisite French support. Even when in office it had shared some of the anxieties of the French, and of its own rank and file, about the dangers of a rearmed Germany and, for this reason, Attlee had announced four conditions for British acceptance of it in February 1951.[9] Once the party went into opposition a major internal dispute erupted over the question (see below) and some Labour leaders, notably Hugh Dalton, were clearly reluctant to accept German rearmament on any terms.[10] The leadership therefore responded enthusiastically to Churchill's proposal for a summit conference, and the postponement of final decisions on the German question during the period of the abatement of tension following Stalin's death.[11] Yet there was never any real doubt that the Labour front bench would support the military integration of West Germany into the Western bloc rather than press an alternative policy against the wishes of the USA and the government and, in a situation of near total party division, it managed to secure the narrowest of majorities for this policy in 1954.[12] It is, however, highly significant that it took this course, not because of any deep sympathy for the West German case, still less because it wished in any way to further the cause of political integration, but because of its fervent desire to maintain a powerful American military involvement in West European defence.[13] Indeed in May 1953 the International Department had actually considered a course which would have taken Britain further into defence integration than Eden's subsequent Western European Union (WEU) formula which brought West Germany into NATO.[14] On the dual premise that the EDC would probably collapse but that the remaining problem was 'to provide for a German defence contribution which shall not constitute an independent army, and ensure continued American commitment', it had thus suggested full British participation in a revamped EDC. However, this proposal for extensive defence integration was to be dependent on the acceptance of two significant decisions:

(1) Although the armed forces would have to be integrated, *the control of these forces would have to be intergovernmental.*
(2) *There would have to be the assurance of a long-term American commitment to Europe.* The new European Defence Organisation would be related to NATO in much the same way as proposed for the EDC.[15]

In other words both the Atlanticist and intergovernmental perspectives remained paramount when the prospect of a crisis within the Western bloc led to consideration of more far-reaching participation in an integrated structure in Western Europe.

The second episode occurred when the Labour leadership, like the majority of observers, believed that the impulse towards supranational integration had been destroyed by the abortive EDC project.

In these circumstances it seriously considered making a proposal (though in opposition) for a diluted form of integration through a new extension of intergovernmental co-operation. Noting that the WEU eliminated the supranational aspects of the EDC, the party thus urged its delegates in Strasbourg to take the opportunity to urge that the Council of Europe (where the Six were in a minority) should resume its original, designated role as the umbrella organisation for the other institutions for West European unification.[16] This indicated a continued belief in a form of West European co-operation which would eliminate the threat of supranationalism.

It is thus evident that leadership policy towards integration underwent no fundamental change during its first period in opposition. The objections to federalism were restated (rather than reexamined) and the NATO/US link was seen as surpassing by far the importance of West European unification *per se*. During the second half of the decade, when the Six regained the initiative with their plans for economic integration, Labour's attitudes followed a similar trajectory to those of the government, to which it offered a policy of critical support. Three points about Labour's policy between 1956 and 1960 are noteworthy.

In the first place, Labour spokesmen continued, as they had in government, to place great emphasis on the Commonwealth. Thus for example, in the November 1956 debate on the government's proposal for a free trade area in industrial products, Harold Wilson claimed that Labour was now the party of the Commonweath.[17] Three years later in the debate on EFTA he took precisely the same line, urging the government not to give all their thoughts to Europe but also to consider a free trade area for the Commonwealth which, he claimed, would strengthen the British position.[18]

Secondly, the Labour leadership, without dissenting from government policy, frequently advocated measures of a radical Keynesian type which, it argued, should be incorporated into any new trading blocs that were created. Throughout these years Labour therefore stressed the need for safeguards on such matters as the maintenance of living standards, freedom for a future Labour government to pursue policies of economic planning, and to defend the balance of payments by import restrictions and foreign exchange controls.[19] In the words of Harold Wilson:

> Where there is a difference between the parties it is on such matters as expansion, full employment, freer credits, on harmonising social policies and on positive and specific action to stimulate industrial development in the underdeveloped parts of Europe in contrast with the more liberal, simple removal of such impediments to trade as quotas and tariffs.[20]

Whilst generally supporting governmental initiatives, Labour's criticisms thus revealed a distinct emphasis which reflected a concern to maintain a capacity at national level for a Labour government to defend the British economy against international trading and currency fluctuations, and to retain the right to pursue interventionist domestic policies for social and employment purposes. Such arguments showed a clear continuity both with those previously used by the Labour Government and subsequently to be advanced against Common Market membership.

The third major characteristic of Labour's policy in this period, perhaps not unlike that of the government, could be described as either flexibility or indecisiveness. The NEC minutes reveal a constant anxiety about taking policy decisions on the subject and a frequent reshuffling of the organisational structure deemed appropriate for analysis of European trade developments. At the same time, however, attitudes were gradually becoming more flexible than their public expression normally implied. For example, when a final breakdown of the free trade area/EEC negotiations occurred in 1958 – an event which the leadership regarded as very serious – the joint report of the NEC European Co-operation Committee and the Finance and Economic Sub-Committee moderated Labour's traditional hostility to supranationalism:

> The continental view of the need for supranational authorities was noted. It was considered that intergovernmental rather than supranational authorities were preferable; it was recognised however that concessions and compromise on this question were required.[21]

Still more significant was the scarcely perceptible shift in attitude towards the question of eventual EEC membership during 1960. In the Commons debate on 25 July 1960, whilst maintaining adamant opposition to membership, Healey was far less intransigent than in previous years and urged:

> our continental friends ... [to] take note of the fact that the sort of Pharisaism towards the Continent which governed the attitude of both parties – I admit this – towards European unity for so many years immediately after the war, is completely dead.[22]

Moreover in a subsequent meeting of the Socialist International Contact Committee between countries of the EEC and EFTA, Wilson went further still. Having argued that all efforts should be made to end the trade divisions between the Six and the Seven, and having claimed that Britain welcomed the political integration and growing economic success of the Six, he continued:

> Earlier British arguments against joining the EEC particularly as
> regards agriculture, the Commonwealth and Social Services,
> [seem] weaker now than two years ago. However, the great
> question [is] whether if Britain offered to join the EEC she would
> be welcomed.[23]

Two important conclusions can be drawn from this brief examination of party policy in the period before British participation in the
EEC became a major issue. First, it is apparent that the leadership
maintained, to a very great extent, the attitudes towards integration
which it had expressed when in government – in particular, a
preference for Atlanticism, an emphasis upon the Commonwealth,
and an anxiety to maintain important tools for economic intervention at national level. Secondly, despite these attitudes, there is
evidence of some softening in the hostility towards participation in
the EEC in 1960, a tendency which was even more marked in the
case of the trade union leadership.[24] In other words, in precisely the
same way as the government, the Labour leadership's opposition
towards membership grew less total as it became clear that the EEC
was more resilient and Britain's bargaining position weaker than
had been realised earlier. However, two further points must also be
noted. First, that even at leadership level, examination of the EEC
had so far been rudimentary; secondly, that outside the leadership
attention to the problem had been almost nonexistent. How would
the existing policy be affected once the issue became 'actual' and
attracted greater attention both within the leadership and the mass
movement?

The Labour Party and the First Application

As soon as it became evident late in 1960 that the British Government was considering making an application for EEC membership,
the Labour Party took serious steps to co-ordinate its various
interested committees and organisations in order to devise a definite
policy on the question. On 7 November the NEC's Home Policy
Sub-Committee asked the Finance and Economic Policy Sub-
Committee to consider the whole question of Britain's relationship
with the EEC. The latter committee then invited representatives of
the International Sub-Committee to deliberate jointly with it on the
subject and also co-opted others (including Labour economists,
Thomas Balogh, Nicholas Kaldor and Robert Neild) to meet with
them.[25] Yet after seven meetings under Ian Mikardo's chairmanship

and the production of a memorandum written up by David Ennals of the Internationl Department, the Committee was unable to agree on a policy or even to write a unanimous report.

After a fairly detailed examination of the issues, Ennals's paper reached the conclusion (endlessly to be reiterated over the next fourteen years) that:

> It is ... not so much a matter of whether we are in principle 'for' or 'against' joining the Six, but rather one of whether the terms on which we might enter and the likely long-term developments of the union are such as would make our joining turn out on balance favourable.[26]

At least six main issues, it was argued, needed clarification and resolution. First, that economic growth would be facilitated and that, in particular, firm assurances would be given that Common Market obligations could be suspended if necessary to ensure that balance of payments difficulties did not impede economic growth; secondly, that some agricultural products, in particular, horticulture, should be granted special protective arrangements; thirdly, that there must be no sudden or widespread contraction of industry, that adequate retraining and reemployment facilities must be ensured, and that no commitment should be made which would limit the scope for future improvements in social security or lead to regressive changes in the form of their financing; fourthly, that other EFTA states which so wished should be able to join at the same time and on similar terms and that special arrangements should also be made to safeguard the economic interests of any who felt unable to join because of their neutrality; fifthly, that Britain should not 'join Europe on terms that injure the legitimate economic interests of Commonwealth members'; and finally that there must be a clarification of the intentions of the EEC, since there would be great objections to Britain's joining if the early establishment of a federal state was planned, for this could mean the end of the Commonwealth and Britain's independent world role. 'If, on the other hand, a slower and more uncertain pace is planned, the objections to our joining are less clear-cut.'

The only recorded criticism of the paper from a left-wing anti-market perspective was a dissenting note from Kaldor. Arguing against the notion (which he attributed to Balogh) that British industry would 'be jolted into a new dynamic mould' by increased foreign competition, he claimed that if this were so, the liberalisation of imports since 1957 should have had such favourable effects, whereas in fact imports of manufactured goods had increased by 100 per cent whilst exports of manufactured goods had increased by only

5 per cent. Instead he argued that, unless accompanied by devaluation, the abolition of tariffs on European imports would probably lead to a severe profit deflation as in 1925–31 and at that time, 'with low profits or continuing losses the incentives or ability to invest in industry were gravely weakened, and we steadily lost in competitive power in the world markets'.[27] Moreover, as British productivity growth continued to lag behind, periodic exchange rate changes *vis-à-vis* the rest of the EEC would be necessary and 'the exercise of any such "freedom" would make nonsense of the whole policy of economic integration, and of the creation of a single West-European Federal State'.

He also found fault with the way in which the political arguments had been stated. The important argument in favour of membership (and the reason for the German and American wish that Britain should join) was, he claimed, that British political stability and cohesion was much greater than that in France or Italy and that British participation would therefore considerably strengthen the stability of any contemplated federation. Against this, however, was the argument that integration in a continental bloc would reduce Britain's freedom of manoeuvre in world affairs and therefore might diminish, rather than increase, her influence. If the Cold War continued indefinitely this would not make much difference since Britain was, in any case, fully committed through NATO:

> But it is not beyond the bounds of possibility that at some time in the future, the maintenance of peace might better be served by Britain not being so fully committed on one side or the other, and being ready to give its support to whichever power or group of powers is more interested in the maintenance of the *status quo*.

And, to emphasise the point, he warned against close involvement with West Germany whose overriding priority was the recovery of the 'lost territories' beyond the Oder-Neisse Line.

Kaldor's arguments, both economic, and more particularly political, were close to the line of Labour left and Communist opponents of British membership and were often to be voiced once the campaign against membership developed during 1962.

The other critical note was written jointly by Roy Jenkins and the economist Robert Neild, who argued that Britain should now apply for full membership. Their main reasons for dissenting from Ennals's paper were explained as follows. First, that it exaggerated the extent to which Britain's Commonwealth links and special position *vis-à-vis* the USA were obstacles to joining the EEC. In this context they maintained (wrongly) that Commonwealth opposition came almost entirely from the old white Commonwealth, particularly from New Zealand, and that the new Commonwealth was, if anything, 'inclined to favour our membership of the EEC'.[28] More convincingly, they continued with the argument that British influence with the new Commonwealth would become less if isolation from Europe led to a condition of relative economic weakness and that:

> So far as our 'special relationship' with the United States is concerned there is surely something faintly ludicrous about our believing we must preserve this by staying out while the United States government is strenuously engaged in urging us to go in. A 'special relationship' is not likely to have much value if it is only cherished by the weaker partner.

Secondly, the fact that some of the policies of the Six, for example on disengagement, were not attractive, was not an argument against membership. It would be more sensible to seek to influence policies from the inside than to believe against all the evidence that a continental bloc could be influenced from without. And an attempt to contract out, even if possible 'only begins to make sense if either now or in the future we shall wish to move in a neutralist direction'.

Thirdly, the EEC was in fact the only proposal for a gradual merging of sovereignty which was 'practical politics' for, neither the Commonwealth unity nor the North Atlantic unity (both mentioned as possible alternatives in Ennals's paper) were either advocated or desired by the others who would be Britain's partners in such unions. If therefore, membership were rejected on grounds of sovereignty:

> it almost inevitably becomes the case, as has indeed emerged in recent arguments, that we are driven into adopting a rather blimpish and nationalistic approach to the surrender of sovereignty, and this we believe is neither a natural or desirable position for a left-wing party.

If this was a well placed criticism, their fourth argument, whilst also forcefully stated, revealed their closeness to the economic assumptions of the Establishment, and of much of the SFIO in the previous decade:

> In recent years Britain has been encouraged not to worry about its economic sluggishness. Going into Europe would make it more difficult to go on with this easy going course, which must in any event lead to extremely undesirable consequences in the long run. Such a sharpening of choice would be wholly desirable. Without

doubt the more conservative choice would be to stay out and the more adventurous choice, and the one more likely to lead to social change, would be to go in; we believe that this factor too should weigh with the Party.

Finally, the Jenkins–Neild note called for clarification of the party's position:

> We believe it is essential at the present time that the Party should first decide the strategy of its approach, i.e. whether its broad desire is to go into Europe or not, and then the tactics, i.e. the question of exactly what should be our approach to Government policy, what terms we should demand, etc. If it confuses the two then the most likely result is that we shall not pronounce on the former question, but shall put forward a series of conditions for going in which everybody who has studied the question both here and on the Continent know to be quite impossible. And as a result our attitude ... will appear both indecisive and faintly hypocritical, and this is something which we must surely avoid.

The logic of this appears impeccable. What it omitted (whether deliberately or not) was the politics of the situation: that is, the fact that it would have been impossible to unify the party on the question except by this failure to differentiate between strategy and tactics, both because of the inevitable party division that a clear decision in principle would have precipitated, and because for many, including Gaitskell himself, the question was not one of principle.[29] Nevertheless, it is significant that at this stage Gaitskell offered some support, in private, to Jenkins's ideas, for in a letter to Ennals he accused the latter of overstating the political commitment involved in accepting the Treaty of Rome and of showing bias against membership. Ennals defended himself vigorously against these charges (which were also made by George Brown, a strong advocate of membership) but because Gaitskell was intent on maintaining an open mind on the subject, he refused to view the matter in any but a 'pragmatic way', insisting that there was no concrete evidence that British independence would be restricted by the existing EEC political institutions.[30]

In any case, it is quite evident that the NEC was totally divided on the issue *before* it even became public, and the minutes of the Home Policy Sub-Committee of 10 July 1961 reveal both this and its policy implications quite clearly:

> Some suggested that the Party should now declare in favour of Britain joining, but only if certain conditions were met: the most

important of these was that the Commonwealth countries should also have the right to join. It was argued that it was now possible to draw up conditions of entry on which most people in the party could agree. It was thought unlikely that the Party could delay a decision very much longer.

Others contested this viewpoint, insisting that the issue must turn on questions which could not be answered until the present visits of Ministers to the Commonwealth were completed and until actual negotiations had begun. The point was also made that with the present spread of Party opinion, a premature attempt at a clarification of Labour's view might lead to a damaging division which would distract attention from splits in the Government's ranks and from the Government's grave mismanagement of economic policy. It was argued that the Opposition had no obligation to make decisions in advance of the Government – particularly when so much important information was not available. It was then AGREED

(a) That no collective view should be presented to the TUC at the joint meeting on July 14th.
(b) Mr Wilson and Mr Gaitskell should be the NEC's principal spokesmen at the meeting, but that other members should be free to put their individual views.
(c) That the main purpose of the meeting should be to exchange views and that we should not therefore seek a joint statement at its conclusion. However, since the Government's attitude to the Common Market was likely to be clarified soon, the question of a further meeting later in the summer should be raised.[31]

The internal conflict, leading to the adoption of the wait-and-see policy, was thus evident as soon as a representative committee of the party even tried to define its attitude on the issue in relative privacy. And this was revealed equally clearly in the subsequent NEC/TUC meeting of 14 July which, in fact, manifested two important divisions.[32] The first was between the Labour leadership and that of the TUC, for dominant forces in the latter, who shared the economic assessment of the industrial elite, wanted a more definite and positive statement of opinion, while Wilson and Gaitskell were clearly anxious to maintain an entirely neutral attitude.[33] The second was between these two Labour leaders and three of the four other NEC representatives who spoke (Richard Crossman, Barbara Castle and Jennie Lee) who expressed more hostile attitudes to the EEC.[34] Nevertheless, despite (or perhaps because of) these cross-pressures the leadership managed to hold its line of pragmatic neutralism on the issue. Moreover, the strength of this position was demonstrated when, in the first public debate on the application for membership in the Commons on 2–3 August, Gaitskell and Wilson both expressed negative views on aspects of the EEC, but still held their backbenchers to the agreed policy of general support for the government against only five Labour-left dissenters, opposed even to the opening of negotiations.

The 1961 Labour conference, which almost coincided with the start of the main negotiations between Britain and the Six, led to no major alteration in policy, but further exposed its ambiguity. For although the leadership was easily able to carry its policy line against a motion of unconditional rejection put by Clive Jenkins and of unconditional support backed by Roy Jenkins, it is significant that the compromise motion was prefaced with a negative:

> This conference does not approve Britain's entry into the Common Market, unless guarantees protecting the position of British agriculture and horticulture, the EFTA countries and the Commonwealth are obtained, and Britain retains the power of using public economic ownership and planning as measures to ensure social progress within the United Kingdom. This conference also calls on the National Executive Committee to convene a meeting of Socialist leaders of Western Europe and Commonwealth countries to discuss the effects of the Common Market.[35]

This then created the paradoxical situation – though exactly appropriate in view of the wait-and-see policy – whereby an overwhelming majority was able to support the motion while thoroughly divided over the merits of entry. Thus the mover of the resolution (John Stonehouse) was a leading member of the Parliamentary Labour Party organisation which opposed membership (Britain and the Common Market), and Clive Jenkins remitted his motion of unconditional opposition in its favour. Yet Sir Alan Birch of the TUC also spoke for the motion, although he clearly wished for EEC entry and George Brown accepted it on behalf of the NEC, while regretting its negative opening. Equally significant was the fact that the motion supporting entry without specifying conditions, for which the principal speakers, apart from Roy Jenkins, were Shirley Williams and Bob Edwards, was overwhelmimgly defeated.

By October 1961 the 'neutral' policy was thus already somewhat negative in tone, and this was reinforced during the first part of 1962 when the NEC began to receive more hostile than positive resolutions on the EEC, and the PLP in March approved entry only with safeguards similar to those that later became formalised as the 'five conditions'.[36] Yet although there were some signs that Gaitskell himself was also becoming more critical of the pro-EEC case, the leader also gave certain contra-indications which tend to confirm his own subsequent claim that he had not yet made up his mind. In particular, on 7 May he submitted a memorandum to a group of friendly trade union leaders which manifested favourable overtones and dismissed much of the opposition case as unfounded, whilst formally maintaining the official line that all was dependent on the five conditions.[37] Such uncertainty was also evident within the NEC although the incipient conflict which lay behind the wavering was normally smoothed over by general agreement that more research and information were necessary. Yet the division became fully apparent in May 1962 in a dispute between Barbara Castle (a member of the anti-EEC Britain and the Common Market Committee) and Fred Mulley (a member of Roy Jenkins's Labour Party Common Market Committee).

The argument was precipitated by an article by Castle in the *New Statesman* in March, entitled 'Planning and the Common Market: The Anti-Socialist Community'. Her main purpose in this was to refute the argument, put about in Brussels and in pro-EEC Labour circles, that the Common Market encouraged planning, and to claim instead that:

> the inherent philosophy of the Community [is] the belief that governments should hold the ring for industry to reorganise on the most efficient basis possible, considered in purely economic terms. Once the basic principles of the Treaty, such as the free movement of goods, labour and capital are accepted, economic considerations will be paramount, for capital moves in the pursuit of profit, not of some politically determined social ends.[38]

Applying this interpretation of the underlying philosophy of the EEC to its policies, she maintained that it would prevent a British government from following a location of industry/development area policy, would lead to regressive financing of the National Health Service, bring about deflation rather than the use of exchange controls and import restrictions as the means to defend the value of sterling and to prevent balance of payments crises, and would encourage multinational monopolies whilst impeding nationalisation except for commercial purposes. Indeed she argued that nationalisation would become 'well-nigh impossible' because of the difficulty in breaking up units which had been internationalised, the encouragement of this tendency being one of the main objectives of the Treaty of Rome.

In the context of the economic philosophy which inspires the Community this means, in effect, that [Britain] would be debarred from pursuing even the cautious and experimental Socialist policy to which the whole of the Labour Party is committed.

Clearly this went far beyond the wait-and-see policy on which the party was theoretically united and pointed to outright rejection of the EEC. Fred Mulley therefore sought to counter the arguments and maintain the existing compromise. His scorn for Barbara Castle's case is evident, but it is also clear that he was politically well to her right in accepting the logic of capitalist economics. He thus maintained that the Treaty of Rome was 'a politically neutral framework and by its requirements of planning it is anti laissez-faire and much closer to Labour Party thinking than to the concepts of Conservatives or Liberals', and that:

> The idea underlying many of Mrs Castle's arguments that we can 'by politically determined social ends' remove our industry from the obligation of covering its costs and selling at economic prices is both political and economic nonsense ... It would also be electorally disastrous. Subsidies can only come from taxes, i.e. from the successful industries. We cannot achieve an expanding economy by taxing the successful to subsidise those who cannot pay their way in a competitive world.[39]

Arguing from these premises, he claimed that the EEC was dynamic rather than static, and would be changed by the entry of British and Scandinavian countries, that its policies were quite compatible with the type of nationalisation and interventionism envisaged in *Signposts for the Sixties*; and that there was no evidence to support some of Barbara Castle's contentions.

Since the Home Policy Committee was unable to adjudicate between these views, the Chairman, Harold Wilson, again smoothed over the conflict by calling for a further research paper: 'Planning and the Rome Treaty'. Yet, in retrospect at least, this indicated the tendency towards a more negative stance within the NEC (as in the party as a whole) for Wilson was politically fairly close to Barbara Castle, and the research paper was to be produced by Peter Shore whose hostility to the EEC was becoming evident. The general overtones of the latter's paper (discussed at the Home Policy Committee on 4 June) proved highly negative. Arguing that balance of payments difficulties had been the main impediment to sustained economic growth in Britain, he pointed out (like Castle) that the EEC would remove some potential protective measures from member states including, for example, those used the previous July by the British Government.[40] Moreover, he reiterated the point that participation in the EEC was bound to weaken economic planning at national level, and that there was no sign that any adequate compensation at community level had been forthcoming. Furthermore, he demonstrated that the adoption by the Community of responsibility for full employment policy would mean a strengthening and development of Community institutions beyond the existing provisions of the Rome Treaty. Continental socialists were, he maintained, ardent federalists, but:

> a federal Europe is not an immediate prospect and while the waiting may not dismay socialists who have virtually no chance of winning effective governmental power in their own countries, it poses a much more serious problem for those, like ourselves, who stand at the threshold of state power.[41]

Yet although Shore's tone was probably indicative of a general hardening of attitudes, it did not lead to any resolution of the internal conflict or an advance towards a decision. Members of the Home Policy Committee still disagreed as to how flexibly the Community operated its own constitution and Gaitskell criticised Shore's paper for overstating the potentially negative effects of entry on the British economy.[42] And although the party subsequently published two detailed and informative papers, highlighting the problems involved in planning should Britain become a member of the EEC, no negative decision on membership was implied.[43]

It is in fact futile to ask when the Labour Party changed its policy because there was no decisive break from the agreed compromise. Rather there was an accumulation of pressure towards a negative stance which was held in check until Gaitskell himself chose to allow full expression to the emotional hostility felt by much of the party. His own role, in acquiescing in the increasing pressure towards a negative stance, was thus of pivotal importance. Yet even this was significant in terms of general attitude rather than actual policy, since the French veto meant that a final decision, to be taken when the full terms were known, was never necessary.

Gaitskell's evolution towards a more negative attitude seems to have occurred between July and September 1962,[44] and it is clear that the hostile reaction of the Commonwealth to the preliminary terms was of decisive importance for him as for much of the party.[45] The original Labour Party amendment in the Commons in August 1961 had sought to ensure Commonwealth acceptance of British entry into the EEC and references to the need to safeguard Commonwealth interests had frequently been reiterated by Labour spokesmen during the subsequent year. Indeed in his broadcast of 8

May, and in his Commons speech a month later, Gaitskell had
pointed to the Commonwealth as the overriding consideration. The
totally unfavourable reaction of the Commonwealth socialists to the
terms, repeated in a more moderate way at the Commonwealth
Prime Ministers' Conference, was therefore bound to provoke
strongly negative attitudes in the Labour Party. The communiqué
issued after the meeting with Commonwealth socialists was thus far
more condemnatory of the government than anything previously
stated by the party and implied the possibility of an eventual
rejection of membership:

> we hold that if Britain were to enter the Common Market on the
> basis of what has so far been agreed great damage would
> inevitably be done to many countries in the Commonwealth and
> therefore to the unity of the Commonwealth itself ... Since the
> terms for Britain's entry as at present known are either too vague
> or too damaging to be acceptable, we urge that no final decision
> be taken by Britain until a further meeting of Commonwealth
> Prime Ministers has been held to consider a more precise and
> satisfactory proposal.[46]

Similarly, before the annual conference, the party issued two
Talking Point statements on the Commonwealth which surpassed, by
far, the criticisms that it had published on the effects of the EEC on
planning, and asserted categorically:

> a warning note should now be sounded. Whatever the marginal
> advantages of membership to Britain may be, if in the view of
> Commonwealth leaders the terms proposed seriously damage
> their interests or threaten to disrupt the Commonwealth as a
> political and economic entity, then Britain could not join.[47]

Gaitskell followed this up with a television broadcast on 21
September in which he criticised the inadequate arrangements for
the Commonwealth and inveighed against any attempt to join a
European federation,[48] and it was a fairly short step (though an
unexpected one) from this to his famous and somewhat demagogic
conference speech. It was in its emotive aspects rather than its
actual content, that Gaitskell went beyond the statement that the
NEC had agreed, with difficulty, on 29 September. It is therefore
this statement, 'Labour and the Common Market', rather than
Gaitskell's speech which reveals the state of internal compromise
which had been attained at that time.

Compromise, leading to inconsistencies in emphasis, was the
hallmark of the document. Thus although the advocates of membership had managed to secure a positive beginning – 'The Labour

Party regards the European Community as a great and imaginative conception'[49] – this impression was soon overshadowed by the insistence that the EEC was a first step towards full economic and politial integration which would present special and serious difficulties for Britain which was 'the centre and founder member of a much larger and still more important group, the Commonwealth', and that:

> although the unification of Western Europe is in itself a great historic objective, it has to be considered in the light of the effect it has on the two transcendent issues of our times: the cold war, with its immense threat of global destruction, and the ever increasing division of the world into affluent nations of Europe and North America and the povery-stricken nations elsewhere.

If joining the Common Market meant mobilising economic resources to help underdeveloped countries and promoting world peace by liberal policies in Europe the case would be strong; but if it meant that the trade of the Commonwealth and less developed countries was to be weakened, and the chances of East–West agreement were to be lessened, the case against entry would be decisive. It was therefore argued that the nature of the Community could be judged only by the terms that were agreed and that the test was the extent to which they accorded with Labour's five conditions, which were then expounded as follows:

1. Strong and binding safeguards for the trade and other interests of our friends and partners in the Commonwealth.

2. Freedom as at present to pursue our own foreign policy.

3. Fulfilment of the Government's pledge to our associates in the European Free Trade Area.

4. The right to plan our own economy.

5. Guarantees to safeguard the position of British agriculture.

If the conditions were accepted the balance would be tilted in favour of entry; if not the present negotiations should be halted for entry was not vital.

The statement then launched its full attack on the government's handling of the negotiations in respect of the first condition (the Commonwealth). The 'totally inadequate' terms which had been published pointed to three conclusions. First, in pursuing its present course, 'with no mandate from the British people', the government had caused a major crisis in Commonwealth affairs which, if allowed to continue, could damage Commonwealth relations beyond repair. Secondly, this surrender on the Commonwealth would make it clear to the Six that no further serious concessions on their part were necessary because the government was so desperately anxious to join. Thirdly, the apparent unwillingness of the Six to pay due regard to the economic problems of hundreds of millions of miserably poor people in the underdeveloped Commonwealth raised the question of whether they were basically inward looking or outward looking. The duty of government ministers was to return to Brussels to present terms which were consistent with their earlier pledges and, if desired by other member states, any new terms should be submitted to a further Commonwealth Conference. At the same time the government must show its determination to comply with the other four conditions in relation to the outstanding issues subsequently to be negotiated. If the demands were not met the negotiations should be halted, but in this case:

> we do not doubt ... that the future will bring, and bring soon, new opportunities for increasing our trade with the Six. Nor do we rule out the possibility that a Labour Government would conduct new and successful negotiations at a later stage.

Finally, the statement ended with some significant indications of the international economic policy Labour would favour in the event of a breakdown in negotiations. Britain should join the USA in an effort to negotiate a reduction in the Common External Tariff and be prepared to make reciprocal tariff reductions. In addition the Commonwealth trade sysem should be reformed and a general expansion of trade between developed and underdeveloped countries should be brought about – a first step being a proposal for a conference of EFTA and Commonwealth countries to consider measures to promote trade and economic development. For the real dangers of the future were not the old rivalries of France and Germany but those that arose from the continuing hostility between the communist and non-communist worlds and from the terrible inequalities between the developed and underdeveloped countries. Britain could not solve these problems alone:

> but more than any other advanced country of the West, we have the greatest opportunity and the greatest incentive to tackle them. For the 700 million people of the Commonwealth, with whom history has linked us, form a truly international society, cutting across the deep and dangerous divisions of the modern world. By its very nature the Commonwealth must think of global not regional problems; of the interests of all races, not just one; of

the problems of age-old poverty as well as those of new found affluence; of non-commitment as well as of cold war.

If we are ever to win peace and prosperity for mankind, then the world community that must emerge will be composed of precisely such diverse elements as exist in the Commonwealth today – pledged, as we are, to friendship and mutual aid. This is our vision of Britain's future – and it must not be allowed to fade.

Two significant points about the statement should be noted. First, the fact that it remained a compromise policy once again enabled both pro- and anti-marketeers to derive support for their viewpoints from it (see below p. 186–91). But secondly, it nevertheless brought overt Labour opposition to the EEC much closer for it made support for any terms negotiated at that time highly unlikely. Given the immense difficulties the Conservative Government had faced in securing the limited concessions which it had announced in the August White Paper, it was almost inconceivable that, even had it so wished and even without de Gaulle, it could have obtained agreement from the Six on the conditions demanded by Labour. But the NEC's denunciation of the present terms was so categorical that it would have been extremely difficult for it to have accepted any new agreements unless they differed very radically from those thus far negotiated. Moreover, although it is true that, after the conference Gaitskell conciliated his pro-market friends on the revisionist right of the party,[50] there were also indications that the party as a whole was maintaining or even increasing its negative outlook on the issue. Thus late in 1962 it chose to publish its views on world government, arguing that this was the only way to lasting peace and denying that a sacrifice of sovereignty at regional level constituted any advance towards the breakdown of barriers at global level.[51] And Peter Shore presented a paper to the NEC in December 1962 in which he argued that, instead of the stiffening of the government's attitude in negotiations and the softening of that of the Six for which Labour had hoped, the reverse had taken place, with no substantial change in the arrangements for the Commonwealth and the French introducing a bombshell in its demand for the financing of the CAP and the scrapping of British deficiency payments to take place from the date of entry.[52] Similarly, the Overseas Department Sub-Committee was informed the next day that the gulf between Labour and the socialist parties of the Six remained as wide as ever and that Barbara Castle had been listened to 'more in regretful sorrow than in anger' when she had reiterated Gaitskell's appeal for continental socialists to try to get better terms for Britain at the November 1962 conference of EEC socialist parties.[53] When, in Paris, in the same month Gaitskell appeared wholly negative and unenthusiastic about entry into the EEC, he was probably expressing the viewpoint which was by then dominant in the NEC.[54]

Although the wait-and-see policy was maintained and entry on the right terms was never precluded, it thus became increasingly probable that the party would have opposed entry on any terms that could conceivably have been negotiated at that time. At the centre of its alternative strategy it was placing reformist interventionism through planning to stimulate the domestic economy, and the revitalisation of Britain's international trade, in which the Commonwealth was to play a pivotal role, in conjunction with EFTA and the USA. It hoped that, in this way, a Labour Government could reactivate the British economy without depending on EEC entry and that the Kennedy round could bring about a liberalisation of the external economic policy of the EEC so as to make eventual membership less problematic.

Gaitskell's decision to give expression to emotional hostility to the EEC rather than standing against the accumulating pressure was clearly of great importance in explaining the unity that had ensued in the party. But why had he chosen this course?

One partial explanation lay, of course, in electoral politics. By August 1962 the government was certainly seeking to derive party political capital out of an issue which was not naturally popular with the electorate and which would become less so if negotiations failed.[55] Gaitskell was therefore probably making a shrewd electoral calculation when he moved into a position of readiness to exploit a governmental failure.[56] Yet he was almost certainly moved at least as much by less machiavellian considerations: first that the government was seeking entry as a last resort because of the failure of its economic policies; secondly, that it was not dealing honestly with the people by refusing to explain the implications of membership; and thirdly, that the terms so far negotiated constituted a betrayal of the Commonwealth and were incompatible with the pledges given by Macmillan in August 1961. That is, there is a strong case for accepting the Labour leadership's own claim that it really had been committed only to supporting negotiations and not necessarily entry, and that it was the government which had shifted from this position.

A second partial explanation lies in the fact that the traumatic divisions within the party throughout the previous decade gave the leader a powerful incentive to seek unity on a question which was, once again, potentially highly divisive. It has already been shown that, even before the issue became public, the NEC was well aware of the danger of a further damaging split, and that this was a major reason for the adoption of the wait-and-see policy. Robins is therefore quite justified in stating:

There is a strong case ... for arguing that ... [Gaitskell] was responding as positively to party management pressures as Attlee before him and Wilson after. The benefits alone that the EEC brought to the Labour Party were sufficient to expect this outcome. From the shattered morale after the Clause IV and defence policy battles, the party united, found electoral confidence and ideological strength in its identity as the 'Commonwealth' Party, and agreed to Gaitskell's continued leadership. All this from an issue which was to come to nothing ... Thus the EEC provided the leader with a balm for the party, providing it did not develop into an issue demanding a clear choice one way or the other.[57]

However, it would be unlike Gaitskell to have sought unity against his own convictions or in such a way as to strengthen the left of the party, and Robins's claim that the five conditions were concessions to the left is more difficult to accept.[58] In particular such a view fails to explain why the party also united on leadership policies in other spheres and ignores the long-term hostility of much of the Labour right towards West European integration.

The motivations of the leadership, and the state of the left/right balance within the labour movement, can be understood more easily if the three most relevant of the five conditions are considered in more depth, paying due regard to the political conceptions of the labour movement as a whole.[59]

The Independent Foreign Policy (Condition 3)

The notion of an independent foreign policy was more ambiguous than it appeared because it was interpreted in very different ways within the Labour movement. For the Communist Party (CP) the demand for independence from the USA had been a mobilising slogan since the onset of the Cold War and, particularly since German rearmament had first been proposed, this had been coupled with a strident campaign against subordination to West Germany.[60] Although the alternative was always stated to be an independent foreign policy, bringing about an era of friendly relations with all countries, the party clearly adhered to the Soviet line. Like the PCF, it was able to provide a plausible economic critique of the Community, but deliberately chose to emphasise foreign policy aspects, arguing that the Common Market was the economic and political arm of NATO[61] and that:

The dream of the Nazis under Hitler was to bring all Europe under their rule and influence in the 'European New Order', to provide expanding markets for the modern and powerful German industry. Adenauer's government pursues the same aim, and is backed by American big business which poured money into Europe on condition that moves were made towards an integrated European economy.[62]

The CP thus called for emergency action to maintain national independence from the American and West German bloc. In August 1962, it even claimed that the march of Macmillan to the Common Market was far worse than that of Chamberlain to Munich: this time the integrated political–economic system of Hitler's New Order was being built before the outbreak of war, and the EEC's central political aim was 'to rebuild the reactionary Munich combination in a far more extreme form'.[63]

If the Communists understood 'independence' to mean withdrawal from the Western alliance, the Bevanite/Tribunite interpretation differed. The major aspiration of this sector of opinion was to bring about *détente* in Europe not, in general, because of pro-Sovietism, but as a means to peace and disarmament. The Tribunite message was thus that the West should avoid 'provocations' to the Soviet Union and, partly for this reason, it had bitterly opposed the rearmament of West Germany and its incorporation within NATO.[64] The Labour left's call for an independent foreign policy was therefore a demand for a Labour government to seek East–West understanding, with a critical detachment from orthodox Western priorities.[65] The European Community was seen as a *general* threat to the success of this policy because it was held to be a product of the Cold War which reinforced the division of Europe and tension between the two blocs.[66] But the more particular fear of the Labour left was that membership of a federal Europe would force a British Government to follow a hawkish Western policy.

There were differences between the Communist Party and Labour-left positions, but both conceived of an independent foreign policy in terms of its *content*. The aspirations of the leadership in general, and of Gaitskell in particular, were quite different. For them independence was defined, not in terms of content, but of *capacity*. This becomes clear if the overriding objectives of its foreign policy are considered.

As was shown in chapter 4, a fundamental foreign policy priority of the Labour Government between 1945–51 had been to maintain the Anglo-American alliance. In Opposition this commitment was maintained, and the leadership rejected any courses of action which would have seriously damaged relations with the United States.

As argued above, it had therefore been almost inevitable that the leadership would eventually endorse German rearmament and even accept new British commitments in order to ensure good Anglo-

American relations and a permanent American military presence in Europe. Ultimately therefore the Labour leadership could not accept Labour-left and Communist positions on German rearmament because, to have done so would have conflicted with the Atlanticist impulses which were so deep seated.[67] For Gaitskell precisely the same consideration was involved in the unilateralist issue. That is, it was because he was convinced that unilateralism would lead to neutralism that he expressed his determination to 'fight and fight and fight again' to reverse the decision of the 1960 conference, and later described his victory over neutralism as the proudest achievement of his life.[68] But the EEC was not an issue of this kind. True, the USA made clear its desire for Britain to join the EEC and this fact weighed heavily with the Labour leadership. However, no catastrophic consequences for the Atlantic Alliance seemed likely if Britain stayed out, and de Gaulle's presence hardly made it certain that the EEC would be the reliable NATO outpost for which President Kennedy was hoping. Moreover the Labour leadership kept in touch with US government circles throughout the negotiations to moderate any conflicts that might arise over the issue.[69]

The leadership therefore believed that close Anglo-American (and Labour–American) relations could withstand a refusal to enter the EEC on unfair terms, in a way that they could not have withstood leadership opposition to German rearmament or acceptance of unilateralism. And this shows the leadership's notion of an independent foreign policy to be different from that of the left who sought independence because the EEC was seen as a creature of the Cold War. Gaitskell's fear was rather that incorporation in a closely integrated federal Europe would prevent Britain from playing a separate world role – and would turn her into an 'offshore island' rather than the centre of a world-wide Commonwealth.[70] The Labour Party condition on EEC entry which affirmed the need for an independent foreign policy was thus (deliberately?) ambiguous. The left meant that they wanted a particular type of foreign policy whereas the leadership simply wished to retain the capacity for a British foreign policy rather than follow that of a federal Western Europe. It was thus significant that the condition spoke of 'freedom *as at present* to pursue our own foreign policy'. (My emphasis.) This meant, in other words, freedom within NATO – certainly not the aspiration of the Communist Party, and hardly as far reaching as that sought by much of the Labour left.

Commonwealth Safeguards (Condition 1)

The Commonwealth should have presented the CP with grave theoretical problems had it taken Lenin's strictures about the importance of communists struggling against their own imperialism seriously. For the notion of a group of former colonies remaining connected to the 'imperialist oppressor' presents serious difficulties from a Marxist–Leninist perspective. But the CP normally avoided such traps by advocating a true Commonwealth based on non-exploitative mutual economic relations.[71] And when opposition to the EEC mounted on the issue of the Commonwealth it readily accepted this and emphasised the question more in its own campaign against the Common Market.[72] Yet although the CP increasingly stressed the Commonwealth when condemning the EEC for being imperialist with regard to the Third World, concern for the Commonwealth *per se* was far more deeply rooted on the Tribune left, although it too emphasised the problems of less developed countries as a whole.

The first Bevanite publications in 1951 had drawn attention to the importance of Third World development and the inability of Britain to make an adequate contribution in this vital matter because of the burden of arms expenditure.[73] Admittedly at this stage the argument had been placed in the Cold War perspective of fighting against communism, but a new emotional commitment to less developed countries on the Labour left emanates from this era.[74] This was reinforced by the setting up of the Movement for Colonial Freedom by Fenner Brockway and the establishment of the first independent black African states in the second half of the decade.[75] And the Suez expedition reinforced emotional feelings of solidarity with the Third World against traditional imperialism, which the Conservative Party was held to embody.

For the Labour left a new role was seen for Labour Britain as the champion of the Third World and non-aligned, with the Commonwealth playing a key role in this constellation.[76] Thus whereas in the 1940s (for a short period) the Labour left had seen 'third force' Europe as a possibility, in the 1950s a longer and deeper commitment to Labour Britain as the centre of Commonwealth less developed countries, in harmony with other non-aligned nations, was formulated. Throughout the decade Britain's future was thus seen to be more closely intertwined with that of the Third World than with Western Europe, with which an increasing lack of sympathy was felt.[77] It was therefore inevitable that the EEC would be viewed as threatening both to this vision of the future and to the multiracial Commonwealth. Such attitudes, constantly expressed in Labour-left statements about the EEC, were epitomised in Tony Benn's speech at the 1962 conference when he argued that Labour could not secure its goals in Europe in an organisation springing from the Cold War or claim that the future depended on countries like India and then place tariffs on them. There were, he claimed, no regional solutions and a

181

belief in a limited region might be even more dangerous than narrow nationalism. Global solutions and the global solidarity of socialists were necessary, and Labour should further such solutions by reinforcing the Commonwealth and the UN.[78]

The political psychology of this commitment to the Commonwealth Third World is, of course, complex. No doubt there was an element of chauvinism within it – a longing for Britain to be able to continue to play a major world role. Certainly, the historical development of Labour's Commonwealth attitudes reinforces such an interpretation, for the Commonwealth had also been an emotive card to play when it had been overwhelmingly white and peopled by 'our kinsmen' and, indeed, such sentiments in the party were still exploited between 1961–63.[79] Yet it would be unduly dismissive to treat the belief in the development of a multiracial Commonwealth as simply chauvinistic or imperialistic.[80] For there was clearly also a basic Labour-left conviction that the EEC was a rich man's club and that the multiracial Commonwealth was capable of being something more. It is thus not difficult to understand why the Labour left rallied to the first of the five conditions.

What about the leadership?

Since the Labour left's commitment to the Commonwealth was based on a liberal humanitarianism, and an element of traditionalist patriotism, it is not surprising that it was shared by much of the Labour right, including Gaitskell himself. Although many on the Labour right had been slow to adapt to the evolution of the Commonwealth and, particularly at the height of the Cold War, had opposed leftist nationalists in the Third World countries, after 1956 they too had rallied to the notion of the multiracial Commonwealth.[81] Indeed in 1957 Gaitskell had opposed the EEC primarily because of its potentially damaging effects on Third World Commonwealth development.[82] Yet however much the leadership believed in the Commonwealth for its own sake, the motives were not purely altruistic. Ennals's NEC memorandum, discussed earlier, makes quite clear the strong elements of self-interest involved in the defence of the needs of the Commonwealth members:

> Surely it is not wishful thinking nor illusions of grandeur to suggest that if [the Commonwealth] nations continue to work together on major political matters – and still more if they succeed in strengthening their economic ties – then Britain will continue to play a leading part in world affairs as far ahead as it is possible to see …

Indeed

> if the future turns on the relationships between white and coloured

people and between the industrialised and underdeveloped countries, *then our influence as a member of such an association is not only of key
importance but is far more likely to grow than decline.* (My emphasis.)
But

> if the Commonwealth is to be held together it is very important that
> we should not join Europe on terms that injure the legitimate
> economic interests of Commonwealth members.[83]

Similar sentiments were of tremendous importance to Gaitskell
who argued that entry into a tight federation would mean the end of
the Commonwealth and the conversion of Britain into a minor power,
and that Britain should join such a federation only if the Commonwealth had already broken up.[84] Thus although the leadership was
motivated by some genuine idealism about the Commonwealth, it
was also influenced by less elevated sentiments. And when, for
example, Denis Healey chided Roy Jenkins at the 1962 conference for
his relative indifference to the Commonwealth it would be misleading
to see in this any major ideological difference in left/right terms
between the two: it was in fact mainly a dispute as to whether British
power and the 'mixed economy' could be safeguarded better in the
EEC or as centre of the Commonwealth.[85]

The defence of the Commonwealth may have been a powerful
rallying cry which attracted left support, but once again it was no real
concession to the left, for it sprang from the autonomous impulses of
the leadership. If foreign policy and the Commonwealth are considered together it can thus be seen that there were solid reasons for a
centre–right leadership to have accepted the increasingly negative
compromise policy of the party.

The Right to Plan the Economy (Condition 4)

The crux of a socialist critique of the EEC would be based on an
analysis of the extent to which it would strengthen capital and
exacerbate the difficulties of any movement seeking to bring about
socialism. Not surprisingly the Communist Party, adhering broadly
to the thesis that the strategy of the left should be the socialist
nationalisation of domestic monopolies, was able to advance a strong
argument that the EEC would strengthen the power of international
monopolies and undermine the objectives of a Labour-left government.

Its first major pamphlet on the subject claimed that the EEC
threatened the British labour movement because it was dominated
by right-wing forces who would seek to thwart socialist measures in
Britain, because it would threaten technically backward industries
and, above all, because it would remove powers from the national
level which would be required by the British labour movement. In
this context it asked how a Labour government could:

undertake even the mildest measures of state planning if our economy were at the mercy of international capitalist monopolies. The Common Market arrangements would encourage agreements between the monopolists of the various countries ...

Any British government planning to operate an anti-monopoly policy or extend nationalisation of basic industries would face great difficulties.

To end industrial stagnation and continually recurring balance of payments crises necessitates far-reaching changes. Membership of the Common Market would tremendously handicap and obstruct any government trying seriously to find a solution to these problems.

British financial interests could organise a 'flight of capital' from Britain, and by taking their money out, undermine the currency. And a British government bound by Common Market agreements, with no control over foreign exchange, would be powerless to stop them.[86]

For the CP, as for the PCF, it was quite clear that the EEC involved a greater subordination to the political and economic power of international capital. Thus the CP's strategy (effectively the anti-monopoly policy, though not yet so called) involved total opposition to British membership. And even though the political–economic analysis was overlaid in the propaganda by inflammatory verbiage the CP provided a cogent critique of the EEC from this point of view.

Was it of equal importance for the Labour left?

As Robins argues, at this stage, foreign policy considerations were more crucial for this section of opinion than economic ones. Yet it would be quite wrong to imply that this aspect of the problem was totally neglected.[87] As long ago as 1952 Bevan had discussed, in a general context, the problematic relationship between national sovereignty and international co-operation. Claiming that he was now more aware than previously that the nation-state was inadequate as an arena for the final triumph of socialism, he nevertheless argued that it was essential to secure economic control at national level before attempting to erect some 'global constitution into which the nation would fit'.[88] This was part of Bevan's long-term belief in the possibility of establishing the essential economic basis for socialism through purposeful use of the parliamentary system, and it was reaffirmed in one of the very rare critiques of West European integration by the Labour left in the period before British membership of the EEC appeared probable. In August 1957 Bevan wrote:

In European political circles, the argument about the Common Market is hotting up. If Conservatives get their way we shall soon be talking about nothing else ... Tariffs, proscriptions in trade and restrictions of various kinds imposed by congeries of sovereign parliaments are vexatious and may constrict production forces. But in the absence of a wider sovereignty, all the conception of a common market does is to elevate the market place to the status now enjoyed by the various European parliaments. It is at this point that Socialists become suspicious of what is intended. Is it the disenfranchisement of the people and the enfranchisement of market forces? Are we now expected to go back almost a century, reject socialism and clasp free trade to our bosom as though it were the one solution of our social evils? ... The conception of the Common Market ... is the result of a political malaise following upon the failure of socialists to use the sovereign power of their parliaments to plan their economic life. It is an escapist conception in which the play of market forces will take the place of political responsibility ... Socialists cannot at one and the same time call for economic planning and accept the verdict of free competition, no matter how extensive the area it covers. The jungle is not made more acceptable just because it is almost limitless.[89]

Once the issue became actual in 1961, the argument that the EEC operated simply in accordance with capitalist priorities and would remove important powers from the armoury of a Labour government was continuously used on the Labour left and, as has been seen, formed part of the internal debate within the NEC, where it was voiced, in particular by Barbara Castle and Jennie Lee, and served by the expert advice of Kaldor and the researches of Peter Shore.[90]

Yet Gaitskell never fully accepted this type of argument and deliberately chose to underplay it in his conference speech.[91] And the agreed statement, 'Labour and the Common Market', did not go nearly as far as had Castle or even Shore in the internal NEC discussions. Rather it stated that some features of economic planning 'cannot be easily combined with membership of the Common Market' and that, although the limitations upon government intervention in the economy imposed by the Rome Treaty 'are not necessarily disadvantageous, they could in certain cases have dangerous consequences for Britain'. In particular it argued that complete free trade with the Six and the free movement of capital could – and, in the short run almost certainly would – intensify Britain's balance of payments difficulties and, if the power of a British government to take corrective measures was limited, prosperity could be damaged. Yet its faith in the Kennedy Round as a means of freeing world trade hardly suggested a deep belief in the importance of retaining major controls over trading policy at national level, and instead of reiterating either Shore's realistic belief that the EEC would not take on a full employment commitment or Castle's interpretation of the Treaty of Rome as necessarily anti-socialist, it simply stated:

> It is ... only simple prudence to secure now either freedom of action for the British government to tackle these problems or binding agreements with the Six on corrective action by the Community as a whole. For the same reason, the voting arrangements finally agreed on in the enlarged Community should be such as to ensure that in economic and social questions British interests cannot be overridden. This would be facilitated by the entry of the EFTA nations.[92]

Instead of taking the line that the EEC was, by its very nature, an organ of monopoly capitalism which was thereby inherently threatening to the introduction of socialism in Britain, the NEC statement simply called for the retention of certain interventionist powers at national level – powers which Gaitskell clearly believed to be compatible with EEC membership in any case.[93] Once again, therefore, the insistence on the right to plan the economy was not such a great concession to the left as it appeared at first sight. Although the terminology of a planned economy appealed to the Labour left, the leadership intended only the mildly reformist interventionism which was to epitomise the strategy of the 1964 Labour Government.

Two further points of relevance to the left–right balance merit discussion: the centrality of the Commonwealth issue, and Gaitskell's refusal to accept a call for unconditional opposition to entry into the EEC.

It is of immense significance, in terms of the internal balance, that the decisive issue was the treatment of the Commonwealth. The emotional commitment to the Commonwealth was, as has been argued, shared by the left and right in the party and it raised none of the fundamentally divisive internal problems. All could accept nebulous, though no doubt sincere, aspirations to stimulate the economic and political development of the Commonwealth and could condemn the Conservative Government for its failure to carry out its responsibilities in this respect. It was thus a naturally unifying issue but, just because it was vague and disguised the basic conflicts which remained, it inevitably tended to bring about unity

186

on the leadership's terms. If, on the other hand, the Labour Party had sought to distance itself from the government on either of the other two major issues – the right to follow an independent foreign policy or to plan the economy – internal conflict would also have been precipitated. For differentiation from the government over foreign policy could easily have revived the internal debate over NATO just when it was subsiding, while far-reaching criticism of the EEC's constraints on national economic planning could have sparked off new arguments about the role of nationalisation in Labour's economic strategy. If the EEC was indeed balm to Gaitskell because it brought about party unity, the furore over the Commonwealth provided him with a unique opportunity to bring about such unity on his own terms.

The resistance to the demand for unconditional opposition was of equal importance in this respect. One reason why Gaitskell would not have yielded to any such demand whatever his personal view had been was, of course, the existence of the pro-EEC faction within the party. Roy Jenkins made it clear to him that a new party row would ensue should the wait-and-see policy give way to one of outright opposition, and Gaitskell naturally wished to avoid this.[94] But Gaitskell would not have adopted such a policy in any case because it would inevitably have tended to strengthen the left in the party. As is evident from the examination of its arguments in this chapter, the CP's position was one of outright opposition to the EEC as a capitalist and anti-Soviet bloc carrying internal and international dangers for the labour movement, and some of those within the Labour Party who took this line were on its extreme left wing.[95] Gaitskell was fully aware of this and, partly for this reason, attributed great importance to the maintenance of a wait-and-see policy rather than the adoption of a totally negative stance.[96] In this way he was able to prevent any advance of CP influence, to prevent the Labour Party taking a doctrinal (i.e., socialist) line rather than an empirical one, and to maintain contact with the political and economic Establishment. Outright opposition would have contained dangers in all these respects.

The left may therefore have rejoiced at their victory in apparently converting Gaitskell to the anti-EEC cause, but the true victor was Gaitskell.[97] This is not to suggest that his policy was opportunistic in a derogatory sense. The fact is that he was able to succeed because on the EEC, as distinct from on Clause IV and unilateralism, his instincts were absolutely in line with those of the party's centre. Because he genuinely saw the matter as one to be settled by considerations of the balance of advantage rather than on principle he was able to adopt a more negative posture when this appeared warranted. Gaitskell's good fortune, or shrewd judgement, lay in the fact that he was able to harness his growing personal antipathy to government policy and scepticism as to its possibilities of success, both to his own advantage within the Labour Party and to use in opposition to the Conservatives. The fact that he was sincerely committed to some conception of Commonwealth development enhanced his ability to exploit this issue, thereby further strengthening opposition to the EEC on centrist rather than socialist grounds.

If this explains the way in which apparent concessions to the left actually strengthened the existing leadership, how did Gaitskell manage to conciliate the pro-EEC minority in the party? In the first place, as has already been noted, concessions were made to this section of opinion both in the leadership's rejection of outright opposition to membership and in some of the positive aspects of the NEC statement. Moreover the fact that the issue never came to a head because the final terms were never known, enabled the proponents of entry (like the outright opponents) to stay their hand in the hope that they could win the support of the leadership at a later stage. Secondly, Gaitskell made overtures to the Campaign for Democratic Socialism pro-Europeans immediately after his negative conference speech and is quoted, significantly, as telling them that he would prefer a new Labour candidate who was pro-EEC, but supported his line on defence, to an anti-EEC opponent of NATO.[98] This leads to a third important factor. Despite the support of a sprinkling of left advocates of entry, mainly from the former committee for a United Socialist States of Europe, of whom Bob Edwards was the most prominent, the leading lights of the pro-EEC minority were firmly on the revisionist right of the party. Thus although Roy Jenkins's closest associates fervently believed in the EEC as a means of securing political hegemony for social democracy whilst modernising the British economy (in precisely the same way as André Philip had argued within the SFIO), they firmly supported Gaitskell on all the other major issues and would not wish to break with him on this question unless he adopted a position of unconditional opposition. Their desire to maintain unity must have been heightened by their awareness of their relative weakness in the party. For while the majority of the proponents of entry were on the revisionist right, it was not the case that the whole of this sector favoured the EEC – Douglas Jay, for example, who had been one of the most strident revisionists at the time of the Clause IV controversy was one of the most vehement opponents of EEC entry.[99] And support for the fervent advocates of entry amongst the party's rank and file was minimal. Not only was the motion for unconditional entry at the 1961 conference overwhelmingly defeated, but Roy Jenkins's Labour Common Market Committee was forced to cancel the only two study schools it had planned because of lack of support.[100]

The fact is there was no specifically Labour or left enthusiasm for the EEC in Britain. For a variety of reasons – both purely emotional and well-conceived – the overwhelming majority of the labour movement either saw Britain's future in quite different terms (and were opponents of entry) or remained to be convinced through empirically based argument that entry would be advantageous (Gaitskell and the centre). In these circumstances the Labour Common Market Committee could make no headway. And because it represented such a minority opinion, and because its majority supported him on all other issues, Gaitskell did not need to fear it provided he maintained the wait-and-see policy. But on this too Gaitskell's genuine position was absolutely in line with the needs of party unity for, as has been shown, he never intended to adopt a policy of intransigent opposition.

There is one further crucial factor to note concerning the bearing of the EEC issue on the Labour Party. In reality, when the issue became salient, most members of the labour movement were relatively ignorant about the EEC and were confused by the vehement but totally contradictory propaganda by opponents and proponents of entry. One of the benefits of the compromise position – again tending to unite the party around the leadership – was its ability to produce a policy which could bring pragmatic opponents and pragmatic supporters of entry together. That is, while it would naturally have been impossible to reconcile CP opponents with revisionist right proponents, it was not so difficult to find a formula to unite a left-centre opponent with a right-centre supporter. The basis for such unity (in addition to the compromise wait-and-see line) lay in the claim that the EEC was not, after all, the crucial issue for Britain's future. What really mattered was the pursuit of the correct economic strategy at home – reformist interventionism, as defined in *Signposts for the Sixties*. The NEC statement, 'Labour and the Common Market', emphasised this belief:

> There is no question of Britain being forced to go in. In particular we reject the widespread but false view that the economic advantages of membership are so great and the economic consequences of non-membership so disastrous that Britain has no choice but to accept whatever terms the Six may offer.

And after neatly setting out four economic arguments in favour of the Community and five against, it further expounded this viewpoint:

> Entry into the Common Market will not offer, in itself, an easy

escape from our economic difficulties. The truth is that the growth of our economy and of our trade will owe far more to our own exertions, to the sensible planning of our economy, to reasonable restraint on incomes based on a fairer distribution of wealth, and to our ability to put investment and exports before home consumption, than to any consequence of our entry or non-entry into the Common Market.[102]

Centrist proponents and opponents could agree to this. Thus George Brown, a strong advocate of membership who had been shocked by Gaitskell's tone, argued that there was no panacea for Britain's economic problems either inside or outside the Common Market, and maintained:

> We have a tremendous need for changes anyway ...
> ... We need a great deal more investment in scientific inventions and machinery, in education and so on, than we are getting.
> One of the reasons ... the Six are going ahead is not just that they are joined together in a common market; it is that they have done so much better than we have in investing a larger share of their national incomes in development and in choosing the right priorities in which to invest it. We need, as *Signposts for the Sixties* said, a National Plan for development ...
> And if we do that, and only if – we shall be in a position to face this decision and to face the consequences either way.[102]

Similarly, in the Commons debate following the Gaullist veto, Harold Wilson, who had become increasingly hostile to membership, expressed a fairly general Labour conviction when he proclaimed that he would 'thank God' if the failure of the Brussels negotiations had brought about a realisation that the future depended on domestic policies, for this was the first condition 'for re-asserting our national strength and our national independence' and, since the past few weeks had brought home 'with sickening clarity' the government's total incapacity to mobilise the energies of Britain in the 1960s, that task must pass into 'other hands'.[104]

Faith in the regenerative effects of Labour's reformist interventionism, which was foreshadowed in the NEC conference statement and which was ultimately to take shape in George Brown's ill-fated National Plan, thus provided a focus for unity on the main lines of economic strategy and enabled all but the most vehement advocates of entry to accept the possibility of the failure of the negotiations with relative equanimity. And if many on the pro-EEC right remained dubious about the NEC commitment to revitalise the Commonwealth, they could nevertheless rally to the attempt to reform the world economy (and with it the nature of the EEC) through support for the Kennedy round. The party as a whole could therefore accept the compromise policy in the conviction that, whatever happened to the EEC application, a British Labour government could revive the economy through a national plan at home, and development in Commonwealth and world trade abroad.

Labour and 'Europe' After the First Application

How then should the situation in 1963 be appraised overall? First of all, it is clear that there were important elements of long-term continuity in Labour's policy. When in government between 1945–51, consideration of the Commonwealth, the world role and the threat to governmental intervention in the economy had been in the forefront of the arguments Labour had used against participation in supranational integration, and these had been reiterated throughout the 1950s. Moreover, as was argued earlier, between 1956–60, when offering critical support to the government attempts to avoid full participation in a common market through the creation of other trading blocs, the Labour front bench had again emphasised the importance of the Commonwealth abroad and interventionist economic strategies at home. The position ultimately adopted in late 1962 therefore bore a striking similarity to its earlier stance.

On the other hand, there was certainly a great difference between the categorical rejection of participation in 1951 and the compromise policy which was adopted ten years later. Moreover, as was pointed out above, there were signs in 1960 and early 1961 that the leadership, influenced by the same considerations as the Conservative Party, was becoming more open to persuasion on EEC entry. The experience of 1961–62 was thus, in part, that of the mass party pulling the leadership back towards the previous and more negative line.

The fact that a negative compromise on EEC membership was reached in 1962 reflects the tentative and partial evolution of governmental policy that was outlined at the beginning of this chapter. Because the elite was not yet convinced that Community membership was an essential goal to which all other interests must be subordinated, it was possible for even the right-wing leadership of the Labour Party to believe that other courses might be preferable. Thus whereas the SFIO had seen 'Europe' as the sole way forward, when centrist political forces had taken this line, Labour leaders, with otherwise similar ideological impulses, could feel that there were alternatives. Economic modernisation could, they hoped, be achieved by domestic investment, a national plan and an export-led boom, rather than by increased competition within the EEC; and the Commonwealth, EFTA and the 'special relationship' could all be reinvigorated by a purposeful Labour government. Indeed there was a general Labour conviction that what was wrong was not the traditional British priorities but the Conservative Party's handling of them. Only a small minority on the revisionist right of the party disputed this analysis and believed, like their counterparts in the SFIO, that modernisation depended on involvement in the EEC, while a still smaller minority of the ex-ILP left saw the Community as a vehicle for socialist internationalism.

The move towards the negative compromise thus occurred in such a way as to unify the party rather than to divide it, because the leadership's alignment with the mass movement led to the marginalisation of the pro-EEC minority. However, this was partly due to the fortuitous circumstances in which no definite decision on membership was necessary. And these circumstances masked two new factors in the situation. First, the beginnings of party political division on the issue were becoming evident now that it was a salient matter in British politics. Secondly, and of more significance to this work, the first application to the EEC saw the beginnings of an internal division within the British labour movement on the issue, leading to the possibility of reproducing within the Labour Party, the conflict between French Socialists and Communists. In 1961–63 the internal cleavage was not simply left/right, but this was more due to division on the right than the left. When the right later adopted the Establishment viewpoint on the Common Market more fully, internal left/right cleavage on the issue was to be almost inevitable, bringing with it a parallel with the French situation in which West European integration was to remain a divisive factor in the labour movement, subject to manoeuverings, conflicts and compromises.

Finally, it must be asked: what was the basis of Labour's increasingly negative attitude in 1962? In particular, is Tom Nairn correct in characterising the situation as follows:

> for years the movement had been torn apart about internationalism and socialism, and its dilemmas in that direction seemed insurmountable. Yet Gaitskell did transcend them, by cleverly seizing on the new issue represented by Europe. Clearly he could do this only by touching on certain more fundamental chords which the different sides in the old disputes shared – on a bed-rock, something even more vital to Labourism than the Bomb and Clause 4. There can be no doubt what that bed-rock was: nationalism ...

192

Thus, unable to agree about socialism, Labour could re-establish harmony over nationalism.[104]

Certainly it is clear that, despite the dispassionate beginning of Gaitskell's speech, it mounted in fervour and, by its use of emotive language, exploited existing prejudices in a demagogic fashion. This applied not only to his notorious reference to 'an end of a thousand years of history' should Britain enter the EEC and cut herself off from the Commonwealth, but also to his treatment of Europe:

> For although, of course, Europe has had a great and glorious civilisation ... there have been evil features in European history too – Hitler and Mussolini ... You cannot say what this Europe will be: It has its two faces and we do not know as yet which one will be dominant.

And, of still more significance, was the passage near the end of his speech when he claimed the best idealistic cause for the young lay not in the EEC but in Freedom from Hunger or the US Peace Corps. He continued:

> You may say: 'You can have this in Europe too.' Yes, but only on our conditions, only if Europe is a greater Europe, only if it is an outward-looking Europe, only if it is dedicated to the cause of relieving world poverty, only if it casts aside the ancient colonialisms, only if it gives up, and shows that it gives up, the narrow nationalism that it could otherwise develop.
>
> There is that possibility. But there is another side in Europe and in the European Movement – anti-US, anti-Russian, pro-colonial, the story of the Congo and Algeria, the intransigence over Berlin. We do not know which it will be, but our terms present what I believe to be the acid test.[105]

Throughout this latter passage ran the implication that Britain represented the forces of light and the EEC those of darkness, that Britain was run by internationalist-minded peace corps workers, whilst the continent was dominated by narrow-minded xenophobic colonialists.

Nor, of course, was Gaitskell alone in appealing to chauvinistic prejudices. The crude use of emotive anti-Germanism by the CP has already been noted, and it was reiterated by much of the left. Perhaps the Forward Britain Movement, an anti-market pressure group of the Labour left, which had considerable influence in trade unions, was the most sensationalist in this respect. Its membership form called upon adherents to state: 'I pledge myself to support the struggles for the independence and sovereignty of Britain and the British people'.[106] And its major themes were that the Germans, having failed to take Britain over twice in war 'now hope to do so without bloodshed with the help of our sell-out British politicians', and that the USA 'told' Britain to get into the Common Market so that it could take over New Zealand, Australia and Canada. An extract from its bulletin of August 1961 indicates its tone. Headed 'The Betrayal of Britain!' it announced:

> The statement of Mr Macmillan to the Commons on Monday, 31st July, that Britain was to seek membership of the European Common Market was the most sombre and far reaching in modern history.
>
> Sombre because although this country has had both defeat and victory in its long history, the Prime Minister's words were the tocsin of betrayal ...
>
> The Government for the Establishment here has decided to get on with the dismantling of Britain and the Commonwealth in a decade. We are to cease existing as a country. Each of the Commonwealth countries must look after itself. The idea is that Canada and Australia will drift into the economic and political thraldom of the USA. Some other constituents will fit in where they can, Britain just to *sink* into Europe ... All this is a part of long-term planning in particular in the USA, at least since 1917; late coming in during the First World War, waiting until we were nearly squeezed dry; late in the Second World War, arms on a 'cash and carry' basis until all British investments in the USA were sold. Then the great pincer movement with dear Dr Adenauer and we were trapped. Only one thing they have not yet calculated for, that is the people of this island and those in the Commonwealth. They will answer this first step of betrayal, and in the end their will shall prevail.[107]

Such shameless tirades which recall some of the propaganda of the PCF would seem to support Nairn's contention. Yet his judgement is based on oversimplification (to be discussed further in the concluding chapter). For the left of the party also used arguments against EEC membership, which were valid from a socialist perspective and which cannot be dismissed as nationalist. And even Gaitskell's invocation of justice to the Commonwealth has at least as much right to be regarded as socialist as Jenkins's commitment to a social-democratic Europe in which Britain would be modernised through exposure to continental competition.

The fact is that 'nationalism' is too emotive a word to encompass the range of Labour and left attitudes. Certainly, the fact that the

EEC was perceived with suspicion and widely regarded as threatening because of its Cold War associations, economic, political and even cultural structure, and its situation as a bloc of rich states, owes much to the British situation: that is, it was clearly a perception of the British left which even left-socialists in France did not share. But to dismiss this as nationalism and Gaitskell's technique simply as 'tear-jerking patriotism and invocation of the imperial relics' is far too easy.

It is pure idealism to suggest that, in 1963, the Labour Party should have adopted a European consciousness, for no such consciousness existed and it could not simply be manufactured. It would thus be as simplistic to suggest that the British left was motivated by sheer nationalism in staying outside the EEC as to suggest that the SFIO was prompted by pure socialism when it had favoured membership. Nevertheless, the European issue was not to go away. Continuity of attitude between 1951 and 1963 was possible because the Labour Party had not had to confront the problems stemming from Britain's changed material circumstances in the same way as the Conservatives; and in any case, even the negative compromise hardly signified a real break with consensus politics. But when the question recurred, would the Labour Party adopt a more socialist policy or would it resume full bi-partisanship on Europe? History was to reveal no clear answer.

Notes

1 Quoted in F.S. Northedge, *British Foreign Policy, 1945–61* (Allen & Unwin, 1962), p. 190.
2 There are many accounts of the reorientation in British policy, but the fullest remains that of M. Camps, *Britain and the European Community, 1955–63* (Oxford University Press, 1964). This can be supplemented with the study of party and pressure group attitudes in R. Lieber. *British Politics and European Unity* (University of California, 1970).
3 For a discussion of the Lee Report, see Camps, *Britain and the European Community*, pp. 281–2.
4 This should not, however, be exaggerated. In 1961 nearly 40% of Britain's imports still came from the Commonwealth, which also still took nearly 40% of her exports. Only 15% of British exports went to the EEC, but they were increasing at twice the rate of growth of exports to the rest of the world.
5 The U2 incident was the ostensible cause of the collapse of the conference, but the lukewarm attitude of the American Government had already been made clear. For a useful analysis of the way in which Britain's decline in power was affecting her international role, see J. Frankel, *British Foreign Policy, 1945–73* (Oxford University Press, 1975).
6 The following are particularly useful on the conflicts of this period: M. Jenkins, *Bevanism* (Spokesman, 1979), M. Foot, *Aneurin Bevan*, vol. II (Paladin, 1975) and P. Williams. *Hugh Gaitskell* (Cape, 1979).
7 The essence of Eden's proposals was that the Council of Europe would continue

to act as the umbrella organisation of West European integration but that for the ECSC, EDC and any other supranational enterprises of the Six only the representatives of the Six should have voting powers, while the other nine members of the Council would have only observer status. At the same time the British Government also suggested that some of the OEEC's functions should be transferred to NATO. The Six justifiably suspected that the British were seeking to minimise the importance of supranational integration. (For a brief summary, see Northedge, *British Foreign Policy*, pp. 144–7). For Labour support, see 'Development of Labour Party Policy towards Western Europe, 1945–53', Memorandum by the International Department, noted at the International Sub-Committee of the NEC, 20 May 1953.

8 NEC resolution on Foreign and Commonwealth Policy, LPCR 1953, p. 150.

9 (1) No German recruitment until the Atlantic Alliance countries had built up their forces in Europe; (2) Atlantic Alliance countries to have priority over Germany in receiving American equipment; (3) German forces to form part of an international army and not a German army; (4) no German army to be begun until the Germans themselves favoured the idea. Attlee's original formulation was slightly more vague, but the conditions were later defined in this manner. See *Problems of Foreign Policy* (The Labour Party, April 1952).

10 Foot, *Aneurin Bevan*, vol. II, pp. 421–3.

11 Attlee's speech in the Commons on 11–12 May 1953 welcoming Churchill's suggestion was also significant in its critical attitude to American policy and its refusal to accept the notion that a united Germany should automatically be allowed to join NATO. The Labour Party published the speech as a pamphlet, *The Way to Peace* (1953).

12 For useful summaries, from opposing viewpoints, of labour's internal struggles on the issue, see D.C. Watt, *Britain looks to Germany* (Wolff, 1965) pp. 124–7, and Foot, *Aneurin Bevan*, vol. II, pp. 421–45. Once the leadership had rallied to the Western position, after the abortive summit conference of February 1954, it released a pamphlet, *In Defence of Europe* (June 1954), which resembled the party's position when in government rather than that implied in Attlee's statement the previous year. In particular, it again fully accepted the right of a united Germany to join NATO.

13 See *Problems of Foreign Policy* (Labour Party, April 1952) and, more revealing, Denis Healey's *Report on the Third Session of the Consultative Assembly of the Council of Europe*, submitted to NEC, 23 Jan 1952, NEC Minutes.

14 Eden's major concession was the incorporation into the treaty of an undertaking not to withdraw or diminish British forces in Europe against the wishes of the majority of her partners. (In fact British forces were reduced in 1957.) Northedge, *British Foreign Policy*, pp. 162–5.

15 'Memorandum on Germany and European Defence' International Department, noted at International Sub-Committee of NEC, 20 May 1953, NEC Minutes.

16 Saul Rose, 'The Council of Europe and West European Co-operation', International Department Memoranda of November 1954 and March 1955; and memorandum of the same title by Alfred Robens and Geoffrey de Freitas, Feb. 1955, NEC Minutes.

17 Lieber, *British Politics and European Unity*, p. 143.

18 House of Commons debates, vol. 615, cols. 1152–62, 14 Dec. 1959; LPCR 1959, report on Commons debate 12 Feb. 1959, p. 71.

19 Lieber pp. 144–51; 'Note on the European Free Trade Area', for discussion at NEC, 26 March 1958, NEC Minutes.

20 House of Commons, 12 February 1959, quoted in *European Trade*, Labour Party Talking Points 13, 1959 (Harvester Microfilm).

21 'Note on the European Free Trade Area'. The Chairman of the European Co-operation Sub-committee was S. Silverman, MP and the members were H.

Earnshaw, Rt Hon. L.J. Edwards, MP, J. Hynd, MP, E. Popplewell, MP, A. Skeffington, MP, F. Willey, MP (F. Gomersall was the Secretary). The membership of the group was probably slightly more 'European' than in the NEC as a whole and it is significant that the NEC had originally found it difficult to recruit members to the committee (NEC Minutes, 25 July 1956) with only Silverman prepared to accept nomination. As the issue became more salient, the matter was dealt with by ever higher bodies: on 27 Jan. 1960 the NEC decided to set up a working party of both NEC and PLP members instead of re-establishing the existing committee; on 21 December 1960 it was agreed not to reappoint this working party (which had never met) but to allow the leadership to establish its own committees with NEC participation to examine the question (NEC Minutes). The workings of this committee will be considered below, but Lieber (*British Politics, and European Unity*, p. 114) is wrong in suggesting that the difference between the TUC and the Labour Party was that the latter handled the matter as an 'international' rather than a domestic economic matter. In fact, as the issue became salient in 1960–61, the Home Policy Sub-committee of the NEC became the dominant committee to examine the matter.

22 Camps, *Britain and the European Community*, p. 301.

23 Socialist International Contact Committee between countries of EEC and EFTA, report to International Sub-Committee, 21 Sept. 1960.

24 For the development of TUC policy, see Lieber, *British Politics and European Unity*, pp. 38–44, 36–8 and 106–115, L. Robins, *The Reluctant Party : Labour and the EEC 1961–75*(G.W. & A. Hesketh, 1979), pp. 14–16. (Robins also contains useful bibliographical information on trade union sources.)

25 The full membership was: NEC I. Mikardo, MP, R.H.S. Crossman, MP, H. Gaitskell, MP, F. Mulley, MP, H.R. Nicholas, H. Wilson, MP; Co-options: Dr T. Balogh, D. Houghton, MP, D. Jay, MP, N. Kaldor, F. Lee, MP, G.R. Mitchison, MP, L. Murray (TUC), R.R. Neild; Representatives of International-al Sub-committee: Mrs B. Castle, MP, D. Healey, MP, R. Jenkins, MP, W. Padley, MP.

26 'Britain and Europe', second draft of report submitted to Home Policy Sub-committee, 12 June 1961.

27 'Commenting and Dissenting Notes' (Nicholas Kaldor) in ibid.

28 'Dissenting Note by Roy Jenkins and Robert Neild', in ibid.

29 For a detailed examination of Gaitskell's attitudes, see Williams, *Hugh Gaitskell*, pp. 702–48.

30 See exchange of letters between Ennals and Gaitskell 11, 12 and 20 July 1961 in the box on EEC Correspondence, Labour Party Library. The same box also contains a letter from Ennals to Brown on the same subject, 7 July 1961.

31 NEC Minutes, 10 July 1961.

32 Report of the meeting of the TUC Economic and International Committees and representatives of the NEC, NEC Minutes, 26 July 1961. (The NEC was represented by Gaitskell, Alice Bacon, MP, Callaghan, Barbara Castle, Richard Crossman, D.H. Davies, D. McGarvey, Jennie Lee, Ian Mikardo, Walter Padley and Harold Wilson, and served by Len Williams, A. Bax, David Ennals and Peter Shore; the General Council, by H. Douglas, H. Collison, Miss B.A. Godwin, R. Hayday, Ted Hill, Sir Thomas Williamson, George Woodcock, and served by Len Murray, J.A. Hargreaves, D. Carline and S. Mukherjee).

33 The report of the meeting records quite clearly the attempt by George Woodcock to secure a more definite statement of attitude and Gaitskell's refusal to be drawn (ibid.)

34 While Crossman and Castle emphasised the Commonwealth, Jennie Lee drew attention to the 'forces at work within the EEC which were working against social equality, and this was particularly true of Italy where the gap between

northern and southern living standards was growing. There were fears that a future Labour government could be prevented from carrying out socialist policies and that the EEC – backed by the United States – was to be another means of intensifying the cold war'. It was also clear that the TUC was not unanimous, Ted Hill in particular being opposed to entry (ibid.).

35 LPCR 1961, p. 211.

36 Robins, *The Reluctant Party*, pp. 33, 40.

37 Williams, *Hugh Gaitskell*, p. 710.

38 *New Statesman*, 13 March 1962.

39 'Planning and the Common Market', submitted to Home Policy Sub-committee, 7 May 1962, NEC Minutes.

40 In July 1961 Selwyn Lloyd imposed a temporary stop on UK company investment in the Six and demanded the repatriation of funds held in UK subsidiaries in the Six. Gaitskell took up Shore's point and referred to the difficulty of repeating Lloyd's action as a member of the EEC in his 1962 conference speech (LPCR 1962, p. 161).

41 Peter Shore 'Planning and the Common Market', Home Policy Sub-committee, 4 June 1962, NEC Minutes.

42 Williams, *Hugh Gaitskell*, p. 709.

43 *Talking Points*, nos. 10 and 11 (1962) (Harvester Microfilm).

44 For details, see Williams, *Hugh Gaitskell*, pp. 724–8.

45 For an outline of the Commonwealth Conference, see Camps, *Britain and the European Community*, pp. 434–43.

46 Statement issued after final meeting, 8 Sept. 1962, quoted in full in 'Commonwealth and Common Market' (2), *Talking Points*, No. 15 1962 (Harvester Microfilm).

47 Ibid.

48 Williams, *Hugh Gaitskell*, p. 729.

49 'Labour and the Common Market', LPCR 1962, Appendix 1.

50 For details, see Robins, *The Reluctant Party*, p. 29 and Williams, *Hugh Gaitskell*, pp. 738–40.

51 'Labour and World Government', *Talking Points* No. 17 (1962). Labour Party concern with world government seemed to grow as membership of the EEC began to appear possible. The NEC had thus begun to consider the formulation of a paper commitment to world government as a policy aim after receiving a letter from Attlee (an opponent of the EEC) signed by 63 PLP members in May 1960 (NEC Minutes, 27 July 1960). Miriam Camps's cynical comment is surely appropriate:'Labour Party spokesmen as a rule preferred the United Nations to the Community and World Government to the institutions of the Six and did so in terms which made it difficult to avoid the conclusion that their preferences owed something to the fact that the United Nationas was weak and World Government comfortably far away' (Camps, *Britain and the European Community*, p. 448).

52 Peter Shore, 'The Common Market Negotiations: Further Developments', NEC Minutes, 3 Dec. 1962.

53 Report by Barbara Castle and Tom Driberg on 5th Congress of Socialist Parties of Member Countries of the EEC, Paris, 5–6 Nov 1962', Overseas Department Sub-committee, 4 Dec. 1962, NEC Minutes.

54 Robins argues that Gaitskell was deliberately provocative in Paris and that this precipitated the Gaullist veto (*The Reluctant Party*, pp. 41–2).

55 Camps, *Britain and the European Community*, pp. 450–66.

56 Even Philip Williams, Gaitskell's highly sympathetic biographer, believes that such considerations played a part in his new emphasis (*Hugh Gaitskell*, p. 721).

57 *The Reluctant Party*, p. 41.

58 Ibid., p. 20.

59 The views of the Communist Party are of relevance since it had exercised a far greater influence over Labour-left views after abandoning its sectarian excesses from 1953 onwards. See Jenkins, *Bevanism*, chs. 8–10 for further discussion of this point.

60 The communist press in 1953 and 1954 was saturated with articles on West Germany, but although the intensity of the coverage declined thereafter it continued as a *leitmotiv* of party publications throughout the period. For example, in March 1960 the Communist Party published John Gollan's 'The German Menace – A Damning Exposure', a highly emotive indentification of Adenauer's regime with that of Hitler, and in September 1961 E. Henri's 'The Strategy of Revenge: The Unceasing Aim of German Militarism', a far better work with the same theme.

61 See, for example, D. Bowman, *The Alternative to the Common Market* (Communist Party, July 1961). (In July 1959 *Labour Monthly* had published an article by J. Jarvie on the EEC which had picturesquely described it as 'NATO with Dungarees on'.)

62 Bowman, *Alternative to the Common Market*.

63 R. Palme Dutt, 'Notes of the Month: Cabinet Changes, Commonwealth and the Common Market', *Labour Monthly*, August 1962.

64 For discussions of the Bevanite campaign against German rearmament, see Jenkins, *Bevanism* and Foot, *Aneurin Bevan*, vol. II.

65 To some extent, ideas originating from the Labour left subsequently influenced party policy. See, in particular, NEC/TUC joint statement, 'Disengagement in Europe', 23 April 1958 (LPCR 1958, pp. 7–8) and the resolution on foreign policy adopted at the 1958 Conference (ibid., p. 186); and NEC/TUC joint statement, 'Foreign Policy and Defence' July 1960 (LPCR 1960, pp. 13–16).

66 See, for example, Clive Jenkins, LPCR 1961, pp. 214–15; *Tribune*, 5 May 1961; *This Changing World*, Victory for Socialism Pamphlet, 1961. In *The Reluctant Party*, Robins also notes that anti-Germanism was used extensively by the Labour left in the argument against the EEC.

67 This is implicit in published statements, such as *Problems of Foreign Policy* (1952) and *In Defence of Europe* (1954), but is more explicit in internal documents, quoted above: e.g. Denis Healey's 'Report on the Third Session of the Consultative Assembly' and the 'Memorandum on Germany and European Defence', 20 May 1953.

68 Williams, *Hugh Gaitskell*, p. 691. (Gaitskell was also referring to the inter-war period.)

69 Williams quotes extensively from a candid memorandum from Gaitskell to Kennedy of December 1962 in which the former explained his motives (ibid. pp. 704–5), and also cites Alastair Hetherington's diary to show that Kennedy had some sympathy for Gaitskell's attitude (p. 743). During the negotiations Wilson visited the USA and reported that, although the USA 'was still very keen for the UK to join the Common Market on political grounds, it was now worried about the possible economic implications of the external tariff' ('The UK and the Common Market: Progress Report', NEC Minutes, 28 Feb. 1962).

70 It is significant that, according to Williams, Gaitskell did not rule out an eventual federal solution *if* the Commonwealth broke up and the alternative was for Britain to be a small island off Europe (*Hugh Gaitskell*, p. 717).

71 At the time of the Marshall Plan, the CP had called for an alternative international economic policy of close co-operation between Britain, the Dominions, and the countries of the Empire in close association with the USSR and the European 'democracies' which were striving to build planned economies. (R. Palme Dutt, 'Notes of the Month', *Labour Monthly*, Sept. 1947). Subsequently the CP had supported Third World liberation movements but had maintained an ambiguous attitude on the eventual role of the Commonwealth.

72 See, for example, R. Palme Dutt, 'Notes of the Month', *Labour Monthly*, Oct. 1962.

73 See, for example, *One Way Only: A Socialist Analysis of the Present World Crisis*, Tribune pamphlet, July 1951.

74 See, for example, Bevan, 'In Place of the Cold War', *Tribune* July 1953 and the pamphlet *It Need Not Happen*, Tribune 1954.

75 The British Guiana crisis of 1953 led to the split, ultimately bringing about the formation of the Movement for Colonial Freedom, because the Labour-left supported Jagan and Burnham while the Fabian Colonial Bureau feared that such leaders would introduce 'totalitarianism' (P.S. Gupta, *Imperialism and the Labour Movement, 1914–64* (Macmillan, 1975 p.360).

76 Bevan's attempt to introduce a new relationship between Labour and such countries as India and Yugoslavia was indicative of these general ideas (Foot, *Aneurin Bevan*, vol. II, p. 403).

77 An important element in this was the increasing alienation not only from French political life in general, but also from the SFIO following the latter party's actions in Suez, Algeria and, finally, in acquiescing in de Gaulle's return to power. At the 1958 Labour Party conference, John Mendelson condemned the SFIO for its failure to defend democractic liberties and called upon the NEC and the Socialist International to admit the PSA as a member, to which Bevan replied (for the NEC) that the situation would be watched carefully (LPCR 1958, p. 244). Shortly before, Bevan himself had written a scathing attack on the SFIO (*News of the World*, 1 June 1958, quoted in Foot, *Aneurin Bevan*, vol. II, p. 604).

78 LPCR 1962, pp. 177–8.

79 Harold Wilson managed to play on two prejudices in a single sentence: 'We are not entitled to sell our friends and kinsmen down the river for a problematical and marginal advantage in selling washing machines in Düsseldorf' (House of Commons debates, vol. 645, col. 1665, 3 August 1961).

80 This is the implication of Tom Nairn's argument in *The Left against Europe?* (Penguin, 1973).

81 Gupta, *Imperialism and the Labour Movement*, p. 372.

82 *The Guardian*, 21 January 1957 (quoted in Williams, *Hugh Gaitskell*, p. 702). See also Gaitskell 'The New Commonwealth', *Socialist Commentary*, March 1958.

83 'Britain and Europe'.

84 Williams, *Hugh Gaitskell*, p. 717.

85 LPCR 1962, p. 175 (Jenkins speech ibid, p. 173.)

86 Bowman, 'The Alternative to the Common Market'.

87 *The Reluctant Party*, p. 24.

88 Aneurin Bevan, *In Place of Fear* (Quartet, 1978), p. 202.

89 *Tribune*, 30 August 1957, quoted in Foot, *Aneurin Bevan*, vol. II, p. 559.

90 See above, pp. 164, 168, 170–2.

91 LPCR 1962, pp. 160–1.

92 'Labour and the Common Market', LPCR 1962, Appendix I.

93 He would not have been so vehement in his criticisms of Shore's paper in May 1962 had he not believed this.

94 *Daily Herald*, 31 Jan 1962, cited in Lieber, *British Politics and European Unity*, p. 172.

95 Three of the four Labour MPs who had voted against the decision to open negotiations in August 1961 were clearly on the extreme left of the party: Zilliacus, H.O. Davies and Emrys Hughes. The fourth was Michael Foot, whose position was always more ambiguous.

96 Williams, *Hugh Gaitskell*, pp. 710, 737.

97 Almost every left-wing opponent of the EEC paid tribute to Gaitskell's conference speech and Frank Cousins, Gaitskell's erstwhile enemy over unilateralism, committed the T & GWU to print a millionn copies of it for free distribution.

98 Williams, *Hugh Gaitskell*, p. 740.

99 Patrick Gordon Walker and Denis Healey, two other Gaitskellites, were also opposed, although Healey's position was less vehement than previously.

100 Minutes of Labour Common Market Committee, 14 Sept. 1961 and 18 April 1962 (Harvester Microfilm).

101 *Labour and the Common Market*.

102 Speech to Labour Party conference, 1962 (Harvester microfilm).

103 House of Commons, 11 Feb. 1963, quoted in 'The Common Market: Breakdown and Aftermath', *Talking Points* no. 7 (1963) (Harvester Microfilm).

104 Nairn, *The Left Against Europe?* p. 40.

105 LPCR 1962, pp. 155–65.

106 *Forward Britain Movement Bulletin,* July 1961 (Harvester Microfilm).

107 Ibid. The FBM's foreign policy ideas (neutralism, development of East–West trade and trade with the Third World, opposition to nuclear weapons, and a vehement emphasis on national independence) were typical of much Labour-left thought and were probably influenced by the CP. But any vestiges of socialism were subordinated to strident nationalism and an attempt to maintain a popular front with Tory right-wing opponents of the EEC.

6

Labour and the EEC, 1964–72

From Consensus Politics to the
Politics of Dissent

The shifts in the Labour Party's attitudes towards the European Community between the Gaullist veto in January 1963 and Britain's entry into the EEC ten years later are legendary and the inconsistencies were to provide the majority of the media and pro-'European' forces with a first-class propaganda target. However, although opportunism was an element in the situation, Labour's volte-faces also emanated from more fundamental processes in the politics of the party and the nation: processes which involved the very nature of the post-war consensus. This chapter explores the interconnections between the changes in the 'European' policy of the Labour Party and the wider context of British politics.

The Labour Government and Britain's Second Application to the EEC

Although the EEC was not a contentious issue in the General Election campaign of 1964 Harold Wilson, the new leader of the Labour Party, used it on occasion to attack the Conservative Government. For example, on 6 February 1964 he challenged the Tories not to consider 'entry into the Common Market on any terms which would reduce Britain's existing freedom to trade with the Commonwealth' and declared 'on behalf of my party, I give that pledge'.[1] Again, in its election manifesto, the Labour Party condemned the Conservative Government for its readiness to negotiate entry under highly unfavourable terms, and stated that, although a Labour government would seek 'closer links with our European neighbours, the Labour Party is convinced that the first responsibility of a British government is still to the Commonwealth'.[2] In office, however, the Labour leadership soon faced difficulties which it had not anticipated and its policy evolved in directions which had not been foreshadowed.

Even during its first year in government there were signs that a change of attitude was taking place. In June 1965, when Wilson spoke of the difficulties of joining the EEC he stressed the problems involved in accepting the Common Agricultural Policy and the associated balance of payments difficulties rather than Labour's five conditions;[3] and at the annual conference in the autumn, and subsequently in the House of Commons, Michael Stewart, the Foreign Secretary, played down the five conditions and made distinctly conciliatory gestures towards the Community.[4] Moreover, at the beginning of 1966 Michael Stewart and George Brown (then in charge of the Department of Economic Affairs) exerted great, and apparently successful, pressure on Wilson to embark on a new EEC initiative.[5]

At this stage, however, Wilson was uncertain as to whether a new application stood any chance of success. Moreover, in the impending General Election campaign he, and the leadership in general, wanted to contrast Labour's 'prudent' approach with the allegedly unconditional attitude of the Conservative Party. However, almost immediately after the Election the pace quickened. In the Queen's speech in April, Wilson intimated that some obstacles to entry had diminished, and a more co-ordinated policy team was established under George Brown, aided by George Thomson. Both subsequently made it clear that they no longer regarded the five conditions as binding.[6] A further and perhaps decisive change came in August when Brown became Foreign Secretary (after threatening resignation over the weakening of the Department of Economic Affairs), and immediately declared that, although the Commonwealth was very important, Britain could be more use to the world and the Commonwealth as leader of the European Community.[7]

The external obstacles to membership, primarily in the shape of General de Gaulle, had not been removed and many ministers remained doubtful as to whether there was any serious prospect of entry in these circumstances. However, the most committed proponents of entry, perhaps persuaded by the Foreign Office, seem to have become convinced that de Gaulle would not be able to withstand pressures in favour of British membership both from his five partners, and from within France herself.[8] The only remaining barrier to a new initiative was therefore the need to secure Cabinet consent.

The Labour Cabinet was totally divided as to the merits of entry into the EEC and an all-day conference on the issue at Chequers on 22 October 1966 did nothing to change this.[9] However, at the end of it, Wilson announced a new and highly significant move: the decision that he and George Brown should visit the capitals of the Six early the next year in order to ascertain whether negotiated entry, on acceptable conditions, appeared possible. In theory this amounted to no more than a diplomatic probe, and Cabinet anti-marketeers reassured themselves with the belief that no decisions had yet been taken. In reality, however, the visits were more akin to informal negotiations, and the opponents of the EEC found themselves unable to contain the impetus that had been created. Thus despite the expression of serious disagreements, the Cabinet voted in favour of making a formal application at the end of April. According to Crossman the only minister (apart from Wilson himself) to have changed his mind during the course of the prolonged discussions was Anthony Benn, the Minister of Technology, who had become 'converted for technological reasons into an ardent Common Marketeer'.[10] Crossman's estimate of the division of opinion on 1 May 1967 was; 'yes without qualification' ten, 'no without qualification' seven, and 'maybe' six.[11] However, Crossman also made the point that Wilson's position was stronger still 'because the six in the middle are nearly all convinced that if any approach is to be made it should be make quickly and with a will'. Despite the shift that had taken place since 1964, Wilson was therefore able to announce the decision to apply to the EEC without the prospect of a major Cabinet revolt; and three months later he forced the resignation of Douglas Jay, who had publicly proclaimed his own opposition to the Community, without any fear that this would provoke any united action by the Cabinet anti-marketeers.[12]

De Gaulle renewed his veto in November 1967, before the formal negotiations had begun, and although the Labour Government 'left the application on the table' the external circumstances only changed during its last few months in office. The Wilson Government was therefore never given the opportunity to engage in the real bargaining which began immediately after it left office in June 1970.[13] But why had the reorientation of policy, which resulted in the 1967 application, taken place? Both international and domestic considerations were of relevance.

In 1962 part of Labour's attack on the Conservative Government had been based upon support for EFTA as an alternative European grouping which had no supranational or restrictive political aspects. However, in October 1964 the Labour Government, which had inherited a massive balance of payments deficit, itself weakened the organisation by imposing a 15 per cent surcharge on EFTA imports in clear contravention of the EFTA treaty. At the meeting of the EFTA council in February 1965, the atmosphere had improved when the surcharge was reduced to 10 per cent, but it was already becoming clear to the government – as to its Conservative predecessors – that EFTA could provide no solution to Britain's balance of trade problems. The emphasis therefore began to switch – again in the same way as with the Conservative government – to that of bridge building between EFTA and the EEC, and in May 1965, Wilson upgraded the EFTA council meeting to Head of Government level in order to increase the impetus in this direction. However, it was rapidly becoming apparent that the Six had little interest in such notions and that full membership might be the only alternative to isolation.[14]

Developments in the Commonwealth were of far greater importance and here too reality failed to accord with the optimistic aspirations expressed in Opposition. The Labour Party had previously insisted that Commonwealth trade could be increased if sufficient will existed, but during Labour's first two years in office it actually declined as a percentage of Britain's total trade.[15] At the Commonwealth Prime Ministers' Conference in 1965 it was agreed that the new secretariat should explore ways of increasing the trade, but this offered no genuine basis for a belief that the trend decline could be reversed, and the government was clearly losing faith in the Commonwealth as a major element in Britain's economic revival. Political events were perhaps of still greater importance and, once again, these repeated the pattern experienced under the Conservatives. Thus in April 1965 the Indo-Pakistan war was settled by Soviet, rather than British mediation, in August the 'new' Commonwealth was alienated by Labour's imposition of immigration controls, and in November the government's failure to act decisively against the white minority regime in Rhodesia led to the severing of diplomatic relations by some African Commonwealth members. All this revealed Labour's earlier aspirations to make Britain the centre of a multiracial world community as wholly illusory.

The final international pressure which had driven the Conservative Government to seek EEC membership had been the decline of the special relationship with the USA and the belief that it could be strengthened by British leadership of the European Community. Here again the Labour Government was to find, like its Conservative predecessor, that its views carried no weight in Washington when they ran counter to those of the American administration. In particular, Wilson's attempts to mediate in the Vietnam dispute – in response to Party pressure – made no impact on President Johnson, who finally undermined British policy in February 1967.[16] Nor did the relationship operate satisfactorily on an economic plane, for the Americans gave sterling little support, increased investment in the EEC more quickly than in Britain, and made it clear from the start of the Kennedy Round trade negotiations that the principal bargaining was to be carried out between the European Community and the

United States.[17] All the international considerations which had led the Conservative Government to turn to the EEC were thus felt by the Labour leadership within their first two years in office. To these were added the domestic factors.

In October 1962 the Labour Party had professed indifference to the EEC in a mood of self-confidence about the ability of a Labour government to transform Britain, and this faith in the regenerative capacities of Labour had been given an immense boost by the election of Harold Wilson as Labour leader early the next year. Indeed, for more than three years he had been able to dominate the party and to provide a persuasive rallying call for all those seeking a progressive alternative to conservatism, with his talk of harnessing 'science to socialism' in the exhilarating task of creating 'The New Britain'.[18] However, the general collapse of this reforming strategy led the Wilson Government increasingly to adopt the expedients of its Conservative predecessor, including the belief that the EEC might solve the overriding problem of relative decline.

A central element in Labour's domestic programme had been the adoption of indicative national planning. This had been predicated on the assumption of growth, based on investment in technologically-based industry leading in turn to an export boom. In fact, from the start, the policy was doomed by Wilson's insistence on maintaining the international parity of sterling, despite the balance of payments deficit; and by July 1966, the National Plan – the centrepiece in the expansionist policy – had been subordinated to an array of orthodox deflationary measures.[19]

While Labour's strategy for the revitalisation of Britain was disintegrating, the government faced increased pressure from the Establishment to adopt an alternative approach based on entry into the EEC. In particular, the Confederation of British Industry (CBI), now more representative of large-scale industry than its predecessor (the Federation of British Industry) saw the Community as the major opportunity for economic revival, and this viewpoint was echoed throughout the elite press. The Conservative and Liberal parties were both unambiguously in favour of membership and, in the depressing economic circumstances of 1966, public opinion polls also showed a rare majority for EEC entry. Finally, and naturally of great relevance, the TUC general council, still dominated by 'moderates', echoed the conviction of big and modern industry that entry would be beneficial.[20] It was in these circumstances that the Labour Government turned to the Community.

In general the justifications for the new policy were extremely similar to those of the Conservative Party. The Labour leadership thus reiterated the view that British and European influence would be enhanced by entry and that this would both strengthen the

Atlantic Alliance and the pressures towards East–West *detente*; and Labour spokesmen also attempted to reassure doubters that more could be achieved for the Commonwealth inside the Market than outside it. However, there was one theme which, though not original, was to be the hallmark of the 1967 application: the imperative of modernisation through technological advance.[21]

Wilson introduced this theme immediately after the Cabinet's decision in favour of the diplomatic 'probe' in autumn 1966:

> We are embarking on an adventure of the kind that enabled merchant venturers of the City of London and other cities in time past to win treasure and influence and power for Britain. We go forward in the same spirit of enterprise today. I believe the tide is right, the time is right, the winds are right to make the effort.
>
> I would like to see a drive to create a new technological inventiveness in Britain and other European countries, to enable Europe on a competitive basis to become more self-reliant and neither dependent on imports nor dominated from outside but basing itself on competitive indigenous European industries.[22]

The message was reiterated both inside the Community and in Britain throughout the next year and was finally given a little more substance on 13 November 1967, just before the veto, when Wilson put forward 'urgent proposals' to create a European-scale industry which would be really competitive with that of the USA.[23]

Analysts have tended to treat such ideas in two ways: as a crude propaganda device designed to reassure de Gaulle about British independence from the United States, and as a means of rallying the Labour Party behind the application.[24] Both interpretations are valid. Yet there was also a third factor. Wilson had previously exuded confidence about the possibility of transforming Britain through modernisation of the capitalist economy: after the failure of the attempt he was now transferring the same assumptions onto the European plane. In his Lord Mayor's speech in November 1967 he thus paid particular tribute to the CBI and urged it to greater co-operation with its counterparts in the EEC, and he advocated the creation of larger units on a European scale as the means to efficiency. His vision was now of a dynamic British economy, which would grow through increased competition and co-operation in Europe.[25]

The Labour Government had taken a major step towards the adoption of the economic assumptions of non-socialist pro-marketeers. Rather than adhering to the belief that modernisation could be brought about by state planning, it had now largely accepted the view that it would result from external competion and private investment. Its hope was that this would induce increased productivity, linked to greater output and growth, and the elimination of the 'stop-go' cycle. This, in turn, would facilitate the payment of higher wages and social benefits and the establishment of a harmonious relationship between trade unions and the owners of industry.

If the government's economic thinking closely resembled that of the Establishment, so too did its political aspirations. The Labour leadership hoped that entry into the EEC would increase British influence, but it wanted as little change as possible in its existing relationship with the USA and the Commonwealth. Nor did it welcome any idea that 'Europe' should follow a distinct policy of its own and, in particular, it opposed de Gaulle's notions of a 'European Europe' as threatening to NATO. In other words, the application for EEC membership in 1967 constituted the reestablishment of consensus politics, which had appeared threatened in 1962 when the Labour Party had assumed a negative attitude to Macmillan's approach.[26]

However, the Cabinet remained deeply divided about the merits of the application and, when the subsequent Conservative administration finally negotiated entry into the EEC, former Labour ministers were to engage in a public dispute as to whether the government would have accepted similar terms in 1967. The two ministers most closely associated with the initiative – George Thomson and George Brown – immediately announced that the agreement would have been acceptable, and this viewpoint was also expressed forcibly by Roy Jenkins and his associates in the Labour Committee for Europe. However, Barbara Castle, Richard Crossman, Fred Peart, Willie Ross, George Thomas and Peter Shore (who only entered the Cabinet in August 1967 after the application had been announced) replied that they would have rejected the terms.[27] Moreover, at the party conferences in 1971 and 1972, both James Callaghan and Harold Wilson himself poured scorn on the notion that the Labour Government would have entered on the conditions secured by the Heath Government.[28] Naturally such arguments had more to do with justifying support for positions taken in 1971 than with establishing the truth about 1967. Yet it is worth speculating as to whether the Labour Government would have entered had the veto *not* been imposed.

It has already been noted that, long before May 1967, the five conditions of 1962 had been quietly jettisoned, to be replaced by two main issues:

(1) Satisfactory arrangements on the Common Agricultural Policy (CAP) including, in particular, a transition period, and a

method of financing CAP under which 'Britain would pay its full budgetary contribution, but would not be called upon to shoulder a totally disproportionate financial burden'.[29]
(2) Satisfactory arrangements for New Zealand dairy producers and Commonwealth sugar growers.[30]

In addition it was stressed that the removal of controls over capital movements could lead to a possible leak of portfolio investment from the UK to North America, against which Britain would seek the freedom to take action herself.[31] The terms which were finally agreed between the Community and the Heath Government failed to meet these conditions.[32] The CAP had been settled, on French insistence, in December 1969 prior to the negotiations, and resulted in a British budgetary contribution which was subsequently to cause a series of crises between Britain and the Community; neither New Zealand nor the Commonwealth sugar producers secured guaranteed agreements for the long term; and the Heath Government accepted, without reservations, free movement of capital to which it was ideologically committed in any case. However, if the discrepancy between the agreements in 1971 and the conditions sought in 1967 provided a basis for the claim that the Labour Cabinet would not have entered on such terms, the case is not as strong as it appears.[33]

In the first place, the extent to which the Labour Cabinet had accepted the EEC should be stressed. In 1967 it was agreed that the Community neither prevented the implementation of domestic economic planning, nor the exercise of an independent foreign policy, and the *principle* of the CAP had been accepted. In addition, the narrowing of the specified Commonwealth interests to the two mentioned above changed the whole emphasis from that expressed in 1962. The argument that the 1967 application was qualitatively different from that of the subsequent Conservative Government cannot, therefore, be sustained. Secondly, it was hardly convincing to contrast the terms demanded in 1967 with those eventually obtained by the Heath Government. After all the Conservatives could have pointed to similar differences between their opening stance and the final agreement, for example, on the size of the budgetary contribution. It is a general feature of negotiations that positions shift during their course. Thirdly, the major reason for the comparative harshness of the terms (which had not been easily predictable in 1967) was the series of decisions on the CAP taken by the Council of Ministers in December 1969. However, the Labour Government had not withdrawn its application at this stage, although this would have been appropriate had it really believed that entry would only be acceptable on the specified terms.[34]

The real issue was not that of the terms in isolation, but of the degree of commitment of the 1967 Cabinet. The terms would have prevented an obstacle to entry at that time only if the application had been tentative or if the anti-marketeers had wielded sufficient strength to have prevented entry on 'unsatisfactory' terms. However, the situation appears to have been quite different.

The presentation of the application indicated a belief that the obstacles could and must be overcome. George Brown's speeches as Foreign Secretary were the most striking in this sense. He told the Commons: 'We shall make our application short, clear, positive and to the point. In the application there will be no "ifs" and "buts", no conditions or stipulations. We shall apply to join.'[35] Two months later he was telling the Western European Union that enlargement would not effect the fundamentals of the Communities and that negotiations should be short for the British would accept precisely the same treaty aims and obligations as the Six.[36] And at the Labour Party conference he claimed that his tour of the capitals with Wilson had shown that there were a limited number of outstanding issues, all of which were soluble and that there was nothing in the Treaty of Rome which could not be accepted, subject to settling the agricultural, balance of payments and financing arrangements. Moreover, he minimised the impact of these problems should Britain join and maximised the costs of staying outside.[37] As a more prudent politician, and one who was somewhat obsessed with quoting himself to demonstrate his own consistency, Wilson was naturally more circumspect in his public statements about membership. Nevertheless, he too stressed the urgency of the application and the overwhelming advantages of membership and played down the conditions of entry rather than emphasising them.[38] Moreover, there is contemporary evidence of a total change in Wilson's attitude, following his tour of the six capitals with Brown, as a result of which he enthusiastically sought a governmental triumph through EEC entry and tended to minimise all the obstacles in the process.[39]

The suggestion that the Cabinet anti-marketeers would have prevented entry on unsatisfactory terms is also unconvincing. First, the personalities involved, their positions in the government and the party, and the dynamics of Cabinet government all make it highly unlikely that a Cabinet revolt would have taken place on an issue in which the prestige of both Wilson and the government were heavily involved, unless a major rebellion in the party had already taken place.[40] (See below.) But there is also a second, and more fundamental reason to view the notion of a Cabinet rebellion with scepticism: the strength of support for the application by the dominant forces in society, and the apparent lack of alternatives to it.

This meant that it was never sufficient for Cabinet anti-marketeers simply to present a negative case on the ill-effects of the EEC, refusing to discuss the alternatives to membership. The generally accepted view was that Britain was now in a situation of prolonged decline in economic strength and political influence, which could be reversed only by a bold initiative. In these circumstances cogent critisms of the balance of payments effects by Douglas Jay or Peter Shore could make little impact (although they may have led pro-marketeers to elevate the importance of the alleged long-term benefits).[41] Attacks by figures such as Fred Peart on apparently less central aspects of the EEC, such as the agricultural impact, made still less impression.[42] For the anti-marketeers to have stood a chance of stemming the tide towards membership, they needed to be both united and to subscribe to an alternative political and economic strategy. Neither condition obtained in 1967. Douglas Jay was on the far right of the party, while Barbara Castle was on the left; Healey, Peart, Shore and Crossman were generally close to Wilson despite their differences on the EEC. Jay vested his hopes in two (impracticable) alternatives: either the type of agreement between the EEC and EFTA which both the Conservative and Labour governments had sought without success, or a wider North Atlantic free trade association, in which the American government showed no interest and which may have been still more threatening to British industry than the EEC.[43] Moreover, his aspirations remained those of the post-war Labour Government: world-wide influence through 'the political kinship of Britain, Canada, New Zealand and Australia ... and the more successful of the newly independent Commonwealth countries'.[44] Not only did these ideas contain no hint of a socialist solution, but they were also now viewed as anachronistic by the political and economic elite.

On the other hand, Richard Crossman differed from the leadership from the opposite point of view. He deplored the whole attempt to maintain Britain as a major power with world-wide influence and believed that adherence to this goal underlay Wilson's wish to enter the EEC. He thus told the Cabinet:

> I was not a Common Marketeer. I was one of the minority who believe in Britain's future as an offshore island, cutting down all our overseas commitments, getting ourselves an economic position as favourable as that of Japan in the Far East and living on our own as an independent socialist community.[45]

And if his own account is to be believed, he constantly urged the ending of the special role of sterling and the defence commitment east of Suez as the means to obtain the socialist 'Little England' that

211

he sought. Such notions, which were probably shared by Barbara Castle, contained the germs of a radical alternative policy to Common Market entry. However, they were unacceptable to other anti-EEC members of the Cabinet and were never even developed by Crossman himself, who actually favoured a 'whole-hearted effort to enter Europe', arguing that the 'possibility of the offshore island' could be considered if the attempt failed.[46] This hardly constituted an alternative strategy.

Overall it therefore seems that the 1967 Cabinet can be described as follows. A minority, on the revisionist right of the party, led by George Brown and Roy Jenkins, was deeply and positively committed to Market entry, and was greatly strengthened by the conversion of some of the pragmatists – and above all Wilson – following the failure of the previous strategy and the strength of pro-EEC opinion in the Establishment. On the other side was a disparate group of sceptics or opponents of the EEC, who acquiesced in the initiative because they had no alternative to offer. The bi-partisan agreement, which had defined Britain's position as the centre of the world-wide Commonwealth in the post-war period had now (temporarily) been reconstituted on a new basis: that is, in the assumption that membership of the EEC would bring about renewed political influence and economic modernisation.

Naturally the Labour Cabinet was not wholly autonomous from the wider labour movement and may have been induced to take a different position had the mass party vehemently opposed entry, as might have been expected given its stance in 1962. Its position must now be considered.

The Labour Party and the 1967 Application

The attitudes of the Labour Party to the leadership's application to the EEC in 1966–67 were contradictory. On the one hand considerable discontent was apparently manifested when over one hundred Labour MPs signed an early day motion in February urging that: 'Britain, in consultation with her EFTA partners, should be ready to enter the EEC only if essential British and Commonwealth interests can be safeguarded.'[47] And after the Commons debate on the application in May, 36 MPs voted against the leadership, while a further 50 abstained (including seven Parliamentary Secretaries, who were immediately dismissed). In addition, there was organised opposition to EEC entry within the labour movement. In the PLP an anti-EEC pressure group (The Britain and Europe Group)[48] claimed over 100 members, and the Chairman of the PLP himself, Emmanuel Shinwell, was a vehement critic who clashed with

George Brown on the issue.[49] On the left, *Tribune* continued a strong and sometimes effective campaign and secured a major coup just before the announcement of the application when it published a statement signed by 74 MPs rejecting the EEC and calling for an alternative approach.[50] (See further discussion below.) Likewise, outside the party, the Communists continued their anti-EEC campaign and bitterly condemned the application.[51] On the other hand, there was no sign of a serious rebellion over the announcement of the diplomatic probe in November 1966, and there was an effective majority for the application at all levels of the party hierarchy: in Parliament, where approximately two-thirds of the PLP voted in favour, in the national executive, where a statement in support of the government was approved by sixteen votes to three,[52] and in the conference where this statement and an unconditionalist resolution were approved, while a cautiously critical resolution was rejected by almost two million votes.[53]

In comparison with the situation either five years earlier or five years later, this degree of party support for (or acquiescence in) membership of the EEC was indeed remarkable, and suggests that the leadership would probably have carried the mass movement in favour of entry.[54] How is this to be explained?

Negative factors were clearly of some relevance, and in particular, the fact that Labour MPs and the conference were being asked to support a decision to negotiate rather than a decision to enter the EEC. For it is clear that the rebellion would have been greater had the rank and file believed that government policy constituted an unconditionalist approach rather than a probe to see if the terms were right.[55] In a formal sense they were, of course, justified in this conviction, but their willingness to accept the leadership's word was reinforced by a second negative factor of some importance: the government's largely successful attempt to avoid internal controversy on the issue by providing as little information as possible about its policy.[56] Before November 1966 this was achieved by arguing that there had been no change in party policy and, thereafter, by insisting that no final decision on entry had yet been made. A third negative factor, which may have played some part in inhibiting potential parliamentary opposition, was Wilson's reimposition of stricter party discipline on 2 March 1967.[57]

Yet even when such factors are given due weight they do not provide an adequate explanation for the quiescence on the issue in 1966–67. When successful party revolts occur there is normally ample evidence of vehement rank-and-file feeling on the subject long in advance: The mass party created no such impression with regard to the EEC at this time. The NEC reflected a general attitude: that is, some anxiety by a limited number of members about 'Europe' and the government's failure to involve the wider party in its policy, but far less widespread concern over this than over other issues.[58] And, in general, Labour Party opposition was comparatively muted in expression. For example, although it was clear from the speech by Frank Cousins at the 1967 Labour conference that the Transport and General Workers Union was anti-EEC, its defeated motion was, in itself, no more negative than that which had been carried at the 1961 conference as a compromise around which proponents and opponents of the EEC could unite.[59] The same pattern was discernible within the PLP. The February 1967 early day motion was thus designed to reaffirm the conditions of entry and could easily be supported by those who simply wished to strengthen the government's negotiating position.[60] Indeed even the intransigent opponents in the PLP who refused to support the application in May 1967 stated, as their reason, the government's failure explicitly to affirm its adherence to the five conditions.[61] It is true that opposition to the EEC, at least until the referendum of 1975, was normally couched in reference to the terms rather than the principle of entry. But the fact that even those who were the most hostile to the Common Market put down comparatively mild motions and were still unable to secure great support demonstrates their defensiveness and the extent to which the government held the initiative.

One reason which has been suggested for the supremacy of the government and the defensiveness of its critics is the effectiveness of the propaganda of the Labour Committee for Europe and its attractiveness to newer, younger and more middle-class MPs elected in 1964 and 1966.[62] There is no doubt that, under Roy Jenkins's inspiration and in close relationship – financial and institutional – with the European Movement, the Labour Committee for Europe (LCE) evolved after 1963 into a highly professional pressure group. In the belief that de Gaulle's veto had eliminated the possibility of early entry into the EEC it had set about its tasks of counteracting xenophobic anti-market propaganda and of converting the PLP and trade union leaders into acceptance of the view that socialism could not be built in Britain alone.[63] In addition it had stressed the technological and political arguments, later to be taken up with such zeal by Wilson, and had emphasised the extent to which socialists and trade unionists in the Six favoured the Community. Thus while anti-EEC groups, such as the Forward Britain Movement, had collapsed almost as soon as the issue had ceased to be salient, the LCE had continued its activities in an attempt to develop generalised pro-Community attitudes, and its access to Cabinet opinion ensured that it was well placed to launch a really active propaganda campaign with a new style of urgency once it became apparent that an application was probable. Its progress was rapid: membership increased from 53 in winter 1964–65 to 60 a year later and 104 in March 1967 with younger, newer MPs attracted to a disproportionate extent. On the other side, although a similar membership was claimed, it was without effective leadership, deprived of resources and unsure of its purposes.[64]

Yet pressure-group activity is, at best, a secondary explanation for governmental supremacy over the party. The LCE grew really rapidly only after the government announced its EEC probe and this suggests governmental domination over opinion rather than any independent LCE influence. Moreover, in the very different circumstances of 1970–71 the LCE declined dramatically although its propaganda was still highly professional and the PLP was even more middle class and potentially pro-EEC in composition than in 1967.[65] Finally, its activity could not explain the quiescence of the conference, for the LCE neither made, nor even tried to make, any inroads into rank-and-file opinion in the trade unions or constituency Labour parties. Governmental dominance must therefore be explained in wider terms.

One part of the explanation is that, though tarnished, the Wilson mystique still held at the time of the application. His stress on the need to create a technological community free from American domination struck a chord with many in the labour movement. The white heat of the technological revolution, as promised in 1964, had not materialised. Could it not be, as Wilson now suggested, because Britain offered too small a market for the research and development costs necessarily involved in technologically advanced production? In reality of course, this suggestion sidestepped all the fundamental problems of political control over private, multinational industry. But perhaps this was its very attraction to many in the Labour Party who sought modernisation of the economy and increased living standards for the British people without confrontation between classes or nations. Similarly, the leadership's political message was bound to appeal to many in the party who had gone through the same sobering experiences since 1964 as Wilson himself: that is, they had found that the Commonwealth did not offer Britain the comfortable world influence to which they had aspired and they found the prospect of being closely tied to the USA less attractive in the era of Vietnam. At the same time dual processes within the EEC – the emergence of Willy Brandt as West German Foreign Minister and of de Gaulle's foreign policy – diminished (temporarily) its associations with the Cold War, and the spectre of a European federation which would necessitate the abandonment of British independence. For the solid centre of the Labour Party the EEC could therefore offer some sense of purpose in the midst of the generally depressing experience of a Labour Government which had not, after all, built a new Britain. In addition to such positive sentiments, basic loyalty to the leadership was also naturally an important factor.

If this accounts for the solidarity of the centre with Wilson's EEC initiative, what of the Labour left? In general, the traditional parliamentary Labour left, and much of the extra-parliamentary movement, remained firmly suspicious of the Common Market for the reasons outlined in Chapter 5. However, two important qualifications must be made. First the Labour left was comparatively weak and disorientated: Bevan had not been replaced as 'leader' and the position was further complicated by the inclusion of Crossman and Barbara Castle in the Cabinet. More important still was the fact that no mass movement had yet been galvanised into action in the way which was subsequently to be the case. Secondly, a minority 'third-force' pro-EEC left had resurfaced, with Eric Heffer as its main spokesman.

Taking socialist internationalism seriously, Heffer argued that the dangers of a loss of sovereignty had been deliberately exaggerated and that those who denounced the EEC as capitalist ignored the socialist potential on the continent and forgot that the suggested alternatives of the Commonwealth, EFTA and a North Atlantic free trade association were at least as capitalist.

> Once we enter into Europe, a united Europe spreading out and getting wider and wider until we create a fully integrated Europe, we will find that the relationship with the United States will be very much different ... Do we not want our independence from the United States? Have we not been a satellite far too long of the United States? Is it not time we created a third force in the world that is big enough and strong enough to stand up to the pressures of both the United States and of the Soviet Union?...
>
> We must fight for a Socialist United States of Europe ... I believe that the way to get there is first to get into the EEC, to fight for its expansion and to fight to turn it into a Socialist economic community.[66]

Heffer and a handful of other Labour-left MPs were also prepared to sign LCE statements clearly designed to counteract the *Tribune* view and such support, though representing only a small minority of the left, provided valuable support for the government, helped the LCE (temporarily) to shed its revisionist-right image and inhibited the formation of a united anti-EEC campaign by the left.[67]

Finally, the opponents of the EEC in the party were impeded by the same factors which weakened the anti-marketeers within the Cabinet: their clear political divisions, and their inability to provide an alternative which could carry conviction in the circumstances of 1967.[68] While the main thrust of opposition still came from the left of the party, in Parliament some of the most prominent opponents tended to be ageing figures on the right, including Shinwell. Communist Party condemnation of the EEC still stressed the anti-Soviet theme, which made little impact on the bulk of the Labour Party, and Trotskyist-inspired criticism secured negligible support. The most coherent critique of the EEC – covering its international, domestic and regional aspects from a socialist point of view – was probably the *Tribune* declaration of 5 May 1967 supported by 74 MPs. However, its political overtones appeared too radical or impracticable for the majority of MPs and trade union leaders at the time:

> The alternative we propose is a move to a wider Europe as a step towards a world community. We ask the Government to enlist the support of the EFTA countries, the Six and the Communist Powers to give the UN Economic Commission for Europe the authority to act as an effective link between the various groupings and to promote economic, financial and technical co-operation.[69]

Nor did it specify a fully coherent alternative for the British economy should this aspiration prove unobtainable, and it entertained the same illusions as Douglas Jay about the reversibility of the trends in trade with the Commonwealth.

Governmental dominance can therefore be explained by Wilson's hold over the centre and right, the incoherence and division of the left, and the inability of the critics to provide a convincing alternative economic or political strategy to set against EEC membership. All this implies that Wilson would have been able to rally the party behind a successful application. If so, this would have represented a full renewal of consensus politics on the new orientation of Britain's external relationships. However, it was not to be, and when the EEC again became a major issue in British politics much had changed.

Before considering the break-down of the consensus, it is instructive to compare the situation with that in France. After all, in Britain in 1966–67 bi-partisan agreement on the importance of the European Community appeared to suggest the kind of support for the EEC that was now being established in France. This would imply that, had de Gaulle not blocked British entry at that time, subsequent attitudes in the British labour movement might have evolved quite differently. Does a comparison substantiate this conclusion?

In 1966–67, when the Labour Government sought entry into the EEC, in one major respect, its justifications for so doing closely paralleled those of the SFIO during the previous decade. That is, Wilson argued that the economic modernisation and political strengthening of Britain to which he was committed, would be realised through membership of the Common Market: Britain would develop through participation in a wider Europe, which would benefit from economies of scale and so compete with the superpowers. But despite the striking resemblance between such arguments and those used earlier by French socialists (see chapter 1), the underlying context was still quite different. The Labour Government had adopted 'Europeanism' entirely pragmatically, without any real shift in political outlook. Harold Wilson still proclaimed that he remained a 'Commonwealth man' and, if it became increasingly difficult to perceive the Commonwealth as the main basis for Britain's economic and political relationships, the nebulous world-wide consciousness associated with it continued to underlie Labour Party attitudes even when expressed in socialist terms. There was, therefore, none of the certainty or inevitability in the European strategy of Labour's front bench, that there had been with their counterparts in the SFIO in the previous decade. Because the leadership had turned to 'Europe' largely as a result of influences from outside the party, it would be susceptible to contrary pressures should these arise. The same was true of 'third-forcism' in the British Labour Party.

In France, left-wing notions of a 'third-force' Europe were deep rooted. They arose from a genuine European consciousness, dislike of Soviet communism (but sympathy for Marxism) and anti-Americanism. In addition, the political importance of such ideas was enhanced by their apparent compatibility with centrist and right-wing support for European independence from the USA. The British situation was quite different. Certainly, on the Labour left there was vehement condemnation of the United States in the era of the Vietnam War and a desire for independence, but only a small minority believed the European Community to have any relevance in this respect. The majority of the left attached far greater importance to the establishment of *détente* between the superpowers and still viewed the EEC with suspicion as a product of the Cold War. Much of the non-communist left aspired to the 'third force' notion of a synthesis between capitalism and Soviet communism but did not believe that it would necessarily be realised in Western Europe.

Finally, the overwhelming majority of the British labour movement remained wedded to the idea of national sovereignty. When urging the party to support the application, both the government and the NEC stressed the argument that the Community was no longer based on the federal principle, and there is no doubt that the movement as a whole was concerned that important powers should not be removed from Westminster. As was shown earlier, in the 1960s and 70s the French Socialists moved closer to communist and Gaullist notions, and also came to emphasise the necessity to maintain national independence. However, two important differences between the French Socialists and the British Labour Party remained. First, the French were emphasising the need to defend national interests within a framework in which they were already operating, and over which the French state had had a major influence. The Labour Party was anxious that the framework itself might constitute the primary threat to national independence. Secondly, despite the reassertion of the national theme *after* the creation of the European Community, in the 1940s and 50s the French Socialists had adhered to the 'European idea' and had believed it vital to transcend the nation-state. The Labour Party, on the other hand, was insistent on the need to protect national sovereignty throughout the whole post-war period, including the time of the application. There was thus always a possibility that, given difficult circumstances either in the domestic sphere or *vis-à-vis* the Community, the national question would assume still greater importance.

Had the Labour Government been able to take Britain into the EEC, the 'European' perceptions of the labour movement may have shifted and converged with those of the French Socialists. In fact, however, significant differences remained, and these were to be reinforced by subsequent developments.

The Erosion of the Consensus, 1969–72

By the time a renewed approach to the EEC appeared to become possible during 1969, there were already signs of a growing unease on the issue within the party. A general dissatisfaction with the government's domestic and foreign policies had led the mass movement to become increasingly suspicious of its motives in any case. And, with the government's deflationary policies after 1967 threatening working-class living standards, the anti-marketeers' arguments about the adverse effects of the EEC on food prices had a greater impact than in 1967, when the promise of long-term benefits had appeared more credible. The new mood was in evidence at the 1969 annual conference and was encapsulated by Jack Jones who stressed the importance of speaking for the 'ordinary people of Britain' who were anxious about the increased cost of living and the threat to jobs posed by entry into the EEC.[70] Although the Transport and General Workers' resolution was, if anything, more hostile than that rejected by the Conference two years previously it was carried without a card vote.[71] Cabinet division on the question was also evident again. For example, late in 1969 a request by Michael Stewart (who had resumed the position of Foreign Secretary after Brown's resignation from the government the previous year) for more members of the Cabinet to make pro-EEC speeches was rejected in favour of a continuation of the existing compromise under which most ministers could remain non-committal.[72] Moreover, both the changing mood in the party and the caution of the leadership were evident when, at the annual conference, Wilson sought to assuage rank-and-file anxieties by promising a detailed evaluation of the economic impact of entry; and subsequently published a White Paper in February which explained (without providing any government opinion) that the adverse balance of payments effects could be variously estimated in a range between £100 million and £1000 million per year.[73] This further fuelled opposition to entry and the trade union movement was becoming increasingly tepid in its attitudes to the EEC by the time the General Election was held in June 1970.[74] Wilson resisted the pressures of Cabinet anti-marketeers to turn the EEC into a major electoral issue, [75] but in March 1970 Peter Shore broke the Cabinet agreement by making a speech with highly negative overtones on the costs of entry,[76] and the Prime Minister's own statements and party propaganda again sought to differentiate between Labour's reservationist position and Conservative unconditionalism.[77]

However, this groundswell of opposition should not be exaggerated. Although Jones's speech at the 1969 Conference was totally hostile to the EEC, he insisted that he wanted only to ensure an open debate, and implied that his motion could be supported by those who favoured membership. And the NEC statement (reiterating that of 1967) which was defended by Brown in unmistakably pro-EEC tones, was also carried without a card vote. Moreover, Wilson's more reserved statements were probably only tactical at this stage and it is reasonable to assume that, had the Labour Party won the General Election, he would have conducted negotiations with the EEC with full commitment. The main shift in Labour's policy thus occurred after June 1970, as the Conservative Government negotiated its way into the EEC. Full accounts of this process have been given elsewhere and it is only necessary to recall the main stages here.[78]

The pre-election position was maintained in the second half of 1970 but from early 1971 increasing pressure was exerted upon the leadership by the mass party, trade unions and members of the Shadow Cabinet to abandon support for the notion of entry into the EEC. Whilst becoming ever more circumspect in his attitudes

Wilson long resisted this campaign, but a decisive stage was reached by July 1971 when the bulk of the negotiated terms became known and the Heath Government launched a major propaganda effort in favour of entry.[79] Following a special party conference on the issue, Wilson thus endorsed the NEC's rejection of 'entry on Tory terms', and distanced himself from the pro-EEC minority.[80] Although 69 Labour MPs subsequently defied the party's decision in the Commons vote in October – thereby providing the government with a majority – the anti-marketeers continued to gain the initiative. By now Wilson had already accepted the notion that the next Labour Government would seek renegotiation of the terms of entry, but a further major step was taken at the end of March 1972 when the Shadow Cabinet accepted the principle of a referendum on the renegotiated terms.

Douglas Jay had suggested a referendum on the EEC issue as long ago as 1968, but the idea had really gained prominence at the end of 1970 when it had been pressed by Tony Benn.[81] At that time Benn had still claimed to favour entry into the Community but, during the course of the next year, he changed his mind and the notion of a referendum became a device by which anti-marketeers in the party tried to shift the decision on the EEC away from the broadly pro-Community leadership. Until March 1972 the proposal had been rejected by both the NEC and the Shadow Cabinet, and the latter's volte-face (influenced by Pompidou's decision to hold a referendum on British membership in France) led to three resignations, including that of Roy Jenkins as deputy leader.[82] At the party conference later that year the next Labour Government was thus pledged to seeking satisfaction on specified points in the renegotiations and holding a General Election or referendum on the result. With this commitment, with Peter Shore as the party's new spokesman on 'Europe', with an NEC/PLP committee with a decidedly anti-EEC majority charged with handling preliminary soundings on renegotiation, with a party boycott of all EEC institutions prior to renegotiation, and with party publications sounding very close to opposition 'in principle', the shift in EEC policy was indeed vast.[83] Why had it come about?

Partly as a result of its own actions and partly through pent-up pressures, the Conservative Government under Edward Heath saw an eruption of overt class conflict on a scale unprecedented since the General Strike of 1926. Conservative electoral rhetoric about the necessity of ending the post-war consensus now appeared to be translated into concrete actions, in particular in the Industrial Relations and Housing Finance Acts.[84] The response of the labour movement was a series of strikes in which the government itself served as the main target – a process which was to culminate in the

221

second miners' strike of 1974 and defeat for Heath in a crisis General Election. Acute conflict between the organised working class and the state also characterised the first two years of the Conservative administration when entry into the EEC was being negotiated and implemented in legislation. Thus in February 1972, while the European Communities Bill narrowly passed its second reading (309–301) stage in the Commons, a miners' strike was almost bringing industry to a standstill; and in the summer of 1972, the final reading of the Bill almost coincided with the imprisonment, under the Industrial Relations Act, of five dockers, and the threat of massive industrial action to secure their release.

In this atmosphere of increased class conflict and political polarisation it was almost inevitable that a linkage would be perceived between the EEC application and the general strategy of the government. This was expressed in its most basic form by various speakers at the special party congress in July 1971, one of whom stated that 'if the Tories are in favour of it … if Ted Heath is in favour of it, I am against it'.[85] In more sophisticated terms, interconnections were held to exist between the right-wing nature of the Conservative Government and the application for membership of the Community: in particular it was often argued that the Industrial Relations Act was a means of aligning British trade union legislation with that of the Continent.[86] And, in a more general sense, Heath's apparent acceptance of confrontation in domestic and foreign policy, made left-wing anti-Community arguments appear far more credible than previously with centrists in the party.[87] It thus became commonplace to argue that the government was interested only in the needs of capital, which would be served by entry into the EEC, and that the adverse effects on the working classes and democracy were of no concern to it.[88]

If the nature of the Conservative administration provided an ideal impetus for the realisation of the anti-EEC potential in the Labour Party, pragmatic politics also played a major role in the reorientation of policy. Because the EEC issue appeared to provide the only major opportunity to bring down the Heath Government before its term of office expired, enormous pressure was exerted on the pro-Marketeers to subordinate their enthusiasm for the EEC to the domestic political struggle.[89] This was evident, for example, in a resolution passed by the NEC (and proposed by Judith Hart) which demanded full PLP opposition to the government in the Commons debate in October:

> The NEC believes that the overwhelming will of the Party is to end the present economic and social evils of this government and expresses the hope that this will be regarded as the absolute

priority on 28th October.[90]

Despite the fact that 69 MPs defied this pressure the next day (aided by a deal between Wilson and the Chairman of the PLP), many of them were to accept the underlying argument during the course of the next year, thereby bringing the Parliamentary Party into closer harmony with the mass movement.

A final reason for the shift in party policy was the virtual elimination of the minority 'third force' left-wing support for 'Europe' which had existed in 1967. The process had begun even before the General Election and can be charted with references to its leading figure, Eric Heffer. In 1969 Heffer had still favoured entry and had spoken in its support, with 'third force' arguments, at the party conference.[91] However, in April 1970, with the new mood apparent in the party, he had announced a change of mind.[92] He took this further at the 1971 special party conference when he declared that he no longer believed that an international socialist Europe could be obtained through the EEC, and that he had discovered before the last General Election that the decisions of the Council of Ministers in December 1969 would prevent a British government from bringing about socialist change within the Community. He continued:

> We have a responsibility to the British people, to the British working class above everyone else. And, in my opinion, the British working class would suffer considerably by joining the European Common Market ...
>
> Those of you who have been pro-Market, examine the realities. Put your responsibility where it is really required, in the interests of the British working people.[93]

This collapse of 'third-forcism' stemmed from a weakness which had characterised it even in 1967. At that stage Heffer's statements gave the impression of someone with a strong belief in the ideal of a socialist Europe and a deep-rooted aversion to British chauvinism, whose actual knowledge of the EEC was superficial. He had thus argued powerfully in favour of membership solely on 'third force' political grounds without any examination of the potential economic effects on Britain.[94] This was possible in 1967 because, despite the efforts of anti-Marketeers like Douglas Jay, the economic and financial implications of membership were not yet widely understood. But once it became a general rank-and-file belief that the concrete economic effects of membership for the working class would be harmful, 'third force' arguments would be viewed as utopian and abstract.

Such processes were at work even before June 1970 and were probably more responsible for Heffer's change of heart than were the December 1969 decisions on the Common Agricultural Policy. However, after the General Election the 'third force' position collapsed as it became increasingly difficult for anyone on the left of the party to adopt anything other than a hostile attitude to membership, with working-class condemnation of the Community mounting and the apparent possibility of overthrowing the Heath Government on the issue. In 1971–72, with very few exceptions (for example, the veteran Bob Edwards), it was therefore the right-wingers in the party who continued to urge the importance of entry into the Community. However, although the Labour Committee for Europe argued in precisely the same way as it had so effectively in 1967, it was placed on the defensive as a minority middle-class group.[95] Indeed throughout the latter half of 1971 and 1972 Jenkins and his associates were under frequent attack as 'MacDonaldite' betrayers of the working class and were warned that if they supported 'the most hard faced bunch of freebooters since the "Coupon" men of 1918, the Party would never forgive them.'[96]

Pragmatists in the leadership were also placed under pressure from the mass movement and anti-Market colleagues such as Benn and Shore, and this led to some startling shifts in position, including a particularly inept double turnabout by Denis Healey.[97] As former 'third-forcists' and pragmatists joined the long-term anti-Marketeers, the pro-EEC body within the party became increasingly weak.

When Britain entered the EEC in January 1973, deep-rooted, traditional national assumptions had been combined with informed critiques, socialist analyses and pragmatic politics to carry the Labour Party into a bitter condemnation of the state's new international orientation. But behind all the emotion, what was the reality and significance of the party's new stance?

The Significance of Labour's Changing European Policies

Once 'successful' negotiations between Britain and the Community had been completed in 1971, total rejection of the EEC by the Labour Party would have involved a far greater departure from the dominant viewpoint than a negative stance in 1962 when membership had been a highly uncertain prospect anyway. In the meantime the political and economic elite had become increasingly committed to the new course and rejection of it, and disruption of the bonds which were being tied, would have been very significant.

Yet although the class and political polarisation of 1971–72 meant that the Labour Party was turning against bi-partisanship, it had not broken totally away from the Establishment consensus.

Despite the shift that had taken place in Labour's European policy, Wilson had headed off strong pressures for a commitment to outright rejection of the Common Market on principle, thereby allowing an escape route for a new Labour government, and maintaining a just credible link between present policies and those favoured in 1967. For example, at the 1972 conference a motion calling for complete opposition on any terms and for withdrawal by a Labour government was defeated. Although a further motion accepting entry, only on impracticable terms, was carried by 3,355,00 to 2,867,000, the NEC's statement, which was more cautious in its demands, was passed by a comfortable majority of almost two to one. This committed the leadership to seeking the following in renegotiation:

(1) Major changes in the Common Agricultural Policy so that it ceased to be a threat to world trade in food products, and so that low-cost producers outside Europe could continue to have access to the British food market;

(2) New and fairer methods of financing the Community budget ... involving a contribution only of such sums as were fair in relation to what was paid and received by other member countries;

(3) The retention by Parliament of those powers over the British economy needed to pursue effective regional, industrial and fiscal policies and an agreement on capital movements to protect balance of payments and full employment policies;

(4) The better safeguarding of the economic interests of the Commonwealth and developing countries, involving the securing of access to the British market and, more generally, the adoption by the enlarged Community of trade and aid policies designed to benefit not only associated overseas territories in Africa but developing countries throughout the world;

(5) No harmonisation of VAT which would require the taxing of necessities.

In addition, Labour was committed to rejecting any kind of international agreement which compelled the acceptance of increased unemployment for the sake of maintaining a fixed parity 'as is required by current proposals for a European Economic and Monetary Union'.[98]

These were extensive demands, but did not involve a rejection of the whole basis of the Community and, in a sense, only the condition

225

regarding the harmonisation of VAT was completely specific. Moreover, although the leadership was committed to advise withdrawal if it deemed the negotiations unsuccessful it had gained some room for manoeuvre by securing the right to decide whether to hold a General Election or a consultative referendum on the issue. Finally, it was notable that, despite the departure from the Shadow Cabinet of Jenkins, Lever and Thomson, the leadership as a whole was broadly similar to that which had formed Wilson's last Cabinet. In fact, as on other central policy questions, the situation at the end of 1972 was ambivalent: there had been a partial advance by the left in the party but the pragmatists retained their hold on the leadership on the basis of ambiguous policies. The bi-partisan consensus on the major question of Britain's economic and political orientation had been broken without being completely shattered.

Despite the infusion of class consciousness and leftward pressures there were thus some close parallels with the situation ten years earlier. Once again the leadership could exploit an issue which was unpopular with the electorate; once again the Conservatives could be charged with a betrayal while it was implied that Labour could achieve better terms in new negotiations; and once again socialist arguments could be coupled with nationalist rhetoric.[99] Moreover, there are parallels on a deeper level than that of internal party management. In 1962 when the Labour Party had adopted a negative stance on Common Market entry, it had – as we have seen – done so in the conviction that it possessed a domestic and international strategy for the regeneration of Britain. The collapse of both spheres of policy had led it to resume the Establishment consensus by seeking to strengthen and modernise the country through entry into the EEC. By 1972 Britain's politicoeconomic crisis was far more profound than it had been ten years earlier. But although the Labour Party had devoted some attention to devising a new internal strategy for its solution – based primarily on co-operation with the trade union leadership and more extensive state control and direction of industry[100] – the question of Britain's international orientation had not been seriously addressed. Indeed, Peter Shore, the spokesman on the EEC, still appeared confident that economic revival could come about through export-led growth on the basis of Britain's existing relationships with the Commonwealth and EFTA.[101] Yet since the war domestic policy had become ever more constrained by pressures from the international capitalist economy and, by the 1970s, this was more clearly the case than ever.

It was in their recognition of Britain's weaker international position, and their criticism of exaggerated claims by anti-marketeers about the existing degree of British sovereignty, that the Labour Committee for Europe had presented its most effective argument.[102] However, in the general rejection of the revisionist-right case, its critique of this aspect of the Labour-left view went unanswered, and it was simply assumed that a restoration of the *status quo ante*, and the election of a Labour government could remedy the weakness in the economy. Yet the previous Labour Government showed the dangers of underestimating the extent of Britain's dependence on external factors and overestimating a Labour government's ability to transform the economic situation without embarking on a radical alternative strategy. If Wilson had adopted the Establishment's option when the National Plan failed in the 1960s, in the 1970s with a less developed international policy, a further decline in the Commonwealth, and a graver politicoeconomic crisis, the temptations to accept the course favoured by non-socialist forces would be that much greater.

Notes

1 House of Commons Debates, vol. 688, cols. 1386–91.
2 Quoted in R. Lieber, *British Politics and European Unity* (University of California, 1962), p. 242. For details of the evolution of Labour Party policy in these years, see L. Robins, *The Reluctant Party: Labour and the EEC 1961–75* (G.W. & A. Hesketh, 1979); U. Kitzinger. *The Second Try: Labour and the EEC* (Pergamon, 1968), and *Diplomacy and Persuasion: How Britain Joined the Common Market* (Thames & Hudson, 1973), esp. pp.266–396; Lieber, *British Politics and European Unity*, ch.9; and M. Camps. *European Unification in the Sixties* (Oxford University Press, 1967), chs. 4 and 5. For revealing insights into Cabinet discussions, see R.H.S. Crossman, *Diaries of a Cabinet Minister*, vols. I–III (Hamilton and Cape, 1975–77) (hereafter Crossman I, II or III).
3 House of Commons, 1 June 1965, quoted in Camps, *European Unification*, p.174.
4 LPCR 1965, p.181; House of Commons Debates, vol. 722, col. 1723, 20 December 1965.
5 Crossman I, pp.365 and 461.
6 Lieber, *British Politics and European Unity*, p.244.
7 R. Pfaltzgraff. *Britain Faces Europe* (University of Pennsylvania Press, 1969), p.184.
8 The impetus in favour of the application appears extraordinary. According to Crossman, as late as 7 July 1966, in private Brown and Thomson believed that there was no prospect of entry into the EEC despite their public statements of confidence (Crossman I, p.563).
9 A long and plausible account of the discussions is given in Crossman II, pp.81–7.
10 Ibid., p.334
11 'Yes, without qualification': Harold Wilson, George Brown, Michael Stewart, Roy Jenkins, Anthony Crosland, Lord Gardiner, Elwyn Jones, Ray Gunter and Lord Longford; 'no, without qualification': Douglas Jay, Fred Peart, Denis Healey, Barbara Castle, Willie Ross, Richard Marsh and Herbert Bowden; 'maybe': James Callaghan, Richard Crossman, Patrick Gordon Walker, Anthony Greenwood, John Silkin and Cledwyn Hughes (ibid., pp.336–7). Kitzinger assesses the line-up slightly differently, but this is mainly through the ommission

of some Cabinet ministers (*Diplomacy and Persuasion,* p.287); Robins counts Greenwood as one of the opponents (*The Reluctant Party,* p.60).

12 While Brown and Wilson had been in Bonn during their diplomatic probe, Douglas Jay had warned Labour back-benchers that Britain would suffer considerably by signing the Treaty of Rome (Robins, *The Reluctant Party,* p. 63). Wilson later claimed that the dismissal was solely because of Jay's age. *(The Labour Government 1964–70 – A. Personal Record* (Weidenfeld and Nicolson and Michael Joseph, 1971), p.427.

13 The Conservative Government was subsequently to make the point that the Labour administration's commitment to EEC entry was so clear that it was able simply to takeover the negotiating brief prepared for Labour ministers. Wilson was to deny this, claiming that nothing had been seen by the Cabinet though much work had been done by officials (speech in House of Commons, 21 July 1971, reproduced in LPCR 1971, pp.73–84). If so, the opposite conclusion can legitimately be drawn: that is, that civil servants were working to directives which they had already received from ministers.

14 For a full discussion, see Camps, *European Unification,* esp. ch.5.

15 The following figures are from P. Foot, *The Politics of Harold Wilson* (Penguin, 1968), p.245.

	1964	1966
Exports to Commonwealth as percentage of UK exports	28	25
Imports from Commonwealth as percentage of UK imports	30	27
Percentage of Commonwealth countries' exports sent to UK	20	16
Percentage of Commonwealth countries' imports from UK	16	14

16 J. Frankel, *British Foreign Policy, 1945–73* (Oxford University Press, 1975), p.211–12.

17 A. Grosser, *The Western Alliance,* (Macmillan, 1980), pp.221–2.

18 For the spirit of the era, see Harold Wilson, *The New Britain* (Penguin, 1964). For a lively critique see, Foot, *The Politics of Harold Wilson.*

19 For a concise critical examination of Labour's record, see D. Howell, *British Social Democracy*(Croom Helm, 1976), esp. pp.241–81.

20 For general outlines of the evolution of pressure group opinion, see Lieber, *British Politics and European Unity,* and Pfaltzgraff, *Britain Faces Europe,* ch.7.

21 For earlier Conservative statements of this type, see Pfaltzgraff, *Britain Faces Europe,* ch.7. For Labour Common Market Committee statements of this kind see, for example, *Newsbrief,* 13 Jan/Feb 1963 (Harvester Microfilm)

22 *The Times,* 15 November 1966, quoted in Foot, *The Politics of Harold Wilson,* p.235.

23 A long extract from this speech is reproduced in Kitzinger, *The Second Try,* pp.307–10.

24 The first interpretation is stressed by Kitzinger in *The Second Try* and the second by Robins in *The Reluctant Party.*

25 Crossman also records Wilson's enthusiasm in Cabinet about the EEC as a means to increased investment and growth (see, for example, II, p.303, 6 April 1967).

26 The extent of the consensus is symbolised by the fact that the Commons vote in favour of the 1967 application constituted the largest majority on any issue since 1945: 488 to 62, with 80 abstentions.

27 Robins, *The Reluctant Party,* pp.93–4.

28 LPCR 1971, pp. 141–3; LPCR 1972, pp.209–15.

29 NEC statement 'Labour and the Common Market', LPCR 1967, p.332. This statement effectively presented the government's view, and the conditions on agriculture were as follows: 'The Labour Party considers that a transitional period to mitigate the effects of Britain's entry into the EEC is more essential in this field than in any other. The Labour Party accordingly welcomes the government's assurance that measures will be taken to ensure that the effect of any price increases does not fall unfairly on those who can least afford to bear the additional burden, such as those with large families and those in the lowest income range. We also support the Government fully in its intentions to negotiate with the EEC:

(i) An annual agricultural price review.
(ii) An assured supply of liquid milk throughout the year
(iii) An equitable arrangement for financing the CAP'.

The sole ground for subsequent claims that the government had not accepted the principle of the CAP concerns its financing arrangements with regard to Britain. In Cabinet on 18 April 1967, Wilson declared that there had to be some long-term arrangements beyond the transition period so that Britain did not have to 'pay an outrageously big proportion of the levies'. This was minuted in Cabinet as 'We should reserve our freedom to seek adjustments in agriculture going beyond transitional arrangements' (Crossman, II, p.318). The basis of the CAP itself was accepted.

30 In his speech to the Commons on 21 July 1971, Wilson claimed that, for New Zealand in 1967, he would only have accepted permanent assured access to Britain or transitional arrangements for a generation (which, he maintained, effectively constituted permanent arrangements). However, the contemporary speeches appear to have been less categorical and the NEC statement read: 'The Labour Party endorses the Government's view that a solution must be found to solve the problem of our trade with New Zealand and to protect the interests of sugar producing countries at present safeguarded under the Commonwealth Sugar Agreement.'

31 See, for example, Brown's speech to the Council of the West European Union, 4 July 1967 (reproduced in Kitzinger, *The Second Try*, pp. 189–201) and Wilson's own account in *The Labour Government*, pp.329–37.

32 For a thorough analysis, see S.Z. Young, *Terms of Entry: Britain's Negotiations with the European Community, 1970–72* (Heinermann, 1973).

33 Nor was the argument strengthened by misleading claims made by the Labour Party in 1971 (see, for example, *Speakers' Notes: Common Market* (The Labour Party, October 1971), and partially foreshadowed in Wilson's speech to the special party conference in July 1971, that the Wilson government had laid down four conditions in 1967 and that two of them had been controls on capital movements and freedom to carry out a regional policy. Wilson was on slightly stronger ground when arguing that the EEC had become less liberal since 1967 on matters such as regional policy, thus implying that specific guarantees had not been necessary in 1967 (LPCR 1972, pp.209–15). But the crucial point is that in 1967 the Labour Government had dropped the fourth condition of 1962 – 'the right to plan our own economy' and had argued instead that the Treaty of Rome presented no insuperable problems.

34 Crossman's diary is interesting in this respect. On 14 September 1969 he regarded Wilson, with Stewart and Brown, as the 'real marketeers' in the Cabinet (III, pp.641–3) and on 6 November 1969, when the Prime Minister sent all Cabinet ministers a letter telling them to be enthusiastic about the Foreign Secretary's policy and not to be obsessed by the terms of entry, he believed Wilson to be 'hell bent' on getting negotiations going as fast as possible (p.718). As late as 10 February 1970, he still thought Wilson was 'fanatically convinced of the need to go in and of the statesmanship required to appreciate this' (pp.811–12). Although he subsequently noted that the Prime Minister then 'back-pedalled' a little (22 February 1970, p.830), he never suggested that Wilson's beliefs had changed.

35 House of Commons Debates, vol. 724, cols. 1513–4, 10 May 1967, quoted in Lieber, *British Politics and European Unity, p.272.*

36 Reproduced in Kitzinger, *The Second Try,* pp.189–201.

37 LPCR 1967, pp.281–5

38 See for example Wilson's Commons speech of 8 May 1967 (House of Commons Debates, vol. 746, cols. 1061–97), and the 'Panorama' interview of the same day (Harvester Microfilm).

39 See for example Crossman II, p.212 (26 January 1967), p.303 (6 April 1967) and p.335 (30 April 1967).

40 It is difficult to see which of the ministers who opposed the EEC would have been prepared to lead a rebellion. Barbara Castle was clearly totally against the application and may have voiced the left-wing position in the Cabinet had opposition mounted in the party but, as Minister of Transport, she was far removed from the crucial spheres of economic and foreign policy. Fred Peart, the Minister of Agriculture, cannot easily be seen in the role of rebel leader, and Peter Shore, the new Minister in charge of the Department of Economic Affairs, was still too junior and dependent on Wilson to act in this capacity. The only person who occupied a key ministry, who could conceivably have headed a dissident group was Denis Healey, the Minister of Defence. However, his general support for Wilson's foreign and domestic policies makes this improbable. The Prime Minister, Foreign Secretary (Brown), former Foreign Secretary (Stewart), President of the Board of Trade (Crosland), Secretary of State for the Commonwealth (Thomson), Secretary of State for Technology (Benn) and Home Secretary (Jenkins) were all strongly in favour, while the Chancellor of the Exchequer (Callaghan) inclined towards membership.

41 The draft EEC declaration put before the Cabinet on 3 July 1967 stressed the political arguments to a greater extent than the alleged economic advantages which had been emphasised earlier (Crossman II, p.406).

42 Crossman, who later said that only Peart and himself cared about agriculture (II, p.318, 18 April 1967), put it as follows: 'Of course Fred Peart and Douglas Jay pushed their objection to the Common Agricultural Policy. But most of us, I think … felt that agriculture is really an ancillary argument' (II, p.83, 22 October 1966).

43 For Jay's views, see his articles in the *Guardian* on 20 and 21 September 1967, reproduced in Kitzinger, *The Second Try,* and also *After the Common Market – A Better Alternative for Britain* (Penguin, 1968).

44 *After the Common Market,* p.125. It is notable that, while he condemned the EEC countries as reactionary, the South African system was apparently seen as no barrier to a close commercial relationship (ibid., p.59).

45 Crossman II, pp.116–17 (9 November 1966). For his general critique of Wilson's foreign policy see II, pp.181–2, 1 January 1967. Crossman's account of his own position is totally credible: he presents himself as vacillating and uncertain – never favourable to the EEC, but often viewing entry as the only practical course for Britain to take (see, for example, II, p.30, 9 September 1966; pp.122–3, 13 November 1966; and III, p.464, 29 April 1969).

46 II, pp.116–17, 9 November 1966.

47 *The Times,* 23 February 1967, quoted in Pfaltzgraff, *Britain Faces Europe,* p.191.

48 This had been reconstituted from the ranks of the 'Britain and Common Market' group and was led by Lord Blyton, Alfred Morris and Raymond Fletcher. For further discussion, see Lieber, *British Politics and European Unity,* p.256 and Robins, *The Reluctant Party,* p.66.

49 Robins, *The Reluctant Party,* pp.62–3.

50 *Tribune,* 5 May 1967. (A long extract is given in Kitzinger, *The Second Try;* and the whole statement is on the Harvester Microfilm).

51 See, for example, 'Notes of the Month: Which Europe?', *Labour Monthly*, June 1967. Asserting that the 'financial-capitalist rulers of Britain [were] using the Labour Government as their servant' and that 'the battle for the future of Britain had now opened' this, and other CP propaganda, still put the political question of 'the EEC as the economic base of NATO' at the forefront of its argument.

52 NEC Minutes, 30 September 1967. On 15 November Crossman evaluated the result of a PLP/government meeting on the EEC as follows: 'In the present mood the Government would have a relatively easy time if, next Spring, after the tour of the capitals, we have very few conditions to make about going in' (II,p.127).

53 The critical motion submitted by the Transport and General Workers Union was defeated by 3,536,000 to 2,539,000 while the 'unconditional' one, submitted by the General and Muncipal Workers Union was carried by 3,359,000 to 2,697,000. The NEC statement was carried by 4,147,000 to 2,032,000 (LPCR 1967, p.285).

54 In *British Politics and European Unity*, Lieber tends to minimise opposition within the Labour Party while, in *The Reluctant Party*, Robins is more cautious, arguing that various strands existed and that party policy was not clear cut.

55 This point is stressed by Robins who quotes the important testimony by the former Labour Deputy Chief Whip, given in the *New Statesman* on 26 February 1971 *(The Reluctant Party*, pp.63–4).

56 There was some disquiet about this in the NEC. In November 1966 the Home Policy Committee cited the EEC as an example of the way in which government policy could change without any discussion by the committee and more consultation was called for (HPC, 7 November 1966, NEC Minutes). It was only at the request of the NEC on 22 March 1967 that Wilson agreed that he and Brown should give a report to the NEC at its next meeting (NEC Minutes, 22 March and 26 April 1967).

57 *The Reluctant Party*, p.62. This factor should not be exaggerated for back-bench rebellions on other issues (notably Vietnam and prices and incomes policy) increased *after* 1967.

58 It is thus significant that when the NEC and Cabinet agreed to hold a joint meeting on 11 June to ensure better mutual understanding it was decided that there was insufficient time to include a discussion of the EEC so it was omitted from the agenda (NEC Minutes, 24 May 1967).

59 It reaffirmed the view of the 1966 manifesto that to enter the EEC without adequate prior protection for essential British and Commonwealth interests would be damaging to the wellbeing of the country and to living standards and therefore called upon the government:'(a) to insist upon proper safeguards for British interests in agricultural policy to avoid increases in food prices ... (b) to maintain the right to plan the economy and pursue an independent foreign policy seeking friendship with all countries. (c) to give full and urgent consideration to alternative policies in close consultation with the Commonwealth and other trading associates throughout the world, (LPCR 1967, p.269).

60 Indeed it attacked the Opposition for its 'unconditionalism' rather than the government (*The Times*, 23 February 1967).

61 *The Times*, 9 May 1967 (quoted in Pfaltzgraff, *Britain Faces Europe*, p.192). The most prominent signatories were Shinwell, Mikardo and Foot.

62 Lieber, *British Politics and European Unity*, pp.252–3; Pfaltzgraff, *Britain Faces Europe*, p 172.

63 See the interesting 'Statement for Discussion on Future Policy' and 'Memorandum on the Future of the Labour Common Market Committee Newsbrief' in Minutes of the Labour Common Market Committee, February 1963 (Harvester Microfilm).

64 The Britain and Europe group included MPs who were not hostile to the EEC but wanted to resist an unconditional application. It was thus not always easy to distinguish from the broadly pro-Market Wider Europe Group (Robins, *The Reluctant Party*, pp.66–7).

65 Kitzinger, *Diplomacy and Persuasion*, p.293.

66 LPCR 1967, pp.280–1.

67 'Britain and the Common Market', a statement signed by 25 Labour MPs in *Europe Left*, no.15, May 1967 (Harvester Microfilm). Other Labour-left signatories, apart from Bob Edwards, were Stan Newens, Sidney Bidwell and Paul Rose. The Centre was also well represented with signatories such as Leo Abse and Ben Whitaker.

68 Lieber quotes one prominent anti-Marketeer, John Mendelsohn, as saying that no alternative strategy was necessary because: 'The alternative to suicide is not to commit it' (*British Politics and European Unity*, p.256).

69 *Tribune*, 5 May 1967.

70 LPCR 1969, pp.309–10 (see also the speeches by the delegates from the Agricultural Workers Union which was far more hostile than in 1967, and the Seamen's Union pp.315–16).

71 The emotive aspects of the resolution went further: 'This conference calls upon the Government in any negotiations for membership of the European Economic Communities to insist on adequate safeguards for Britain's balance of payments, cost of living, National Health and Social Security systems, and power of independent decision in economic planning and foreign policy. Conference further rejects the proposal for a nuclear-armed Federal European State, including Britain' (LPCR 1969, p.309).

72 Crossman III, p.718, 6 November 1969.

73 'Britain and the European Communities, An Economic Assessment', Cmnd 4289.

74 In *Diplomacy and Persuasion*, pp.266–76, Kitzinger provides a useful account of the shifts in trade union opinion between 1969 and 1972. The decisive change occurred in 1970–71 but, whereas before 1967 the TUC had been generally more favourable to the EEC than the Labour Party, this was no longer the case by 1969.

75 Crossman III, p.894, 20 April 1970.

76 In his speech on 25 March 1970 Shore stressed the formidable disadvantages to entry and maintained that the people, as well as the politicians, should decide (ibid., p.874, 26 March 1970).

77 See for example Wilson's speech in Camden Town Hall, 21 February 1970, quoted in Wilson, *The Labour Government*, pp.761–4; and Labour's 1970 manifesto, 'Now Britain's Strong, Let's Make it Great to Live In'.

78 For full details see Robins, *The Reluctant Party*, ch. 6, and Kitzinger, *Diplomacy and Persuasion*, pp.293–396.

79 Wilson had already made a speech with hostile overtones in April and Callaghan had been even more critical in a widely publicised speech on 25 May 1971. But it was only when no more delay was possible that Wilson finally accepted the majority position within the party.

80 The NEC resolution stated: 'Conference having studied the government's White Paper ... OPPOSES entry on the terms negotiated by the Conservative government; REGRETS the government's refusal to give the nation the facts necessary for a full appraisal of the continuing cost of entering the Communities against the possible long-term benefits, and in particular the Prime Minister's refusal to set up a select committee to examine the facts available to the government; and further CONSIDERS that Conservative economic and social policies so weaken and divide the nation that Britain's ability to improve the living standards of our people inside or outside the Market have been undermined; and since, in the words of the present Prime Minister during the election, "no British government could possibly take this country into the Common Market against the wish of the British people", CALLS on the Prime Minister now to submit to the democratic judgment of a general election.

It therefore invites the Parliamentary Labour Party ... to unite wholeheartedly in voting against the government's policy' (LPCR 1971, p.114).

This had been carried by 16 to 6 in the NEC, the dissenters being Tom Bradley, Jim Diamond, Roy Jenkins, Fred Mulley, Walter Padley and Shirley Williams (Kitzinger, *Diplomacy and Persuasion*, p.308).

81 Jay, *After the Common Market*. Benn first suggested the referendum in a 'letter' to his constituents in December 1970.

82 The other two resignations were those of George Thomson and Harold Lever.

83 The composition of the special committee, established in November 1972, was: NEC members – Bill Simpson, Ian Mikardo, Jim Diamond, Michael Foot and Alex Kitson (all anti-EEC except Diamond); PLP – Harold Wilson, James Callaghan, Tony Benn, Peter Shore and Denis Healey (Shore and Benn were vehement opponents and the rest were pragmatists on the issue).

84 For an interesting critical account of the evolution of Conservatism, see A. Gamble. *The Conservative Nation* (Routledge, 1974).

85 Delegate from Southend East Constituency Labour Party, LPCR 1971, p.306.

86 Jack Jones, LPCR 1971, p.168. For further discussion and references on this type of linkage see Robins, *The Reluctant Party*, p.81.

87 One of Heath's most provocative foreign policy initiatives was the decision to resume arms supplies to South Africa. On the rightward shift in Heath's general foreign policy, see Frankel, *British Foreign Policy*, pp.202–3, 223–5, 311–21. The fact that Heath had also advocated Franco-British nuclear co-operation since 1965 (see Document 13 in Kitzinger, *The Second Try*) also enabled Labour to argue that British entry into the EEC could lead to a Common Market 'bomb'. Heath denied that he had discussed any such proposal with Pompidou but Wilson still pointed to it as a danger (LPCR 1971, pp.313–20).

88 Even Callaghan attacked the EEC from this perspective at the 1971 Conference (LPCR 1971, pp.141–3).

89 Robins also suggests that the left was deliberately using the issue to weaken the revisionists in the party and oust Jenkins from his position as Deputy Leader (*The Reluctant Party*, p.103).

90 NEC Minutes, 27 October 1971. This motion was passed by 15 to 8 but Benn, as Chairman, disallowed a stronger one – proposed by Alex Kitson – from being put to the vote, on the grounds that it was submitted too late.

91 LPCR 1969, pp.316–17.

92 *New Statesman*, 17 April 1970.

93 LPCR 1971, pp.338–9.

94 LPCR 1967, pp.280–1; interview in *Europe Left*, no.18, October 1967 (Harvester Microfilm).

95 For an example of LCE views, see 'The Labour Party and the European Communities', September 1971 (Harvester Microfilm). Even the strongly pro-European Uwe Kitzinger accepts that the elitism of Jenkins and his associates alienated working-class opinion in the mass movement (*Diplomacy and Persuasion*, pp.309–11, 325).

96 J. Brooks, Cardiff South East Constituency Labour Party, LPCR 1971, p.136.

97 For details see Kitzinger, *Diplomacy and Persuasion*, pp.303–5. Tony Crosland also shifted his position in June–July 1971.

98 Summary of NEC Resolution, LPCR 1972, p.383.

99 For Nairn the parallels were so close that he was totally negative about Labour's 'Great Debate': 'Did it in the smallest degree help the growth of a clear class consciousness or give a more articulate general expression to the working-class malaise of the moment? Did it move one millimetre towards that renovation and

233

reorganisation of the socialist left which is so long overdue in the country? Or did it simply provide a little deoderant to cover the smell of decaying Labourist and national tradition?' (*The Left Against Europe?*, Penguin, 1973, p.118.)

100 The first major statement, outlining such policies, was that of the joint TUC/Labour Party Committee, 'Statement on Economic Policy and the Cost of Living', February 1973. It was preceded by an agreement in July 1972 that a future Labour government would immediately replace the Industrial Relations Act with an act establishing a Conciliation and Arbitration Service, and with legislation granting new rights for workers and unions.

101 Peter Shore (anonymous) *Special Pamphlet on the EEC*, (New Statesman, 1971) (Harvester Microfilm).

102 See, for example, John Mackintosh, *Europe Left*, vol.2, no. 1, February 1971 (Harvester Microfilm).

7

Renegotiation, Referendum and ... Withdrawal?

The Labour Party and the EEC, 1974–81

Between 1974 and 1981 the vacillations of the British labour movement over the issue of membership of the Community continued and culminated in the decision of the Labour Party conference in 1980 (confirmed and strengthened in 1981) to withdraw from the EEC. This commitment, which hastened the departure of much of the revisionist right from the party, was deplored by the overwhelming majority of the political and economic elite, and celebrated as a major breakthrough by the left. In the latter part of this chapter its immediate and long-term significance is discussed. However, it is first necessary to recall the major stages in the tortuous evolution of policy.

From Renegotiation to Withdrawal, 1974–81

When the Labour Party returned to power in March 1974, after a crisis election in the midst of a miners' strike and a state of emergency, there had been little change in its EEC policy. If anything, the intensification of Britain's economic problems during her first year of membership, meant that the mood of the party had grown still more intransigent, and at the 1973 conference a resolution opposing entry on principle had only narrowly been defeated. However, the new government did not fully reflect the party's hostility to the EEC.

A supreme pragmatist, James Callaghan, became Foreign Secretary and took overall charge of negotiations. He was aided by a pro-marketeer, Roy Hattersley, as Minister of State for European Affairs and an anti-marketeer, Peter Shore, as Secretary of State for Trade. Fred Peart, who had also been an opponent of the EEC in the last Labour Government, became Minister of Agriculture, and the

Cabinet's European Strategy Committee reflected the division of opinion within the government. It thus contained three EEC enthusiasts (Roy Jenkins, Harold Lever and Shirley Williams), four opponents (Michael Foot, Peter Shore, Eric Varley and John Silkin), two whose views were uncertain (Edward Short and Fred Peart) and three pragmatists (Harold Wilson, James Callaghan and Denis Healey). In the event however, it seems that policy was largely determined by Callaghan in close liaison with Wilson.[1]

A month after taking office, the new Foreign Secretary made his first public speech to the government ministers of the Community states, outlining the Labour government's position.[2] Although this contained all the major demands of the party's programme and was said to have caused a furore in Community circles, a partial retreat was already evident, for Callaghan now implied that satisfaction of the government's demands might be possible without revision of the Treaties. No doubt soundings in continental capitals and advice from the Foreign Office had led him to conclude that there was no possibility of inducing the Community in general, and the French in particular, to change the fundamental basis of the EEC. However, this early decision was to have major implications for, if interpreted literally, the full demands agreed when in opposition could not be achieved within the existing legal framework. Moreover, this was only the beginning of the retreat for Callaghan's second major speech to the Community at the beginning of June was far more conciliatory in tone. The emphasis was now switched to settling problems as part of the continuing business of the Community in the interests of all members rather than those of Britain alone, and Callaghan talked of the future 'when', rather than 'if' the outstanding issues were settled.

Little more occurred in public until after a second General Election in October 1974. Thereafter it became clear that the gulf between the leadership, as personified by Wilson and Callaghan, and party activists was growing.

At the party conference at the end of November the mood was overwhelmingly hostile to the EEC and, against the wishes of even the anti-Community NEC, an emergency resolution was carried which demanded complete safeguards on:

> the right of the British Parliament to reject any EEC legislation, directives or orders, when they are issued or at any time after ... to bring any firm in Britain under public ownership, and to control and regulate industry by financial or other means ... to restrict capital inflows and outflows ... to determine its own taxation policy ... to subsidise food and import food free of duty ... to control labour movements into Britain ... to independently

determine its own defence policy ... and for the Commonwealth and under-developed countries to export to Britain on terms at least as favourable as before Britain entered the EEC.[3]

However, there were numerous signs that Wilson and Callaghan were eager to agree a settlement with the EEC in the near future. Without seeking NEC approval Wilson invited Schmidt to address the annual party conference, obviously knowing that he would counsel against a British withdrawal from the Community, and the two stayed together at Chequers that night.[4] A week later Wilson announced that, if satisfied that renegotiation was successful, he would commend the terms to the electorate and recommend that Britain should play her full part in the development of the Community. The probable purpose of this statement was to signal to the EEC that, if some concessions were made, Wilson would play a positive role in seeking to convert the public to favour support for membership, rather than simply allowing the referendum to take its course without any governmental recommendation.

The subsequent negotiations with the EEC can be summarised briefly.[5] On 9–10 December 1974 a summit was held in Paris. No details of any agreements were published but Wilson showed his willingness to make the necessary gestures to the 'Community spirit'. Although he reserved Britain's position on the issue of direct elections he accepted the declaration that, on economic and monetary union (EMU), the will of the heads of government had not weakened and their objective had not changed. (Subsequently he was to explain – in terms that were simultaneously candid and cynical – that he could subscribe to this because, for all practical purposes, the goal of EMU had been abandoned and that 'its realisation in the forseeable future ... [was] as likely as the ideal of general and complete disarmament which we all support and assert')[6]. In addition they stated that the time had come for agreement, as soon as possible, on an overall concept of European union and, as a small step in that direction, the heads of government pledged themselves to meet, accompanied by Foreign Ministers, at least three times a year. In return for Wilson's adherence to these statements he secured two concessions. The Regional Fund was established (albeit on a far less generous scale than that proposed by George Thomson, the Commissioner responsible) with Britain as the second largest beneficiary. Secondly, the Commission was invited to:

set up as soon as possible a correcting mechanism of general application which, in the framework of the system of 'own resources' and in harmony with its normal functioning, based on

> objective criteria and taking into consideration in particular the suggestions made to this effect by the British government, could prevent, during the period of convergence of the economies of the Member States, the possible development of situations unacceptable for a Member State and incompatible with the smooth working of the Community.[7]

This hardly constituted a major move towards Labour's position.

Between the Paris Summit and the European Council meeting in Dublin on 10–11 March 1975 most of the other outstanding issues were resolved. The Lomé convention, partly negotiated by Judith Hart, placed trade between the EEC and the African, Caribbean and Pacific countries on a less overtly unequal footing than the earlier agreements, and was viewed by the Labour leadership (though not eventually by Judith Hart herself) as meeting the manifesto commitments to the Third World in general and Caribbean sugar producers in particular. The CAP was basically accepted, with the Community pledging itself to a thorough review of its operations and with arrangements for New Zealand dairy produce still to be agreed. On the issues of British autonomy over regional and fiscal policy, the government generally expressed satisfaction with the flexibility of the EEC *in practice* and demanded no real renegotiations, although it informed the Community that it might subsequently ask for a Treaty amendment on steel.[8]

By the time the Dublin summit took place the government therefore sought satisfaction only on two points: New Zealand dairy produce (on which Wilson himself had been so vehement when in opposition), and Britain's budgetary contributions. The Community's concessions were hardly extensive on either issue. On New Zealand butter the quantities for import in the first two years after the end of the transition period were indicated only in broad terms with a provision for subsequent arrangements (but no firm commitment to them), while the question of cheese imports after 1977 was left completely open. The agreement on the corrective mechanism for the budget was too complex for summary here, but it is perhaps sufficient to note that the problem was not solved so that the amount of Britain's contribution was once again to become a major domestic political issue almost as soon as the transitional period ended, and the Conservative Government was forced to negotiate a new interim concession in 1980. Nevertheless, Wilson returned from the summit determined to recommend acceptance of the terms both to the Cabinet and to the nation.

The Cabinet supported him by 16 votes to 7 on 18 March and, following a decision which Wilson had already foreshadowed in January, collective responsibility was suspended on the issue so that dissident ministers could publicly campaign against the government. However, 18 out of 29 NEC members rejected the new terms as falling 'very far short of the renegotiation objectives ... embodied in our last two Election Manifestoes' and recommended to the forthcoming special conference 'that the Party should campaign for the withdrawal of the United Kingdom from the Common Market'.[9] And this conference subsequently approved an NEC document which was highly critical of the renegotiations and called for a 'no' vote in the referendum.

None of this deterred the Cabinet majority and the pro-Market campaign then exploited to the full the advantages which it possessed. While the Labour left faced the greatest difficulty in working with the Conservative right in a pressure group against the government, the social-democratic wing of the party had no comparable problems in working with 'moderate' Tories and Liberals. The 'Britain-in-Europe' campaign, financed by the European Movement, had patiently waited for Roy Jenkins to step into the Presidency once the Cabinet had voted in favour of the terms (it would have appeared illegitimate for him to have assumed this position before the Cabinet decision!) and Shirely Williams and Dickson Mabon took leading positions in a Labour offshoot of this organisation. Wilson, Callaghan and other front-bench pragmatists took the objectively specious, but politically effective, stance of neutrality between the pressure groups.[10]

Thus with overwhelming press and media support, unanimity between the best known leaders of all three parties, and a general identification of 'moderation' with market membership and 'extremism' with withdrawal, the electorate voted by two to one in favour of continued membership in the referendum of 5 June, with a turn out of 63.2 per cent. Labour voters and the working classes were less enthusiastic than the middle classes and Tory and Liberal voters but, in general, they too showed a majority for membership.[11]

The extent to which the referendum indicated any real public conviction about the EEC is highly dubious. Nevertheless, for the moment, Labour's 'Great Debate' appeared to be over. The government announced its decision to assume the role of a full member and, from then until its fall in May 1979, the leadership never again called Britain's membership into question. On the other hand, it exhibited little warmth towards the Community, and individual ministers remained overtly hostile to it. Even at Cabinet level attitudes were ambivalent and divided and, overall, the government was more Atlanticist than *communautaire*.

Meanwhile in June 1975 the party, and particularly the left wing, faced the fact that it had been hoist with its own petard in the referendum. For the immediate future it had no choice but to recognise the verdict. Thus Benn announced:

> I have just been in receipt of a very big message from the British people. I read it loud and clear. It is clear that by an overwhelming majority the British people have voted to stay in, and I am sure everybody would want to accept that. That has been the principle of all of us who have advocated the referendum.[12]

In the circumstances, the only option for Labour anti-Marketeers was to adopt a line closely resembling that of the PCF: that is, to accept membership, but to oppose anything which appeared to further the goal of integration.

The most immediate 'European' issue following the referendum was that of direct elections to the European Parliament. At the beginning of 1976 Callaghan tried to steam-roller a proposal to hold the elections through both Cabinet and Parliament, arguing that he and Wilson had already committed Britain to participate in these in European Council meetings, and indeed claiming that they were a consequence of membership of the EEC. Predictably, the Cabinet anti-marketeers expressed outrage on learning that a further commitment had apparently been entered into without prior discussion and they succeeded in slowing down the timetable for implementation without, however, preventing the government from signing the Convention authorising the direct elections on 20 September 1976.[13] This did not deter the NEC from taking the contrary line in a document which was presented to the annual conference two days later.[14] This paper argued, in precisely the same way as the PCF, that as the party should oppose further integration which would threaten national sovereignty, it could not accept direct elections because these brought with them the risk of enhancing the power of the European Parliament over national Parliaments. This line was upheld by 4 million to 2.2 million votes – an insufficient majority to make it party policy but sufficient to indicate the movement's continuing hostility to the EEC and induce caution in the government. This was only the formal public opening of a battle over the very principle of direct elections which was to continue for the next two years. Eventually the hand of Callaghan (who became Prime Minister in April 1976) was greatly strengthened against party dissent by the evident need to hold the elections as part of the price of the Liberal–Labour pact of April 1977.[15] By then, however, Labour Party criticisms of the *economic* implications of membership had grown increasingly severe.

During 1975 and 1976, the government had introduced a rigorous deflationary policy with serious effects on working-class living standards. In this situation the call for import controls, as a partial alternative means of reducing the balance of payments deficit and strengthening manufacturing industry, had ceased to be a minority left-wing demand and was entering into the mainstream of British Labour politics. The EEC could be blamed simultaneously as the cause of the deficit and the obstacle to the solution and, only a few days after the 1976 annual conference, a government minister, Peter Shore, appeared to lend his weight to this contention. Arguing that the European Parliament must remain legislatively impotent whether there were direct elections or not, he insisted that the £2,000 million trade deficit with the Community in manufactured goods was a far more important issue since export led growth was the basis of the government's whole economic and industrial strategy:

> If the Community means anything ... [this problem] is one for which a Community solution must be found – indeed it is a real test of the EEC ... But if it is not dealt with collectively then it must be solved by the British government and people – if need be alone.[16]

Throughout the next year Labour Party disquiet about the apparent economic implications of the EEC, and the obstacles which membership imposed to any solution, mounted and were reflected in the NEC. In an attempt to thwart demands for withdrawal or a new referendum Callaghan therefore wrote a long letter to the National Executive in September 1977.[17] The thrust of his argument was that:

> the real long-term effects of Community membership cannot be properly measured because this period has coincided with a five-fold increase in oil prices and the worst world recession in 40 years. I do not think that enough weight is given to this coincidence when we measure the dissatisfaction felt in Britain about the effect of membership.

Where aspects of Community policies did not work in British interests, the solution was not to withdraw which would:

> cause a profound upheaval in our relations with Europe but also more widely – and particularly in our relations with the United States.

Rather

> Our main purpose should be to define our aims and objectives so that the British people can see clearly that Labour's policy is best designed to promote their interests inside the Community and to strengthen the unity of the people within a democratic framework.

Yet when he outlined six key elements in such a programme the general tone was negative, with emphasis placed on the need to maintain power at national level, to reform the CAP, and to protect

British regions and sources of energy.

In the event the comparative restraint of the NEC was sufficient to defeat calls at the 1977 Labour Party conference for fighting the next election on an anti-EEC programme; but it is evident that the government, whose own attitude to the Community remained as divided as ever, was forced on to the defensive on the issue in the face of the mounting tide of protest. This trend continued, moreover, in the next year, when the proposal for a European monetary system was put forward, and the NEC, no doubt reinforcing opposition within the Cabinet, reminded the government that the 1976 party programme rejected 'any form of economic or monetary union which compelled us to accept unemployment for the sake of maintaining a fixed parity'.[18]

By now indeed party discontent over the EEC was escalating and becoming increasingly difficult to contain. The 1978 annual conference thus passed the following composite resolution:

This Conference calls on the National Executive Committee, when formulating the Party's manifesto for the next election, to ensure that it contains pledges to:

(a) amend the 1972 European Communities Act so as to restore to the House of Commons the power to decide whether or not any European Economic Community regulation, directive or decision should be applicable to the United Kingdom;

(b) fundamentally reform the Common Agricultural Policy so as to permit imports of food from the world market, abolish food mountains and allow member states to adopt a deficiency payments system;

(c) rewrite the Treaty of Rome so as to curtail the powers of the Commission and give express recognition to the rights of member States to pursue their own economic, industrial and regional policies.

(d) reject any moves towards economic and monetary union and any other encroachment on the rights to self government of member States, including any extension of the European Economic Community Assembly's powers;

(e) ensure that the benefits of this country's indigenous fuels are retained for the British people;

(f) transform the European Economic Community into an enlarged, reformed and more flexible institution in which independent States can meet and discuss issues of mutual concern.[19]

In this situation Callaghan resumed a more critical line on the EEC. In a well publicised speech at the Guildhall on 13 November 1978 he thus called for a diminution in the projected budget contribution, reform of the CAP, and an adjustment in Community policies so as to benefit Britain. And he urged a revival of the original objective of the Community's founders: 'to strengthen the economies of the Community members and, by reducing regional differences, to ensure their harmonious development'.[20] The next day he and the Foreign Secretary, David Owen, sought to dispel any impression that the government was threatening withdrawal, but the negative sentiments expressed by the Prime Minister were naturally bound to stimulate further attacks by the left.[21]

Now that the decision to participate in the European elections had been taken, anti-marketeers were determined to campaign on the issue of membership itself and were claiming that approximately 60 of the 81 candidates would be hostile to membership.[22] The continuing split in the Cabinet was revealed by the fact that Benn, Foot and Shore supported a document sent by the Labour Common Market Safeguards Committee to all aspiring candidates, which threatened withdrawal if the extensive demands of the annual conference were not met; and the Home Policy Committee, under Benn's chairmanship, incorporated a pledge into the manifesto for the European Elections, that the Labour Party would consider withdrawal unless the EEC was fundamentally reformed.

By January 1979 it thus seemed that the party crisis over EEC membership was recurring. The NEC adopted the draft manifesto by 19 votes to 4 and the attempt by Shirley Williams to insist that this was not a final decision because the PLP should have been consulted first, was defeated by 15 votes to 5. Nor was Callaghan able to veto the inclusion of the sentence threatening withdrawal (his proposal being defeated by 17 to 8), and the depth of the conflict was underlined when the press conference scheduled for announcing the contents of the manifesto had to be cancelled because Callaghan effectively prevented Benn from addressing it.[23]

Yet Labour drew back from the brink of total internal warfare over the issue. Two factors facilitated this. The first was the pragmatism of Callaghan who was anxious to exploit the electoral advantages of the unpopularity of the Community and to preserve the semblance of party unity, and therefore continued publicly to express the grievance over the budgetary issue. Moreover, while generally battling successfully to ensure that the manifesto for the General Election was safely 'moderate' he accepted the inclusion of harsh words about the EEC, which even advocated import controls 'to protect employment while the necessary changes and modernisation of our industry takes place', and 'the protection of our own interests' if there was no speedy reform of the CAP. This tended to isolate the vehemently pro-EEC right, now led by Shirley Williams, thereby partially placating the left. The second factor was the willingness of the left to observe some constraint: that is to condemn the EEC and to call for fundamental (and unrealisable) reforms, but not to campaign for withdrawal. Thus in the spirit of the 1978 Conference resolution the whole basis of the EEC was condemned in party statements and the manifesto for the elections for the European Parliament maintained that 'Labour Assembly members will act as representatives of the dissatisfaction with the EEC that exists in Britain today'. Nevertheless, rather than calling for immediate withdrawal the contentious sentence was vague and open-ended:

> if the fundamental reforms contained in our Manifesto are not achieved within a reasonable period of time, then the Labour Party would have to consider very seriously whether continued European Economic Community membership was in the best interests of the British people.[24]

And while aware that Labour's policy for industrial and regional regeneration would fall foul of the Treaty of Rome, party documents reaffirmed the objective as 'to gain the co-operation of our socialist allies [in the European Economic Community] in promoting powerful socialist industrial policies within each of the member States' and asserted that:

> In re-affirming its resistance to Community rules and regulations which protect existing social structures, the Labour Party is indicating an area of common interest and co-ordinated action for all those striving for social justice and equality.[25]

Before the General Election in May 1979 Labour Party policy on the EEC was thus ambiguous and contradictory, with the continuation of conflicts within the Cabinet and between the leadership and the mass party. Hostility to membership was growing and in the elections to the European Parliament, which took place less than a month after the General Election, the majority of Labour candidates expressed very negative views on the Community. (Only 17 were elected as a result of low turnout, the general swing to the Conservative Party and the rural bias in the constituency boundaries.) Nevertheless, the party as a whole appeared to be just about reconciled to the continuation of British membership.

Within the next year all this was to change, as the existing compromise broke down and by 1980 the renewed conflict over the Community was evident at leadership level. Shortly before the annual conference, Michael Foot (on the eve of becoming leader) and Peter Shore were thus desperately trying to maintain the pre-election front-bench policy against the revisionist-right 'gang of three' (William Rogers, Shirley Williams and David Owen), who had issued a public statement announcing full support for Community membership, and John Silkin, who had declared his intention to vote for withdrawal at the forthcoming conference.[26] However, the withdrawal commitment was taken by the 1980 conference and given more concrete form, at the 1981 conference, which also determined, by a majority of 4,758,000 that no further referendum on the issue should be held.[27] By then the revisionist right had formed the nucleus of the new SDP.

The Labour Party's decision to withdraw from the Community was therefore an important contributory factor in finally creating a split in the Labour Party and a realignment in British political parties. What was the significance of this commitment in the longer-term context of Labour policy towards West European Integration?

The Significance of the Commitment to Withdraw

As was argued in chapter 6, rejection of the EEC on Tory terms in 1971–72 has been one aspect of the break with consensus politics, and left-wing activists regarded it as an integral part of the radical Labour Party programme adopted in 1973. Similarly, in the 1974 Government, it was, for the most part, the left who were most committed to withdrawal, with Benn, the *bête noire* of industrialists, the most consistent in putting a socialist case against the Community.[28] The victory of the pro-marketeers in the referendum therefore constituted an unmistakeable defeat for the left within the party, and opened the way for further retreats on the 1973 programme.[29] Moreover, there was a direct connection between the triumph over the left on this issue, and the leadership's general move to the right after 1975, for the argument over the Community had become inextricably connected with a more fundamental dispute over the whole thrust of governmental policies.

By the mid 1970s the long-term left-wing hostility to the EEC was reinforced by a further consideration: the severe weakening of the competitive position of British capitalism. This brought with it the fear that the weakness was being exacerbated by membership of the Community, and the belief that the problem could only be remedied by the reassertion of control over the economy at the level of the state. In other words, there was a growing belief on the left of the party (supported by the Communist Party) that reformist intervention at home, through planning agreements, nationalisation, and the National Enterprise Board, could succeed only if the increasing incorporation of Britain into the world economy was reversed.

245

Such ideas developed only gradually: for example, the Labour Party programme of 1973 still expressed a belief in the importance of multilateral free trade whereas, during the course of the decade, import controls came to be viewed as a central part of the Labour left's programme.[30] By 1975, the so-called Alternative Economic Strategy (AES) was being advocated by the same political forces who were at the forefront of the anti-EEC campaign. In January 1975 the Tribune Group thus advocated the introduction of selective import controls in order to:

> encourage the growth of firms concerned with import substitution, to ensure that key industries have the raw materials and components they need, to see that the whole plan is not frustrated by excessive import bills and to maintain full employment.[31]

And the next month such ideas were advocated, without success, by Benn, within the Cabinet.[32]

Similarly, although the NEC document in the referendum campaign did not call for import controls, it constantly stressed the importance of maintaining the ability, at national level, to implement socialist policies.[33] By 1975 the retention of national economic sovereignty had indeed become the preeminent issue in the Labour left's case against the EEC.

The defeat of the left thwarted the development of such ideas at Cabinet level and constituted a victory for those who maintained that Britain's crisis could be solved by forcing British industry to modernise through increased competition and reduced labour costs. One result of this was a governmental retreat on the interventionist strategy, embodied in the original conception of the National Enterprise Board and the Industry Bill, an acceptance of market forces and the implementation of an orthodox deflationary policy.

The renewed strength of the anti-marketeers at the end of the decade not only reflected the increasing power of the left wing in the party, but also a more widespread acceptance of the AES and the belief that withdrawal from the EEC was the necessary precondition for its implementation. Finally, the NEC statement 'Withdrawal from the EEC', which was overwhelmingly approved at the 1981 Conference, made the interdependence between Labour's domestic programme and withdrawal quite explicit:

> By the time Labour returns to office, the British economy will have been dangerously weakened by the years of Tory economic policy. Labour will have no choice but to carry through a radical, Socialist economic strategy ... On trade planning, on selective aid for industry, on providing access to our markets for lower-priced

food imports, on the direction of investment and capital flows, and on many other issues, our policies are in conflict with either the letter or the practice of the Treaty of Rome.

And:

[EEC membership] has seriously hindered, and could prevent altogether, Britain adopting a coherent socialist strategy for industrial and economic regeneration. Withdrawal is thus not a substitute for Labour's alternative economic, industrial and social strategy. It is a necessary condition for its success.[34]

At first sight it would thus seem that in 1981 the Labour Party had not only broken away from consensus politics, but was at last in possession of a coherent alternative strategy. But was it really true that Labour's vacillations over the EEC had been resolved, and that the movement was united on a different course? There was cause for scepticism about this.

The first reason to question the strength of Labour's commitment to withdrawal was the nature of the front-bench personnel involved. Certainly, the defection to the SDP of the leading pro-EEC enthusiasts had weakened this section of opinion at all levels of the party, although it had not been totally eliminated. However, as was shown earlier, the 1974 Cabinet had been 'balanced' rather than pro-Community and policy had not been determined by the pro-EEC enthusiasts in either 1967 or 1975. With Denis Healey as deputy leader and Michael Foot, who had played a conciliatory role on the issue in 1974–75, as leader, there was good reason to believe that a new compromise would eventually be sought. Moreover, even many of the long-term anti-marketeers on the front benches opposed the Community for reasons other than concern to implement the AES. Peter Shore, who was rapidly emerging as one of the major opponents of the left in the party, still adhered to the ideas of the 1960s rather than the AES, and put national arguments at the forefront of his case against the EEC. Even John Silkin, who was a member of the Tribune group, harped on the issues of the CAP and Britain's budgetary contrbution rather than presenting socialist arguments against the Community and maintained: 'I'm not saying, I never have said, that the EEC is a bad institution if you happen to be French or German. It's probably right, but for us, it's always been wrong.'[35] Indeed, after Tony Benn was dismissed from the Shadow Cabinet, there were few front-bench opponents of the EEC who put the AES at the forefront of their arguments. It therefore remained a strong possibility that, in office, much of the leadership would favour a new compromise with the Community, for example, on the CAP and budgetary issues.

However, there were more fundamental reasons for doubting whether a Labour government would implement the withdrawal commitment. These can be highlighted by further consideration of a relevant episode in the past: the renegotiations and referendum of 1974–75.

Lessons from the Past: The Renegotiations and Referendum

The Role of the Party

It might be argued that the party would prevent a Labour government from abandoning the withdrawal commitment and, indeed, the changes in the party constitution following the 1979 election were designed to prevent any reneging on aspects of the programme. However, the experience of 1975 is pertinent in this respect for, at that time, the Cabinet recommended the results of the renegotiation against the wishes of the majority of the party at all levels, including both the PLP and non-Cabinet ministers.[36] How was this achieved?

At rank-and-file level it was, in 1974–75, very difficult to know what was happening during the renegotiations and what was entailed in the agreements. Lack of knowledge was not, however, the problem at Cabinet or NEC level. Indeed as soon as Callaghan adopted a conciliatory tone to the Community in his speech in June 1974 a minor, but significant, crisis erupted in the higher echelons of the party. In Cabinet on 13 June the anti-EEC ministers (of whom the most vehement were Benn, Shore, Foot and Castle) attacked Callaghan for taking this new line without consultation, and further arguments over the speech – and a public dissociation from the government's EEC policy by Benn – took place early in July.[37] Although this led Callaghan to make veiled threats of resignation, a still more serious row took place in the NEC, again involving anti-EEC ministers.

In May the NEC had established an EEC Monitoring Sub-Group and, under the chairmanship of Anthony Benn and with a membership of Ian Mikardo, Alex Kitson, Bill Simpson, Lena Jeger and Judith Hart (with Peter Shore and Roy Hattersley co-opted), it was – apart from Hattersley – wholly anti-EEC in composition. At its meeting on 27 June, chaired by Benn, Callaghan's speech was criticised and the Committee asked the Research Department to prepare a paper for the next meeting which would compare and contrast Callaghan's speech with his earlier statements and the manifesto commitment. When this was produced for the Committee's next meeting, it was to cause a major rumpus.[38]

The paper was particularly critical of the Foreign Secretary's remarks on the CAP and on the issue of sovereignty over regional, industrial and fiscal policies, and questioned whether Callaghan's statements were compatible with party policy. In the ensuing discussion at the meeting of 10 July Mikardo, the Chairman of the NEC, emphasised that if the government had abandoned its opposition to the principles of CAP the matter should be brought to the full NEC and, in the meantime, it was agreed that a meeting should be sought with the Minister of Agriculture (Fred Peart). Moreover, on the issue of sovereignty and industrial policy, Shore implicitly criticised his own government by arguing that the implementation of party policy could mean the repeal of section 2.1 of the European Communities Act of 1972 (that is, a change involving a treaty amendment of the type already precluded by the government). The Committee also passed a resolution on the issue, presumably also accepted by Shore: 'It was agreed that the June 4 statement was not as comprehensive as was needed, and that future negotiations would need to take account of those issues not covered by the June 4 statement.' Finally, it also expressed a wish for a meeting with Callaghan and for a paper to be submitted by the government to the Committee.

Well-placed critics of the leadership were thus well aware that the renegotiations were being handled in a limited way, and sought to impose new checks on the government. The problem was not one of knowledge. Nevertheless, this was to be the Committee's swansong. With the pretext that the document criticising Callaghan had been leaked to *The Times*, Wilson announced a ban on ministers attending its meetings and Callaghan managed to torpedo discussion of the matter in the NEC.[39] Wilson had thus preempted the eruption of a new party row which could easily have arisen if the anti-EEC ministers who had been unable to control governmental policy in the Cabinet were to participate in an attempt by the NEC to keep the leadership to the position agreed in the party programme. Why then had the dissident ministers and the NEC allowed Callaghan and Wilson to escape detailed control?

As in 1967 it was difficult for the party to move unless the minority in the Cabinet did so. But the latter would not force the issue. The front-bench anti-marketeers were united neither in the totality of their opposition nor in their reasons for it, and for many the domestic priorities and the running of their own departments assumed far greater importance. A further pressure for unity on the EEC issue stemmed from the consideration that the trade union leadership was naturally preoccupied with ensuring that the government repealed the anti-union legislation of the previous administration, and they would not have welcomed the eruption of a dispute over the EEC which could jeopardise the position of the government. In addition, a potential leader of the Cabinet dissidents, Michael Foot, urged restraint so as not to damage the prospects of the party in the forthcoming election.[40] Finally, Wilson chose his moment shrewdly. The ban on ministerial attendance at the Monitoring Committee took place in the summer and after the recess intraparty disputes were postponed in preparation for the October election.

Yet the dissident ministers had not only allowed Wilson and Callaghan to evade detailed control, but had also established the pattern which was to condition the situation after the election: that is, that total party/governmental confrontation over the EEC was avoided so as not to jeopardise the general position of the government and in order to maintain party unity.

After the October Election the tension within the Cabinet mounted on the EEC question. Wilson's report of the December summit caused a major argument, with the anti-marketeers maintaining that he had entered into commitments which had never been discussed and arguing that a Cabinet meeting should have been held before rather than after the summit. However, conflict was then reduced with the decision (at the suggestion of Michael Foot) that it was now most important to reach agreement as to how to disagree publicly once the renegotiations were completed.[41]

Further heated exchanges on aspects of the renegotiations occurred in the Cabinet over the next two months but by early March the dissident ministers were certain that Wilson was going to recommend acceptance and that he would secure a Cabinet majority for this policy. Led by Barbara Castle, they now began to organise their riposte and, although this precipitated a major row in the short term, its final impact was softened by the fact that agreement to differ had already been legitimised.[42]

Before the Cabinet vote had even been taken arrangements for the dissenting ministers to issue their own statement in a press conference after the Cabinet meeting had been made in secret and, on the same day, a meeting of anti-EEC Labour MPs was called to gather signatures for an Early Day Motion, which embodied the declaration of the dissenting ministers, and to urge MPs to campaign for the withdrawal of Britain from the EEC. (Over 100 signatures were gathered that day.)[43] Most significant of all, it was the dissenting ministers who arranged for Ian Mikardo to obtain the signatures of the 18 NEC members (out of a total of 29) for the motion which condemned the new terms and recommended a party campaign for withdrawal. This motion caused a crisis for it could have led to the very situation which Wilson had sought to avoid: one in which the whole weight of the party machine, supported by dissenting Cabinet ministers, was mobilised against the government on an issue of major importance. According to Barbara Castle's account, Wilson and Callaghan therefore threatened resignation if the motion were carried by the NEC and, at this point, Foot once again acted as peacemaker.[44]

At the Cabinet meeting on 20 March, which Wilson insisted on devoting to the affair, Foot suggested a compromise formula and although he was subsequently unable to secure total support for it from Mikardo he obtained tacit agreement from all concerned that the issue should not be pushed to crisis point. The essence of the plan was that the party's General Secretary, Ron Hayward, should neutralise the party machine so that all individuals and constituency Labour parties should be allowed to put their own viewpoint in the forthcoming referendum campaign, while Transport House serviced both sides. The underlying rationale for the strategy was summed up by Hayward himself at the meeting of the NEC on 26 March when he pleaded passionately 'that we should not tear ourselves apart over this: "The unity of the party is a damn sight more important to me than the question of the Market".'[45]

Here was the real strength of the suspension of collective Cabinet responsibility. It allowed the leadership to secure a *quid pro quo* which masked the extent of the conflict between the majority of the Cabinet and the majority of the party (including even the majority of the government and PLP).

The next two months revealed the extent to which the anti-marketeers, in their understandable wish to avoid a governmental crisis, had disarmed themselves once they had agreed not to mobilise the party machine against the government. For although the subsequent special conference predictably approved an NEC document which was highly critical of the renegotiations and called for a 'no' vote in the referendum, this made little difference to the general position as, once again, politicking at the top largely neutralised the effects of the decision.[46] Without recourse to the mass party base, the dissenting ministers were fatally weakened in any case, but further factors contributed to their failure to stem the success of the government in the forthcoming referendum. Despite their original intentions, they were unable to maintain a united front not only because of the pressures of departmental responsibilities but also because of policy differences between them.[47]

Because the anti-marketeers in the Cabinet had been reluctant to mobilise the whole weight of the movement against the leadership, it was difficult for the party to take a bolder line. In the same way as the Cabinet dissidents, the majority of the rank and file wished to avoid a situation in which they weakened their own government. The campaign was therefore very restrained in comparison with the bitterness that had characterised it in 1971–72.

There were some special features about the situation in 1975 which might not be repeated on another occasion. In particular, party–Cabinet conflict was softened at that time by the expedient of the referendum, and in 1981 the party voted to preclude a recurrence of this. However, in all other respects the experience appears highly relevant. In particular, once again a general loyalty to the government, especially within the Cabinet, the NEC and the party machine, and a desire to avoid total conflict, could be anticipated. Secondly, and still more significant, in the event of a Labour victory in a General Election, the party would again surely attach greater importance to the implementation of immediate measures to diminish unemployment, reflate the economy and repeal anti-union legislation, than the EEC. If a Labour government appeared to be tackling these problems, it could probably secure acquiescence by the party – or a token conflict only – if a new compromise was sought with the Community.

The Attitude of the Socialist Parties in the European Community

As was noted above, before the election of 1979 Labour Party statements had emphasised the importance of striving for a common stance by the socialist parties of the Community against aspects of the Treaty of Rome. After the withdrawal commitment had been made, anti-marketeers within the Labour leadership still hoped that such an alliance might be possible, and that support from socialists within the Community would facilitate a Labour government's task in negotiating an orderly withdrawal. However, in this respect also, the renegotiation experience demonstrates the lack of reality in such expectations.

In 1973 it was decided that the most effective course of action that the Labour Party could take, while in opposition, would be to seek support for its position from potential sympathisers on the Continent in a series of bilateral meetings.[48] A possible source of encouragement appeared to lie in the West European social-democratic parties outside the EEC and, perhaps in order to show that the party was not committed to membership, discussions began in August 1973 with a bilateral meeting with Swedish Social Democrats. This was an occasion for sharp talk by the wholly anti-EEC delegation of Bill Simpson, Michael Foot, Ian Mikardo and Peter Shore.

Shore claimed that the negotiated terms 'reflected the Tory government's total defeatism' and maintained that on the CAP Labour would be seeking either a complete change or an exemption protocol for Britain. Foot was similarly vehement. He stressed that a Labour government would press the issue of renegotiation with the utmost seriousness and would not be content 'with a mere face-

saving formula' for, without renegotiation of the terms, 'the implementation of the Party's policies as set out in Labour's programme
would not be possible'. However, the Swedes gave them no encouragement to withdraw from the EEC and were only lukewarm
about the suggestion that Britain might rejoin EFTA should it
withdraw from the EEC.

In any case, it was always clear that whatever support other states
could give, the crucial meetings would be with EEC parties and, in
particular, with the French Socialists, for the attitude of the PS to
Labour's demands would throw much light upon the feasibility of
renegotiation. A high-level delegation, including Wilson, Shore and
Mikardo therefore met their counterparts, including Mitterrand,
Defferre, Pontillon and Jospin on 21 September 1973 in Transport
House. The subsequent press release claimed that: 'There was
substantial agreement on the necessity for important changes in the
structure and mechanisms of the EEC. The French will pursue them
from within whilst the Labour Party would pursue them from
outside.'[49] In fact the meeting was largely a 'dialogue of the deaf'
with the French delegation showing little sign of the critical attitude
to the EEC that might have been expected following the signature of
the Common Programme and before the defeat of the CERES line at
the forthcoming special party conference.

Mitterrand's reply to Shore's call for major changes in the
Community so that 'Britain's security, prosperity and democracy
were no longer at risk' was characteristic. He agreed that the
Community was imperfect, but claimed not to understand the basis
of Labour's fundamental objections. After having subjected the
British delegation to an interrogation on this point, he insisted that
the only result of a wish for renegotiation would be British withdrawal. He did not want this and went on to stress that the
Community could be modified despite the Treaty of Rome, and that
electoral victory by the PS and Labour Party would facilitate this
task. However, he maintained that the EEC would continue even if
Britain left it, because the other countries felt that they could not
separate if they were to remain independent of the superpowers.

Ian Mikardo failed to move Mitterrand either with the argument
that the Treaty of Rome presupposed an open, competitive capitalist
system precluding any possibility of moving towards socialism, or
with the suggestion that the consolidation of the European power
blocs was divisive and could threaten the Conference on Security
and Co-operation in Europe which, if successful, could be the greatest
contribution to the welfare of the peoples of Europe. And the gulf
between the two parties was revealed when Gaston Defferre questioned the Labour Party's willingness to fight American multinationals and the US government, and reiterated the Gaullist argu-

ment that British entry had been vetoed to prevent further Atlanticism in the Community. The meeting ended without result after Wilson had summarised the aspects of the present terms which were unacceptable and stressed that 'since January the feeling in Britain had been one of utter disappointment'.

No further discussions with Community parties were held because the domestic and international crises were soon to develop and to preoccupy the party and its leaders. However, it was already quite evident that a Labour government could rely on little active support from socialists in the EEC if it sought thoroughgoing renegotiation or threatened withdrawal, and this consideration was no doubt a further influence on the leadership once it was returned to power.

In 1981 it was therefore predictable that precisely the same pressures would be felt by the Labour front benches and this proved to be the case. Claude Cheysson, the French Foreign Secretary, ridiculed Labour's policy and in the autumn, during a visit to Mitterrand in Paris, Michael Foot was informed that a British Labour government seeking withdrawal from the Community would receive no help from French Socialists. It was reported in the British press that this experience had a sobering effect on Foot.[50] If so, the impact was reinforced by a meeting of the socialist parties of the European Community early in 1982 which made it clear that a Labour government could count on no more support from these parties than from the West European centre or right.[51] No doubt it was this fact, coupled with the other considerations inducing a reappraisal of the withdrawal commitment, that led Michael Foot, in the autumn of 1982, to emphasise the importance of maintaining good relations with European socialists when implementing Labour's programme.[52] The implication was that withdrawal was no longer a top priority and that it might be as important to retain the West European left as allies.

Withdrawal and Politicoeconomic Crisis

The experience of 1974–75 provides a third reason for questioning the strength of the commitment to withdraw: the fear of the consequences in a situation of domestic and international crisis.

The acute politicoeconomic crisis, in which the Labour Government had assumed power, had not been resolved by 1975. In January, Britain's balance of payments deficit was the highest ever recorded and domestic inflation, stemming largely from the rise in oil prices, increased rapidly during the first half of the year reaching an annual rate of almost 30 per cent in May, with wage demands running at a similar level. With export markets curtailed by the world recession, the owners of industry were threatened with a severe squeeze on profits. In these circumstances, there was a major conflict between industrialists and the government, with threats of an investment strike if the state assumed compulsory powers of intervention in private industry in the forthcoming Industry Act.[53] The EEC issue was inevitably intertwined with the more general question as to whether the government would press ahead at the risk of serious confrontation with the owners of capital or retreat to win their co-operation. For there was no doubt that large scale industry would vehemently oppose withdrawal and could be expected to launch a major campaign, arguing that there was no alternative to membership and that withdrawal would be a disaster. With the majority of the Cabinet anxious to pacify the industrial elite, there was therefore a definite incentive to accept the new *status quo* and remain within the Community, rather than to precipitate a new crisis by advocating withdrawal.

In the early 1980s both the international and domestic economies were in a still more precarious state, and withdrawal from the EEC would be liable to provoke an even greater crisis than in 1975. It is clear that the owners of capital within Britain, the EEC and the United States would exert enormous pressure on a Labour government which attempted this course, that speculation against sterling on a major scale would take place, and that private investment would fall, at least in the short run. A severe immediate threat to Britain's export market in the Community could also be anticipated.

Many of these issues were discussed, in a sober fashion, in the documents published by the Labour Party in 1981.[54] However, in crucial respects the party's thinking appeared inadequate for the scale of the problems that would be encountered. For example, its suggestion that import controls against the EEC would not provoke serious retaliation, and that there might therefore be no significant reduction in British exports to the Community was surely over optimistic.[55] Similarly, the notion that new trading partners would be found outside the EEC, and that countries like Australia would reorientate their production towards British needs seemed utopian. Furthermore, the implication that other Community states would respect Labour's timetable for negotiations over withdrawal was naïve in the extreme. On the contrary, it could be predicted with confidence that the Community (and particularly France) would place every conceivable obstacle in the way of Labour's plans and attempt to undermine its will to succeed.

There is thus no doubt that withdrawal would be a radical policy and, if coupled with the implementation of the AES, the scale of the confrontation with the owners of capital would surpass that of 1975. By 1982 even many of the intellectual authors of the strategy were beginning to have second thoughts as to its adequacy, and doubts were also expressed in the TUC general council.[56] It was therefore

255

very questionable whether a Labour government would possess
sufficient will and unity to carry through the programme in a situation
of acute crisis when it had failed to do so in 1975.

The Ambiguous Commitment

If Labour's past experience suggested reasons for doubting the
strength of the withdrawal commitment, the strategy could also be
criticised from a quite different viewpoint: namely, that if the party
had really moved far enough to the left to make the implementation
of the AES likely, it would be incongruous to regard withdrawal
from the EEC as its prerequisite.[57]

Withdrawal would be an incredibly complex and time-consuming
affair, engaging the full attention of many ministers, and probably
the whole Cabinet, for long periods.[58] If it were a crucial and central
part of the programme, this time and energy would be unavoidable.
Even then it would have grave drawbacks for it is clearly preferable
for a radical government to implement its programme while public
support for it is at its greatest and the Opposition is weakened,
rather than allowing disaffection to mount and to be exploited by
anti-governmental propaganda. But *was* withdrawal from the EEC
the key part of the programme on which everything else depended?
Despite the Labour Party's argument – supported by many of the
proponents of the AES – this appears improbable.

Between 1974–79, in comparison with the pressures exerted by
domestic capitalists and the International Monetary Fund, the EEC
was a peripheral factor in shifting the Labour Government from its
programme. Similarly – as the NEC document on withdrawal itself
recognised – it was of still less importance in leading the Thatcher
Government to seek the freeing of capital from all restraints. Finally,
as was shown in chapter 3, the immediate experience of the
Mitterrand Government appeared to suggest that the major external
obstacle to a radical strategy comes not from the European Commission, but from international capital in general and from the other
Community governments. None of this is to deny that the implementation of the AES is incompatible with the Treaty of Rome.
However, it does suggest that Labour Party thinking on the EEC
has mainly concerned the hypothetical future: if a Labour government really sought to implement the party's Alternative Economic
Strategy, leading to state intervention against the operation of
capital, it would encounter opposition over a whole range of policies
by the European Commission. It was therefore seen to be necessary
to withdraw so that this particular set of obstacles to socialist
measures should be removed.

This was a curious way to make a frontal attack on capitalism:
instead of seeking to implement the domestic programme at the risk

of conflict with the European Community (amongst other forces) an incongruous legalism was effectively dictating the postponement of radical change until the constitutional position with the Community was regularised. However, in this way, the AES might be deferred for years, until the impetus for socialistic measures was lost.

The AES may, or may not, be a viable policy. However, if the Labour Party was really committed to it, it would seem more logical to adopt a different approach. As Barbara Castle was to suggest in September 1982:

> Instead of arguing that we *know* we couldn't carry out socialist policies within the Community, let us announce that we are going ahead with our own policies and make the European authorities react to us. If they then rule us out of court, the responsibility for the breach will be theirs, not ours. They will have proved our case.[59]

The result of such a policy could still be that major conflict with the Community would occur, leading to eventual withdrawal. However, it is not certain that this would prove necessary, particularly as the Labour Party might then have a greater chance to promote wider and deeper co-operation with the left in the other EEC countries, with the eventual aim of transforming the nature of the Community.

This stance would appear more logical for a party seriously committed to a radical strategy, and it would also make a further volte-face less probable. It nevertheless remained far more likely that the ambiguities in Labour's position would continue at least until after the next General Election, and that, if returned to power, further dramatic shifts could then be expected. The reason is that policy is not determined by argument alone, but by the interplay of forces within the movement.

Despite the qualms of some of the authors of the withdrawal commitment, and the doubts of the leadership, the labour movement was not in a mood or position to rethink the EEC strategy. Hostility to the Community had become an article of faith amongst the rank and file: it was simultaneously a tactic for weakening the revisionist-right tendency in the party, and part of the definition of being left-wing. This meant that, despite the leftward shift which had taken place, there were strong elements of continuity between Michael Foot's position and that of Wilson in 1972 and Gaitskell in 1962. In each case, the left had played the major role in driving the party against the EEC when in opposition and in each case the leader preferred to acquiesce in this mood than to confront it. Gaitskell's premature death had prevented him from experiencing pressures to change this stance when in government, but Wilson had succumbed to them in 1966–67. Again between 1972 and 1974 Wilson had calculated that further clarification of the renegotiation objectives would only reopen the division in the party and had therefore waited until reelected before tackling the question. After 1981 Foot's dilemma was similar: reexamination of the issue would excite suspicions on the left that the leadership was intent on driving the party back towards the centre. Rather than risk a renewed major split, it was therefore seen to be preferable to ignore the issue as far as possible until governmental office made its resolution necessary.[60] However, the probabilities were that the left would then be disappointed once again.

In 1981 Labour's 'European' problem had not been resolved and, indeed, it appeared as intractable as ever. Whereas in France the differences on the issue between the Communists and the Socialists, and within the *Parti socialiste*, were susceptible to compromise, in Britain each agreement was little more than a temporary truce in a constant battle. This difference stems in part from the Labour Party's specific character as a terrain for conflict between various forces on the left. But it is also attributable to the contrasting role of the European Community in French and British economic and political life. Because West European integration has appeared beneficial to a wide coalition of interests in France, CERES and the PCF are ultimately prepared to compromise on the issue despite their strong ideological objections to the Community. In Britain, however, long-term hostility to integration, coupled with the immediate problems experienced by a relatively weak economy opening its market at a time of generalised recession, has meant that the majority of Labour's traditional clientele have continued to perceive 'Europe' as a threat. No genuine compromise has therefore been possible. It is, moreover, difficult to see how this can change unless the British economy revives, the Community is transformed, or the Labour Party undergoes a metamorphosis. None of these appears likely in the near future. Any Labour commitment for or against 'Europe' will therefore remain ambiguous and, probably, short lived.

Notes

1 This is the overwhelming impression given in Barbara Castle's *The Castle Diaries, 1974–76* (Weidenfeld, 1980). This provides much relevant information and convincing insights on Cabinet decision-making on the issue.
2 Speech to the Council of Ministers, 1 April 1974. This summary is based on that in U. Kitzinger and D. Butler. *The 1975 Referendum* (Macmillan, 1976), pp.30–34.
3 LPCR 1974, p.251 (this is a summary of the resolution and not the verbatim text).

4 Mikardo complained to the party's General Secretary that the NEC had not invited Schmidt, and warned that there could be a hostile demonstration if he attempted to interfere in Labour's internal affairs; Barbara Castle advised the West German embassy similarly. *The Castle Diaries*, pp.218, 224.

5 A fuller account is given by Butler and Kitzinger, pp.38–9.

6 House of Commons, 18 April 1975, quoted in ibid. Wilson had also used this argument in Cabinet on 12 December 1974, but had failed to placate the anti-marketeers (*The Castle Diaries*, pp.248–50, 12 December 1974).

7 The Commission's paper, 'The Unacceptable Situation and the Correcting Mechanism' was communicated to the Council in January 1975 and formed the basis for the subsequent agreement. J. Pinder, 'Renegotiation: Britain's Costly Lesson?', *International Affairs* vol. 51, no.2, April 1975.

8 Section 15 of the Labour Government's Iron and Steel Act of 1967 gave the British Government the power to control private investment, but this had been repealed in the European Communities Act as incompatible with the Treaty of Paris. In Cabinet on 27 February 1975 Wilson agreed that the Community should be informed that the government intended to overhaul the European Coal and Steel Community so that this power could be reassumed if Britain remained in the EEC (*The Castle Diaries*, p.322, 1 March 1974). It was agreed at the subsequent summit that Britain should study how best to do this, but in fact the power was never reassumed.

9 The complete text is reproduced as Appendix III in *The Castle Diaries*, p.750.

10 Butler and Kitzinger, *The 1975 Referendum*, pp.93–4.

11 A. King, *Britain Says Yes: The 1975 Referendum on the Common Market* (American Institute for Public Policy, 1977), p.132.

12 Ibid., p.133

13 *The Castle Diaries*, pp.635–6 (29 January 1976), pp.650–1 (12 February 1976), pp.705–6 (26 March 1976).

14 'Direct Elections', NEC statement 1976 (Harvester Microfilm).

15 In 1977 the Labour Government and PLP (though with a great number of dissenters) accepted proportional representation for the Direct Elections as part of the Liberal–Labour pact, but this Bill was lost at the end of the session. It was reintroduced at the next session, but Conservative opposition ensured the defeat of proportional representation. The NEC statement of 1976 had explicitly opposed a change in the electoral system.

16 Speech to the Labour Common Market Safeguards Committee, 28 September 1976 (Harvester Microfilm).

17 Labour Party News Release: 'The Prime Minister's Letter to the September 1977 meeting of the NEC about the Common Market' (Harvester Microfilm).

18 Labour Party News Release: The European Monetary System', 26 April 1978 (Harvester Microfilm).

19 LPCR 1978, Composite Resolution 42, quoted in *Labour and Europe: Recent Statements of Policy* (The Labour Party, 1978) (Harvester Microfilm).

20 *The Times*, 14 November 1978.

21 *The Times*, 15 November 1978.

22 *The Sunday Times*, 19 November 1978. In the event this number was not so high. David Butler and David Marquand estimate that 30 of the candidates were pro-marketeers (*European Elections and British Politics* (Longman, 1981), p.64).

23 *The Guardian*, 25 January 1979.

24 'European Assembly Elections: NEC Manifesto', January 1979 (Harvester Microfilm).

25 *The Labour Party Campaign Handbook: The EEC*, (The Labour Party 1979) (Harvester Microfilm).

26 *The Times*, 9 June 1980.

27 The evolution of the party's EEC study group illustrates the way in which the change of policy came about as a result of left-wing pressure from the mass party rather than because of any particular episode in British relations with the EEC. Before the 1980 conference the study group, under Benn's chairmanship was still considering various policy options. It was only after the shift in policy by conference that it confined its attention to withdrawal and produced the statement presented to the 1981 conference.

28 This is not to suggest that his arguments were always convincing for, on occasion, he was simplistic and sensationalist. For example on 18 May 1975 he claimed that 500,000 jobs in Britain had been lost through entry. This led to public attacks on Benn by front-bench pro-marketeers, including Healey and Roy Jenkins, and also clearly embarrassed other anti-marketeers (Butler and Kitzinger, *The 1975 Referendum*, pp.180–2). Benn's justification for this figure (which he defended four years later in *Arguments for Socialism* (Cape, 1979, pp.104–5) was to set Britain's negative trade balance with the EEC in manufactures against its positive balance with the world as a whole. This calculation was untenable since it ignored the trade trends prior to entry and assumed that the deficit would not have arisen outside the EEC.

29 In the immediate aftermath of the referendum Wilson transferred Benn from Industry to the less controversial post of Secretary of State for Energy and dispersed the other Industry ministers. Judith Hart had already resigned from the Cabinet.

30 *Labour's Programme 1973* (The Labour Party, 1973), p.16. Nevertheless the programme incorporated many of the features of the emerging AES. In particular, it stressed the importance of exchange control and control over capital movements.

31 Quoted in D. Coates, *Labour in Power?* (Longman, 1981), p.236.

32 *The Castle Diaries*, p.355n. (Benn had circulated his paper to the Ministerial Committee on Economic Strategy but had not even succeeded in getting it discussed in Cabinet.)

33 'The Common Market Re-negotiations: An Appraisal', NEC paper, April 1975 (Harvester Microfilm).

34 'Withdrawal from the EEC' NEC Statement for 1981 Labour Party Conference, pp. 2 and 3.

35 Speech at TUC annual conference 1981, quoted in 'File on 4', BBC Radio 4, 16 September 1981.

36 In the Commons debate on 6–9 April 1975, 38 ministers voted against the government, 9 abstained and only 45 voted in favour. (Eric Heffer, the Minister of State for Industry was dismissed for flouting the guidelines on permissible dissent.) Of backbenchers, 107 voted against the leadership, 24 abstained and 92 voted in its favour.

37 *The Castle Diaries*, p.113 (13 June 1974), pp.125–6 (2 July 1974), p.128 (5 July 1974).

38 Ibid., pp.143–4 (11 July 1974).

39 Butler and Kitzinger, *The 1975 Referendum*, p.36; *The Castle Diaries*, pp.143–4 (11 July 1974), pp.152–3 (24 July 1974). Immediately after the election Benn contrived to ensure the establishment of a new body with the more diplomatic name of the EEC Liaison Sub-committee (ibid., pp.204–5, 30 October 1974) but this only held its first meeting on 3 February 1975 when many of the crucial decisions had already been made. Alex Kitson was chairman and five ministers, including Callaghan, were full members. The change in composition lessened the extent to which the Committee united in opposition to the government and led to a situation in which intra-Cabinet disputes were reproduced, without conclusion. In any case it only held two meetings.

40 See, for example, the dispute between Foot and Benn on the issue on 2 July 1974 (*The Castle Diaries*, pp.125–6).

41 Ibid., pp.248–50 (12 December 1974).

42 Barbara Castle's account also shows quite clearly that the dissenting ministers had organised their response in advance and had worked in liaison with backbenchers and the NEC (ibid., pp.326, 341–3, 348).

43 The motion was organised by Joe Ashton, Benn's PPS and secured 140 signatures before being abandoned.

44 *The Castle Diaries*, pp.344–9.

45 Ibid., p.355.

46 The special conference voted by 3,724,000 to 1,986,000 to support an NEC statement asserting the belief 'that on both economic and democratic grounds, the best interests of the British people would be served by a "No" vote in the coming referendum'. At the NEC meeting on 1 May Hayward announced that the party organisation would not be mobilised for a campaign around this resolution, and this was agreed (Butler and Kitzinger, *The 1975 Referendum*, pp.111–13). Benn had already acted in a conciliatory manner at the NEC on 23 April, when he had successfully moved that a paper prepared by the Research Department ('The Common Market Re-Negotiations: An Appraisal') and bitterly condemned by Callaghan, should not be adopted by the NEC, but should be distributed as an information paper, along with the government's statement (*The Castle Diaries*, p.375).

47 Peter Shore was to the right of the other dissenting ministers and appeared happiest when concentrating his attack on the implications of EEC membership on parliamentary sovereignty. Foot adopted a similar stance and, in any case, was inhibited in attacking his own government. Benn took an increasingly strident line against the EEC, but Barbara Castle obviously found this simplistic and believed that the 'real anti-EEC case' was not being put (*The Castle Diaries*, p.383 (1 May 1975), p.390 (2 May 1975), p.403 (1–6 June 1975).

48 This was agreed at the first meeting of the joint PLP/NEC committee on 8 March 1973. (The SPD had suggested a joint SPD/Labour Party expert study group on the Labour Party's objections to membership of the EEC in June 1972, but the Labour Party was wary about accepting this invitation).

49 News Release by Labour Party Information Department, 21 September 1973.

50 *The Times*, 27 November 1981. Nor was the CERES left sympathetic (see article by Didier Motchane, *The Times* 26 October 1981).

51 *The Times*, 12 February 1982; *Sunday Times*, 14 February 1982. The gulf between the Labour Party and the other Community socialist parties was also acknowledged in a confidential report by the Labour Party international department in April 1982 (*The Times*, 15 April 1982).

52 Speech to Labour Party conference, 29 September 1982.

53 For a full account of the government's relations with industry, see Coates, *Labour in Power?*, chs. 1 and 3.

54 The issues are outlined in the main statement 'Withdrawal from the EEC' and discussed in greater depth in the five research papers published with it: 'Britain's Trade with the EEC'; 'Agriculture'; 'Fiscal and Financial Implications of Withdrawal'; 'Implications for Industrial Policy'; 'Miscellaneous'.

55 'Withdrawal from the EEC', pp.14–15;'Withdrawal from the EEC: Research Paper 1', pp.9–11. Since more than 40% of Britain's trade was with the EEC by 1981, the policy was inevitably attacked by Establishment sources (see, for example, David Wood, *The Times*, 14 September 1981), but the assumptions on which it is based have also been criticised from the left (A. Glyn and J. Harrison, *The British Economic Disaster* (Pluto, 1980), pp.158–60). By October 1982 even Stuart Holland, one of the authors of the strategy, appeared to have lost faith in the efficacy of unilateral action, protected by import controls, as a means of reflation (*The New Socialist*, November 1982).

56 See, for example, F. Cripps and T. Ward 'Labour and the Economy', *The New*

Socialist, July 1982. See also the confidential report by TUC Economic Committee, 'The European Economic Community', extracts of which appeared in *The Times*, 11 February 1982.

57 For two useful left-wing critiques by John Palmer, see 'The EEC – An Overview', *Socialist Economic Review*, 1982, and 'Britain and the EEC: The Withdrawal Option', *International Affairs*, autumn 1982, vol. 58, no.4.

58 It would presumably preoccupy the Foreign Secretary, Ministry of Agriculture, and all ministers associated with industry, trade, employment, economics and finance; the Leader of the House and all ministers with legal and constitutional responsibilities. In addition, the Defence ministers would no doubt devote considerable attention to American reactions, the Home Secretary would need to deal with changes in immigration laws, the Secretary of State for Social Security would need to review the whole system of reciprocal arrangements with the EEC; and even the Secretary of State of Education would be involved in new decisions about the equivalence of qualifications. For an informed discussion of the problems involved in redrafting Britain's international trading agreements, see Palmer, 'Britain and the EEC'.

59 *New Statesman,* 17 September 1982.

60 In this respect, it was significant that the NEC did not put the EEC on the agenda for the 1982 Labour Party conference.

Summary of Part Two

When the post-war Labour Government opposed the suggestion that Britain should participate in supranational integration in Western Europe, its attitude stemmed largely from national rather than specifically socialist considerations. The immediate experience of victory in the Second World War, following a long-term historical development in which Britain's material interests and consciousness had been defined in insular and imperial terms, made any such participation appear inconceivable to the overwhelming majority of the British elite, including the Labour leadership. However, these fundamental determinants of the government's policy were reinforced by political perceptions specific to the labour movement: in particular, by the notion that continental Western Europe was dominated by conservative forces and the belief that any quasi-federal state established there would therefore be based on *laissez-faire* principles which would threaten the newly-created Welfare State. Left-wingers who dissented from such a judgement were in a small minority and were weakened still further as the Cold War polarisation of the late 1940s eliminated Labour-left support for the notion of a 'third force' Europe.

By the time the Conservative Government took power in 1951 there was therefore a national consensus with regard to Europe and Britain's international orientation, even though there were sharp differences on particular issues. Both the Conservative and Labour front benches agreed that British interests lay with the Commonwealth and the USA, and that close involvement with a supranational Europe should be avoided. The Labour left was less enthusiastic about the United States than the leadership but shared much of the general national outlook, particularly as regards Europe. The Conservative Government's subsequent conversion, in 1961, to the view that British interests could best be defended within the EEC induced a partial breakdown in bi-partisanship. The Labour left now defined its aspiration for Britain as that of potential leader of non-aligned and Third World countries, with the Commonwealth playing a pivotal role, while the centre and leadership continued to adhere to the former Atlanticist and Commonwealth vision. Only a small minority on the right of the party enthusiastically grasped the new policy as a means of building a social-democratic Europe, while the left-wing Europeans had now shrunk to insignificant proportions.

The Labour Government's application to the EEC in 1966–77, emanating from considerations which closely resembled those of its Conservative predecessors, carried the party for a short period but, even before the loss of the General Election in 1970, rank-and-file hostility to the Community was again increasing. The return to power of a Conservative Government, determined to secure entry and simultaneously seeking to undo much of the post-war domestic consensus, unleashed a volcano of pent-up working-class anger which spilled over on to the European issue. National and socialist arguments and emotions were combined with tactical considerations to result in an official commitment to renegotiate the terms of entry and withdraw from the Community if the results were deemed unsatisfactory. In the event, the subsequent Labour Government accepted minor changes in the terms and secured electoral support for this stance in a referendum. However, this policy had been disavowed by a majority in the party at all levels except that of the Cabinet itself, and the Community remained unpopular with the rank and file and with the public. In 1980, after pressure, primarily from the left, the Labour Party became officially committed to withdrawal.

Since the Conservative, Liberal and Social Democratic parties, as well as the industrial and financial elites and the media, were intent upon remaining in the EEC, Labour's new policy implied a significant break with consensus politics, particularly when taken in the context of other elements in its programme. Moreover, even though it sought to rally general support for its defence of the 'national interest', the party proclaimed that its *socialist strategy* was incompatible with continued membership of the Community. The British left was also embarking on a course which contrasted completely with that of its counterparts in France. Apparently convinced that a radical transformation of the Community was inconceivable in the near future and that membership constituted an insurmountable barrier to national regeneration and socialist policies, the Labour Party was opting for a new course. Whereas the predominant forces in the French left believed it possible to combine Europeanism with the pursuit of their own reforming goals, the British left now argued that its Alternative Economic Strategy (AES) could be followed only if Britain withdrew from the Community.

According to one of its proponents:

> The main condition for the implementation of the alternative economic strategy is the substantial severing of the ties that bind the British economy to the world economy. Only then can full economic sovereignty be regained, only then will the measures it takes not be undermined by foreign pressures. From the Labour left's standpoint a social democracy can only be created if the British state regains control over the national economy.[1]

Yet this point had been made more than thirty years earlier when the Labour Government had resisted involvement in the integration process on the grounds that this would undermine its Welfare State and full employment policies. If successive Labour governments had been unable or unwilling to maintain Britain's national economic sovereignty when she was comparatively strong, it was surely paradoxical to suggest that it could be recaptured when – as the Labour left constantly stressed – she was now so weak. There therefore remained grounds for a suspicion that the AES might not, after all, imply a new move towards the adoption of a viable socialist policy, but a continuity in the Labour Party's ardent, and probably illusory, faith in the capacities of the British nation-state.

However, this is not to suggest that the Labour left should now simply accept the European Community and conform with its rules and regulations. Any party that has a serious commitment to socialism is bound to come into conflict with the goals and behaviour of the EEC and, while this remains in its present form, passive acceptance of it would be tantamount to acquiescence in a further weakening of Britain's manufacturing base. It would also legitimise the political arguments of the Liberals and SDP, thereby reinforcing the position of Labour's right wing. It would thus seem that the only viable long-term strategy for the Labour Party to adopt would be that of antagonistic co-operation with the Community. That is, it could accept Community co-operation in areas which seemed useful or unobjectionable, suggest alternatives which appeared beneficial, undermine or evade policies which appeared threatening, and seek to block new moves which might impose constraints on left-wing governments. Simultaneously it could seek wider and deeper co-operation with the left in other countries with the eventual aim of transforming the Community through the power of socialist forces both in the domestic politics of each member state and internationally.

In other words, the professed goals of French Socialists would seem to provide a suitable model for emulation by the Labour Party.

Yet there are dangers in this course too for it can lead, as it often has with the French Socialists, to the rationalisation of capitalist goals with socialist rhetoric, and the defence of national interests with high-flown sentiments about the need to build a socialist Europe.

Overall, the British labour movement therefore faces an acutely difficult situation containing contradictions which will not easily be resolved in the immediate future. This is the general plight of socialist parties in capitalist society.

Notes

1 A. Gamble, *Britain in Decline* (Macmillan 1981), p.184.

8
Conclusion

Three questions were raised in the Introduction to this study. It is now time to attempt explicit answers to them by drawing on the material which has been discussed in the preceding chapters.

Why has West European Integration Posed Such Problems for the Left in Both France and Britain?

As argued in the Introduction, the integration process has presented the left with immense difficulties because it has introduced a new, and perplexing, dimension into the labour movement's political task. The left has traditionally sought change within the nation-state whilst talking of the need for international working-class unity. The establishment of a degree of internationalism on a capitalist basis has thus presented it with a series of acute dilemmas. The problematic nature of the issue has been reflected in a number of symptoms: the divergencies within the labour movements of each country and the vacillation that has often been evident; the difficulties in constructing a persuasive socialist case capable of securing widespread support within and across national boundaries; and the divergencies between the British and French parties.

The problem for left-wing opponents of integration has not been the lack of cogent reasons for socialist opposition, but the elaboration of these in a programme. From the start of the process, left opposition has arisen from Western Europe's association with the United States and hostility to the Soviet Union, its capitalist basis and elevation of free market economic principles, its potentially negative impact on democratic control and accountability and its tendency to further the concentration of capital and to deprive peripheral regions and the Third World of resources. Had condemnation of the emerging European Community been expressed purely in doctrinal, socialist terms, the basis of the criticism would have been clear. However, neither the PCF nor the Labour Party has ever presented a wholly socialist case. Each has argued that it has been defending the interests of the nation as well as the working class.

Throughout this study, it has been maintained that it is simplistic to assert that such arguments necessarily constitute nationalism. In both countries, the mainstream of the labour movement had, in the late nineteenth and early twentieth centuries, come to believe that the nation-state was something more than a committee for managing the affairs of the bourgeoisie, and that it was also subject to working-class influence. The conviction that it would be regressive to remove key powers from national level and relocate them in a supranational body, dominated by capitalist interests, was therefore natural for all who held that the existing States could be influenced or used for progressive purposes. Both the Labour Party and the PCF did believe this (even though their eventual aspirations were different) and part of their hostility to West European integration was (and still is) explicable in these terms. Similarly, the more critical attitudes of French Socialists towards the EEC since the mid–1960s sprang largely from such assumptions.

However, as this study has also emphasised, there has been a very marked tendency within the PCF, and sometimes within the Labour Party also, for such beliefs to be expressed in a chauvinist manner and for a potentially socialist argument against West European integration to degenerate into a traditional nationalistic campaign. Why is this?

Socialism has not, so far, proved to be a hegemonic ideology within the working classes in either France or Britain. Nor has the left in either country secured the support of the whole of the working class or achieved governmental office without capturing the votes of a middle-class minority. It therefore faces a general problem in defining alternative policies, for these must appear practicable and realistic to a non-socialist electorate. This difficulty is intensified on the 'European' issue because any change in the policy currently being pursued by the state always appears to have 'dangerous' implications. When the PCF campaigned against French involvement in the integration process, the consequence of accepting its line was thus seen to be a total reorientation of foreign policy, resulting in French abandonment of the West and alignment with the Eastern bloc. When the Labour Party attempts to argue that an alternative economic strategy is possible outside the EEC, it is claimed that this will lead to a siege economy or autarchy. In such circumstances, there is a tendency for the anti-integration left to abandon the attempt to persuade through rational argument and instead to seek interclass support through explicit appeals to nationalism in its more traditional sense: a nationalism in which specifically socialist arguments are underplayed so as not to lessen the resonance of the purely national appeal to a non-socialist audience.

Such lines of argument came naturally to much of the Labour leadership in the early post-war period because it was, in any case, far more deeply influenced in its foreign policy by the dominant conception of the national interests and outlook than by socialism, except in a very restricted sense. Elements of this remained in Hugh Gaitskell's speech to the 1962 Labour Party conference, in Peter Shore's contributions at the time of the referendum thirteen years later and, indeed, in some of the attitudes to the withdrawal policy expressed in 1981. In theory, the PCF is motivated by Marxism, and in theory again, Marxism and chauvinistic nationalism are incompatible. In practice, however, as we have seen, the French Communists have often elevated the national, anti-German, argument over socialist ones and at times this has appeared to be the major feature of their policy statements.

If mass parties of the left are often tempted to use the national question in order to win support, the temptation will be increased when the stakes appear particularly high, or when the party's general position appears to be threatened. For example, PCF nationalism reached its maximum intensity during the campaign against the European Defence Community when success on a major issue seemed possible and during 1978–81 when it was struggling against marginalisation. A closely connected danger is that the European Community serves as a scapegoat in such situations. Thus in the 1970s and 80s, with Britain's politicoeconomic crisis deepening and its resolution becoming ever more problematic, there was a tendency for the Labour Party to imply that a solution was possible *if only* power could be restored at national level. This could easily have a diversionary effect in that less attention could then be devoted to the specific nature of such a solution, particularly as the leadership has normally been more concerned to maintain party unity and to use the 'national card' against the Conservative Party than to define radical alternative policies.

The role of the national question in left-wing opposition to West European integration has therefore been paradoxical. It has been the left of the movement (that is, the PCF, Labour left, PS left) that has tended to be the most hostile to 'Europe' and, in general, for socialist reasons. However, they have often allowed the nationalist arguments to assume disproportionate importance in order to win wider support. This has not always worked to the advantage of the left of the movement, for the right of the Labour Party and PS can often partially absorb the national argument and subordinate the specifically socialist criticisms to it. This happened most obviously within the Labour Party in 1962, but has also occurred within the French left, where the increasing stress on national independence by the PS leadership has partly neutralised CERES and the PCF. Moreover, it has often been the case that conservative forces outside the labour movement have derived the principal advantage because of the interclass appeal of nationalism. Thus it was de Gaulle who exploited the emotion behind the goal of national independence in the 1960s, even though the PCF had pressed the demand relentlessly throughout the whole post-war period; and the Falklands campaign in 1982 was to demonstrate that the Conservative Party was far more able to exploit popular nationalism than the Labour Party.

The first major problem of left-wing opponents of West European integration in both countries has therefore been to present the argument against the Community in terms of the nation-state, without either giving the advantage to non-socialist nationalists or appealing to emotions difficult to reconcile with socialism. If, in theory, it is not nationalism to argue that the potential for socialist change at state level is weakened if powers are transferred to a semi-supranational capitalist bloc, in practice both the PCF and the Labour Party have often found it difficult to maintain the distinction. However, the problems and dilemmas of the left are not eased if support is given to the EEC.

Much of the most enthusiastic pro-'European' opinion has been found on the revisionist right wing of the Labour Party and the social-democratic wing of the French *Parti socialiste*. This is scarcely surprising since West European integration has been closely connected with developments in the international capitalist economy and the consolidation of the Western alliance, and those who have accepted the basic economic and political structure would therefore be the most likely to support 'Europe' once the modernising elite did so. This sector of opinion did not normally find it problematic to reconcile integration in Western Europe with socialism, because its major aspiration was for limited reform within capitalism and it seemed that 'Europe' was compatible with, or advantageous to, the pursuit of this objective.

However, support for integration has been experienced as a direct problem by those socialists – numerous in France and a tiny minority in Britain – who have had a strong commitment to the goal of European unity, but have also been antagonistic to integration on a capitalist basis.

In the 1940s and early 50s there was, amongst sectors of the French socialist left, a genuine belief that the creation of a semi-federal Western Europe would lead to the destruction of capitalism, which was seen as inextricably wedded to the nation-state. By the 1960s disillusionment with the form taken by the EEC had already set in, but there was still much active debate as to how it could be reestablished on an independent socialist basis, and the extent to which this could be furthered by action at both national and Community levels. However, by the 1970s even in France interest in the issue had become much less intense. It was viewed as a given factor in the situation rather than either a major threat to domestic progress or a creative possibility. General support remained, except in CERES, but the socialist left was finding it more difficult to demonstrate that the Community could positively aid the attainment of socialism within France, particularly in view of the rightward shift in the majority of member states.

In Britain, except for two short periods in the immediate post-war years and in the mid 1960s, integration has never been supported by left-wing socialists. For the tiny minority who favoured entry in 1970–72 or the continuation of membership since then, the objective has been negative rather than positive: to seek to convince the movement as a whole that the EEC was not necessarily immediately damaging in the way the majority believed, rather than to demonstrate any dramatic advantages stemming from membership.

By the 1980s the pro-Community left in both countries thus faced problems, even though they were far more dramatic in Britain. And, more generally, it is clear that the parties in question have confronted major difficulties whatever attitude they have adopted to 'Europe'. Such dilemmas are inescapable for the left in a domestic and international environment dominated by capitalism.

Why do the Dominant Forces on the French Left Now Accept Community Membership While Their Counterparts in Britain Reject It?

In the Introduction, the suggestion that the differences stemmed from divergent *national interests* was rejected as inadequate for, it was argued, national interests are not neutral, objective entities. On the contrary, the perception of national interests is dependent upon ideological perspectives and the socioeconomic interests which are represented. On the other hand, this study has constantly emphasised the importance of differing *national situations* as a crucial determinant of the contrasting attitudes in the two countries.

The distinction is an important one for the national situation is a much wider notion, comprising the totality of national historical development, economic and political organisation and cultural outlook. Whereas the idea that there are objective national interests which determine party policies is misconceived, it remains true that the nation-state has existed as an objective reality and focus of consciousness. The notional common interests of the international working class have not been the principal concern of any of the parties: all have been influenced by the national situation in which they have been operating, though not all in the same way or by the same aspects of that situation.

In the case of the leaderships of the British Labour Party and the French Socialists – particularly when in power – the definition of national interests made by the dominant forces in society have clearly been of great importance. Thus even when they have justified their respective policies with socialist arguments, their behaviour has often been compatible with that of the non-socialist elite. The fact that the French Socialist leadership opted for West European integration in the immediate post-war period while the Labour government rejected it can therefore be explained by the divergent interests of the respective nation-states as defined by the whole policy-making elite: divergent interests which were rooted in long-term historical development, immediate wartime experiences and the existing stage of economic development. The socialist justifications for those policies were no doubt often sincere and may have been persuasive within party circles, but were not of decisive importance in policy determination.

The situation has remained broadly similar throughout the whole post-war period. Thus, for example, although it could appear that the PS was moving closer to the 'European' policy of the PCF in the late 1960s and 70s, it was simultaneously acquiescing in the new definition of state interests made by the Gaullist elite. Despite his socialistic arguments in favour of the European Community, therefore, Mitterrand actually followed the evolution in attitudes established by non-socialist forces and in 1981 was prepared to implement a 'European' policy which would not differ fundamentally from that of his right-wing predecessors. In Britain the position has been equally ambiguous but not wholly dissimilar.

Until 1961 the 'European' policy of the Labour leadership reflected that of the non-socialist elite. Between then and the mid 1960s there was a difference between the front benches of the two major parties, but this was less significant than it appeared. First, the Establishment itself was only just beginning to redefine its view of the national interest and there was still argument as to whether the European Community was really of crucial importance. Secondly, the Labour Party was in Opposition at the time and the leadership was therefore more susceptible to rank-and-file pressure than when in government. However, once Harold Wilson became Prime Minister he soon followed a 'European' policy which accorded with the elite's position and, in reality, so did the Labour Government of 1974–79. That the renegotiation occurred was, no doubt, the result of rank-and-file pressure when in Opposition. Yet the fact that Britain was seen to have a grievance against the Community also sprang from the relatively weak position from which she had negotiated entry into the EEC. After all, even the subsequent Thatcher Government effectively sought a renegotiation of the terms.

However, it would be simplistic to treat the leadership as a wholly autonomous force from the mass party. It is clear that the 'European' policy of the Labour leadership has been influenced by opinion within the party both in 1962, and, more particularly, in 1971–72 and 1979–81. This has not occurred in the same way in France. How is this contrast to be explained?

Once again long-term differences in national experience and national situation are of crucial significance. To the SFIO membership, the Nazi Occupation and Vichy Government, followed by an unstable parliamentary regime, offered little reason to elevate the importance of the nation-state, and good reason to hope for more from 'Europe'. To the rank and file of the Labour Party on the other hand, military victory against facism, followed by electoral success against Churchill, and the construction of the Welfare State appeared to provide every reason for confidence in the nation-state. Nor did the subsequent decade really alter the situation: the threat of Civil War in France in 1958, and the Gaullist takeover, again persuaded French Socialists that the threat was at home rather than abroad. And the success of the bargaining by the French nation-state in 1956–57 meant that the Community could be viewed as an opportunity rather than a threat. Meanwhile the spectre of Gaullism in France and Adenauer in West Germany did nothing to alter the 'European' attitudes of Labour's rank and file, while the comparatively liberal conservatism of the affluent 1950s meant that the labour movement failed to realise that British capitalism was entering an era of structural crisis in which radical international changes would be sought.

If subsequent history is to be understood two other fundamental differences in national situation must be appreciated: the organisation of the left, and the differences in internal political development. Because the Labour Party has been the focus of left-wing politics in Britain – notwithstanding the proliferation of leftist groups since the 1960s – pressures within the mass movement have been reflected in some way in Labour Party policies, at least when in Opposition. Thus the apparently cyclical process by which the Labour Party has adopted a different EEC policy when in government from that favoured in Opposition, is characteristic of much of the party's behaviour, and ultimately reflects the party's contradictory position. In Opposition it has been a vehicle for working-class and socialist forces; in government it has been subject to pressures from the Establishment and has adopted policies in conformity with the interests of the elite. The vacillation over the EEC has followed from these fundamental contradictions.

In France the situation has always been different because of the institutional division of the left and the fundamentally different role of trade unionism. Although many of the policies of the SFIO in power differed from those in Opposition, competition with the PCF always imposed limits upon the extent to which this was allowed to affect the fundamental nature of the party. From the early post-war period, commitment to 'Europe' became part of the self-identity of French socialism and a feature in its differentiation from the PCF. Socialist attitudes to the EEC were to become far more critical after the mid 1960s, but there has been no renunciation of 'Europeanism'. The same has been true of the PCF. So much of its self-identity has been bound up with the attempt to combine the appeal to the nation and the working class that positive support for the European Community, in the manner of the Italian Communist Party, has been unthinkable. Indeed the more reformist it has become, and the weaker it has been *vis-à-vis* the PS, the greater has been the temptation to reassert its *national* credentials as a primary defining characteristic. Moreover, whereas in Britain the tradition of unitary trade unionism also constrains the Labour Party at least in Opposition, to adopt policies in conformity with the perceived interests of the working classes, French trade unionism is in no position to do this. On the issue of the EEC, the different confederations have therefore normally adopted the political views of the party with which they are associated, rather than exercising any independent influence on the development of those views.

Such organisational characteristics have been important in explaining the different outlooks of the labour movements in the two countries. However, they have probably not been decisive, for fundamental political and economic processes limit the independent influence of organisational structures. The final, and crucial, factor is thus the differing domestic developments of the two countries in the post-war era.

In France, a combination of phenomena including economic modernisation and the impact of Gaullism, have brought about a situation in which the left has been increasingly dominated by forces which have believed that further socialist reform is possible without the overthrow of the institutional structure of the Fifth Republic. This stems in part from the revival of the *Parti socialiste*, which had begun to outpace the PCF long before the 1981 elections. However, the whole thrust of PCF policy since 1962 had, in any case, been to seek re-entry into the mainstream of French political life by moderating elements of its former intransigence. Subsequently, the assumption of political power by the left as a whole appeared to necessitate the adoption of those policies of the right which were reasonably popular with all social classes, and the compromise on the EEC was one part of this more general process.

In Britain political and economic development has taken a quite different course. Economic decline and the failure of Labour governments either to halt this process or to bring about a redistribution of wealth renewed fundamentalist thought on the left. The majority of the Labour left came to believe that the consensus politics of successive governments, including the desire for membership of the EEC, contributed to the dire straits of Britain in the 1970s and early 80s. In these circumstances, the left did not seek to emulate the policies of the right, but to set British politics on a new course which also involved a rejection of the EEC.

The contrasting attitudes of the dominant forces on the left in each country must therefore be explained on various levels. Original differences in the respective national situations, which have continued, coupled with organisational and ideological divergencies in left-wing politics, and a move towards greater polarisation in Britain and greater consensus in France have all combined to bring about important contrasts in attitudes.

Is there any Possibility of Cross-national Unity on the Issue?

Post-war history provides little grounds for optimism in this respect. In the 1940s and 50s the Labour Party regarded the SFIO and other continental socialist parties as federalists whose socialism was little more than a rationalisation for their willingness to co-operate with conservative forces. On their side the French Socialists saw the Labour Party at best as a devotee of the doomed doctrine 'socialism in one country' and, at worst, as a nationalist party whose objections to integration really stemmed from the desire to maintain a world empire. In the 1960s the French Socialists supported British membership of the Community and condemned de Gaulle's vetoes, but were no more prepared to change the nature of the EEC to meet British demands than was the French right. Meanwhile the Labour Party attached little importance to the views of the French Socialists, whom they had not forgiven for the Suez invasion or the suppression of the Algerian rebellion. The same degree of mutual misunderstanding has continued throughout the 1970s and early 80s. At the time of Labour's renegotiation the PS was, as we have seen, notably unsympathetic to its demands, and the withdrawal commitment has been ridiculed or dismissed with contempt by the PS. Such attitudes have been fully reciprocated by the Labour Party which has tended to regard the PS, in the external sphere, as a French nationalist party which milks the Community in general and the British in particular. These mutual suspicions on the 'European' issue have been reinforced by differences on other related questions. To the PS, the Labour Party appears Atlanticist and therefore fundamentally non-socialist. Similarly, the fervent PS belief in a nuclear defence policy alienates much of the British left.

If the Labour Party's relations with the PS have often been strained, those with the PCF have been virtually non-existent. During the years of *deténte* and the apparent evolution of the PCF towards Eurocommunism, some leading members of the Labour Party – notably Eric Heffer – hoped that it would be possible to transcend the historic split between communist and socialist politics and move towards a synthesis in Western Europe. However, the subsequent reversion of the PCF towards pro-Sovietism – particularly with regard to the invasion of Afghanistan and the repression of Solidarity in Poland – crushed such ideas. Nor has the PCF ever adopted anything but a critical attitude towards the Labour Party, which it has regarded as totally imbued with the twin evils of Atlanticism and reformism, and devoid of any grounds for claiming to be socialist. Moreover, it has rejected Labour criticisms of the Community whenever these have involved threats to interests in France which it supports. It thus opposed Britain's entry into the Community in the first place and has constantly resisted her demands for lowering the British budgetary contribution. Indeed, in May 1982, when the British veto on increased farm prices was ignored, the PCF joined in the cheering in the French national assembly, despite its fervent belief in the necessity for the mainte-nance of a French national veto. In such circumstances Labour Party co-operation with the left in France, and indeed in the other member states, has been modest.

After the 1975 referendum it joined the Socialist Group within the Strasbourg Assembly and then, the next year, the Confederation of Socialist Parties of the European Community, whose aim was to consider problems of a more long-term nature than the Socialist Group. The Confederation, which is itself attached to the Socialist International, has clearly been increasing in importance partly because the common Community membership of all the parties gives it a sharper focus than the much wider International. Howev-er, despite agreement on many of the immediate and long-term problems affecting Western Europe – including even a theoretical consensus that the CAP should be reformed – transnational co-operation by the socialists has, so far, had a minimal impact on the divergencies analysed in this book.[1]

Problems have been experienced at the most basic levels of collaboration. Indeed, before joining the Socialist Group, the Labour MEPs even considered the possibility of forming an independent body, largely because the socialist parties of the Six had a federalist tradition and the British therefore feared that they would remain. in a permanent minority. Although this was resolved in favour of membership of the Group, co-operation remained very difficult. Thus in 1977 the Labour delegates refused to participate in any of the four working parties (on economic policy, social policy, democracy and institutions, and external relations) established by the Confederation because the objective of these was to form a basis for a common programme for the Community socialist parties. The Labour Party did not accept the legitimacy of this aspiration both because of the implicit support it would provide for the goal of integration and because any such programme might conflict with its domestic priorities. The difficulties were then compounded by the fact that the Labour Party was the only member of the Confederation to oppose the principle of direct elections to the European Parliament. Moreover, the results of those elections and subsequent events exacerbated the tensions. The majority of new Labour MEPs were hostile to the Community and, once the party became committed to withdrawal the next year, meaningful co-operation grew ever more problematic. A large minority of Labour's MEPs again advocated withdrawal from the Socialist Group and, although this line was not carried, relations with the other parties (and indeed amongst the Labour MEPs themselves) deteriorated. Not one other socialist party sympathised with the withdrawal commitment, and when Michael Foot and Eric Heffer tried to explain Labour's policy in Brussels in February 1982, the exasperation of the other parties was barely disguised. Moreover, because of the salience of the agricultural issue in British complaints against the Community, and in French support for it, mutual Anglo-French bitterness within the Group has often been the most visible, despite full consciousness both in the Labour Party and the PS of the potential importance of collaboration.

There is one other significant difference in the role of British and French MEPs. The PS (and indeed the PCF) nominated prominent figures to serve in the European Parliament, and they continued to play an important role in policy-making within the domestic and European spheres. In Britain, however – with the exception of Barbara Castle – relatively unknown people were chosen for the Strasbourg Parliament, and they have been unimportant in the development of party policies. This difference is partly attributable to the specific tendency in France for politicians to accumulate positions of responsibility at all levels of government. But, more fundamentally, it follows from the differing role of the Community in national and party policy-making. Because the PS attached importance to the EEC as a vehicle for furthering its policies, it inevitably sought to harmonise decision-making in the domestic and 'European' arenas, and was prepared to allow its MEPs to participate at both levels. However, since the Labour Party was so ambivalent about the Community, domestic politics remained fundamental and MEPs therefore played a subordinate role in determining 'European' policy, and no role at all in general policy-making.

Past and present trends therefore provide little basis for confidence that cross-national unity will develop in the near future. However, it would be misleading simply to blame the British Labour Party for this and to assume that a united socialist strategy could easily be achieved if the Labour Party accepted membership of the Community and participated fully in the activities of the Socialist Group and the Confederation.

The Labour Party has been explicit in its belief that the domestic sphere is of primary importance and that the Community must not be allowed to impinge on the sovereignty of the nation-state or Labour's freedom to determine its own policy. In theory the PS and other socialist parties have disputed this. However, in practice, when their own interests have been concerned, they have adopted a similar attitude. Thus, for example, while the Labour Party refused even to discuss the notion of a common programme, the plan was ultimately dropped not only because of Labour's objections, but because other parties also decided that it might create difficulties at home. In particular, the PS itself feared that acceptance of a European socialist programme would provide fuel for PCF and Gaullist propaganda attacks against the Socialists for subordinating themselves to foreigners.

This episode again pinpoints the primacy of the national situation in policy determination. In the case of the Labour Party, this has resulted in total opposition to the Community and, in reality, PS 'Europeanism' is also rigidly constrained by domestic considerations. While this remains the case, cross-national co-operation by socialists in the Community will inevitably be partial and subject to internal pressures. Acceptance of membership by the Labour Party would diminish some of the immediate barriers to co-operation but would not, in itself, fundamentally alter the situation.

To ask whether there is a possibility of a major change is therefore to ask if the conditions which give rise to national primacy are likely to be transcended. In other words, is a fundamental transformation in the role of the West European nation-state taking place?

In the nineteenth and early twentieth centuries France and

Britain were fully independent nation-states. Even then their national sovereignty was circumscribed to an extent by their transactions with other states but, as great powers, their domestic affairs were relatively immune to external pressures. In such circumstances, it was entirely appropriate for parties of the left to believe that the attainment of state power would mean that their goals could be implemented within the national arena.

By the 1980s much had changed. Both states remained medium-range powers in the international context, and there was still some potential for the implementation of socialist goals within the nation-state. However, national developments were also severely constrained by the system of international capitalism, by membership of the Atlantic Alliance and European Community and, more generally, by East–West tensions and the problem of limited resources. Moreover, by the early 1980s all the countries of the EEC were suffering from substantially similar problems: in particular, the danger of de-industrialisation and mass unemployment, and the threat of nuclear war in Europe.

In these circumstances, the dilemmas of the West European left have become more acute than ever. On the one hand it is difficult to share the faith of either the PCF or the Labour Party in the capacity of the nation-state to resolve such problems. On the other hand, further integration on a capitalist basis would exacerbate the tendency to mass unemployment (particularly in weaker economies), and would further reduce the capacity of the left to ameliorate the situation at national level. Socialist solutions would then be postponed until the hypothetical future when the left might attain power throughout the Community.

The labour movement is thus operating within an environment which inevitably presents it with a series of contradictions. If the left confines its activities to the nation-state, it is unlikely that major progress can be made. Yet thoroughgoing cross-national co-operation would be possible only if the national situation ceased to be the dominant influence on left-wing parties, and this could probably come about only if political power was already seen to exist at supranational rather than national level. However, any such transference of power from the nation-state could weaken the left and strengthen capitalism politically and economically.

These contradictions will not easily be resolved. Yet at some stage it is likely that the relative failure of the left in each country to attain its goals will bring about a transformation of consciousness. No doubt this will only occur when there is a clear change in material circumstances. However, a beginning would be made if the Labour Party accepted that the decline in the relative power of the British nation-state was irreversible, and the PS acknowledged that the

Treaty of Rome cannot be used to promote socialism even if it defends established French interests. Immense problems would remain in combining national and cross-national strategies against capitalism, but at least the respective national situations would then have been transcended. In this event, the left in France and Britain would at least be in a position to contribute to the establishment of socialism and European unity.

Notes

1 For further details of co-operation, and its limits, see G. and P. Pridham *Transnational Party Co-Operation and European Integration* (Allen & Unwin, 1981), esp. pp.135–52.

Appendix I: Main Stages in the Development of West European Integration

1946	Sept.	Amidst increasing tensions in East–West relations, Churchill calls for United Europe in Zurich speech and subsequently forms campaigning committee.
1947	Mar.	'Truman doctrine' speech marks public announcement of 'Cold War'.
	Mar.–May	Dismissal or resignation of communists from governments of Italy, Belgium and France.
	June	Marshall calls for American aid to Europe on the basis of a programme agreed by the European nations.
1948	Mar.	Treaty of Brussels between France, Britain, Belgium, Luxembourg and Netherlands: incorporates proposals for economic, social and cultural collaboration as well as military co-operation.
	Apr.	Convention of OEEC established to undertake elaboration and execution of Marshall Aid programme.
	May	Hague Congress attended by 750 non-communist delegates of European countries (including many members of parliament and government) to promote European unity. The European Movement, established in 1947, becomes a major cross-national pressure group.
1949	Apr.	Signature of the NATO treaty.
	May	Establishment of the Council of Europe.
	Aug.	First General Election in newly established Federal Republic of Germany.
1950	May	Announcement of Schuman's proposal for a coal and steel community.
	June	Beginning of Korean War and increased American pressure for West German rearmament.
	Oct.	Pleven proposal for a European Defence Community.
1951	Apr.	Signing of Treaty of Paris, establishing Coal and Steel Community.
1952	July	Beginning of active operations of Coal and Steel Community.
1953	Mar.	Draft treaty of European Defence Community; death of Stalin in same month and apparent possibility of East–West detente reinforces French opposition to idea of Defence Community.
1954	Aug.	French Parliament votes against ratification of EDC.
	Oct.	Signature of Paris agreements establishing the Western European Union, and allowing West Germany and Italy to enter the Brussels Treaty and NATO (enters into force in May 1955).
	Dec.	British sign formal agreement of association with Coal and Steel Community (enters into force in September 1955).
1955	June	Messina Conference of foreign ministers of the Six to increase pace of West European integration.

	Oct.	Formation by Jean Monnet of new, and influential, pressure group, The Action Committee for the United States of Europe.
1956		Discussions through the year by the Six of proposals to form an economic community and EURATOM.
1957	Mar.	Signing of the two treaties in Rome establishing the EEC and EURATOM.
1958	Jan.	EEC begins to operate.
	May	Crisis of the 4th Republic and de Gaulle's return to power in France.
	Nov.	Breakdown in negotiations between EEC and British-led group seeking free trade area.
1959	Dec.	Finalisation of Convention for establishment of EFTA (enters into force in January 1960).
1960	May	EEC ministers agree on plan to expedite development of Common Market.
1961	July	Macmillan announces British application to join EEC.
1963	Jan.	De Gaulle ends negotiations by announcing veto on British application.
1965	July	EEC crisis between France and the other five on agriculture and supranationalism begins.
1966	Jan.	Luxembourg Accords (compromise) on voting in Council of Ministers and agreement on Common Agricultural Policy.
	Nov.	Wilson announces high level approach to ascertain whether conditions exist for fruitful negotiations between Britain and the EEC.
1967	May	Wilson announces new application for British membership of Community.
	July	Merger of EEC, ECSC and EURATOM.
	Nov.	De Gaulle announces second veto on British membership.
1968	July	Complete abolition of customs duties within EEC.
1970	Apr.	Council decision on replacement of financial contributions from member states by Community's own resources.
	June	New Conservative Government in Britain begins negotiations with EEC.
1971	May	Anglo-French summit leads to agreement on enlargement of Community.
	July	Labour Party announces determination to renegotiate terms of British entry into EEC.
1972	Jan.	Treaty of Accession signed between EEC and new members – United Kingdom, Ireland, Denmark and Norway. (Norway later decides against accession following referendum).
	June	French Socialists and Communists sign Common Programme, including agreement on the EEC.
1973	Jan.	British entry into EEC.
	Oct.	Arab–Israeli war, followed by increase in oil prices and deepening economic crisis.

1974	Mar.	New Labour Government takes office with commitment to renegotiation.
1975	Apr.	Wilson announces success of renegotiations; Cabinet remains divided and Labour Party states opposition to continued membership of EEC.
	June	British referendum endorses government's decision to remain in EEC.
1976	Sept.	European Council decision on direct elections to the European Parliament.
1977	Sept.	Disintegration of unity of the left in France leads to increase in mutual polemics and readoption of more hostile attitude to the EEC by the PCF.
1978	Dec.	European Council decision to establish European Monetary System (without British adherence).
1979	June	Direct elections to the European Parliament (turnout in Britain at approximately 30% is far lower than in any other member state).
1980	May	British Conservative Government (elected the previous May) secures interim agreement on rebates on British budgetary contributions to EEC.
	Sept.	Labour Party Conference votes for withdrawal from EEC.
1981	Jan.	Entry of Greece into EEC.
	May–June	Overwhelming victory of the left in French presidential and legislative elections.
	Sept.	Labour Party Conference confirms policy of withdrawal and precludes further referendum on the issue.
1982	May	Status of Luxembourg Compromise called into question when British veto on increased agricultural prices is ignored.

Appendix II: Legal Problems for a Left-wing Government in The European Community

Preliminary Remarks

(1) The following is intended as a brief introduction to some of the problems a government of the left might encounter as a result of the treaties which established the European Community. It does not examine secondary legislation, directives, judgements by the Court, or the experience of governments with regard to Community law. Nor does it deal with the wider institutional framework – i.e., the general impact of the Community on democratic accountability and sovereignty.

(2) It concentrates on the EEC since the Coal and Steel Community and EURATOM were, in effect, incorporated into the wider Community with the merger treaty of 1967. However, three Articles of the Coal and Steel Community (established under the Treaty of Paris of 1951) are also mentioned since they provided the High Authority (now the Commission) with specific powers which have no counterpart under the Treaty of Rome.

(3) To identify potential problems does not necessarily mean that they are specific to the EEC (i.e., some apply to GATT and the IMF); nor does it necessarily imply that they are insurmountable by determined or ingenious governments.

Socialism and European Unity

The Economic Assumptions of the Treaties

The underlying assumption of the treaties of the European Community was that the economy of the whole area would become more efficient and dynamic if internal barriers were progressively reduced, and if competitive conditions were equalised. (See, for example, Articles 2 and 3 of the Treaty of Rome). It would be misleading to suggest that the treaties showed no concern for the social conditions and living standards of the working classes (see, for example, The Preamble of the Treaty of Rome, and Articles 117–26). Nevertheless, the treaties were clearly based on a belief that problems could be solved if the European Community was converted, as far as possible, into a single capitalist economy. The legal structure which was established as a result of this conviction inevitably imposed prima facie problems for a left-wing government committed to state intervention in the capitalist economy in order to counteract the effects of the market on major areas of activity. These potential difficulties became more apparent during the 1970s and early 1980s, with the tendency towards economic contraction and increasing unemployment rather than the expansion envisaged in the treaties. Since many on the left (particularly in Britain) attribute the deterioration in domestic conditions, at least in part, to the removal of economic barriers, the *creation* of the Community is viewed as inherently damaging. However, this question is not discussed here. The aims are: (i) to identify those parts of the treaties which could impede governments of the left who were seeking to reverse the present trend towards deindustrialisation, high unemployment, and regional deprivation; (ii) to note those parts of the treaties which such governments might conceivably be able to use to further their domestic goals.

(i) Potential Constraints Under the Treaty of Rome

In general, the type of constraint stems from Community hostility to state intervention which it regards as a distortion of competitive conditions. However, the Labour Party claims two additional grievances against the EEC which are said to exacerbate the weakness of the British economy and make regeneration far more difficult: the Common Agricultural Policy (CAP) and the method of financing the Community (largely through duties on imports from outside the Community) which was adopted in April 1970 and came into full effect in January 1975. (As the CAP accounts for more than 70 per cent of EEC expenditure the two grievances are closely connected).

Because a high percentage of British imports are from outside the Community, Britain pays the second highest net contribution to the Community although her GNP is third highest and, on per capita income, she is one of the poorer members. Furthermore, since agriculture accounts for a smaller percentage of Britain's GNP and employment than that obtaining in any other member state, she receives comparatively little support from the funds devoted to the CAP. The CAP and the system of budgetary contributions can therefore legitimately be regarded as a constraint on a British government seeking domestic economic regeneration and any such government would be expected to demand a reform of CAP and/or the method of financing it, and/or an increase in the relative proportions of Community expenditure devoted to other budgets (e.g., social and regional policies). However, despite the importance of such matters in the British context, they are mainly specific to it. The constraints listed below are of more general relevance and may ultimately be of greater significance to governments of the left in Britain also:

Article 3: defines the methods by which the EEC shall be created (emphasising the removal of internal barriers of all kinds).

Article 5: stipulates that members shall abstain from any measure which could jeopardise the attainment of the Community.

284

Article 9: prohibits customs duties on imports and exports (and all charges having equivalent effect) between member states.

Article 37: calls for member states progressively to adjust any state monopolies of a commercial character to ensure that no discrimination regarding the conditions under which goods are procured and marketed exists between nationals of member states. (*Author's note:* this would, for example, prevent a state from purchasing exclusively from a national company or issuing a monopoly position within the nation to a national company or consortium.)

Articles 67, 69 & 70: call for the progressive implementation of freedom of movement of capital (with the Commission having the right to issue mandatory directives on this) within the Community and the co-ordination of exchange policies (in the direction of easing exchange controls) with non-Community states.

Article 85–89: anti-cartel and anti-monopoly clauses. (*Author's note:* it is stated quite explicitly that associations and concentrations will be permitted if they seem beneficial and necessary and do not cotravene other parts of the Treaty. The effect of this could be that a government which sought to prevent the establishment of a private cartel or concentration which the Commission had allowed, could itself be accused of interfering with conditions of competition.)

Articles 90–91: member states are neither to enact nor maintain in force any measure contrary to the Treaty of Rome in the case of public undertakings or undertakings to which member states grant special or exclusive rights. (*Author's note:* this means that states cannot give special privileges to nationalised industries which contravene the Treaty's competition policies.)

Article 92.1: 'Save as otherwise provided in this Treaty, any aid granted by a member state … in any form whatsoever which distorts or threatens to distort competition by favouring certain undertakings or the production of certain goods shall, in so far as it affects trade between member states, be incompatible with the common market.' (*Author's note:* the remainder of the article lists categories of aid which will or may be regarded as compatible with the Treaty. These are discussed below under (ii).)

Article 107: rates of exchange are to be treated as a matter of common concern. If a member state alters exchange rates and 'seriously distorts competition' the Commission may authorise other states to take necessary counter-measures for a strictly limited period.

Article 116: member states shall, in respect of all matters of particular interest to the common market, proceed within the framework of international organisations of an economic character, only by common action. (*Author's note:* this could, for example, preclude a left-wing government from taking a different stance from the rest of the Community in international negotiations on aid and development for the Third World.

Additional Constraints in the Treaty of Paris (Coal and Steel Community). Three articles of the Treaty of Paris grant the Commission (formerly the High Authority) specific powers which have no real counterpart under the Treaty of Rome:

Article 54: the Commission can impose fines if it finds that state financing of the coal and steel industries would involve subsidies, aids, protection and discrimination contrary to the Treaty, and its judgement in this respect is disregarded.

Article 58: in the event of a decline in demand leading to 'manifest crisis' (or the threat of such a crisis) the Commission can impose a system of production quotas. *Author's note:* the decision is largely removed from the control of governments, thus weakening national control over the protection of employment. This occurred with the Davignon plan in the late 1970s.)

Article 61: allows the Commission to fix minimum and maximum prices in coal and steel.

Socialism and European Unity

(ii) Possible Uses of the Treaty of Rome

Preamble: affirms 'as the essential objective ... the constant improvement of the living and working conditions' of the peoples of the Community and claims to be anxious 'to strengthen the unity of their economies and to ensure their harmonious development by reducing the differences existing between the various regions and the backwardness of the less favoured regions'.

Article 2: states the task to be 'to promote throughout the Community a harmonious development of economic activities, a continuous and balanced expansion, an increase in stability, an accelerated raising of the standard of living and closer relations between the States belonging to it'. (*Author's note:* protective measures could be justified as means of meeting the objectives of the Preamble and Article 2, but the problem would be to secure recognition by other states that the situation in one country was particularly grave. This would be still more difficult if the other governments were ideologically opposed to state intervention as a solution to economic problems.)

Article 36: states that the preclusion of prohibitions or restrictions on imports and exports (specified in Articles 30–34) shall not apply if justified 'on grounds of public morality, public policy or public security; the protection of health and life of humans, animals or plants; the protection of national treasures possessing artistic, historic or archaeological value; or the protection of industrial and commercial property'. (*Author's note:* this may enable ingenious governments to justify certain import controls. However, the same article stipulates that such measures 'shall not ... constitute a means of arbitrary discrimination or a disguised restriction on trade between member states'. The European Court tends to interpret the article very strictly.)

Articles 48–51: these articles establish the right of free movement for workers, and seek to facilitate this by calling for the abolition of discriminatory practices in employment and social security benefits. (*Author's note:* although such articles may ease the conditions of migrant workers, they could also mean that member states would be precluded from enacting national legislation in the interests of workers if such legislation was deemed to contradict the objectives of the common market by rendering the attainment of equal conditions more difficult. (This caveat also applies to Articles 117–119, mentioned below, and to Article 120 which calls on member states to endeavour to maintain the *existing* equivalence between paid holiday schemes.)

Article 73.1: the Commission may authorise a state in which movements of capital lead to disturbances in the capital market to take protective measures. (*Author's note:* the Commission is to determine the conditions and details.)

Article 73.2: on grounds of urgency or secrecy a member state in difficulties may take such measures on its own initiative. (*Author's note:* the Commission may decide that the state concerned shall amend or abolish the measures.)

Article 92.2: two relevant forms of aid are stated to be compatible with the common market: (a) social aid, granted to individual consumers, provided that such aid is granted without discrimination related to the origin of the products concerned; (b) aid to rectify damage caused by natural disasters or other exceptional circumstances.

Article 92.3: The following may be compatible: (a) aid to promote the economic development of areas where the standard of living is abnormally low or there is serious unemployment; (b) aid to promote a project of common European interest or to remedy serious disturbance in the economy of a Member State; (c) aid to facilitate the development of certain economic activities or economic areas, where such aid does not adversely affect trading conditions to any extent contrary to the common interest; (d) other categories of aid specified by the Council. (*Author's notes:* (1) the conditional nature of 92.3 means that the Commission could prohibit such aid if it judged it as liable to distort competition. (2) Following the Thomson report of 1973 the European Regional Development Fund was established in 1975, with the largest share of 40 per cent granted to Italy, 27 per cent going to the UK and 17 per cent to France. A government of the left could secure additional resources from this fund, but it is small in comparison with the CAP and its use is still subject to Article 92.1.)

Article 104: 'Each Member State shall pursue the economic policy needed to ensure the equilibrium of its overall balance of payments and to maintain confidence in its currency, while taking care to ensure a high level of employment and a stable level of prices'. (*Author's note: despite the Treaty's assumption that such goals could be attained by economic liberalism, it would theoretically be possible for a state to claim that its balance of payments, employment level, currency and price levels were all being damaged by the operation of the EEC and that protective measures were necessary.*)

Article 108.1: where a member state is in difficulties or seriously threatened with difficulties as regards its balance of payments the Commission shall investigate and recommend measures for the state to take. (*Author's note:* this is not necessarily advantageous since the recommendations, though not binding, might urge deflation.)

Article 108.2: if such actions prove insufficient, the Commission shall recommend to the Council the granting of mutual assistance.

Article 108.3: if mutual assistance is not granted or proves insufficient, the Commission shall authorise the state to take protective measures. (*Author's note:* these measures will be determined by the Commission and can be revoked, or the details changed, by the Council, acting on a qualified majority.)

Article 109.1: in a sudden balance of payments crisis, a member state may take the necessary protective measures. These must cause the least possible disturbance in the functioning of the Common Market and not be wider than strictly necessary.

Article 109.2: the Commission may recommend mutual assistance. *Author's note:* Article 109.3 stipulates that the Council may, on a qualified majority, decide that the state concerned shall amend, suspend or abolish the protective measures. This could negate the effects of Article 109.1 and add to the difficulties of a left-wing government.)

Article 117: asserts that member states agree on the need to promote improved working conditions and living standards.

Article 118: stipulates that the Commission is to promote close co-operation particularly in employment, labour law and working conditions, basic and advanced vocational training, social security, prevention of occupational accidents and diseases, occupational hygiene, the right of association and collective bargaining (*Author's note:* Articles 117 and 118 are unspecific and have no binding force.)

Article 119: each member state shall maintain the application of the principle that men and women should receive equal pay for equal work.

Articles 123–128: permit the use of the European Social Fund to 'improve employment opportunities for workers ... and to contribute thereby to raising the standard of living'. *Author's note:* this operates on the basis of needs rather than national quotas and supplements national aid rather than replacing it. (In 1980 Italy received 32.4 per cent, Britain 22.7 per cent and France 19.3 per cent of such aid). It was originally envisaged as coping with problems arising from declining industrial regions and sectors. However, with the development of mass unemployment in the 1970s its scope has been widened and its funds increased. Nevertheless it still comprises only approximately 5 per cent of the total Community budget.

Article 130: permits the use of the European Investment Bank, which operates on a non profit-making basis to grant loans and facilitate the financing of projects, including those for the development of less developed regions.

Index

288